Praise for *Spirituality in Mission: Embracing*

For decades, Bill Taylor and his global colleagues have encouraged our pursuit towards being "reflective practitioners." *Spirituality in Mission* is the masterpiece collection of guidance towards that goal. In a day of hyperactivity, exhaustion, and ministry burn out, this resource—written by an amazing collection of global Christian leaders—provides the challenges and the tools needed for long-term personal depth and ongoing organizational renewal. Slow down, read this book reflectively, and reenter ministry work strengthened.
Paul Borthwick, Senior Consultant Development Associates International (USA)

Mission organizations, Bible agencies, and church planters are coming together in unprecedented ways in the twenty-first century. They are working together to build God's kingdom. As a result, they're developing a broader vision and experience of what it means to be the body of Christ. Those of us on the journey like to reference Psalms 133—it is wonderful and pleasant when brothers and sisters live and work together in harmony! Harmony is precious and refreshing, resulting in God's blessing. May your reading of this book give you new insight, blessing, and refreshment for your own journey.
Bob Creson, President/CEO Wycliffe Bible Translators, USA

Century after century, missionary vision and dynamism have always come from churches and persons that enjoyed spiritual vitality. Missionaries that I have known who left a mark in mission history were women and men that practiced regularly the spiritual disciplines of prayer and meditation of the Bible. The value of this new book, *Spirituality in Mission*, is how it explores and expounds its subject through personal testimony, reflection, and Bible exposition. The diversity of authors and subjects make it a milestone in missiological literature.
J. Samuel Escobar, Facultad Protestante de Teología UEBE, Spain;

Starting with the phrase "the use of means," William Carey inaugurated the modern missionary movement as fundamentally pragmatic. As we move into a new era of mission far more diverse and richer, we must infuse that pragmatism with the aroma of Christ in new ways. *Spirituality in Mission* does just that, offering perspectives on the spiritual journey that is not constrained by the task at hand. Be warned, though, that some essays will not paint a picture of spirituality that is void of reality. Rather, what emerges is an interior life of the Spirit that is both global and local, and enriching to all.
Dr. Ted Esler, President Missio Nexus, USA

Here is a true gold mine of life experience and wisdom, unearthing new facets of Christian spirituality through a fresh theological understanding. It is an eye-opener to enriching voices of the majority world and a corrective to the sacred-spiritual Western dichotomy, with its individualistic spirituality. The imagery of a "lifelong journey" and the "finishing well" perspective provide important food for thought with missions too often marked by quick fix, short-term, and numbers. This resource displays an authentic, all-embracing understanding of Christian spirituality as the "undivided longing for God's glory to shine out to the world." This book is a crucial toolkit for reforming the spirituality of our churches and mission organizations, of mission workers and pastors alike.

Prof. Dr. Anne-Marie Kool, Professor of Missiology, Evangelical Theological Seminary in Osijek, Croatia

Spirituality in Mission is well written, accessible, intellectually engaging, and comprehensive in its subjects and issues. As a mission educator and cross-cultural mission practitioner, I am pleased that the contributors are well known and globally diverse, representing both experienced mission practitioners and thoughtful academics. I loved the case studies from different cultural and geographical contexts. Do not neglect the concluding annotated bibliography. It is a valuable resource to those engaged in mission practice, education, and training, and also for those engaged in missionary care. This book is greatly needed, useful, and a timely resource.

Rev. Canon Dr. George Iype Kovoor, Chaplain to The Queen, Rector at St. Paul's Episcopal Church Darien, Connecticut, USA

There is much of profound value in this anthology. The outstanding treasure for me was the sense that we are not alone on our spiritual journey. Chapter by chapter it is as if each contributor joins the reader and shares from their cultural and personal experience of spirituality in mission as we all walk the road together. At the outset, Rose Dowsett instructs, "Authentic spirituality is profoundly communal," and that is well represented by this volume. It is a communal work. Own this book and let the diverse global voices encourage us all to stay and grow, together, on mission.

Dr. Jay Matenga, Executive Officer, Missions Interlink New Zealand

Spirituality in Mission addresses a vision of the spiritual life that forms and feeds mission. The variety of cultural contexts of the mission scholars and practitioners give weight to the rich expressions of spirituality. The authors bring together mission and spirituality through biblical and practical exploration. The thoughtful consideration of the various approaches and aspects of spirituality present a broad range of perspectives. I found the practical reflection and application section at the end of most chapters perfect for individual study or small group discussions. This book is refreshing and convincingly shows that spiritual formation and missional living are a dynamic, interrelated process.

Monika Mench, Recruitment Director, DMG, Germany

Comprehensive in content and often deeply convicting, this volume treats the topic of spirituality in missions from every conceivable angle. Seasoned leaders from around the globe lend their voices to various aspects of spirituality in ways a solitary worldview could not. Topics ranging from the missionary call all the way to the conclusion of a missionary's life are insightfully touched upon. This newest mission resource should be referenced by every aspiring missionary and current message-bearer, to guide him or her through their ministry journey.

Dr. Marvin J. Newell, Senior Vice-President Missio Nexus, USA

At last, a timely, comprehensive, and foundational resource for missions in the twenty-first century! It is filled with gems of wisdom, grace, and helps for the beginners, "wounded warriors," and thriving missionaries. The future of missions depends on many more of God's people successfully embracing it as a life-long journey. Such an endeavor is usually too much for individual missionaries without a caring and understanding missional community behind them. Together, we will have the needed spirituality to embrace it life-long and to finish strong and well. Thus, this book is also invaluable for every Christian engaged in the Great Commission.
Dr. Andrew Ng, Missions Consultant SIM East Asia, Singapore

Spirituality in Mission redefines spirituality right now and surely in the future mission scenario. I know most of these writers; they walk the talk. How we will do mission will be based how we practice spirituality in the future. Our mission world has changed from ethnocentric to polycentric missions, from everywhere to everywhere with the dynamic of global North and global South missions. Terms like missionary, mission, and mission-field will also change. I am happy this book came out after ten years in the making. Readjust your spirituality for future missional and leadership effectiveness.
Dr. K. Rajendran, Chairman Global Innovative Voices and Associates [GIVA]; Former Chairman of World Evangelical Alliance Mission Commission, Bangalore, India

Seldom does one come across the range of spiritual depth and geographical breath as harvested in this well-represented tome on *Spirituality in Mission*. At a time when the foundations of evangelical identity and expression are being shaken, the key markers of evangelicalism—a vital spirituality overflowing into missional obedience—are winsomely connected and articulated in this latest effort by the World Evangelical Alliance Missions Commission. This work will be required reading in my classes relating to the most important reasons for Christian existence—spirituality and mission.
Dr. Ramesh Richard, President, Evangelism and Church Health [RREACH], Professor of Global Theological Engagement and Pastoral Ministries, Dallas Seminary, USA

This new publication is an invaluable resource—for a number of reasons. With voices and perspectives from the global Christian community, we have a vision for Christian spirituality and maturity in Christ that is trinitarian, biblical, and ecclesial and addresses the deep longing of the church to know the fullness of life in the Spirit. The diversity of voices is crucial here: representing the reality that our theology and practice of Christian spirituality need to be informed by both the ancient witness and the contemporary witness that fosters learning across cultures and ethnicities. This resource is an essential text for courses in spirituality across of the spectrum of denominations, East and West, North and South.
Dr. Gordon T. Smith, President Professor of Systematic and Spiritual Theology, Ambrose University and Seminary, Calgary, Canada

Spirituality in Mission is an extraordinary compendium of biblical insight and godly wisdom that provides life-giving commentary to the classic Rene Padilla observation that "true spirituality requires a missionary contemplation and a contemplative mission." Showcasing thoughtful Christ-followers from across God's global kingdom, this resource breaks down dualistic thinking and presents a wonderfully holistic view of gospel-living that speaks both to individual

transformation and the flourishing of church and community across cultures. It is a well-written, well-edited volume worthy of not only a permanent spot on your bookshelf (or handheld), but a permanent place in the church's ongoing conversations on what it means to be fully Christian in the twenty-first century.
Harold B. Smith, President and CEO, Christianity Today, USA

This book brings together many voices from diverse Christian traditions, organizations, and locations. On the surface, it may be overwhelming as the writers raise a wide spectrum of issues from spiritual warfare to suffering, from Scripture to cultural context. But on deeper reading, we discern the underlying unity reminding us that it is the Triune God who directs mission by relating to us and reconciling the world to himself. This excellent resource helps us to think more deeply about spirituality and how every Christian, with one heart and voice, can do God's mission, every day and in every way.
Rev. Dr. Robert M. Solomon, Bishop Emeritus The Methodist Church in Singapore

Research conducted in South Africa during 2016 revealed that the greatest challenges Christian leaders faced focused on intimacy with Christ. There was a profound sense that a lot of leaders were so busy with good and even great activities but often became either burnt out or disillusioned because so much was done out of self-energy and effort. This reality personally sobered me. *Spirituality in Mission* is an invaluable contribution to the spiritual formation of leaders around the world. It is highly recommended!
Peter Tarantal, Chair, World Evangelical Alliance Mission Commission; Associate International Director, Operation Mobilization (South Africa)

Carefully crafted over the span of a decade, this anthology provides a solid, multicultural biblical foundation on spirituality as experienced within mission contexts. *Spirituality in Mission* is an excellent and indispensable global resource that will greatly enrich the missionary movement. It offers a variety of mission-experienced contributors who bring their unique and practical perspectives to the subject matter. This is a must-read for those serious about engaging in significant and transformative missionary activities and in all arenas of the church on mission.
Bishop Efraim M. Tendero, Secretary General, World Evangelical Alliance, Philippines

The editors and writers are all pilgrims. Their book is global in scope, contains in-depth analysis, and is soul stirring. They summon us to a life-long journey with the Master as traveling-servants in the *missio Dei*. *Spirituality in Mission* is a timely contribution that I enthusiastically endorse to all reflective practitioners.
Dr. Sadiri Joy Tira, Catalyst for Diasporas, The Lausanne Movement (Canada)

The WEA MC has pioneered researching and resourcing global mission and missionaries. As with *Too Valuable to Lose* and *Worth Keeping*, this new volume addresses the person of the missionary. Our life with God is the soil and source of our missional engagement, and conversely, our missional engagement shapes and sharpens our spiritual lives. The diverse authors of *Spirituality in Mission* explore the nexus of these two dynamics of the Christian life. This is a treasure for the entire church. So all of you, Christian, missionary, pastor, justice worker, evangelist, professor: pick up this book, read, and linger with the transforming truth.

Rev. Cliff Warner, Rector, Christ Church Anglican, Austin, Texas; Dean, Diocese of Churches for the Sake of Others, Texas, USA

Some years ago the WEA Missions Commission published *Too Valuable To Lose* after a major research project on the causes of missionary attrition. I'd like to think that this splendid anthology is proof that fruitful and painful lessons have been learned over the years since then. Certainly I hope that one impact of the wide reading that this collection of biblical and experiential wisdom will deservedly have, will be fewer "losses" in the future. I love the combination of solid biblical and theological reflection—so utterly essential to a truly Christian spirituality—and the breadth and depth of lived experience in multiple cultures and lifetimes. It is hardly a book to read all at once, but then, it rightly aims to accompany "the lifelong journey."
Rev. Dr. Christopher J.H. Wright, Langham Partnership (UK)

Spirituality
in Mission
Embracing the Lifelong Journey

edited by
John Amalraj
Geoffrey W. Hahn
William D. Taylor

forwards by Bertil Ekström and C. Rosalee Velloso Ewell

Spirituality
in Mission
Embracing the Lifelong Journey

edited by
John Amalraj
Geoffrey W. Hahn
William D. Taylor

forwards by Bertil Ekström and C. Rosalee Velloso Ewell

Published by William Carey Library

1605 E. Elizabeth St.

Pasadena, CA 91104 | www.missionbooks.org

Koe Pahlka, copyeditor and interior design

Jay Matenga, cover design

Goran Vučićević (unsplash.com), cover photo

William Carey Library is a ministry of

Frontier Ventures | www.frontierventures.org

Printed in the United States of America

22 21 20 19 18   5 4 3 2 1 BP1000

Library of Congress Cataloging-in-Publication Data

Names: Amalraj, John, editor.

Title: Spirituality in mission : embracing the lifelong journey / [edited by]
    John Amalraj, Geoffrey W. Hahn, William D. Taylor.

Description: Pasadena, CA : William Carey Library, 2017. | Includes
    bibliographical references and index.

Identifiers: LCCN 2017050756 | ISBN 9780878080564 (alk. paper)

Subjects: LCSH: Spirituality--Christianity. | Christian life. | Missions.

Classification: LCC BV4501.3 .S66355 2017 | DDC 248--dc23 LC record available at https://lccn.loc.
gov/2017050756

Contents

Along the Journey: Discerning Organizational Spiritualities: Issues and Case Studies

Along the Journey: Preparing and Engaging

Along the Journey: Caring for Companions

Along the Journey: Finishing Well

Along the Journey: Appendix

Along the Journey

Setting the Stage

Dedication

To the Triune God, the Author and Finisher of our faith;

To His children, following their Master as cross-cultural servants.

To our life companions and children who have walked with us, shaped us, stirred us;

To our ministry colleagues, who encourage us on our journey.

Foreword

Bertil Ekström

What is spirituality? How do we understand spirituality in our different cultural, ecclesiastical, and family backgrounds? What characterizes biblical spirituality and how is that shown in our daily lives? Is it only an issue of inner life or does spirituality have something to do with the way we express our faith in words and deeds? How does spirituality relate to mission and how does mission engagement express spirituality?

These and many other questions and issues are dealt with in this new book produced by the World Evangelical Alliance Mission Commission. Authors from eighteen countries give us their perspectives on biblical principles and cultural expressions of spirituality particularly as the church engages in God's mission. Following the pattern adopted by the WEA Mission Commission of "listening to the grassroots" and "responding with a global perspective," reflective practitioners look at the relationship between spirituality and mission. The anthology of texts enriches our understanding of the depth and the meaning of being spiritual and the diversity of forms to live out the Christian faith.

God created humans as religious beings and we are "incurable" religious, reflecting something of the image of God in us. It is amazing to see the enormous diversity of religious expressions around the globe and the creativity in performing spirituality in the many religious systems. The question of course is how much of all these expressions correspond to the God-intended relationship to the Creator. Also how much is just human efforts to compensate the lack of understanding and of desire to relate to the true and loving God. Spiritual behaviors are often more an attempt to manipulate and appease supernatural powers, and even God himself, than to humbly submit to the biblically revealed God in a correct fear of him.

The mission of God is a direct result of God's love and comes from his inner spiritual being, a desiring heart for complete restoration of the whole creation and for humankind to be reconciled with him. The reconciliation with God is primarily a spiritual process although it affects all dimensions of human life.

Therefore, mission has everything to do with spirituality. Both in the way men relate to God and in the fact that mission happens in a spiritual sphere many times in opposition to evil spiritual powers and false gods. Missionary effort is often part of a spiritual encounter and performed in spiritual battles.

The unfortunate dichotomy between the spiritual and the secular has many times influenced our understanding of mission. Particularly up to the 1960s the emphasis in evangelical circles was basically on the vertical relationship with God. Although there was mission practice that corresponded to a more holistic approach to the human being, the main focus was on the need for "saving souls."

A broader understanding of mission and what true spirituality is about came from the growing social concern from the 1960s onwards, partly already shown in ecumenical circles, but very much out of a new evangelical theology and missiology as seen in the Lausanne Covenant and in Latin American missiologists. Interestingly, this more holistic concern regarding God's mission and the church's vocation had already been seen in the Protestant Reformation.

2017 is the year when we celebrate 500 years of the Reformation. In many ways the reformation of Martin Luther, Phillip Melanchton, John Calvin, and Huldrych Zwingli had to do with the understanding of spirituality and the missionary vocation of the church. It was initially not so much the aspect of sending missionaries to evangelize other nations but to make God's love and grace known to all. The reaction was primarily against the middle age church that had lost most of the biblical principles. Taking advantage of the fear that people had of final condemnation and the lack of direct access to Scripture, the church sold indulgences and charged for the different ceremonies that people had to go through. Spirituality had become blind obedience to religious laws and to religious leaders that put themselves as mediators between God and men.

Visiting Wittenberg a short time ago, I realized that Martin Luther did not post the ninety-five theses on the entrance of his own church, the parish church where he preached more than 2,000 sermons over the years. He went to the Schlosskirke, the Castle Church, a few hundred meters from the parish church, and that was owned by a family and frequently used for ceremonies such as the graduation of students from the University of Leucorea. It was also in the Castle Church that Luther himself had received his doctorate in theology in 1512. The church was a symbol of both the wealth of the church and of the exploitation of the poor who had to buy freedom from sin through the indulgences. The date chosen by Luther was also symbolic. Nailing the theses at the door of the Castle Church on the eve of October 31st, they would be seen by all church attendants on the morning of November 1st, the day of All Saints, one of the most important religious holidays of the Roman Church.

The ninety-five theses did not only protest against theological heresies but also the way people were oppressed and exploited, kept in poverty many times without basic rights. The religious system did favor those in power and the hierarchy of the church and gave very little to the population in general. Aspects of justice, human relationships, and welfare are therefore also part of Luther's manifest. It was clearly a holistic approach to the gospel and to the mission of God that the church should stand for and make known to all. There was no real spirituality if it did not affect all the areas of life.

Luther defined a spiritual person as a Christian who had the Spirit of Christ and who was in a process of sanctification. The holiness would be obtained by means of life and works. So it was not just the inner life that was at stake. Spirituality should also be shown in daily life in society, following the example of Jesus and living according to gospel principles.

Interestingly, the counter-reformation that happened within some parts of the Roman Church did emphasize the same aspects. Ignacio de Loyola, who started the Society of Jesus in 1534, affirmed that the Jesuits should follow the example of Jesus in incarnational spirituality, giving practical action to the gospel values.

Micah, one of the prophets in the Old Testament that could be called "reformers" of their time, expresses true spirituality by the words: "He has shown you, O man, what is good. And what does the Lord require of you? To act justly and to love mercy and to walk humbly with your God" (Micah 6:8).

The issue today is how spirituality should direct and guide a daily life as followers of Jesus in the engagement in the mission of God. No doubt that it has to do with our inner life and our relationship to God, but it is in showing our love and concern to others that we prove our love to God, according to the Apostle John (1 John 4). Mission without spirituality will only be a human effort to convince people of religious theories. Spirituality without a missionary involvement of the church will not express God's desire that the transforming gospel reaches every person.

There are certainly many ways of defining and expressing spirituality, and you will see some of them in this book. The danger I see is that we so easily add to the "five solas" other aspects that we think are essential for true spirituality. During my forty years in ministry as a missionary, I have seen too much of division, frustration, people leaving the church, condemnation and judgment of others based on the "added" requirements for a correct spiritual life. At the same time that we respect each other, the different traditions we come from and the diverse cultures we live in, it is important to go back to Scripture for a theological basis and to the example of Jesus for the right model of spirituality.

A special word of thanks goes to the editorial team formed by my friends and colleagues John Amalraj, Geoffrey W. Hahn, and Bill Taylor. They represent different traditions and generations and have done an outstanding job putting together this volume. The diversity of themes discussed in the different chapters shows also that spirituality has to do with everything in life and that it is both individual and collective in its nature.

This book will help you rethink your understanding of what is spiritual, revisit your own spiritual journey, and appreciate the different forms of spirituality as they are described and performed around the globe. If the text has helped you to go through a "new reformation," to have a deeper understanding of what God's mission is about—as much as it is needed in your particular context—and to find new ways of expressing your discipleship to Jesus in words and action, the book has fulfilled its purpose.

The Holy Spirit, the one who best understands what spirituality is about and who leads the church in its missionary vocation, will guide you in the reading and study of this book!

Rev. Bertil Ekström is a third culture kid, born in Sweden and raised in Brazil. Married to Alzira, the couple lives in Campinas and has four children and four grandchildren. Bertil is an ordained pastor linked to the Swedish Mission Interact and to the Brazilian Convention of Independent Baptist Churches (CIBI), and has worked with theological education and mission movements in Brazil and Latin America for many years. He served as the executive director of the WEA Mission Commission from 2006 to 2016 and is currently part of the staff team of the MC and coordinator of the Global Missiology Task Force. He has a BTh and a MTh from the Baptist Theological Faculty in São Paulo and a PhD in Missiology from the Open University of England.

Foreword

C. Rosalee Velloso Ewell

In ancient Greece, journeys are epic—they are dramatic stories of people caught up in the natural and supernatural battles, cultures, and romances of their times. This collection of essays might also be called epic. It does not water down or simplify our preconceived ideas of "spirituality" and "mission." Rather, each in their own way, these chapters draw us into the narrative of the Triune God's activity in the world and God's calling upon a people to be on a lifelong journey towards God and witnessing of the good news of the gospel of Jesus.

But don't let the epic character of this book suggest it is inaccessible. Not at all! It is a book that itself takes us on a journey with the authors and editors even as it illuminates and challenges our own lives and the lives of our communities. The volume covers a whole range of topics and themes, ranging from theological reflections upon types of spiritualities to case studies that illustrate and bring to life the issues others have faced in their own life of discipleship and ministry.

From analyses of the costliness of bearing the cross to a recognition that the yoke of the gospel is light and is in fact made easy because of Jesus, these chapters teach the reader about grace and forgiveness, about discipline and discernment, about prayer, liturgies and life in community.

The personal narratives in some of the chapters remind us of the specificity of God's calling upon each life and of the global implications of such a specific call. A few chapters include study questions and suggestions for small group reflection which, when brought alongside the biblical narratives, offer the reader a wealth and depth of knowledge and understanding about contextual missiology and spirituality.

This is a book for all people, young and old, women and men, who want to learn and grow in Christ and who know that we learn best from experience. This is a book for all people because it is about experience—about the way God's Spirit works in the lives and cultures of people all around the globe, challenging, healing, teaching, giving new life and purpose for mission.

Christian spirituality can sometimes be seen as an abstract mental or emotional practice. That is not the case with this book. The value of this volume is that it reminds the reader of the very concrete and contextual nature of our lives in Christ and of our calling to participate in God's mission. Like the disciples on the road to Emmaus (Luke 24:13–35), we can often be blinded by our focus on the past and not see that Jesus is right there, walking with us. Such blindness hinders our work in mission until our eyes are opened and we are enabled to see Jesus. Ultimately, it is my hope that these chapters will enable readers around the world to see Jesus more clearly and to see that God's call to mission goes hand-in-hand with a life of discipleship and a spirituality grounded in the variety of our contexts and in the texts of Holy Scripture.

Dr. C. Rosalee Velloso Ewell is the Principal of Redcliffe College (www. redcliffe.ac.uk) and Executive Director of the Theological Commission of the World Evangelical Alliance. She is a theologian from São Paulo, Brazil, with a PhD from Duke University (USA). Rosalee currently lives with her family in Birmingham, England. Rosalee is married to Sam, and they have three children. She and her family are involved in revitalizing urban neighborhoods around gardening, cooperatives, and community meals. They are also engaged in prison ministries, in teaching and writing.

Introduction

Preparing for the Journey: Reflections from the Editorial Team

William D. Taylor, with John Amalraj and Geoffrey W. Hahn

The Backdrop of this Global Publication

You have in your hands a resource with a long gestation season. The first vision of its potentiality and initial ideas emerged about ten years ago in worldwide discussions with our mission colleagues as we attempted to discern key global issues in our world of polycentric mission. Of the many important ones, the theme of spirituality and mission—Christian spirituality in the real context of cross-cultural mission—emerged at the top of our concerns due to its undeniable reality and the need to engage it in our own life journey. It also had major application to the diverse players in our mission structures—intercessors and mobilizers, missionaries and senders, pastors and teachers, churches and agencies, training programs and schools, networks and pastoral care resources. We need them all; we serve and lead many of them. We could not find any other publications that would specifically address these themes with a global, cross-cultural, evangelical perspective and with writers from diverse ministries and geographies, all reflective practitioners.

John Amalraj led our first group conversation at the 2006 Goudini Spa, South Africa global consultation convened by the World Evangelical Alliance Mission Commission. Some of us have clear memories of those garden discussions.

The second forum took place in Pattaya, Thailand at the MC 2008 global consultation. In that venue, John led another creative discussion which in turn led to the third step towards this publication, the 2009 issue of *Connections: The Journal of the WEA Mission Commission*. John was the appointed guest editor of that issue. You will find that

"Mission and Spirituality" publication online in two locations, http://en.calameo.com/books/002708321d0ead3813df1 and https://mc.worldea.org/resources/connections.

If you visit the journal and compare the contents and writers of both journal and this book, you will find shared themes, titles, and authors.

The fourth step took place in Stuttgart, Germany at the 2011 MC global consultation with John again at the helm, but moving closer to the process that would lead to the book. The final critical discussions took place at the 2014 MC global consultation in Izmir, Turkey. The general structure of the book emerged that week, the first writers volunteered, and the editorial process began in earnest.

By then, Geoffrey W. Hahn was a coeditor, with Bill completing the team due to his passion for the themes of our book and experience in the production of MC publications. The editorial team has been in constant dialogue and correspondence over the final months of manuscript production, having selected and invited the writers, then shepherding and encouraging them in their own writing process.

The Nature of MC Publications

The book is global, with forty-one women and men from eighteen nations: Australia, Brazil, Canada, Germany, Guatemala, Hong Kong, India, Kenya, Korea, Nigeria, Scotland, South Africa, Spain, USA, and Singapore. This listing of nations does not include the geographical arenas our writers have served, yet that experience greatly enriches our overarching background and contribution.

Our writers represent a diversity of mission leadership and structures—mission-minded churches, sending bodies, country and regional leaders, network facilitators, younger and older, pastors and mentors, mission teachers and trainers, ministries engaged in grassroots service to the vulnerable and broken.

As stated earlier, our writers are reflective practitioners. What does this refer to? They are "women and men of both action and reflection committed to God's truth; obedient in the power of God's Spirit to the Great Commission in all its fullness; servants who are globalized in perspective; citizens of their own culture but also of the world; leaders who are passionate of heart and who also reflect the heart of Christ.[1]

Our authors craft their words from experience and commitment. They are women and men in different stages of the journey, a few from the earlier laps, many in the height of their pilgrimage, and some on the last laps. All reflect a life of tested spirituality. Nobody is "Photoshopping" reality in this book.

---

1   William D. Taylor, *Global Missiology for the Twenty-first Century: The Iguassu Dialogue* (Grand Rapids: Baker Academic, 2000), 5.

We write for you, the readers. You represent the same diverse mission ministries and leaders as your writers. The book is primarily designed to nurture you, the reader; it is also produced to help re-form our mission structures and their unique spirituality; it is designed to serve as a classroom text.

What Is "Out There" on the Subject?

Visiting Google, and Amazon to get a sense of what is "out there," the results were overwhelming (due to the broadest definition of the search terms), and this is only in English. On spirituality: 133,000,000 results; on Christian spirituality: 7,620,000 results; on Christian spirituality and mission: 1,130,000 results; on Christian spirituality and cross-cultural mission, 1,280,000 results. There seems to be a lot "out there."

Amazon on the topic of "Christian spirituality and mission" listed 8,091 books; but when narrowed down with "cross-cultural mission," we were reduced to only twenty-six published results. However, this search was not really helpful in that most of the books we surveyed were tangentially related to our topic.

Hence the vital importance of the book you now own and hope to read. It is our prayer that we will both change and shape the nature of the discussion of what it means when we speak of *Spirituality and Mission: Embracing the Lifelong Journey*.

Our Metaphor

The editorial team discussed our title at length and over a long time. What were we truly trying to say? What were our dreams? What needs were we attempting to address? What pictures or metaphors were applicable? What was our title and what was our subtitle? Which goes first?

What did we mean by "embracing the lifelong journey"? Well, first we affirmed the theme of the "journey," and that it was a "lifelong" one. We discussed whether to use the term "pilgrimage," which many have done and with rich value, some using it as a synonym for "journey." But we selected "journey." "To embrace" can imply something as distant as "hold" or more intimate, as to "hug." It can mean to "encircle or clasp." It can be the act of holding someone or something closely in one's arms, with different degrees of affection and intimacy. We use the term in the sense of affirming the journey, of holding it closely in our arms as pilgrims on this long-distance walk of God, faith, mission, life, finishing well. And the embrace is not only for one stage of the journey but rather for the entire, lifelong relationship with the Trinitarian community.

The Holy Spirit is integrally involved in God's mission, making it a distinctly spiritual activity, and this is deliberately represented by the title on our cover. Jay Matenga designed the cover, intersecting the flourishes of "spirituality" in and out of "mission." This is laid over a misty forest path photo by Goran Vučićević (unsplash.com) that shows the path turning a corner in the mist. We don't know what is around the corner, but we do know there we will find God and the Spirit is leading us there

Facets of the Broader Discussion

This discussion of spirituality and mission flows first of all from Scripture, the holy narrative of God—spirituality, many times in conflict with other spiritualities—from other religious as well as secular variants. That tension continues today. It also flows out of lifelong debates on the spirituality streams that God works through, from the profoundly liturgical-sacramental on through to the other side of deeply emotional-individualized. It visits the desert fathers and mothers, the Celtic saints in isolated islands and mountains, the saints and martyrs whose spirituality was tested in cells and dungeons, on the rack and the pyre. It attempts to engage with the more contemporary discussions about this intimate walk with the Father and Son, in the empowering presence of the Spirit.

Somehow God blesses this diversity, for core values find their origin in the fundamental hunger for the Triune God, to know him in truth and in Spirit and in experience; and all of this in the context of cross-cultural mission in our complex world.

This new book emerges out of a context of both experience and questions, of praxis and service. This is what makes us a community of "reflective practitioners." Here are some of the questions that have led us to this book.

Some Personal Items:

- What kind of spirituality gets us into cross-cultural ministry—whether close to home or distant? We all remember those experiences, theologies, songs, sermons, challenges, prayers, numbers, and much more.
- But then, what happens sooner or later when "stuff happens," when our most fundamental beliefs and passions are tested, when we are cut to the bone, when we bleed in silence (or in public), when God ever so clearly does not conform to what we expected? In other words, we have "hit the proverbial Wall."
- What happens when we minister cross-culturally with those who come from spiritually vibrant but different evangelical streams, whose spiritual emphases differ from, and potentially challenge, our own?
- And then, what will we do? Dig deeper into our theology and spirituality? Seek the God-resources in other streams and reflection on spirituality? Deny its pain, stuff it, or bail out as some have done (but stuff will come out, sooner or later)? Do we careen from one spirituality (or theological) extreme to another?
- And then what kind of spiritual convictions and hopes, tensions and transitions will emerge to re-shape us along the journey?

- For those of us in the latter laps of our journey, what spirituality will carry us to the very end of life? How will we resolve the pain of unanswered prayer, of unfulfilled labor, of broken family, of children whose faith crisis leads them far from Christ?

Some Intriguing Queries:

- Are there organizational spiritualities unique to each church, school, or mission organization? How do we engage them?
- What insight do we learn from the different streams of Christian-evangelical-charismatic-reformed spirituality, as well as Anglican Orthodox and Roman Catholic voices—the liturgical sacramental streams?
- What are other issues of spirituality that we must study, grapple with, internalize, and apply?
- What is happening in our younger generations of emerging mission partners in our polycentric mission world, those cross-cultural workers coming out of the contemporary global cultures and spiritualities and brokenness?
- What new insights are helpful for us? What new resources are there, in print and online?

While each of our spirituality stories is unique, there are commonalities and core truths and experiences. We find a vast literature on historic Catholic and Orthodox spirituality, but we do not have time and space for those themes in this book. We are keenly aware that organizations, schools, agencies, teams, and networks have their own spiritual and subtle culture and ethos. Not always is that easy to discover, but discover it you will, especially if you join that organization, whether it be small, medium-sized, or huge. YWAM spirituality is different from Wycliffe spirituality; a radically charismatic church culture is certainly different from a Bible church culture; an Assembly of God culture is different from a dispensational mission agency; a much older mission compared to a younger one; a Nigerian one compared to a Korean one; a "finish the job in this decade" one compared to a long-horizon one; a reductionist team compared to a wholistic one. Yet at the same time a fascinating reality is emerging, in that many mission structures (schools and agencies) are opening themselves to a broader vision and experience of the body of Christ. Thus is it not strange to find within the same organization a fabric of active supernaturalism (open charismatics) woven together with those from a more cessationist position on the Spirit's gifts. What's fascinating is to observe these two streams over time modify and create what some call the "empowered evangelical."

In Search of Applicable Definitions of "Spirituality"

We are aiming for the evangelical dimensions of our themes, and that focuses the task. While we were surprised in our literature search to discover the large number of references on the broader topic, we are not surprised to note the reduced number on Christian spirituality and Christian mission. As you read this book, you will discern a diversity of understanding of the meaning of this key term, and that's our challenge. There is no single definition that satisfies us all. But there are shared values.

Here are some working definitions that guided us, and we applied them all to the journey of cross-cultural mission realities and its servants-partners-workers-missionaries.

A. Barus writes about spirituality in the *Dictionary of Mission Theology: Evangelical Foundation*:

> Its connection with mission begins with the God of mission, who draws us into relationship with himself in order to engage us in participation with him in that mission. This is the source of a 'spirituality of mission' as an expression of that relationship with God which initiates and empowers mission commitment.[2]

John Amalraj, one of our three coeditors, wrote in *Connections*:

> True spirituality is a live, continuous, personal relationship with the creator God that fulfills my deepest human longings for inward and outward peace and gives me meaning and purpose for everyday life. Spirituality is of no use if it is not of earthly use. True spirituality is discovered in human relationships built on the foundation of a relationship with God.

Another helpful definition comes from Gerald L. Sittser, in *Water from a Deep Well: Christian Spirituality from early Martyrs to Modern Missionaries*.[3] He captures the inner core of spirituality as "what it means to seek, know, and experience God." He goes on to develop the theme on a historical journey that is profoundly significant to all thoughtful believers, and it has special application to those of us who have lived the cross-cultural life.

Here are some other definitions-descriptions. "Christian spirituality embraces devotion to the Triune God, abiding in Christ, pursuit of holiness, and cultivation of virtues—in short, the whole of life lived under the direction and power of the Holy Spirit." Bruce A. Demarest, *Four Views on Christian Spirituality*.[4]

---

2   John Corrie, ed, *Dictionary of Mission Theology: Evangelical Foundation* (London, Inter Varsity Press, 2007), 371–373.

3   Gerald L. Sittser, *Water from a Deep Well: Christian Spirituality from early Martyrs to Modern Missionaries* (Downers Grove, IL, IVP, 2007), 18.

4   Bruce A. Demarest, *Four Views on Christian Spirituality* (Grand Rapids, MI, Zondervan, 2012), 17.

"Christian spirituality is the study and experience of what happens when the Holy Spirit meets the human spirit"—Dr. Edith M. Humphrey, *Ecstasy and Intimacy: When the Holy Spirit Meets the Human Spirit.*[5]

"Christian spirituality concerns the quest for a fulfilled and authentic Christian existence involving the bringing together of the fundamental ideas of Christianity and the whole experience of living on the basis of and within the scope of the Christian faith."—Alister E. McGrath, *Christian Spirituality.*[6]

How to Read this Book

Well, why not start out thanking God for what you hold, for the writers and their vulnerability to tell their stories, for the way they encourage us? Peruse the table of contents to familiarize yourself with the unique nature of this resource.

Study the major categories of the book. We start by setting the stage for the journey; then we establish the biblical, theological, and pastoral foundations of the journey; we examine eleven critical issues of our journey; we develop a unique section on the spiritual dynamics that flow out of different organizations and their own theological distinctives; we focus on related issues that prepare and then engage us as we walk out our pilgrimage, followed by a set of chapters addressing how best to care for our fellow servants on their lifelong marathon. We then draw our discussion to an end with some final reflections by the editorial team and a brief annotated bibliography on the subject.

This is not a novel, so your approach is different. Be sure to read the foundational chapters to capture the broader picture; select some of the themes closer to your own reality; consider then the chapters that relate to your family and ministry colleagues.

Note that while we have an annotated bibliography at the end, our writers have also shared with us some of their own story, a key biblical passage, and a prime resource that has shaped their journey. These nuggets are pure gold. Cherish them.

Words of Gratitude

We first of all thank our writers who carved time and creativity out of an already-busy life of servanthood. You know who you are, and we are profoundly grateful. We could not have done this without the expert eye, heart, and hand of Koe Pahlka, our gifted copy editor who has again produced another MC publications. We thank Esther Christensen and David Nettles from the SIM team who helped us in so many ways,

---

5   Dr. Edith M. Humphrey, *Ecstasy and Intimacy: When the Holy Spirit Meets the Human Spirit* (Grand Rapids, MI, Eerdemans, 2005), 17.
6   Alister E. McGrath, *Christian Spirituality* (Hoboken, NJ, Wiley-Blackwell, 1999), 2.

and Jerusha Justin, an Interserve volunteer who assisted in the early days of contact with the authors.

We thank God for our readers, friends, family, colleagues, fellow pilgrims in the life of constant obedience and struggle on the journey. Some of them still walk with us; others have transitioned Home. They also form part of that phalanx of witnesses who encourage us from just the other side of the "thin place" that separates us.

Drawing to a Close

We pray that this introduction will encourage you. We have worked hard to avoid duplication, though significant but perhaps healthy overlap will take place. After all, we are all working on a global tapestry as we invest our heart and mind, time, and discipline into writing something that will serve the global mission community for a long time.

We envision this book as a prime resource for all emerging and current longer-term mission servants. We see mission pastors giving a copy to all potential volunteers in this global community. We see it as a text in mission training schools and seminaries. We see mission agencies giving a copy to all of their new team members. We see parents giving a copy to their cross-cultural servant children. We see veteran servants picking it up to see what might still apply to them. We see it as a crucial tool that the Spirit of God will use to sharpen us, to mature us, to encourage us, to shape us as we serve in these challenging times.

God's rich and insightful blessings upon you as you embrace your journey and accompany these global pilgrims.

Psalm 84:5-8 (*New Living Translation* and *The Message*)

> Happy are those who are strong in the Lord,
>   who set their minds on a pilgrimage to Jerusalem.
> When they walk through the Valley of Weeping,
>   it will become a place of refreshing springs,
>   where pools of blessing collect after the rains!
> They will continue to grow stronger,
>   and each of them will appear before
>   God in Jerusalem.
> O Lord God Almighty, hear my prayer.
>   Listen, O God of Israel. (NLT)

And

> And how blessed all those in whom you live,
>   whose lives become roads you travel;

They wind through lonesome valleys, come upon brooks,
    discover cools sprigs and pools brimming with rain!
God-traveled, those roads curve up the mountain, and
    at the last turn—Zion! God in full view! (TM)

Editors

John Amalraj, son of a pastor, trained as a lawyer, further studied political science and human resources development and started his career in the corporate sector. He responded to the invitation to servr with India Missions Association (A national mission movement of agencies in India) in Chennai, New Delhi and Hyderabad involved in networking mission organizations, developing leaders and enabling strategic thinking. He also studied theology in Singapore while working with migrant Indian workers along with a local Methodist church. John served as the Executive Secretary (National Director & CEO) of Interserve-India from January 2006 until December 2017 envisioning, equipping and enabling Christian Professionals to be involved in global missions transforming communities through whole life mission.

John sits on the Governing boards of Union Biblical Seminary, Pune, the South Asian Institute for Advanced Christian Studies, Bengaluru and the Christian Institute of Management, Chennai. For ten years he has also been a member of the Council for Global Engagement and Leadership of Taylor University, Indiana, USA. During this book project, he led a team of "Reflective Practitioners" for the Globalization of Missiology Task Force of WEA Mission Commission. He is presently reading, learning and reflecting on leadership.

John is married to Jessie, an English Language trainer. They both are blessed with Jason in the University dreaming to become a fictional novelist and photographer and Joash studying business and psychology in High School. They presently make their home in Pune, in the western part of India.

Scripture: *Genesis 12:1-3 ("The Lord had said to Abram, "Go from your country, your people and your father's household to the land I will show you. "I will make you into a great nation, and I will bless you; I will make your name great, and you will be a blessing. I will bless those who bless you, and whoever curses you I will curse; and all peoples on earth will be blessed through you")*

Resource: Listening to real life stories of mission work from my grand aunt who preached the gospel to the tribal peoples in Central India.

Geoffrey W. Hahn accepted Christ at a young age, and when he was a teenager God called him to cross-cultural missions. He completed his BA at Wheaton College, MDiv at Trinity Evangelical Divinity School, and doctorate at Denver Seminary (with a thesis on cross-cultural partnerships).

Geoffrey's Scottish wife, Fiona, is a nurse by training and holds a Master's degree in public health. Her ministry focus is on compassionate ministry that protects and empowers populations that are marginalized or vulnerable to exploitation. Geoffrey and Fiona's sons, Greg and Gabriel, and daughter-in-law, Kandace, are all serving others with the unique gifts and skills God has given them.

Before beginning in overseas missions, Geoffrey served in pastoral roles in Chicago area churches. As missionaries, God opened doors for him and his family to serve in rural and urban settings in Ecuador, including in evangelism, discipleship, leadership training, founding an eye clinic and radio station, and developing structures to mobilize and send Latin American missionaries.

In mission leadership Geoffrey has served as both country and area director and on SIM's International Leadership Team for twelve years, currently as Deputy International Director. Along with geographic leadership responsibilities for North, Central, and South America, Geoffrey also provides global leadership for partnerships and mobilization, and for diaspora, sports, and business-based ministries.

Geoffrey seeks to empower others for effective ministry responses to the ever-changing ministry settings and realities in our world.

Scripture: *Micah 6:8 ("He has shown you, O mortal, what is good. And what does the LORD require of you? To act justly and to love mercy and to walk humbly with your God.)*

Resource: *The Brothers Karamazov,* by Fyodor Dostoevsky

William D. Taylor was born and raised in Latin America (dual nationality—Costa Rica and USA). His studies include Dip (Moody Bible Institute), BA (University of North Texas), ThM (Dallas Theological Seminary); PhD (University of Texas—Austin). He lived in Latin America for thirty years, seventeen of them with Yvonne in Guatemala under Camino Global at Seminario Teológico Centroamericano, and worked with a creative church-planting team in Guatemala City. He has served global mission for over fifty years in diverse capacities: student work and teaching, leadership development and church planting, global networking, consulting and mentoring, writing and speaking to address key global and personal issues.

From 1986-2006 he was Executive Director of the Mission Commission of World Evangelical Alliance, and for another decade its Senior Mentor. He is a writer and editor of a number of mission publications in English and Spanish.

As president of TaylorGlobalConsult (2011), Bill now invests his life in selective mentoring-apprenticing-life coaching and writing, consulting and teaching, teaching—in both local and global arenas.

Married since 1967 to pianist-artist and spiritual director, Yvonne, a native Texan, they have three Guatemala-born children and eight grandchildren. Based in Austin, Texas, they worship at Christ Church-Anglican. In this later stage of life, they desire to serve and strengthen Christ's worldwide Church and finish their journey with faithfulness and integrity.

Scripture: *Luke 4:14–21 ("Jesus returned to Galilee in the power of the Spirit, and news about him spread through the whole countryside..."); 2 Corinthians 1:3–7 ("All praise to God, the Father of our Lord Jesus Christ ...")*

Resource: *Water from a Deep Well: Christian Spirituality from Early Martyrs to Modern Missionaries*, by Gerald L. Sittser (Downers Grove, IL: InterVarsity Press, 2007).

Along the
Journey

Theological Implications

CHAPTER 1

Biblical and Theological Reflections on Christian Spirituality

Rose Dowsett

Introduction

The word "spirituality" does not appear in either the Old or the New Testaments, though the New Testament in particular has a great deal to say about the meaning of "spiritual." On the other hand, both testaments have much to say about "holiness" or "godliness," and about true discipleship impacting every dimension of life. I shall argue that it is these terms that are the true meaning of biblical spirituality, and indeed that until very recently in the course of church history, it is these that Christian believers would have employed.

So, what may have caused this shift in language and terminology? What does it say about both the church and the world?

A Curious Story

In the English-speaking world, the term "spirituality" was originally coined by a group of pantheistic poets and then used by the Spiritualist movement of the nineteenth century: a profoundly anti-Christian group whose main preoccupation was communicating with the dead through séances. In the twentieth century, the music group the Beatles brought the term into mainstream use during their phase of immersion in Eastern mysticism, yoga, and Hindu and Buddhist meditation. In each case, the concept of spirituality involved a deliberate distancing from Christian belief, indeed a rejection of it.

> Today the term [spirituality] has been hijacked by anyone and everyone to represent some warm inner glow, some extrasensory experience, something totally subjective and vague, the result of almost anything.

Today the term has been hijacked by anyone and everyone to represent some warm inner glow, some extrasensory experience, something totally subjective and vague, the result of almost anything. It is usually assumed to be mystical in some way, beyond rationality, personal and individual. It can be entirely independent of ethical behavior, can be religious or secular, or simply a synonym for chosen lifestyle.

It was only in the later part of the twentieth century that the term "spirituality" came to be commonly used among Protestant Christians as a description of the particular ways in which different believers expressed and lived out their faith (although the term may have been used a little before this by Roman Catholic and Orthodox writers). It also came to be used retrospectively to describe the distinctive expressions of discipleship of the past—Celtic spirituality, Quaker spirituality, for instance. It frequently involved a strong element of mysticism and focus on the mystery of God as opposed to knowing him through the person of Jesus Christ, and a greater emphasis on the Holy Spirit.

> What does matter, however, is that we are clear about what (in this case) Christian spirituality is and the ways in which it differs from the world's usage of the term.

There is no particular problem for us as Christians in using a term with a dubious history. In fact, both the Bible and traditional theology have many examples of absorbing a word or practice and investing them with new meaning and significance. That may be a matter of contextualization or simply recognition of the way in which language evolves. What does matter, however, is that we are clear about what (in this case) Christian spirituality is and the ways in which it differs from the world's usage of the term. Further, what may rather vaguely be thought of as experience of the supernatural does not necessarily equate with genuine experience of the true and living God.

Mystery, Mysticism, and the Holy Spirit

It is beyond dispute that no human being can know all there is to know about God: there is indeed mystery, beyond our ability to grasp. This side of Glory there will always be things we do not understand. He is infinite; we are finite. He is eternal; we are temporal. He is not bound by time and space as we are. He is absolutely just, as we are not. Our minds and understanding are clouded by our fallenness—even though redeemed—and we only "see through a glass darkly" (1 Cor 13:12). The Apostle John could write, "No one has ever seen God" (John 1:18, 1 John 4:12), while also insisting that we can be assured that, "If anyone acknowledges that Jesus is the Son of God, God lives in him and he in God" (1 John 4:15). The Lord Jesus, in response to a question from Philip, replied, "Anyone who has seen me has seen the Father" (John 14:9). It is in looking at, responding to, and trusting in the Lord Jesus Christ that we see all that we need to know about the nature and character of God. In him, mystery and revelation are brought together.

It is also the clear testimony of Scripture that the Holy Spirit's ministry is supernatural, often miraculous, and sometimes mysterious (see, for instance, the Pentecost narrative in Acts 1 and 2), but not fuzzily mystical: his activity is always in harmony with the Father and the Son and to forward the Trinity's purposes in relation to creation. A mystical experience that does not in some way further those purposes or point to the true and living God is not a Holy Spirit experience. A true experience of the Spirit will lead to focus on God, not self. Sadly, even some so-called Christian spirituality is in fact a form of narcissism: a glorying in an experience, a rush of adrenalin, a seeking after "something uplifting that will make me feel better" rather than an undivided longing for God's glory to shine out to the world.

The Christian church has from its very earliest days had its mystics and its solitaries, especially those who withdraw from the rough and tumble and contamination of "the world" in order to focus completely on God. Christians did not invent these patterns, simply adapting them from already existing ways of life among a variety of religious practitioners, including Jewish Essenes and others. Some took to bizarre ways of life, from those who lived at the top of a high pillar to those who lived in caves or alongside a remote shrine. Some formed silent, enclosed monastic communities whose sole purpose was prayer and communion with God.

The very best of the monastic orders combined much time in prayer and worship with strong commitment to taking the Christian story to the pagan world (most of what we now call Europe, for instance, was evangelized in this way) and to care for the poor and sick. This was not the introversion of mysticism and total preoccupation with "making one's own soul," but the upward and outward focus summarized in the two Great Commandments (Matt 22:37–40). There may be today those who are genuinely called by God to a life that is primarily solitary and wholly devoted to prayer, but this is the exception rather than the rule and should not be regarded as a more spiritual way of life. Both Old and New Testaments are far more concerned with living out faith in God in all the concrete realities of life.

Authentic Spirituality Is All-embracing

The Lord Jesus, following the Old Testament summary of the Law, taught that we are to love God with our total personality—body, mind, soul, emotions, or whatever other categories you care to use, though Hebrew culture did not see these as separable; there was no such thing as a disembodied "spirit," detached from body and mind, character, and behavior. We too often read into Scripture Greek dualism, thus profoundly misunderstanding texts that speak of the soul (e.g., Matt 16:26). Modern Western culture, in the wake of the Enlightenment, emphasizes (entirely falsely) that the spiritual and the rational/material are totally separate, the latter being objective and the former subjective and beyond verification (and therefore unreliable).

> Modern Western culture, in the wake of the Enlightenment, emphasizes (entirely falsely) that the spiritual and the rational/material are totally separate.

By contrast, both Old and New Testaments bear consistent witness to the call to worship the Lord with all that we are, all that we have, in every dimension of life, and that this is the essence of genuine spirituality. Inner experience that does not issue in whole-person transformation is spurious and worthless. Paul, following on from an outburst of worship, citing the glorious nature of God, puts it like this:

> Therefore, I urge you, brothers, in view of God's mercy, to offer your bodies as living sacrifices, holy and pleasing to God—this is your spiritual act of worship. Do not conform any longer to the pattern of this world, but be transformed by the renewing of your mind. Then you will be able to test and approve what God's will is—his good, pleasing and perfect will. (Romans 12:1–2)

It is for this reason that the Ten Commandments combine our relationship with God with our relationship with those around us, along with personal behavior. It is also why the Lord Jesus in his ministry heals the sick, feeds the hungry, goes fishing with his friends—alongside teaching and preaching, going to synagogue and Temple, praying and celebrating Passover. It is why he challenges the distortion by the Pharisees of what it means to serve God: the preoccupation with ritual cleanliness while ignoring the hypocrisy and dirtiness of their own hearts (Matt 23:23–26); the despising of a poor widow because she has only two tiny coins to offer to God (Luke 21:1–4); the outrage that a man should carry his mat on the Sabbath, rather than rejoicing that a life-long invalid should, at last, know the liberation of being healed (John 5:1–18); and many more. It is why Jesus says there will be those at the Last Judgment who have been highly religious but who will not be accepted into eternal life because they have ignored the needs of the poor (Matt 25:41–46) and who seem to know nothing of love and compassion and grace towards others. And it is why so much of the Epistles are devoted to the practicalities of living out Christian faith in every dimension. This is what it means to reflect the nature of God to a watching world.

Often in the history of the Christian church, movements have emerged to correct some imbalance or other. In turn they have often themselves then created another imbalance. So the Pietist movement was a needed correction to an outward practice of religion that ignored personal discipleship, the need for personal repentance and conversion, and attention to the study of God's Word, prayer, and other spiritual disciplines. More recently, Liberation Theology, though often based on a faulty Marxist analysis of society, brought much-needed attention to God's concern for justice, his anger at the exploitation of the poor and powerless, and the pressing need to address endemic structural evil.

> Authentic spirituality involves the whole person, in the whole of his life, in every dimension.

The truth is that we need the whole word and wisdom of God and not just select parts of it. Authentic spirituality involves the whole person, in the whole of his life, in every dimension.

Authentic Spirituality Is Profoundly Communal

Too much contemporary Christian literature about spirituality is addressed to individuals in separate self-contained units. But the emphasis of Scripture is on the believing community together being the primary place where faith and character are developed and honed, where the quality of our relationships together is to exemplify kingdom reconciliation, and where children and new disciples, rubbing shoulders with others, are to be brought into ever-growing understanding and concrete lived-out reality of new life in Christ.

> The emphasis of Scripture is on the believing community together.

That community may be the home and family, which Luther famously described as "God's little church," it may be the formal congregations where most of us belong, or it may be some other configuration of believing people such as a mission agency or peer group where faith and obedience and transformation are stretched and grown. It is no accident that the majority of the New Testament Epistles, with so much rich theological content and so much applied practical wisdom, are almost all written to groups rather than to individuals, and indeed only make full sense in the context of communal life, set within the even broader context of an unbelieving world. Those letters that are written to individuals have a very easily discerned specific purpose—and even these we read as God's inspired word with significance for us all, not just for the original recipients.

Some Western cultures have become strongly individualistic, and this has rubbed off on many believers. For example, guidance and choice and decision-making may be assumed to be a purely personal affair. Sometimes Christians are urged that they owe it to themselves—and to God—to focus strongly on their personal uniqueness and the fulfillment of their personal giftings; the issue of how these are to serve the body to contribute to a healthier whole may be ignored. The gifts of the Spirit are not in fact given for our own gratification but to help equip the Lord's people together for every work of service (1 Cor 12:1–31; Eph 4:11–16). Similarly, we need one another to help us all in our struggle against sin and in our pursuit of Christlikeness. When we try to do these things on our own, we set ourselves up to fail.

Some cultures are much more communal and interdependent. This makes it more instinctive to expect the living out of Christian faith to be communal, too. It is also why, in those cultures, evangelism needs to be to whole families, or to whole villages or networks, rather than just to individuals. Western mission has not always understood that, and the result has been either that an individual professing faith has been totally alienated from and rejected by his family and community; or that he or she has found it impossible to continue in the faith. The Lord's example in the Gospels is a fascinating mix of dealing with individuals, with households, and with crowds. The contemporary phenomenon of so-called "people movements" is a dramatic illustration of the importance of seeing significant groups of people come to faith together. At the same time, there is a needed warning that unless individuals within such movements come to genuine personal faith and experience true spiritual new birth, there may be new waves of "culture Christians" rather than genuine disciples of Jesus Christ.

In today's global church, we also have the privilege and duty to listen carefully to brothers and sisters from all over the world as they share their understanding of authentic discipleship. This too is an exciting but also sobering part of our family-ness in the twenty-first century. It is too easy to be divided by culture and language, and even personal preference, but the Lord calls us to be a body together to worship, learn, engage in witness and mission, and to glorify the one and only living God.

Authentic Spirituality Is Rooted in Scripture and Theology

It should go without saying that true Christian spirituality will always be compatible with and informed by God's revelation in his word. One of the problems with the loose and vague way in which the word "spirituality" has come to be used is that it can be used to validate any experience, whether or not it is commensurate with the teachings of the Bible, and however much it may bypass the use of our intellects. This is particularly a snare for those attracted by mysticism or who do not weigh carefully and discerningly the utterances of those who claim to have a message from God (e.g., 1 Cor 14:29–33, 2 Pet 2:1). It is inevitable that as we read Scripture we will read it and listen to it through the grid of our own presuppositions and experience—there are no infallible interpreters other than the Holy Spirit himself—but we can all work hard and with humility at studying the Word with others, of our own culture and of other cultures.

In today's world, there are many different voices all claiming authority over us or insidiously shaping our minds and lives. Much modern media is highly influential and nowhere is it neutral. As we read, watch, listen, we need constantly to be measuring it all up against what God's Word has to say. Christians will always be called to be counter-cultural as well as "in the world, but not of it," and our grasp of biblical truth will be fundamental in working this out. This involves applying our whole mind and intellect as well as our heart and emotions.

> As we read, watch, listen, we need constantly to be measuring it all up against what God's Word has to say.

"Theology" is simply the study and wisdom of God, though it is sometimes equated with certain ways of organizing biblical revelation into thematic categories. Scripture is not always so tidy as some theologians and systems of theology would like us to embrace. However, there are clearly big themes in Scripture that we need to have informing and shaping our spirituality. So, for instance, because the New Testament revolves around the person, cross, and resurrection of the Lord Jesus Christ, so must our spirituality. Because God cares passionately about the world he created, so we too must include stewardship of creation in our understanding of spirituality. Because he loves and yearns over his world, so must we. Because he is just and looks for justice in human societies, we must work for justice too, with special care for the widows and orphans and aliens (migrants) whose number explodes today all over the world. In a world fixated on acquiring wealth and status we will live by different values of simplicity and humility, generosity and thankfulness. In a world that sees this life as all there is and an end in itself, we will live in the light of eternity and that infinite canvas against which earthly life is painted. In a world often obsessed with avoiding suffering and seeking comfort, we will accept that suffering is an intrinsic part of following Christ as he calls us to take up not a sofa but a cross.

All this is part of authentic discipleship, authentic spirituality, the desire to "be holy as I am holy" (1 Pet 1:16, 2:9).

Conclusion

The Puritans understood that true spirituality (which, in line with Scripture, they called godliness or holiness) looks for all life to be doxological, that is, an offering of worship. That means that whether I am preparing a meal or writing a letter, driving the car or giving practical care to an elderly neighbor, this is as much the arena for offering myself up to God in worship as when I read the Scriptures and pray at the start of the day, prepare a sermon or write a chapter for a Christian book. No part of life is apart from him.

> The Puritans understood that true spirituality (which, in line with Scripture, they called godliness or holiness) looks for all life to be doxological, that is, an offering of worship.

This integrated life of discipleship, seeking to grow more and more like the Lord Jesus, will make it natural to bear witness to the grace of God as we meet both believers and unbelievers; make serving others a joy not a frustration or resented curtailment of personal freedom; stretch mind and heart; inspire us with humble but confident hope that death is the gateway to life face-to-face with the Savior; enable us to help one another "toward love and good deeds" as we "draw near to God with a sincere heart in full assurance of faith, having our hearts sprinkled to cleanse us from a guilty conscience and having our bodies washed with pure water" because the Lord Jesus has died and risen, once for all and perfectly, to make a living way to the very throne of God (Heb 10:19–24).

May our understanding and practice of authentic spirituality bring glory to the Triune God.

Rose Dowsett, with husband Dick, served forty years with OMF International before retirement. A Bible teacher and missiologist as well as a mother and grandmother, Rose continues to write, research, and teach, and is currently working on two more books. She was formerly vice-chair of the WEA Mission Commission and co-led the Global Missiology Task Force. She remains passionate about world mission. She lives in Scotland.

Scripture: *Matthew 6:33 ("But seek first...")*; *Colossians 1:15–20 ("The Son is the image...")*

Resources: *Dynamics of Spiritual Life* by Richard Lovelace (Downer's Grove, II: InterVarsity Press, 1979; *A Passion for Holiness* by Jim Packer (Nottingham: Servant:USA/ Crossway,1992).

CHAPTER 2

What Shapes Our Spirituality in Missions?

K. John Amalraj

India is a land known for her spirituality. Magnificent temples, ancient sculptures, images, idols, and pictures of gods displayed all over provide a spiritual environment not necessarily seen in any other land. The quest for true spirituality draws people from around the world to come to India. It has attracted many seekers from the West and East searching for the truth behind this form of spirituality. Is there a difference between spirituality and the religiosity that seems to encompass the subcontinent?

Job Anbalagan quotes from a newspaper article as follows:[1]

> On the summit of one of the mountains of the Kailash Range was a deserted Buddhist temple, and rarely visited by man. A few miles from this temple dwelt the great saint known as the Maharishi of Kailash, in a cave some 13,000 feet above the sea level. All this region is the Olympus of India, the seat of Hindu holy myths, and it is associated in Hindu sacred books with the names of great and devout souls of all times.

> In the summer of 1912, Sadhu Sundar Singh (d. 1929) traveled through these regions alone and on foot. He would never forget the day when, struck with snow-blindness and almost wearied to death, he staggered drearily on over snowy and stony crags, not knowing whither he went. Suddenly he lost his balance and fell. Recovering from the fall, he awoke to one of the greatest experiences of his life, for he opened his eyes to find himself lying outside a huge cave, in the shelter of which sat the Maharishi of Kailash in deep meditation.

> Sundar realized that thus, unexpectedly he had succeeded in his search after a holy man, and as soon as he could command his voice, he spoke to the aged saint. Recalled from his meditation, the saint opened his eyes and, casting a piercing glance upon the Sadhu, amazed him by saying, "Let us kneel and

pray." Then followed a most earnest Christian prayer ending in the name of Jesus. This over, the Maharishi unrolled a ponderous copy of the Gospels in Greek and read some verses from the fifth chapter of Matthew. Sunder heard from his own lips the account of his wonderful journey from Alexandria to the Himalayas, from reading the Quran to the Gospels. The Sadhu had long conversations with him about holy things and heard many strange things from his lips. The Sadhu had visited the Maharishi three times.

What Shapes Indian Spirituality?

The spiritual environment in India has given birth to many religious sects of Hinduism like Buddhism, Jainism, Sikhism, etc., and has fostered religions like Christianity and Islam that came to her shores. Hinduism, Buddhism, and Islam spread into the South East and the Far East through Indians commissioned by kings as well as through traders who took their spices and religion to all the islands in the Indian Ocean. Indian spirituality has been exported successfully to the West through jet-setting gurus who have built religious communities among the natives in North America and Europe to be their followers through their syncretistic teachings. New Age spirituality and one of the expressions of it in Yoga or Transcendental Meditation, for example, draws its source from Hinduism and is sweeping the younger generation in the West much more than those in India itself. Indian spirituality is best expressed in performing rituals, contemplative meditation, pilgrimages, and celebrating the stages of life. The climax of spirituality is in the act of renouncing the pleasures of the world, family relationships, and choosing to live and die as a hermit.

> Indian spirituality is best expressed in performing rituals, contemplative meditation, pilgrimages, and celebrating the stages of life.

Muslims in India faithfully express their spirituality in the cultural form that has been passed on to them through the influence of the Mughal Empire for nearly one thousand years. There are some contextual exceptions to this. Unfortunately most Indian Christians express their spirituality in the form of European or American denominational subcultures that were handed down to them. The Gothic structures, the English hymnals, the pipe organs, the three-piece suit for Christian Bridegrooms, and the wedding rings are all symbols of Christian spirituality. Mother Theresa, serving the poor, has become a symbol of Christian spirituality in India. She is now venerated as a saint by people of all religions and even worshiped as a goddess! No wonder the public opinion in India perceives Christianity as a Western religion. There may be exceptions, but they are scattered and too few to make an impression.

I once overheard a pastor say to the young organist, "Practice well since we are the only custodians of the liturgical music which the churches in England have thrown out." For the pastor, the eighteenth-century liturgy was an important expression of his spirituality, but he was totally ignorant of the fact that there are millions of Indians seeking true spirituality within their cultural expressions.

What Shaped My Own Spirituality?

I am an Indian. But you will be disappointed to know that there is very little of the Indian spirituality that I can discover in my own spiritual expressions. Four generations ago my great-grandparents chose to follow Jesus Christ and embraced Christianity. I was baptized as a Lutheran, confirmed in the Anglican tradition, discipled by parachurch agencies to be an evangelical, and influenced by charismatic experiences. I have grown up rebelling against various forms of superficial spirituality that I encountered. This made me question all forms, functions, and meaning of the expression of spirituality, but I cannot escape the reality that my spirituality was shaped by denominational Christianity.

What Shapes the Indian Christian Spirituality?

The history of Christianity in India goes all the way back to the first century with Apostle Thomas's martyrdom in the southern tip of India. However, it is the influence of the Syrian ecclesiastical order, European, and American missionaries that have left a mark on how Indian Christians express their spirituality. The denominational mission societies faithfully planted their form of spirituality in the new churches they established. Most of the Indian missionaries from the south who went to north India imitated the Western missions in their own mission enterprise, which includes structures, policies, and methodologies. It is similar to the mission enterprise from the northeastern states of India as well as the churches in east, west, and northern India.

Describing True Spirituality

Spirituality may have to be defined in its context, and it is not a term exclusive to the followers of Jesus Christ. There are many hundreds of definitions for spirituality in various dictionaries and writings, but I want to suggest my own understanding of spirituality.

True spirituality is a live, continuous, personal relationship with the creator God that fulfills my deepest human longings for inward and outward peace and gives me meaning and purpose for everyday life. Spirituality is of no use if it is not of earthly use. True spirituality is discovered in human relationships built on the foundation of a relationship with God.

True spirituality is a live, continuous, personal relationship with the creator God that fulfills my deepest human longings for inward and outward peace and gives me meaning and purpose for everyday life.

What Shapes Our Spirituality in Missions?

There are many factors that shape our spirituality in missions. If we seek to express true spirituality in our life and work in a modern, global mission context we need to stop and look back to what shapes our spirituality.

Life Stages: Our expression of spirituality changes as we advance in our age. Some of us who are younger leaders are excited at every new opportunity that comes before us and we jump on to that. We assume that our generation can finish the job of the Great Commission and so put all our energy to the task. Being active and busy in the ministry sounds very spiritual. However, as we advance in our age and life stages, we are mellowed with experience. Our energy level drops, we slow down and start talking about leadership succession and the need for sabbaticals. As we near the grave, our spirituality is expressed more visibly. We confess our regrets, failures, and disappointments and naturally begin to devote more time to spiritual disciplines.

There is a need for intergenerational participation at every level of mission work so that there is more of a balanced expression of spirituality. Do age and the stages in life shape our spirituality in missions?

> There are many factors that shape our spirituality in missions. If we seek to express true spirituality in our life and work in a modern, global mission context we need to stop and look back to what shapes our spirituality.

Personality: The simplest of personality types say that we are either extroverts or introverts. Though I may be wrong, I tend to think that most extroverts love to express their spirituality in charismatic form of worship, compared to introverts who may like a more liturgical form of worship. We might assume that an introvert whose image is that of being very contemplative looks more spiritual than an extrovert who does the opposite. We normally talk of leadership styles that differ based on personalities. Some leaders are perceived to be more spiritual than others but the perception may simply be personality differences. What is the influence of our personality and our leadership style in the way we express our spirituality in missions?

Culture: The study of the relationship between culture and spirituality is complex and vast. This is where contextualization of spirituality becomes an issue. Christ shared his revelation in simple Semitic terms with stories, images, and parables that arose out of his own Jewish culture. The Sermon on the Mount (the Beatitudes) is a counter to the kind of spirituality practiced by the Pharisees and the Sadducees. Later, as Greco-Roman philosophical concepts were established, those conceptual terminologies became normative. Adaptation, nativization, and contextualization became part of several pioneering ministries.

The Westerners understanding of spirituality is influenced by the Greek dualism of secular and sacred or physical and spiritual. Asians and Africans, on the other hand, incorporate the spiritual realm into every aspect of their daily life—a more wholistic understanding of spirituality. It is normal for them to think spiritually. Many of the mission fields in rural areas of India normally report miracles, deliverance from demon possession, and even the healing of their milking cows, goats, and poultry which led to people deciding to follow Christ.

Western culture expresses its spirituality in the form of abstract philosophies boxed into systematic theology. We are labeled as either Calvinist or Wesleyan, an evangelical, liberal, or an ecumenist. Why cannot we combine the richness of all of them into an expression of spirituality without these labels? In the context of Asia and Africa, these distinctions generally do not matter except for the funding! The theologians and denominational leaders have influenced our thinking process. Why do we have to continue the centuries of theological debates and denominational wars in Asia and Africa? For many of us it is an expression of spirituality to defend our pet theology or denomination. These distinctions may be important in the Western historical context but not necessary in many other cultures. This has direct implications for the kind of church planting that takes place on the mission field.

> Asians and Africans on the other hand incorporate the spiritual realm into every aspect of their daily life—a more wholistic understanding of spirituality.

The Roman Catholic missions were the pioneers to develop Asian Christian spirituality led by the courageous efforts of Matteo Ricci (d. 1610) in China where he attempted to retain Buddhist expression of spirituality in his life and witness. Francis Xavier (d. 1552) had earlier attempted to adapt to the local culture in Japan. In India, Roberto de Nobili (d. 1656) emulated Ricci, adapting saffron dress and other symbols including an Indian name to express his spirituality within the Indian culture.[2] Many others including Protestant missionaries followed in their footsteps, but their efforts were isolated and scattered and have never become mainstream in Indian spirituality.

Worship is one of the most visible forms of the expression of spirituality within a culture. There are efforts in developing indigenous music and songs on the mission fields. The African style of worship with rhythm and dance and the Asian way of worship with rituals and symbols adds diversity to our worship.

Spiritual disciplines like prayer and meditation of Scripture is also related to cultural expressions. Mass prayer and the early morning prayers are Korean cultural expressions. The inductive Bible study method is primarily a Western cultural practice, whereas the meditative approach to the study of Scripture reflects the Asian culture.

---

2   Basil Pennington with Simon Chan, "Spirituality, Christian," in *A Dictionary of Asian Christianity* (Grand Rapids, MI: Eerdmans, 2001), 790.

How Does Culture Shape Us in the Expression of Spirituality in Missions?

Religious Traditions: Richard Foster's monumental work in collecting stories from historical, biblical, and contemporary paradigms and clearly distinguishing the strengths and weaknesses of each of these traditions is a very useful work in the study of how religious traditions influence our spirituality. Foster says,

> There are streams of spiritual life: the Contemplative, Holiness, Charismatic, Social Justice, Evangelical, and Incarnational traditions. In reality these traditions describe various dimensions of the spiritual life. It is Jesus who models them in his life in its most complete form. [3]

Although most of us would attempt to identify in which tradition we have been influenced, there will always be a mixture of traditions. Foster does not discuss much about the spirituality tradition of the Eastern Orthodox, where the liturgy in itself is a demonstration of the gospel and has been designed to help people worship God and through that bring others to worship God.

> Although most of us would attempt to identify in which tradition we have been influenced, there will always be a mixture of traditions.

The spirituality that was expressed by Sadhu Sundar Singh (d. 1929) during his time was unique. He was a convert from Hinduism and the religious traditions of Hinduism shaped his expression of spirituality. It was close to the monastic tradition and similarities can be identified in most of the religions. There are men and women who dedicate their lives totally to living the deeper spiritual dimensions of their religious beliefs. The mandate of the Vatican Council II says, "Let them reflect attentively on how Christian religious life may be able to assimilate the ascetic and contemplative traditions whose seeds were sometimes already planted by God in ancient cultures prior to the preaching of the gospel."[4] Sadhu Sundar Singh, after a lot of hesitation, accepted baptism by the Anglican tradition but soon after that renounced all identification with the traditional churches and took on an ascetic lifestyle, traveling barefoot all over India and even to Tibet preaching the gospel. His teachings were once popular in the West as a tool to aid deeper spirituality.

In a similar way, the first generation Buddhist background believer, Muslim background believer, Sikh background believer, animistic background believer, and others will have a spirituality that is influenced by their own religious tradition background. The expression of spirituality in our mission fields will vary according to the traditions. How do traditions shape our spirituality and eventually affect our missions?

---

3   Richard Foster, *Streams of Living Water* (New York. HarperCollins, 1998).
4   Pennington, 792–94.

Gender: Women are considered more spiritual than men in most cultures. Women are the bearers of culture. If we take a survey of attendance on Sunday worship, prayer meetings, revival meetings, crusades, and outreaches we will generally find more women than men. History bears witness to the sustenance of mission movements because of the role of women in providing prayer support. In the Indian context, it is the devout women who sacrificially set aside money, rice, wheat, etc. for the cause of giving to missions. It is the mothers who most often dedicate their sons to become pastors or missionaries. It is the mothers who are always praying for the prodigal son or daughter. Most of us come from a male-dominated society and fail to recognize the influence of our own mothers, wives, sisters, and daughters who are in the forefront of expressing their true spirituality. It is women who shape the spirituality of their children and family and pass it on to the next generation. This is true not just in Christianity but even in other religions. It is an irony that women are not involved in official roles in religious organizations or structures. Maybe this is why we sometimes lack a sense of spirituality in our missions! We would have a richer experience of spirituality if we involved more women in our gatherings, meetings, committees, and consultations! Does gender shape spirituality in missions?

Understanding of Vocation: All personnel who are involved in missions will relate to the "missionary call"—how do we understand the relationship between one's spirituality and calling? Does our spirituality relate to how we respond to our calling? As a pastor's son in a conservative evangelical tradition, my family expected me as the eldest son to follow in the footsteps of my father. I resisted this family pressure and ended up studying law and management. Eventually I became involved in mission organizations using my training and experience in the corporate world. I never heard a voice or saw a vision or had somebody lay their hands on me and prophesy. A mentor saw the potential in me and invited me to be involved in missions. I do have the assurance that I am fulfilling the purpose of God in my life but how I understood calling depended on who and what shaped my spirituality.

The word "call" has its roots in the Latin word *vocario,* which in English means vocation. All people are called to their respective vocation. A teacher needs to have a sense of call if she is dedicated to her work. A doctor needs to have a sense of calling to excel in his profession. A businessman also needs a calling to be involved in business. We become frustrated when we have to work to sustain ourselves and our families without having a choice to fulfill our potentials. God has gifted us with natural abilities and spiritual gifting for certain specific vocations. A missionary who has lost her sense of calling will be a total failure on the field. Similarly, a pastor who has lost his sense of calling will just be doing the routine without concern for his congregation. All mission organizations have extensive procedures and systems to test the calling of individuals into missions. How we understand each individual's calling is based on the spirituality expressed in the organization. Is there something different in the way we understand a missionary calling to that of a calling to a profession? Why does a missionary or a pastoral vocation somehow seem to be more spiritual than the other vocations? Are we being dualistic? Does this understanding of spirituality make us expect that only a few in the church are called to missions and all others just stay where they are? The Filipino churches envision their womenfolk to serve professionally as maids and sent them out to the Arab world as witnesses. Hundreds of young women came back with stories of transformation. A silent spiritual revolution is happening because of the faithfulness of the Filipino maids.

The hidden years of Jesus' life have fuelled a lot of speculation. The last we hear of Jesus' childhood was when he was just twelve years old and in the temple answering questions. I think it is right to believe that Jesus was a fulltime carpenter, initially as an apprentice with his earthly father Joseph and later as the responsibility fell on him to earn a livelihood to support his family—his mother Mary, his brothers, and sisters. His public ministry lasted only a very brief period, but his life as a carpenter also had a mission to fulfill. The influence of his spirituality in the everyday life was a way of fulfilling his mission. Those hidden years were not just a time of waiting or preparation for his "main" public ministry. Jesus was sent by the Father to redeem the world, and it included the long silent years of work as a carpenter. He did become a Rabbi in his public ministry. It is good that we do not have more information about his carpentry work otherwise we would have institutionalized the vocation of carpenter and turned all the tables, chairs, or furniture made by him into museum articles. If we understand who and what shapes our spirituality then our understanding of vocation and the missionary enterprise will be different.

> Jesus was sent by the Father to redeem the world and it included the long silent years of work as a carpenter.

Organizational Spirituality: In the study of organizational behavior it is said that organizations have their own subcultures. In large multinational organizations, different departments may even have their own subcultures. I have had the privilege of working in the corporate world for a brief period before starting to work with mission organizations. I realized that organizations are human structures, whether in the business world, or in missions, or in the church arena. The same interpersonal challenges are present in both kinds of organizations except that in Christian organizations the expectations from one another are much higher than in business organizations. I believe that we can use the field of knowledge in management, governance, and organizational behavior to strengthen the capacities of our organizations to be more effective. However, in the early stages of my involvement in mission, I was told not to use my knowledge of management because these skills were not spiritual. Many organizations have gone into crisis simply because they refused to adopt common management principles.

What kind of spirituality do our organizations have and how does it impact missions on the field? Why do we call only some mission organizations "faith missions" and not all of them? The fundraising policies, the member care policies, the organizational structure, and the governance model of our organizations are different according to our culture, but more than that they are different because of the spiritual traditions which shaped the founders and leaders of these organizations. Let me suggest two large organizations that express their spirituality differently. I have good friends in both these organizations: Operation Mobilisation (OM) and Youth with a Mission (YWAM). I have yet to meet someone who has migrated from OM to YWAM or the reverse. Recently I had conversations with friends who successfully made a transition between international organizations. I asked them three questions as follows:

1. Have you noticed any differences in how God's call is understood in these organizations?
2. Have you observed any differences in the process of organizational decision making that has affected your journey in missions?
3. Are there any significant differences in the exercise of leadership in both these organizations other than cultural?

The fundraising policies, the member care policies, the organizational structure, and the governance model of our organizations are different according to our culture, but more than that they are different because of the spiritual traditions which shaped the founders and leaders of these organizations.

In summary, their responses to these questions was eye-opening. They value the sincere and deeply God-focused way the organizations seek to walk their journey in mission given the context in which they were founded and the traditions they inherited. It is not about either/or, good/bad, or spiritual/or not. They treasure the maturing and growing that has happened through the transitions.

Conclusion

I am not an anthropologist, biblical scholar, or even a missiologist. Thank God for the Igassu Consultation that gave us the term "Reflective Practioners" which best describes our journey. We need to reflect on why we do what we do and who or what actually shapes our expressions of spirituality in missions? Let us not judge one another in the expression of our spirituality. Let us not become legalistic and lay down norms of spirituality. Let us enrich our spirituality by being inclusive of one another's diverse spiritual expressions and experiences. In a globalized context of missions we need to develop integration into every aspect of our life and mission so that God's name may be glorified for ever and ever!

Now all glory to God, who is able, through his mighty power at work within us, to accomplish infinitely more than we might ask or think. Glory to him in the church and in Christ Jesus through all generations forever and ever, Amen (Eph 3:20–21).

References

Comer, Kim, ed. 2003. *Wisdom of the Sadhu*. Farmington, PA: The Bruderhof Foundation.

Foster, Richard J. 1998. *Streams of Living Water*. New York: HarperCollins.

Moreau, Scott A, ed. 2000. *Evangelical Dictionary of World Missions*. Ada MI: Baker Books.

Pennington, Basil with Simon Chan. 2001. "Spirituality, Christian." In *A Dictionary of Asian Christianity*. Sunquist, Scott W., ed. Grand Rapids, MI: Eerdmans Publishing Co.

Sunderaraj, Francis, ed. 1990. *World Missions: The Asian Challenge. Compendium of Asian Missions Congress*. New Delhi: Evangelical Fellowship of Asia.

John Amalraj, son of a pastor, trained as a lawyer, studied political science and human resources development, then started his career in the corporate sector. He responded to the invitation to serve with India Missions Association (A federation of mission agencies in India) in Chennai, New Delhi, and Hyderabad. He is involved with networking mission organizations, developing leaders, and enabling strategic thinking. He studied theology in Singapore while serving with migrant Indian workers along with a local Methodist church. John now serves as the Executive Secretary of Interserve India envisioning, equipping, and enabling Christian Professionals to be involved in global missions. John is married to Jessie, an English Language trainer. They are blessed with sons Jason and Joash, and they make their home in Pune, India.

Scripture: *Genesis 12:1–3 ("The Lord had said to Abram, 'Go ...'")*

Inspiration: Listening to real-life stories of mission work from my grand aunt who preached the Gospel to the tribals in Central India.

CHAPTER 3

Mission and Spirituality

Kirk Franklin

Introduction

South African missiologist David Bosch observes how monks in the monastic movement understood that there was no such thing as a "quick-fix mentality" with spirituality in mission because mission spans from one generation to the next.[1] The church in God's mission might see "a momentary advance," but without "a spirituality of the long haul" this may not be sustained.[2]

Understanding spirituality means we must consider "the practices and beliefs of the religion with which it is connected."[3] Scott Sundquist identifies seven practices and beliefs that are fundamental for spiritual formation for Christian mission: 1) *silence*: the "secret" of the spiritual life is to learn to wait upon the Holy Spirit who gives his gifts that enable participation in his mission; 2) learn and memorize *Scripture*; 3) *community*: communal witness reflects the presence of the Triune God; 4) *repentance* "opens the doorway to spiritual power [through] honest weakness;" 5) *action*: a "gentle dance of the personal and communal, of silence and action, and of study and reflection;" 6) *attentiveness*: learn to pay attention to the needs all around; and 7) without *love*, a missional life is like "a clanging symbol or a noisy gong (1 Cor 13:1)."[4]

Defining Terms

There are three key terms to consider:

---

1   David Bosch, *Transforming Mission: Paradigm Shifts in Theology of Mission* (Maryknoll, NY: Orbis Books, 2011), 238.
2   Patrick Henry, "Monastic Mission: The Monastic Tradition as Source for Unity and Renewal Today" *Ecumenical Review* XXXIX (1987), 280.
3   Chris Starts and Peirong Lin, "The Search for Spirituality in the Business World," in *Leadership, Innovation, and Spirituality*, eds. Patrick Nullens and Jack Barentsen (Leuven: Peeters, 2014), 37.
4   Scott Sunquist, *Understanding Christian Mission: Participation in Suffering and Glory* (Grand Rapids, MI: Baker Academic, 2013), 299ff.

1. *Mission*: As its foundation and source, the mission of God is the salvation activity of the triune missionary God as Jesus Christ is proclaimed, through the blood of his cross, as savior for all.[5] The church is God's instrument for his mission that reaches across all barriers (linguistic, cultural, religious, ethnic, ideological, socioeconomic, and so forth) in order to introduce people to Christ by "announcing the gospel in speech and social action."[6]

2. *Missional:* An adjective describing something related to mission or something characterized by the mission of God. Being missional "means to participate in God's mission as he and we work out his will in the world."[7]

3. *Missional spirituality* (or spirituality in mission): Spirituality is not concerned just with spiritual disciplines and habits (such as prayer, Scripture reading, church attendance, or an ethical list of behaviors). Instead, "spirituality is informed by the *missio Dei* and the theological reflection of the church."[8] Spirituality in mission is fundamentally connected with examining the foundations for mission such as discerning the work of the Holy Spirit, discovering what God is doing in the world and joining with him. Missional spirituality is "lived in and fuelled by awareness of the *missio Dei*" as the Holy Spirit enlivens it.[9]

Some Insights from the Bible

First and foremost, spirituality is about loving God: "Love the Lord your God with all your heart and with all your soul and with all your strength" (Deut 6:5). It is about focusing on God: "Set your hearts on things above… Set your minds on things above… your life is now hidden with Christ in God" (Col 3:1–3).

God's Word influences our spirituality: "Blessed are those… who delight in the law of the Lord, and who meditate on his law day and night" (Ps 1:1–2; also Ps 51:6). To be spiritually alive requires relying on the Holy Spirit's guidance: "Live… according to the Spirit" (Rom 8:4; also John 14:17).

Spirituality comes from living a holy life: "Just as he who called you is holy, so be holy in all you do" (1 Pet 1:15; also Matt 5:6). The evidence of a spiritually alive life is inner peace: "You will keep in perfect peace those whose minds are steadfast, because they trust in you" (Isa 26:3, TNIV; also Rom 8:6 and Rom 14:17).

---

5   Stephen Bevans and Roger Schroeder, *Prophetic Dialogue: Reflections on Christian Mission Today* (Maryknoll, NY: Orbis Books, 2011), 2.

6   Robert Gallagher, "Missionary Methods: St. Paul's, St. Roland's, or Ours?" in *Missionary Methods: Research, Reflections and Realities*, eds. Craig Ott and J.D Payne (Pasadena, CA: William Carey Library, 2013), 4.

7   Roger Helland and Leonard Hjalmarson, *Missional Spirituality: Embodying God's Love from the Inside Out* (Downers Grove, IL: InterVarsity Press, 2011), 27.

8   Robert Webber, *The Younger Evangelicals* (Grand Rapids, MI: Baker, 2002), 240.

9   Darryl Balia and Kirsteen Kim, *Edinburgh 2010, Volume II: Witnessing to Christ Today* (Oxford: Regnum Books, 2010), 223.

Spirituality Is Context Sensitive

Missional spirituality takes place in and is deeply influenced within a cultural context. As God works around the world, we hear stories and descriptions of what the spirituality of God's people looks like. This provides tangible learning experiences about the rich diversity of spirituality, spiritual practices, and traditions. These remind us of the diversity in God's mission.

Take for example, missionary preparation of over one hundred years ago: In the era of the 1910 Edinburgh World Missionary Conference, preparation focussed on the "quality of spirituality" that was evident in missionary training which sought to cultivate "a deeply rooted spiritual life" that was not dependent upon external aids but instead on the "personal advice of experienced Christian friends."[10]

Throughout mission history, renewal and expansion are accompanied by new spiritual dynamics and renewed forms of spirituality. The concerted missionary efforts over the past 100 years have demonstrated this with "the strongholds of Christian spirituality" shifting from the West/North to the global South.[11]

> Throughout mission history, renewal and expansion are accompanied by new spiritual dynamics and renewed forms of spirituality.

Christian spirituality is vulnerable. Andrew Walls notes how some world religions have maintained allegiance across the centuries but not so with the Christian faith.[12] Do we remember that Yemen was once a Christian kingdom, Syria had a church influence that led the Christian world, and Christianity was strong in the whole Euphrates valley (modern Iraq)? Walls therefore concludes, "Christian advance is not steady inevitable progress. Advance is often followed by recession. The spread of the gospel does not produce permanent gains that can be plotted on a map." Why is this so? Because at the very heart of the gospel is the "vulnerability of the Cross and the fragility of the earthen vessel."[13] As the Apostle Paul states, "We have this treasure in clay jars, so that the extraordinary power belongs to God and does not come from us" (2 Cor 4:7).

I shared this observation about the gospel's vulnerability with a church in Yaoundé, Cameron. As I spoke, there was a noticeable commotion, though I could not tell the source. Later over lunch, some of the elders met with me. They had stern looks so I apologized in advance for anything I said that had caused offence. They replied to the

---

10   Ann-Marie Kool, "Changing Images in the Formation for Mission: Commission Five in Light of Current Challenges a Western Perspective," in *Edinburgh 2010: Mission Then and Now*, eds. David A. Kerr and Kenneth R. Ross (Pasadena, CA: William Carey Library, 2010), 159–60.

11   Samuel Kobia, "Cooperation and the Promotion of Unity: a World Council of Churches Perspective," in *Edinburgh 2010: Mission Then and Now*, eds. David A. Kerr and Kenneth R. Ross (Pasadena, CA: William Carey Library, 2010), 246.

12   Andrew Walls, "Demographics, Power, and the Gospel in the 21st Century," presented at the Wycliffe International Convention and the SIL International Conference (Waxhaw, NC, June 2001), 1.

13   Walls, 1.

contrary. The commotion was actually women weeping. They were sad to realize that the Western churches that had brought them the gospel and that they had embraced, many of those same churches, in places like Scotland and Wales, were now boarded up or had found new life as cafes, libraries, and community centers. Their sadness was compounded when they realized the same could happen to their congregation. Due to the inherent vulnerability of Christian spirituality, within one generation their congregation could disappear.

Missional Spirituality in Community

The eternal existence of God "has been in community."[14] The relational character of God is expressed in the Trinitarian nature of God himself. The relationship among the Father, Son, and Holy Spirit becomes the model for relationship among God's people.

> As God's people relate to each other in community, their individual and mutual spirituality is strengthened.

As God's people relate to each other in community, their individual and mutual spirituality is strengthened. This has missional impact because it fulfills Jesus' desire for the unity of community as a witness to the watching world (John 17:23).

The importance of community to strengthen spirituality in mission was an outcome of a missiological reflective consultation that my agency hosted in Accra, Ghana a few years ago. We brought together a dozen mission leaders from ten countries for two days to consider the topic of "Community as an expression of the mission Dei." The discussion notes were used as the foundation for a document called *The Wycliffe Global Alliance in Community* (Principles of Community) which we posted on our website. There are four principles that are intended to strengthen spiritual missional communities:

1. We are created for community and called to community (creation and calling).
2. We are God's people, called to consistently and lovingly relate and behave according to the instruction of his Word and the example of Christ (identity— who we are together).
3. Living and serving in community glorifies God and provides a tangible example of the gospel in action. We reflect the image of God through intentionally modeling authentic community (how we live together).
4. A community that glorifies God attracts people to God and his mission (what we do together).[15]

These principles articulate core values for missional spirituality. A number of years ago, I was given the responsibility of forming an intercultural missional leadership team

---

14   Jedidiah Coppenger, "The Community of Mission: The Church," in *Theology and Practice of Mission: God, the Church and the Nations*, Bruce Ashford (Nashville: B&H Publishing Group, 2011), 61.
15   WGA, "The Wycliffe Global Alliance in Community (Principles of Community)" (Unpublished paper, 2014), 1.

comprising of Christians from many nations. As the team was forming, I faced the challenge that no one really knew each other and yet they were expected to work closely together. They also needed to work virtually as they were spread around the world. Therefore, before we started working together, we gathered, including spouses, for a three-day retreat. Each couple was given two hours to share their testimony, and then the rest of the group prayed for the couple. We also did recreational things together and had fellowship over meals. This created the foundation for a community where we placed a high value on our spiritual journeys. Since then, each time we meet we spend several hours catching up with our personal, spiritual, and ministry journeys. When new team members join us, we give them ample time to introduce themselves and join us in the spiritual journey of our leadership community. For many, this is the first time they have ever been treated this way.

Missional spirituality, according to Joke van Saane, can be like a journey: "The final destination is not so important, but the journey itself with all the barriers and challenges forms the most important part."[16] The spiritual journey for participants in God's mission provides important lessons to be learned and passed on to others.

Mission Spirituality in Reflective Practice

Missional spirituality grows through personal devotions, prayer, and holiness. While we need to "retreat and reflect" we must also "engage and act."[17] Otherwise we could disengage. Mark Sayers proposes a process of "withdrawal-return" so that a leader gets "critical distance [from] the myths and illusions" of one's culture in order to "break their spell."[18] Once balance is regained, the leader returns refreshed and ready to lead again.

> Missional spirituality grows through personal devotions, prayer, and holiness. While we need to "retreat and reflect" we must also "engage and act."

Rene Padilla states, "True spirituality requires a missionary contemplation and a contemplative mission."[19] In the process, Henri Nouwen believes the leader needs to constantly learn to listen to God's loving voice and in it alone find the courage and wisdom to address any issues that appear.[20]

William Taylor uses the concept of a "Reflective Practitioner" which he defines as "women and men of both action and study; rooted in the Word of God and the church of Christ; passionately obedient to the fullness of the Great Commandment

16   Joke van Saane, "Spirituality and the Psychology of Leadership Credibility: an Analysis of from the Psychology of Religion," in *Leadership, Innovation, and Spirituality* eds. Patrick Nullens and Jack Barentsen (Leuven: Peeters, 2014), 47.
17   Helland and Hjalmarson, 49.
18   Mark Sayers, *Facing Leviathan: Leadership, Influence, and Creating in a Cultural Storm* (Chicago: Moody, 2014), 126.
19   Balia and Kim, 2010, 241.
20   Henri Nouwen, *In the Name of Jesus* (New York: Crossroad, 1989), 45.

and Great Commission; globalized in their perspective; yet faithful citizens of their own cultures."[21] According to Taylor's definition, the fundamental characteristics of a reflective practitioner is one who anchors his or her action and study upon the Bible; has an awareness of global realities and the church; and understands how to integrate these components into their response to God's invitation to join him in his mission. The reflective practitioner's goal is to demonstrate an integrated nature—action and study that is glocal and global, Christ-centered and biblical.

Socrates' maxim that the unexamined life is not worth living applies here. A reflective person learns the importance of self-examination. In doing so, he or she develops courage to deal with difficulties, stands firm for what he or she believes, admits mistakes, and successfully battles inner turmoil or external opposition.[22]

Spirituality in Missional Leadership

In a qualitative research study I conducted of fifteen members of my agency's leadership team, I analyzed their personal leadership philosophies. These consisted of their individual beliefs, values, ideals, and practices about leadership that were related to their understanding of the Bible, culture, personal experiences, training, temperament, gifting, and abilities. The team's individual leadership philosophies were based on their authentic experiences without relying on the efforts (articles, books, etc.) of other leaders.

In the sampling, eight (53%) were from Western countries and seven (47%) were from countries in the global South. The sample base was 60% male and 40% female. Over two-thirds (66%) were aged between 51–65 (due to the higher level of experience and maturity needed to fulfill their global responsibilities) with 13% aged between 45–50 and 20% aged between 66–75.

Through analyzing the key words, themes, and concepts of each of the individual leadership philosophies, I observed the importance of spirituality in the life and practice of an experienced leader in God's mission. There were professional and personal characteristics, such as being flexible, discerning complexity, taking thoughtful risks, demonstrating courage in the midst and demands of leadership, understanding the importance of continuous communication, and maintaining personal integrity. However, what stood out were the spiritual values which I placed in four clusters:

1. *Relationship with Christ and reliance upon God's Word:* Practice personal devotion through prayer and guidance from the Bible to discern God's will in all contexts.

---

21   William Taylor, *Global Missiology for the Twenty-first Century: The Iguassu Dialogue* (Grand Rapids, MI: Baker Academic, 2000), 1.
22   Eddie Gibbs, *LeadershipNext: Changing Leaders in a Changing Culture* (Downers Grove, IL: InterVarsity Press, 2005), 136.

2. *Christ is the ultimate leadership example:* Lead as a "first follower" of Christ—willing to lead in and from "unconventional and unfamiliar" ways.[23]

3. *Align with God's missional plan:* Understand God's missional heart as one faithfully uses his/her spiritual gifts in leadership.

4. *Commit to spiritual transformation:* Live a spiritually intimate life in Christ based upon personal holiness, integrity, spiritual renewal, and guidance from the Holy Spirit.

These spiritual characteristics provide important foundations for leadership: Christ is the ultimate leadership example for the leader. The leader learns how to depend upon the Holy Spirit's creativity, which flows out of a personal relationship with Christ and reliance upon God's Word. As a result, the leader gains insights into how to align with God's missional plan. The leader is committed to continuous personal growth and development. A result will be the spiritual transformation of the leader and the community he/she leads.

> The leader learns how to depend upon the Holy Spirit's creativity, which flows out of a personal relationship with Christ and reliance upon God's Word.

Mission Spirituality and Discipleship

Missional spirituality calls for a renewed commitment to discipleship that is open to the working of the Holy Spirit. Let me share from personal experience: After four years of intense mission leadership responsibilities, the Board of Directors to whom I report enabled me to have a two-month sabbatical. Each day on my sabbatical I spent time lingering in the Scriptures, starting from Genesis 1 and making it to Judges. At the end of each Bible session I wrote down thoughts, impressions, or actions the Lord was speaking to me about.

For example, there was Enoch who "walked with God" (Gen 5:24); Noah, "a godly man ... blameless among his contemporaries [who] walked with God" (Gen 6:9); and Moses who also walked with God and gave insights into life for the Israelites while they were in captivity in Egypt, when they were released, and their 40-year wandering in the wilderness. As participants in God's mission, are we known as ones who walk with God? Can the same be said of our agencies?

God gave instructions for how the Israelites were to conduct their lives, including the Ten Commandments. God decreed in Exodus 20:8, "Remember the Sabbath day to set it apart as holy ... from the other days." The weekly cycle of rest is restorative and thus for our own good and yet, how many of us take one day a week to completely rest (not even looking at work-related emails)?

---

23   Leonard Sweet, *I Am a Follower: The Way, Truth, and Life of Following Jesus* (Nashville, TN: Thomas Nelson, 2012), 12.

At the end of the sabbatical I had the conviction that I needed to be a better example among those whom I served. Therefore, during a gathering of over 200 such people, I confessed and repented in these areas:

- I confess my neglect of my relationship with the Lord.
- I confess that many times I have spoken inappropriately about other people.
- I confess that at times I have placed my work above my love for the Lord.
- I confess I have relied more on my organization rather than on my God.
- I confess that I experience a weariness that comes from my endless pursuits of working harder and not following a healthy pattern of rest, and thus I am a poor role model in this respect.
- I confess that I am prone to covet whatever it is that I think God has deprived me of but that he has given to someone else.

After sharing this and receiving feedback, many people in the conference were positively impacted. Some claimed they had never heard one of their leaders confessing and repenting in this way. It brought encouragement and a personal challenge to them about the need to cultivate one's spirituality as one participates in God's mission.

Conclusion

Spirituality from a missional perspective can be summarized as: 1) a description of the relationship between God and a believer made alive in Christ and empowered by his Spirit; 2) this relationship is intended to be transformational (a noticeable change in one's character) because it takes the believer from their pre-Christ state to what they are today and provides motivation for future spiritual maturity; 3) people should see something different in the believer that is only possible because of Christ and God's Word upon which the believer's life is built; and 4) his relationship with God is intended to initiate and empower missional commitment.

Discussion Questions

1. How does the concept of "a spirituality for the long haul" help in envisioning God's mission as one with sustained impact?[24]
2. Scott Sundquist outlines seven fundamentals for spiritual formation for mission.[25] His fifth fundamental is "action" where he describes spirituality as "a gentle dance

---

24   Patrick Henry, "Monastic Mission: The Monastic Tradition as Source for Unity and Renewal Today" *Ecumenical Review XXXIX* (1987), 280.
25   Sundquist, 399ff.

of the personal and communal, of silence and action, and of study and reflection." What are ways that you can apply these to missional spirituality?

3. What are reasons that the spiritual transformation of a leader in God's mission may have wider implications for the missional community he/she leads?

References

Balia, Darryl and Kirsteen Kim. 2010. *Edinburgh 2010, Volume II: Witnessing to Christ Today*. Oxford: Regnum Books.

Bevans, Stephen B. and Roger P. Schroeder. 2011. *Prophetic Dialogue: Reflections on Christian Mission Today*. Maryknoll, NY: Orbis Books.

Bosch, David. 2011. *Transforming Mission: Paradigm Shifts in Theology of Mission*, 20th Anniversary ed. Maryknoll, NY: Orbis Books.

Coppenger, Jedidiah. 2011. "The Community of Mission: The Church." In Bruce R. Ashford, *Theology and Practice of Mission: God, the Church and the Nations*. Nashville: B&H Publishing Group.

Gallagher, Robert L. 2013. "Missionary Methods: St. Paul's, St. Roland's, or Ours?" In *Missionary Methods: Research, Reflections, and Realities*, eds. Craig Ott and J.D Payne, 3–22. Pasadena, CA: William Carey Library.

Gibbs, Eddie. 2005. *LeadershipNext: Changing Leaders in a Changing Culture*. Downers Grove, IL: InterVarsity Press.

Helland, Roger and Leonard Hjalmarson. 2011. *Missional Spirituality: Embodying God's Love from the Inside Out*. Downers Grove, IL: InterVarsity Press.

Henry, Patrick G. 1987. "Monastic Mission: The Monastic Tradition as Source for Unity and Renewal Today." *Ecumenical Review* XXXIX, 3:271–281.

Kobia, Samuel. 2009. "Cooperation and the Promotion of Unity: A World Council of Churches Perspective." In *Edinburgh 2010: Mission Then and Now*, eds. David A. Kerr and Kenneth R. Ross, 237–249. Pasadena, CA: William Carey International Press.

Kool, Ann-Marie. 2009. "Changing Images in the Formation for Mission: Commission Five in Light of Current Challenges a Western Perspective." In *Edinburgh 2010: Mission Then and Now*, eds. David A. Kerr and Kenneth R. Ross, 158–180. Pasadena, CA: William Carey International Press.

Nouwen, Henri. 1989. *In the Name of Jesus*. New York: Crossroad.

Sayers, Mark. 2014. *Facing Leviathan: Leadership, Influence, and Creating in a Cultural Storm*. Chicago, IL: Moody Publishers.

Start, Chris and Peirong Lin. 2014. "The Search for Spirituality in the Business World." In *Leadership, Innovation, and Spirituality*, eds. Patrick Nullens and Jack Barentsen, 31–39. Leuven: Peeters.

Sunquist, Scott W. 2013. *Understanding Christian Mission: Participation in Suffering and Glory*. Grand Rapids, MI: Baker Academic.

Sweet, Leonard. 2012. *I Am a Follower: The Way, Truth, and Life of Following Jesus*. Nashville, TN: Thomas Nelson.

Taylor, William D. 2000. *Global Missiology for the Twenty-first Century: The Iguassu Dialogue*. Grand Rapids, MI: Baker Academic.

van Saane, Joke. 2014. "Spirituality and the Psychology of Leadership Credibility: an Analysis of from the Psychology of Religion." In *Leadership, Innovation, and Spirituality*, eds. Patrick Nullens and Jack Barentsen, 41–56. Leuven: Peeters.

Walls, Andrew. 2001. "Demographics, Power, and the Gospel in the Twenty-first Century." Paper presented at the Wycliffe International Convention and the SIL International Conference. Waxhaw, NC, June.

Webber, Robert. 2002. *The Younger Evangelicals*. Grand Rapids, MI: Baker.

WGA. 2014. "The Wycliffe Global Alliance in Community (Principles of Community)." Unpublished paper.

Kirk Franklin, PhD, grew up in Papua New Guinea (PNG), the son of US Bible translators. As an adult, Kirk served in PNG in media-communications, where he met his Australian wife, Christine, and their three children were born there. Since 1991, Kirk and his family have lived in Melbourne where Kirk has held leadership roles with Wycliffe Australia. Since 2008, Kirk has been the Executive Director of the Wycliffe Global Alliance. He has had formal studies in theology, missiology, and leadership from institutions in the US, Australia and South Africa. Kirk and Christine are members of Warrandyte Community Church.

Scripture: *Psalm 27:14 ("Wait for the Lord; be strong and take heart...")*

Resource: *Hearing God: Developing a Conversational Relationship with God*, by Dallas Willard, (Downers Grove, IL: InterVarsity Press, 2012).

CHAPTER 4

Grace on the Journey

Geoffrey W. Hahn

The spiritual journey involves unexpected turns that lead to surprising panoramas as each missionary strives to follow God's lead. While the trail God blazes for each missionary is unique, there is an item everyone needs to pack for their amazing journey regardless of where God leads them. What is this indispensable supply? As a passport is critical on any significant excursion beyond national borders, grace is critical for the missionary endeavor. God calls his followers to be people characterized by grace in their mission journey, each and every day. The process of being refined by God as people who exude the virtue of grace is foundational to spiritual growth and to ministry efficacy. Only by living out grace can a missionaries' living testimony be congruent with the gospel message.

The centrality of grace theologically distinguishes genuine Christianity from all other religions. Grace, or treating others with unmerited favor, is essential to the Christian paradigm of missions. It is the very foundation of biblical Christianity and it is the essence of Christ-likeness. Grace is a core quality of God himself. So as missionaries strive to be Christ-like, to be godly, surely growth in grace is critical to attaining that goal. Followers of Christ are to be a living expression of grace.

> The centrality of grace theologically distinguishes genuine Christianity from all other religions. Grace, or treating others with unmerited favor, is essential to the Christian paradigm of missions.

The grace-grounded challenge that Paul gives in Romans 15:7 is to "accept one another then, just as Christ accepted you." This admonition is crucial for vibrant ministry teams, especially with the complications introduced in a cross-cultural setting. The verse demonstrates that grace has both vertical and horizontal dimensions. Vertically, God puts grace on full display by sending Jesus to die for human sin, and forgiving sin results in new life for those who believe. Horizontally, Christians are expected to follow Christ's model: to grow in grace and to put grace on full display in their interactions with others.

The identity of missionaries is not only individual, but it is also found in their relationships with other members of the body of Christ and particularly in their relationships with those on their team. Accepting one another's differing gifts, personality, and cultural heritage allows missionaries to demonstrate grace to each other in cross-cultural ministry. The identity and purpose of all missionaries must encompass living out grace and working together in unity. The ministry team's ability to witness is inescapably connected to the depth and quality of the team's relationships and fellowship. According to 2 Peter 3:18, as Christian communities make every effort to pursue holiness, they are to "grow in the grace and knowledge of our Lord and Savior Jesus Christ."

Central to living out grace is that of fostering a caring, uplifting community. As members of a team care for one another, grace is being practiced. In contrast, as Kenneth Gangel comments, "What could be less effective in fulfilling the Great Commission than inviting unsaved people into a congregation scarred by complaining, bitterness, criticism, and hypocrisy?"[1] It is worth noting that the epistles are often addressing specific local churches, and the local church is not the same as a missionary team. However, the principles associated with working in unity are relevant to all contexts where believers work together. In any context of ministering together with fellow believers, each person only has some gifts and therefore is reliant on the gifts of others to function as a body. Likewise, the principle of being people characterized by grace is foundational to all Christian communities, whether they are local churches, ministry organizations, or missionary teams. David Pollock puts it well: "The Great Commandment and the Great Commission are inseparable. The second cannot be done without the first."[2]

> Central to living out grace is that of fostering a caring, uplifting community.

Grace and Missionary Retention

While gracious, caring relationships are difficult to form and maintain, they are a key to missionary retention. God created all people, including missionaries, with the desire to have deep and meaningful relationships with others, and he meets this need through community. Community is a gift from God. The human responsibility is, by God's power, to ensure that community is characterized by grace. Without gracious relationships among missionary teammates, missionary attrition is inevitable. The longing we have for grace-filled community is a gentle reminder that we are created in God's image. The Holy Spirit within us causes us to long for authentic fellowship with fellow believers.

> While gracious, caring relationships are difficult to form and maintain, they are a key to missionary retention

If a missionary team does not model care for one another it fails to embody both grace and the transformational work of the Holy Spirit. Conversely, when unity and care are embraced in the life of a mission community, this often results in spiritual growth for each member. The team becomes a living witness of God's transforming grace, and the

---

1   Kenneth O. Gangel, *Ministering to Today's Adults* (Waco, TX: Word, 1999), 275.
2   David Pollock, "Developing a Flow of Care and Caregivers," in *Doing Member Care Well: Perspectives and Practices from Around the World*, ed. Kelly O'Donnell (Pasadena, CA: William Carey Library, 2002), 23.

team becomes an attractive ministry partner for other Christian groups and even non-Christian groups. "Unity, genuine community, or oneness is a gift from God, a witness to the world and necessary if the church is to fulfill God's purpose."[3] To move forward on the missionary journey with greater kingdom effectiveness, missionaries must strive to develop teams characterized by grace.

Grace and the Trinity

The journey of grace in missions begins with God as Trinity. In whatever God undertakes, the three persons of the Trinity, full of grace, function together—never independently of each other. This reveals much of God's character, the way that he relates, and what he expects of his followers. The Trinity reveals that God is fundamentally communal and that the Father, Son, and Spirit work together in unity: a holy harmony, embracing diversity. God expects Christians to work together in that same unity, and in Ephesians 4:4–7, Paul calls followers of Christ to walk in a unity modeled on the Trinity.

Gilbert Bilezikian writes concerning the Trinity, "Father, Son, and Holy Spirit are united in a relationship of mutual reverence and deference that expresses itself in reciprocal servanthood."[4] So it should not come as a surprise that God's plan for his followers is that believers work together in unity: "He values community supremely because he experiences the dynamics and the synergy of three in one. Thus, when he creates in his image, he creates community."[5]

From God's character flows gracious community, cooperation, and collaboration. Certainly each person was made to be in community, as God is in community. Indeed, it is part of what it means to be created in the image of God. God created humans with a built-in need to work together in order to be as effective as possible for his work. Regardless of personality, cultural heritage, and gifting, no person is created in such a way that they are meant to carry out God's work alone. Grace must be cultivated as the glue that holds the community together: "To each one of us grace has been given as Christ apportioned it" (Eph 4:7).

> From God's character flows gracious community, cooperation, and collaboration.

Grace and Collaboration

Ministry teams thrive when they are characterized by grace. Although grace-full community is difficult to achieve and maintain, God clearly expects missionaries to

---

3   Roberta Hestenes, "Developing Christian Community," *DMP/L* 2030, Denver Seminary Doctor of Ministry Program (Denver, July 15–19, 2002).
4   Gilbert Bilezikian, *Community 101: Reclaiming the Local Church as Community of Oneness* (Grand Rapids, MI.: Zondervan Publishing House, 1997), 200.
5   Ibid., 18.

strive to be people of grace. "God himself taught us to meet one another as God has met us in Christ."[6] In Pauline theology, grace is repeatedly emphasized in discussions about working together with others. Where communities of grace exist, collaborative opportunities increase as other Christians, churches, and Christian organizations are attracted to that grace and desire to participate in the gracious environment. Grace sets the foundation for flourishing teams and extensive partnering.

Throughout Paul's writings, words and phrases such as "unity," "together," and "one another" continually surface. God created humanity with a need to cooperate in order to be as effective as possible for his work. Regardless of personality, cultural heritage, and gifting, we are created in such a way that we need others in order to carry out God's work. In 1 Corinthians 12 Paul elaborates how each Christian is unique in the body of Christ, requiring us to work together in order to function as God intended. No one person possesses all the gifts. In missions then, the spiritual gifts that each of us receives are given for the good of others, and one person can only be effective in fulfilling their calling in the Great Commission with the help of others. By God's design, as we collaborate with fellow team members our ministries have the greatest impact in this world.

> By God's design, as we collaborate with fellow team members our ministries have the greatest impact in this world.

Collaboration in missions requires community, which requires an abundance of grace. Christian community then is a blessing on the journey of grace. Dietrich Bonhoeffer has said, "It is easily forgotten that the fellowship of Christian brethren is a gift of grace, a gift of the kingdom of God."[7]

In Ephesians 4, Paul fleshes out the behavior that is appropriate to the Christian community: "As a prisoner for the Lord, then, I urge you to live a life worthy of the calling you have received" (Eph 4:1). This calling is directly connected to God's work of grace on behalf of believers, flowing through Ephesians 1, where unity is achieved through Christ's work on the cross. So, "to live a life worthy of the calling you have received" arises out of the God's grace and ultimate purpose "to bring all things in heaven and on earth together under one head, even Christ" (Eph 1:10). Christian community is only possible by God's grace, and flourishes as a result of grace displayed within the community.

As Christ's coworkers, we are not only to give praise for the grace we have received so freely; we are expected to proactively respond with specific behavior toward others in a manner that is congruent with the work of grace and God's eternal plan for his people. "Now they are exhorted to 'walk,' to live out their new life in Christ and the unity that is theirs in the church. They are part of God's grand design for the world, which includes the uniting of all things in heaven and on earth (1:10)."[8]

---

6   Dietrich Bonhoeffer, *Life Together* (San Francisco, CA.: HarperCollins, 1954), 25.

7   Bonhoeffer, *Life Together*, 20.

8   Arthur Patzia, "Ephesians, Colossians, Philemon," *New International Biblical Commentary* (Peabody, MA.: Hendrickson, 1984), 154.

Grace and Leadership

Because individual missionaries can behave as if they exist and minister in isolation, missions need to be proactive in building up Christian community. As exciting as the vision of gracious community might be, it does not happen automatically. A vital role of leaders of teams is to be proactive in building community in the team. To establish gracious community and to see it thrive over time requires prayer, dependency on God, a continual pressing into growth in grace, ownership of the vision, and daily cooperation by the whole team. The missionary team should be able to say: "We care for each other as we carry out the kingdom work. We invest in each other as well as investing in our particular ministry roles. We recognize and celebrate that God, though his leading, has brought us together as a missionary team to accomplish his purposes. We are committed to each other as we are jointly committed to following God together." Such a team is demonstrating a community of God's grace.

Biblically, grace is far more than an abstract concept—it is a practice. For all of us, including team leaders, there must be a practical outworking of grace in our everyday lives. As God's people, "We need an environment where we sense the freedom to be who we are, within boundaries framed by values and a common goal. We need to feel we are safe and supported as whole people who have significant things to contribute despite our differences."[9] How can the missionary team grow into an authentic community of grace? This is the challenge facing leaders today.

Grace involves carrying each other's burdens, accepting one another as equals, valuing one another, treating others as better than oneself, and respecting cultural differences. Grace lived out in community involves putting into practice the "one another" admonitions of the Bible—be patient, bearing with one another (Eph 4:2), be kind and compassionate to one another, forgiving each other (Eph 4:32), love one another (John 13:34), accept one another (Rom 15:7), stop passing judgment on one another (Rom 14:13), carry each other's burdens (Gal 6:2), encourage each other (1 Thess 4:18). As a leader, I have found it wonderfully helpful as a team exercise to brainstorm together and create a list of concrete behaviors that would characterize us as we grow more as a team characterized by grace.

> Brainstorm together and create a list of concrete behaviors that would characterize us as we grow more as a team characterized by grace.

In the missions context, a vast majority of working with others is voluntary, rather than being dictated or required. If a team member is judgmental, contentious, and devalues others (that is, generally lacking in grace), why would anyone choose to minister with them? Team members who lack in grace tend to be proactively avoided. Instead, for missionary teams to flourish they must look for members who treat others with mutual respect and dignity, who are a joy to minister with because they are filled with grace.

---

9   Roberta Hestenes, *Turning Committees into Communities* (Colorado Springs, CO: NavPress, 1991) 38.

And grace must be practiced, even through the inevitable trials that will come, when the best teams will experience times of miscommunication and misunderstanding, and when relationships will deteriorate if grace is not extended and relationships are not intentionally nurtured.

Grace and Effectiveness

As missionaries, we need to explore how our ability to live out grace as individuals impacts the effectiveness and productivity of our team's overall ministry. Individualistic approaches and those that are divisive and isolationistic are ultimately ineffective in their approach. To combat this perspective, David Bosch suggests that, "We need to retrieve togetherness, interdependency … The 'psychology of separateness' has to make way for an 'epistemology of participation.' The 'me generation' has to be superseded by the 'us generation.'"[10] This has implications for our effectiveness.

Grace can lead to increased productivity and effectiveness in ministry as people work together in synergy:

> A synergistic effect in physiology speaks of a body organ that cooperates with others to produce or enhance an effect. One observer states that "synergism occurs when the output is greater than the sum of the inputs." … Synergy comes from partnerships; and we want to seek kingdom partnerships for world missions.[11]

As I have shown above, God has made people in such a way that we must work in community, and as we grow in grace we collaborate to be effective and productive in ministry. He has given each person unique gifts: "These resources and skills need not necessarily be equal in quantity or quality, but they must be recognized by both partners as equal in value."[12] Hans Finzel, borrowing from Peter Drucker, states: "All work is work for a team… The purpose of a team is to make strengths productive and weaknesses irrelevant."[13] According to God's perfect plan, only by graciously valuing those differences and working together with others can multiple gifts, abilities, and talents be combined, thereby covering for each other's weaknesses.

---

10   David J. Bosch, *Transforming Mission: Paradigm Shifts in Theology of Mission* (Maryknoll, NY: Orbis, 1991), 362.

11   William D. Taylor, "Introduction: Setting the Partnership Stage," in *Kingdom Partnerships for Synergy in Missions*, ed. William D. Taylor (Pasadena, CA: William Carey Library, 1994), 6.

12   Luis Bush and Lorry Lutz, *Partnering in Ministry: The Direction of World Evangelism* (Downers Grove, IL: InterVarsity Press, 1990), 62.

13   Hans Finzel, *Empowered Leaders* (Nashville, TN.: Word Publishing, 1998), 131.

Grace and Cultural Diversity

In order for missionary teams to thrive in the context of vast cultural differences, the journey together needs to be characterized by relationships of grace: "The heart of the gospel is restored relationships. God longs for Jesus' finished work to be demonstrated in our relationships. Investing time in getting to know, understand, and genuinely appreciate each other isn't optional."[14]

As soon as two people link in ministry collaboration, multiple talents and numerous differences become available that can be capitalized on to help develop a highly effective work. "The simple fact is that a shared vision, a united effort, and a combination of resources always bring greater efficiency and power to accomplish specific tasks."[15] However, the differences can also trigger tension and conflict, unveiling pride, fear, and prejudice. There are few people in the world who do not believe, at the bottom of their hearts, that they are the ones who are normal. Are there any countries in the world that do not view at least one other country or group within its borders as problematic? Members on teams, especially highly diverse teams, inherit these biases, which need to be overcome as we grow in Christ and minister together.

> However, the differences can also trigger tension and conflict, unveiling pride, fear, and prejudice.

Colleagues must build on each other's strengths rather than to be mired in judging differences. Cultural understanding is not enough. "Getting to know one's teammates is, at first, most exciting … but reality soon sets in when the most normal ways of interacting become gnawing irritations or puzzling encounters."[16] Says researcher David Livermore, "We want to move from the desire to love across the chasm of cultural differences to the ability to express our love."[17]

A teammate can understand the differences between themselves and a colleague of a different culture, yet still behave in a way that is highly judgmental of those differences. All human beings are susceptible to ethnocentrism, and it takes a discerning leader to work through this with a highly diverse team. Grace involves acceptance and appreciation of the cultural differences, as well as respect for the other, with genuine love and mutual regard. To affirm, even to celebrate differences is critical to effective teams. Healthy, productive mission teams celebrate what unites them in Christ, as well as their shared ministry vision and goals to see people transformed by Christ. Recognizing their diversity, members genuinely value and respect one another.

---

14   Phill Butler, *Well Connected: Releasing Power, Restoring Hope through Kingdom Partnerships* (Waynesboro, GA.: Authentic Media, 2005), 16.

15   Howard L. Foltz and Ruth Ford, *For Such a Time as This: Strategic Missions Power Shifts for the Twenty-first Century* (Pasadena, CA: William Carey Library, 2000), 25.

16   Lianne Roembke, *Building Credible Multicultural Teams* (Pasadena, CA: William Carey Library, 2000), 105.

17   David A Livermore, *Cultural Intelligence: Improving your CQ to Engage Our Multicultural World* (Grand Rapids, MI: Baker Academic, 2009), 11.

When we work alongside Christians from other cultures, a common response can be to judge differences as sinful. However, before casting judgment, missionaries require the discipline to extend the grace of suspended judgment. They must consider if the differences may actually be cultural diversity that falls within biblical parameters for godly living. "Can we accept people who look, act, and even believe differently than we believe if we know it will release their potential? This doesn't mean we just tolerate them; it means we extend unmerited favor to them, namely grace. Can we admit our own frailties, declare our own strengths, and receive the strengths of others despite their weaknesses?"[18]

As soon as two or more people come together, they have multiple talents and numerous differences to capitalize on to help each other become a highly functioning team. "Though one may be overpowered, two can defend themselves. A cord of three strands is not quickly broken" (Eccl 4:12). However, the worldview differences in a cross-cultural relationship can cause tension and conflict, and ministry colleagues need to learn how to build on each other's strengths rather than be mired in judging the differences. Transformation from within is what is needed most.[19] This is where the missionary needs to model grace and expect grace from all members of the ministry team. Kenneth Gangel states, "Believers are to exhibit grace in all their relationships. They show forgiveness; they exercise the freedom to be different, and for others to be different; they understand and utilize genuine flexibility. In a word, they are the least judgmental people on earth for they remember the grace God has extended to them."[20] This is the journey of grace.

Concluding Reflections

Missionaries have compelling reasons to explore the virtue of grace, as the application is vital to successful missions. Differences inevitably surface when we work with people of various cultures. In the face of these differences, grace is necessary to prevent our teams from eroding into relationships characterized by misunderstanding, judgment, and accusation. Conversely, an atmosphere of grace attracts people regardless of culture and is critical for journeying together in ministry.

God exhorts us to work alongside others in Christian community. When we capture God's vision for community, we "seek to become servants to others, to be sensitive to needs, to meet other people's desires and wants, to care and to share, to give and to receive, to forgive and to be forgiven."[21] Regardless of the ministry context, we are to follow the biblical mandates and principles of genuine care giving for one another and of working together graciously in Christian community.

---

18   Bill Thrall, Bruce McNicol, and Ken McElrath, *The Ascent of a Leader: How Ordinary Relationships Develop Extraordinary Character and Influence* (San Francisco, CA: Jossey-Bass, 1999), 39.
19   Livermore, 13.
20   Kenneth O. Gangel, *Coaching Ministry Teams* (Nashville, TN: Word Publishing, 2000), 155.
21   Bilezikian, 182.

Missionaries may well develop innovative strategies to reach the lost, but more important than our strategies is God's hand on our hearts, transforming us into people of grace who can minister in a Christ-like manner. As we journey cross-culturally with grace, we fulfill God's ultimate purpose to unite all things in Christ, including people of every tribe, tongue, and nation (Eph 1:10; Rev 5:9,10).

> Missionaries may well develop innovative strategies to reach the lost, but more important than our strategies is God's hand on our hearts, transforming us into people of grace who can minister in a Christ-like manner.

References

Bilezikian, Gilbert. 1997. *Community 101: Reclaiming the Local Church as Community of Oneness.* Grand Rapids, MI: Zondervan.

Bosch, David. *Transforming Mission: Paradigm Shifts in Theology of Mission* (Maryknoll, NY: Orbis, 1991), 362.

Bonhoeffer, Dietrich. 1954. *Life Together.* San Francisco, CA: HarperCollins.

Bush, Luis and Lorry Lutz. 1990. *Partnering in Ministry: The Direction of World Evangelism,* Downers Grove, IL: InterVarsity Press.

Butler, Phill. 2005. *Well Connected: Releasing Power, Restoring Hope through Kingdom Partnerships.* Waynesboro, GA: Authentic Media.

Finzel, Hans. 1998. *Empowered Leaders.* Nashville, TN: Word Publishing.

Foltz, Howard L. and Ruth Ford. 2000. *For Such a Time as This: Strategic Missions Power Shifts for the Twenty-first Century.* Pasadena, CA: William Carey Library.

Gangel, Kenneth O. 1999. *Ministering to Today's Adults.* Waco, TX: Word.

———. 2000. *Coaching Ministry Teams.* Nashville, TN: Word Publishing.

Hestenes, Roberta. 2002. "Developing Christian Community." *DMP/L 2030,* Denver Seminary Doctor of Ministry Program. Denver, July 15–19.

———. 1991. *Turning Committees into Communities.* Colorado Springs, CO: NavPress.

Hibbert, Evelyn and Richard Hibbert. 2014. *Leading Multicultural Teams.* Pasadena, CA: William Carey Library.

Livermore, David A. 2009. *Cultural Intelligence: Improving your CQ to Engage Our Multicultural World.* Grand Rapids, MI: Baker Academic.

Patzia, Arthur. 1984. "Ephesians, Colossians, Philemon." *New International Biblical Commentary.* Peabody, MA: Hendrickson.

Pollock, David. 2002. "Developing a Flow of Care and Caregivers." *Doing Member Care Well: Perspectives and Practices from Around the World*. Ed. Kelly O'Donnell. Pasadena, CA: William Carey Library.

Roembke, Lianne. 2000. *Building Credible Multicultural Teams*. Pasadena, CA: William Carey Library.

Taylor, William D., ed. 1994. *Kingdom Partnerships for Synergy in Missions*. Pasadena, CA: William Carey Library.

Thrall, Bill, Bruce McNicol, and Ken McElrath. 1999. *The Ascent of a Leader: How Ordinary Relationships Develop Extraordinary Character and Influence*. San Francisco, CA: Jossey-Bass.

Geoffrey *W. Hahn* accepted Christ at a young age, and God called him to missions when he was a teenager on a short-term medical mission trip. He completed his BA at Wheaton College, MDiv at Trinity Evangelical Divinity School, and doctorate at Denver Seminary, with a thesis on cross-cultural partnerships. Geoffrey and his wife, Fiona, have two young adult sons. They served in pastoral roles in Chicago area churches and as SIM missionaries in rural and urban settings in Ecuador. In mission leadership Geoffrey has served as a country and area director, and on SIM's International Leadership Team as Director of Ministry Development and currently as a Deputy International Director. Geoffrey seeks to empower others for effective ministry responses to the ever-changing ministry settings and realities in our world.

Scripture: *Micah 6:8 ("He has shown you…")*

Resource: *The Brothers Karamazov,* by Fyodor Dostoevsky (originally published 1880).

CHAPTER 5

Spirituality and the Prophet Jonah

Duncan Olumbe

The prophet Jonah elicits both admiration and rebuke for the manner in which he responded to God's call to go to Nineveh—perhaps because he uncomfortably mirrors our spirituality, especially our personal struggles in obeying God. In so doing his story unveils that deeper interrelatedness between our spirituality and mission. Indeed Jonah forces us into some introspection to reevaluate our spirituality as mission leaders and to seek concrete changes in the way we model spirituality in our leadership. Jonah is an intensely personal story and is therefore good for drawing personal implications which are critical for embracing the lifelong journey of spirituality and mission. In this chapter I offer a brief examination of the prophet Jonah with a heavy emphasis on our personal walk with God as I have increasingly realized that this is an area many, if not all of us, struggle with.

Overview

Little is known about Jonah. He was the son of Amittai and from Gath Hepher (2 Kgs 14:25), a prophet during the reign of king Jeroboam (793–753 BC) just before the Exile. He had seen the fulfilment of his prophecy as the northern kingdom of Israel enjoyed dominance over her enemies, the Arameans of Damascus (2 Kgs 14:25).

Jonah is a great favorite in mission circles, especially for mission mobilization where he is often treated as the "black sheep" of mission—the example not to follow. However, I believe that he reflects most of our struggles in seeking to obey God's call in his mission and thus offers us deep nuggets of truth in our personal walk with God.

So join me in the high drama of God's unmatched grace in redefining Jonah's spirituality and personal ministry in a kind of roller-coaster pilgrimage. I will explore this in three broad themes:

1. Come Follow Me: God's call to his mission (Jonah 1:1–17)
2. Come Back to Me: Repentance and restoration in our spiritual pilgrimage (Jonah 1:17–2:10)
3. Come with Me: Following God into his mission (Jonah 2:10–4:11)

Come Follow Me

God's Call to His Mission (Jonah 1:1–17)

Jonah's story starts with God's distinct call: *The Great Invitation—Come follow me to Nineveh!* It is instructive that God initiates the journey/drama: "The word of the Lord came to Jonah" (v 1). This underscores the missiological foundation that mission is God's mission (*missio Dei*). Thus the beginning point of redefining our mission engagement has to be God's call upon our lives. Even though the term "call" has been overused/misused, I believe that God's call into his mission is paramount over our voices, reasoning, or prevailing needs.

> Reflection: Might it be that God's call to his mission has been filtered by our human ingenuity? Perhaps we need to ask ourselves afresh: How "in touch with God" are we as missionaries? Or could it be that like the days of Eli the High Priest, "The word of the Lord ...[is] rare" (1 Sam 3:1)?

The second issue in chapter 1 of Jonah is what I call *active disobedience*. Jonah, in spite of clearly hearing "the word of the Lord" to go to Nineveh, actively decides to run away from the Lord and go to Tarshish. The reasons for Jonah's decision are not immediately clear. Perhaps he feared the great evil city of Nineveh or the overland journey with its perils. Or by heading to the opposite direction, he intended to go as far away as possible from God's voice. It is only towards the end of the book (4:2) that Jonah reveals his real reason—he feared that God would simply use him and then forgive the wicked people of Nineveh, thus rendering his prophecy useless/pointless. We shall revisit this later.

The third lesson from this chapter is the *challenge of exercising obedience to God's call in mission*. The fact that Jonah was a prophet did not insulate him from running away from God. He not only chose to disobey God but he actively planned to run away from the familiar to the unfamiliar where he was most likely unknown and obscure. It is intriguing that his disobedience affected and threatened not only his life but that of the sailors as well. And despite the fact that he knew his theology well (1:9), he was a living contradiction of his beliefs!

From Jonah we learn the basic lesson in our spirituality that often the challenge is not in hearing God's voice but obeying him. We tend to settle down in whatever God has called us to, and God's still small voice slowly gets dulled by other cares. Sometimes God calls to the untidy fringes (margins) and we find ourselves negotiating with him and trying to rationalize our disobedience. Or sometimes success in our mission efforts clouds our spiritual sense to hear God. Furthermore, God's call to his mission is not a one-off affair; it demands of us daily obedience (Matt 16:24). And at the core of such daily obedience is the commitment to maintain a vibrant personal walk with the Lord. Yet this is the one area that gets easily chocked by the

> From Jonah we learn the basic lesson in our spirituality that often the challenge is not in hearing God's voice but obeying him.

daily grind of ministry even in mission circles. Sadly the fact that we're in mission tends to obscure any disobedience to God's voice. Ultimately running away from God and the familiar leads to isolation; isolationism in the context of disobedience can be a deadly combination for missionaries!

> Ultimately running away from God and the familiar leads to isolation; isolationism in the context of disobedience can be a deadly combination for missionaries!

> Reflection: How do we ensure that we maintain a life of daily obedience to God? Could it be that God is calling us to move to other areas/aspects of mission service but we're making excuses? Might it be that we are actively disobeying God's call? Are we willing to confront the "skeletons in our closet" and allow God in? May God help us to reestablish the daily spiritual discipline of obeying him!

The fourth lesson from Jonah chapter 1 is that it forces us to *reinvestigate God's amazing grace in realigning us to his mission.* God still pursued and confronted Jonah in his disobedient flight to realign him back to the original call. Furthermore, God's grace is amplified by the fact that he uses the margins—(unbelieving) sailors and the storm—to get Jonah back to his senses. The (probably) non-Jewish sailors (and the whale) appeared more obedient to God than Jonah; no wonder at the end they "greatly feared the Lord… offered sacrifices… and made vows to him (v 16)!" However, we must credit Jonah for not dismissing "the margins" used to correct him.

I stand in awe at God's mercy and grace in spite of my human weaknesses in his service. I think Cece Winan's song, "Mercy said No; I'm not gonna let you go," echoes God's stubborn grace! It is humbling that God would use the "unconverted" to draw us back to his will. In fact it seems nonbelievers are sometimes able to discern God's dealings more than us missionaries!

> Reflection: Could it be that we can get so deaf to God's voice that it takes unbelievers to confront us? Might we be too proud of our "missionary status" that we dismiss God's correction? Might we be so "totally asleep below deck" that we miss out on God's warning signals? Might we be missing the tell-tale signs of God's extended grace upon our lives? How do we hear the "still small voice" through physical calamities, endless conflicts, barren ministry, etc.? While appreciating God's grace how do we ensure that we do not continue to sin that grace may abound (Rom 6:1ff) or take God's grace for granted? Might it be that we've settled in our comfort zones and are unwilling to follow Christ to new fringes of mission?

Come Back to Me

Repentance and Restoration in Our Spiritual Pilgrimage (Jonah 1:17–2:10)

Chapter 2 of the book of Jonah outlines for us the distress of being cut off from God's presence, the humble cry of repentance, and the joyful celebration of forgiveness and restoration. We are invited into the inner sanctum of a man utterly broken so much like king David (Ps 51). Jonah's cry, from the belly of the whale, epitomizes a life-transforming encounter with God in the abyss of desolation.

The first lesson here is the *recognition of the distress of being cut off and outside God's will.* Distressed, alienated, and literally "dead," Jonah prayed to God. His experience felt like literal death: "Depths of the grave" (v 2) or banished from God (v 4). He recognized God's hand in "hurling" and "banishing" him into the depths of the sea. The reality of the distress of being cut off from God's will is real and scary.

Like Jonah, hard moments in life have a great ability to draw us closer to God. How I long to see more of this brokenness and restoration in mission circles! However, it takes great humility and courage to seek repentance in the midst of God's restoration process. I believe repentance has to be firmly rooted in the recognition of this distress and the fact that against God and God alone have we sinned. Without a sense of sin, repentance is hollow. A general lack of remorse and repentance where sin is involved especially among missionaries is disturbing. This leads to cover-ups; I am alright until I am discovered!

> It takes great humility and courage to seek repentance in the midst of God's restoration process.

> Reflection: It is scary to be in missions and experience the desolation of being cut off from God's will. Might it be that we have lost spiritual sensitivity to be able to sense this distress in being cut off from God? Or is it that our conscience is so seared that we totally fail to experience remorsefulness of sin? Might we have lost the centrality of remorse and repentance in our instant-gratification society?

The second lesson is the need to *refocus on God in the midst of engulfing and burying realities of disobedience.*" Jonah went beyond being remorseful; he refocused on God right in the belly of the whale. He still believed in and called upon God (v 7). And God heard him; God was there for him at his lowest point (v 5–6)

Jonah teaches us to realize that God is with us right in the middle of any messy situations. He is only a prayer away even if/when we do not feel like praying. God hears our prayers even when we're too bruised to utter a word. Before we even say a prayer, God already knows our innermost heartaches. As missionaries we have to confront the human nature of turning a blind eye to sin and refusing to confront sinfulness in a godly way. However, the element of love is critical in helping people grope their way back to God in the engulfing and burying messy realities of repentance and restoration. God in his grace brings us back to life from the pit; he restores our faith in him!

> Reflection: How can we help ourselves and those we minister to refocus on God rather than the mess of disobedience? How might we confidently cry out to God, "Draw me close to you, never let me go"? How can we truly be dependent on God and echo the song, "This is the air I breathe. And I am desperate for you, lost without you"? And like David, how can we cry out, "Create in me a clean heart, renew a right spirit within me"?

The third lesson is on *rejecting the worthless idols of our time*. As Jonah felt his life ebbing away, he remembered God and prayed to God (v 7). In remembering God, he profoundly experienced the grace of God which eludes those who cling to worthless idols. It would seem that Jonah's idol was the design and pursuit of his own call instead of obeying God's call.

I believe one of the insidious idols of current global mission is the idol of being too busy! Too busy even to pray! For those from the global South, we have to reject the worthless idols of dependency, subservience, manipulation, inferiority complex, etc. For others from the global North, we have to daily confront the idol of power and control which insists that our ways are better than the Lord's or others; we have to learn to obey God and to respect others. Otherwise, we can so very easily forfeit the grace that could be ours. And the absence of a regular experience of God's grace and forgiveness creates an amazing level of self-righteousness and callousness which is one of the cancers of our current mission leadership.

> The absence of a regular experience of God's grace and forgiveness creates an amazing level of self-righteousness and callousness which is one of the cancers of our current mission leadership.

However, it is in experiencing God's grace and forgiveness as a daily experience that keeps us eternally indebted and sufficiently tender to those around us who fall into sin. We can thus sing, "I'm forgiven… Amazing love how can it be."

> Reflection: What does it mean to reject the worthless idols of our times? What are some of the worthless idols of our mission enterprise which we need to confront? How may we embrace and extend the awesome experience of God's grace in the context of forgiveness?

The fourth lesson is the joy of *recommitment and realignment to God's mission*. We see Jonah finally able to sacrifice to God with a song of thanksgiving, keep his vows (v 9), and ultimately experience/discover that "salvation comes from the Lord" (v 10). This was an expression of recommitment and realignment to God's purposes for him.

I believe that the evidence of genuine repentance is restoration to God's purposes. Ultimately, fresh obedience to God is the hallmark of repentance and restoration. Sadly some of our discipline is not geared towards restoration but seems to be aimed at literally killing our wounded soldiers.

> Reflection: In the business of mission service might we have lost the joy of God's salvation? And in our discipline systems, might we be guilty of "killing our wounded soldiers"? How can we instead nurse them back to service? Where is the much-needed balance between discipline and restoration in our leadership? How do we handle the apparent reality where we seem to have many perfectionists as mission leaders who often tend to impose almost-impossible-to-achieve standards?

Come with Me

Following God into His Mission (Jonah 2:10–4:11)

The last two chapters of Jonah are full of lessons. First we see Jonah *experiencing God's second chance in his disturbing mission.* God's word "came to Jonah a second time" (3:1). A restored Jonah is recommissioned to Nineveh and this time he obeys God (v 3). I hear echoes of Jesus restoring Peter after his betrayal (John 21:15–19). Repentance leads to restoration which leads to recommissioning. God calls us into his mission not as perfect beings but as fallen-restored-and-recommissioned sinners. Those of us who have experienced God's second chance are forever grateful for his unfathomable mercies. I have been profoundly moved by Jimmy Baker's book, *I Was Wrong,* and Gordon MacDonald's book, *Rebuilding Your Broken World.* Unfortunately, such stories are scarce and hushed.

> Repentance leads to restoration which leads to recommissioning.

> Reflection: How can we embrace God's second chance without making grace cheap? Where are our generation's stories of restoration and recommissioning within the Mission Commission circles?

The second lesson is that *God's mission is often way beyond our imagination.* The repentance and revival experienced in Nineveh were phenomenal (3:6–10). The king's message reveals an amazing understanding of God, his mercies and grace. It is like a full mission statement. At the heart of Nineveh's revival was a deep understanding of their evil ways and violence in light of God's compassion, which led to a cry for God's mercy and grace. This episode reminds me that God is often already at work among nonbelievers even before we get there with the gospel message. We are not "taking the gospel there," God is already there with his message; we're simply going as signposts of his great message of reconciliation to the nations. Genuine revival is not manufactured

> We are not "taking the gospel there," God is already there with his message; we're simply going as signposts of his great message of reconciliation to the nations.

or manipulated (as sadly is sometimes the case in our days). It is purely a work of God way beyond our human efforts and sphere of influence. Indeed, "God works in mysterious ways, his wonders to perform." And God is at work even in totally hopeless contexts.

> Reflection: How might we be able to experience a fresh genuine revival sweeping across the global mission scene? Might it be that we have no faith in God actually doing more than we can ask for or imagine? And how might we allow ourselves not to manipulate God and the manner in which he acts?

The third lesson here is about God's prodding on Jonah to *relinquish power and control to God*. God provided Jonah with shelter from the sun but then sent a worm which caused it to wither (4:5–9). While Jonah enjoyed the comfort of the vine, he was very happy (v 6), but when it withered he became very angry (v 8). At the root of Jonah's complaint was the issue of power and control; he not only thought that he was entitled to the vine but that he could control it. On the contrary God sought to demonstrate that he is the one fully in charge of even the "small" details in Jonah's life.

We need to confront the temptation of self-focus vis-à-vis others-focus. This is a big challenge in our "me" generation and culture. While we daily enjoy God's "small mercies," may we never be tempted to think that we're entitled to them and demand them from God. We can thus sing, "Blessed be the name of the Lord… You give and take away, my heart will choose to say." God is the one who gives and takes away. The story challenges us to be more vulnerable and dependent on God's power.

The last but perhaps most fundamental lesson is the call to *regaining God's heart for the lost*. Instead of being happy at God's mercy to the people of Nineveh, Jonah got very angry and depressed. He wondered "How could God let go such evil and brutal people so easily without punishing them?" Why did Jonah have to go through all the trouble if God was going to forgive them anyway in spite of Jonah? Did Jonah have to go?

God is concerned for any and all who are lost in sin, who do not know their right hand from their left. A significant redefinition of our spirituality has to confront our self-righteous hangover which attempts to make God predictable. Having enjoyed God's forgiveness, it is shocking that we can turn around and not appreciate the same grace extended to others. Could it be that we are behaving very much like the elder brother to the prodigal son by not celebrating that the one who was lost is now found? Oh that we would regain God's heart for the lost; a deep passion for the lost!

> A significant redefinition of our spirituality has to confront our self-righteous hangover which attempts to make God predictable.

> Reflection: Might it be that we secretly rejoice at the suffering of the wicked? Should we not be concerned like God about those who are lost in sin? Might Jonah be mirroring some Christians' jest at HIV-AIDS sufferers, or response to Islam (i.e., how did we react when Osama bin Laden was killed?), or our

response to homosexuality and/or disasters/calamities? Might it be that we actually do not want people to come to the Lord en masse because it would mean that we as missionaries will be "out of a job"? Could it be that we've made mission not a calling but a job which we have to defend at all costs including even if it means barring sinners from coming to Christ? What yardstick do we use to define success? How come sometimes we get shocked at God's doing; is this a manifestation of our unbelief? Lord I believe; help my unbelief!

Conclusion

The book of Jonah has a lot of lessons for us, especially in redefining our spirituality within God's mission. I pray that we shall be willing to review our spirituality even as we serve in the context of God's mission. First and foremost, I pray that we shall be willing to accept and obey God's "Great Invitation" to come and follow him into his mission. Secondly, I pray that we shall be open to experience and extend God's restoration and recommissioning as a regular feature of our mission spirituality. And thirdly, I pray that we shall be willing to humbly walk alongside the awesome deeds of our great God as he draws people to himself, often in ways beyond our imagination.

The call to daily obedience in the sometimes mundane grind of mission service cannot be overstated. The centrality of a vibrant walk with the Lord is indispensable. And the refining fire of God's restorative justice and grace is painfully regenerative. Our human inclination to prejudge others as unworthy of God's grace is scary. The cry for more tender mission leaders in our generation is loud and clear. God is calling us to individually and collectively realign our mission engagement and spirituality to his mission agenda. May we be ready to experience and extend God's restorative grace and passion for the lost as we seek to model a spirituality for the long haul. Amen.

Duncan Olumbe is the Executive Director of Mission Together Africa, which seeks to mobilize and equip people from Eastern Africa into God's mission. He is passionate about newer models of mission funding, Diaspora missiology, contextualized mission training, using the Internet for mission, and mentoring younger leaders. He lives with his family in Nairobi, Kenya from where he serves both locally and globally.

Scripture: *2 Corinthians 4:1–2 ("Therefore, since through God's mercy we have this ministry…*

Resource: *I Was Wrong: The Untold Story of the Shocking Journey from PTL Power to Prison and Beyond*, by Jimmy Baker (Nashville, TN: Thomas Nelson, 1997).

CHAPTER 6

Spiritual Warfare in Missions

The Origin, the Nature and the Context of Spiritual Warfare in Missions

Reuben Ezmadu

The Lord cast his plan for the redemption of mankind from the Fall in a warfare context when he announced as follows: "And I will put enmity between you (i.e., the serpent) and the woman, between your offspring and hers; he will crush your head and you will strike his heel" (Gen 3:15). The deliverance of the people of Israel from slavery in the land of Egypt (a typical missionary enterprise) took place in the context of warfare, more of spiritual contests and maneuvering, as evidenced in the successive encounters between Moses/Aaron—who were employing the instructions and directions from God on one side to secure the release of the people of Israel from slavery—and Pharaoh/ Egyptian magicians—who were invoking and employing satanic powers on the other side to resist the deliverance of the Israelites from bondage (Ex 7:10–12:36).

These are conditions which describe the state of the people who are subjects of the missionary enterprise:

1. Living in an abode of wickedness: Psalms 74:20
2. Shut up in prisons: Isaiah 42:28
3. Plundered and exploited: Isaiah 42:28
4. Hardened and blinded: 2 Corinthians 4:3–4
5. Harassed and scattered: Matthew 9:36
6. Under the chain of the evil one: Acts 8:9–11
7. Shut-off and guarded by a very strong man: Matthew 12:29

> Spiritual warfare is the battle that is being waged between the agents of God's kingdom and the opposing forces of the evil one in a bid to set mankind free from bondage to sin and oppression of the devil.

We cannot, therefore, contemplate getting such people out of that kind of condition without definitely encountering some spiritual conflicts. Hence, spiritual warfare is the battle that is being waged between the agents of God's kingdom and the opposing forces of the evil one in a bid to set mankind free from bondage to sin and oppression of the devil.

Spiritual forces opposed to the gospel and their earthly agents are variously summarized as follows:

1. Psalm 2:1–3 describes "a conspiracy by nations and their rulers against Christ and his gospel."
2. Paul, in his writings to the Ephesian Christians (6:12), calls such opposing forces "rulers, authorities, powers of this dark world, and spiritual forces of evil in the heavenly realms," which oppose God's purposes on earth.
3. 2 Corinthians 4:4 describes "the god of this age (which) has blinded the mind of unbelievers so that they cannot see the light of the gospel of the glory of Christ, who is the image of God," and therefore should be overcome, uprooted, and dislodged for mankind to have access to the benefits of God's salvation (Eph 6:11, 13–18; 2 Cor 10:3–6).
4. The opposing forces also manifest as "ancient gates," traditions, cultures, customs, rules and regulations, practices, etc., which prohibit the penetration of the gospel (Ps 24:7–10) and deny people the right to decide to follow Jesus Christ (John 4:13–34), distract others from hearing the gospel (Acts 13:6–12), infiltrate missionary teams to undermine their effectiveness (Acts 16:16–20), oppose and discourage missionaries (Acts 19:23–32), perform counterfeit miracles to discredit the gospel (Acts 19:13–20).

The Lord, who himself encountered spiritual warfare in his earthly ministry, warned us about the same experience in our own era as we continue with his mission here on earth (Matt 10:16–22; John 16:33). Hence, he assured us of his presence and power to overcome and emerge victorious in the spiritual battle to be encountered in taking the gospel to the nations (Luke 10:19; Matt 24: 20; Mark 16:17).

Spiritual Warfare in Modern Missions

Even though spiritual warfare had always been part of the missionary enterprise right from the beginning as indicated above, this reality has unfortunately been overlooked, ignored, and not recognized in many of the missionary endeavors, especially by some of the older mission sending structures. As a result, many labors have been unfruitful, many missionaries became casualties in the fields, and much effort has been frustrated, resulting in a very high toll on manpower and resources. There was also the misconception that evil forces operated more among the tribal and animistic cultures, fuelling the delusion by the devil that civilized and developed societies are no-go areas for demonic operations. Such ignorance or misconception has contributed to the present situation that prevails in modern and postmodern societies where demons, under various guises, have woven a "civilized," polished, technologically advanced, satanic empire with their fangs in media, education, government, business, and even religion. This phenomenon thereby redefines the unreached and ripe mission fields to extend beyond the traditional concepts of the unreached.

For us in Africa, spiritual warfare has been (and will continue to be) part of our holistic approach to missions. It is a common feature of the African church to thrive in the midst of spiritual battles, physical limitations, limited resources, social upheavals, and insecurity. In fact, the church in Africa exists in such contexts and flourishes within that kind of environment. The church in Africa is increasingly becoming a missionary church, even in the face of such limitations, oppositions, and challenges. The contexts of religious pluralism, ethnic and cultural diversities, multilingual realities, unwavering belief in the supernatural, tenacity and persevering spirit, adaptability, creativity, now strengthened by spiritual fervency, have placed the African church in a position to contribute more towards the final push in world evangelization and missions, albeit in cooperation and partnership with other sections of the body of Christ worldwide—especially our brethren in Asia, Latin America, Middle East, and Central Asia who share similar experiences.

> The contexts of religious pluralism, ethnic and cultural diversities, multilingual realities, unwavering belief in the supernatural, tenacity and persevering spirit, adaptability, creativity, now strengthened by spiritual fervency, have placed the African church in a position to contribute more towards the final push in world evangelization and missions

How Spiritual Warfare Advances the Kingdom Agenda

There are several examples in the Bible in which encounters with opposing forces to the realization of God's purposes on earth ended up in advancing the same agenda instead of hindering it. A few of these examples include: The encounter Moses and Aaron had with Pharaoh and his magicians in the battle for the emancipation of the Jews from their bondage in Egypt (Ex 8:5–8; 16–19; 12:31–36, 41). Elijah's encounter with the prophets of Baal (1 Kgs 18:20–40). The church in Jerusalem's encounter with the leaders of their days (Acts 4:13–31) and with Herod (Acts 12:5–12, 21–24). The encounter Paul and Barnabas had with Bar-Jesus (Elymas) the sorcerer (Acts 13:6–12); the encounters Paul and Silas had with the owners of the girl fortuneteller (Acts 16:16–40) and with the devotees of Diana of Ephesus (Acts 19:23–41). In our own case, we have had several such encounters which eventually opened the door for the gospel to thrive in hitherto hostile communities. One of the the most prominent was the encounter we had in our first mission field among the Ibarapas (a subpeople group of the Yorubas in Oyo State of Nigeria).

The Ibarapas had a traditional festival devoted to the worship of one of the Yoruba ancestral deities through a cult called the Oro. By their mythology, a woman is not supposed to see the masquerades which come out during the period of the festival. As such, a curfew is imposed throughout the festival period, most importantly during the night. One night, our team in that particular community had an all-night prayer meeting which ended in the early hours of the next morning. Members of the team, who included ladies not aware of the curfew because they were new to that community, were on their way back to the houses where they were staying when they ran into a group of the masquerades. This provoked an angry reaction from the worshipers. They dragged the team members to the traditional ruler demanding that the women be sanctioned and our group be banned. God gave us favor in the sight of the traditional ruler who said to the devotees of Oro to allow their "god" to fight for itself since it had power to instantly destroy women who have seen the masquerades. They watched these sisters throughout the day, and the days dragged into weeks and months, yet none of the ladies had even a headache, much less any health-problems or death. This was how the Oro cult and that festival went into extinction in that community. The Lord crowned the victory with the conversion of the Chief Masquerader who, at age seventy and illiterate, was granted divine ability to read, preach, and teach from the Yoruba language, starting with some of the Oro devotees.

Winning the Battle

In commissioning the church to carry on with his mission on earth, the Lord implied that there will be battles which will involve a dislodging and a dispossession of the strong man of his long-held positions and captives (Matt 12:29). So we are destined to win this raging spiritual warfare in missions! But there are certain things we need to know and do about spiritual warfare in missions if we are to complete the task before us.

1. Not be ignorant of the devices (the schemes and modus operandi) of the devil (2 Cor 2:11).
2. Sharpen our spiritual senses of "discernment" so as to easily identify the devices and operations of the evil one (Matt 16:15–17 cf. 22–23; Acts 16:16–18; 1 Cor 2:10–14).
3. Train and equip missionaries in the awareness of the realities of spiritual warfare in missions and in the assurance of Christ's power to overcome the evil forces arraigned in opposition to the gospel (Mark 3:13–15; Luke 10:19; Luke 4:16–18; Matt 28:18–20).
4. Understand the nature of the warfare, distinguishing between the victims (humans) and the villains (the spiritual forces at work) so as to know who to target in the fight (Eph 6:12).

5. Master the weapons at our disposal to wage the warfare and understand how to appropriate them in the various circumstances, contexts, and purposes (Eph 6:11, 13–18; 2 Cor 4:1–5; 10:3–6).

6. Trust and rely on the leading and direction of the Holy Spirit because he alone knows the target and the right weapon to apply under any circumstance of warfare (John 14:26–27; 1 Cor 2:10–14).

7. Always walk in the confidence of the assurance of Christ's presence, power, protection, provision, and preservation as we face the challenges of penetrating the strongholds of the enemy to set free his captives (Matt 28:18–20; Matt 10:26–31).

Reuben E. Ezemadu is currently the International Director of the Christian Missionary Foundation Inc. He served as the pioneer General Secretary and later as the Chairman of NEMA (Nigeria Evangelical Missionary Association) as well as the pioneer General Coordinator of the Third World Missions Association (TWMA). At the moment, he is the Continental Coordinator of the Movement for African National Intiatives (MANI). He has authored and edited a number of books on Missions, as well as contributed several articles to other publications, including the most recent titles: *Sending and Supporting African Missionaries in the 21st Century*, and *Models, Issues, and Structures of Indigenous Missions in Africa.*

Scripture: *Psalm 32:8 ("I will instruct you and teach you…")*

Resource: *The Social Conscience of the Evangelical*, by Sherwood Eliot Wirt, (London: Scripture Union Publishing, 1968).

CHAPTER 7

Where There Is Lament

Suffering and Spirituality

Miriam Adeney

Suffering produces perseverance,
perseverance produces character,
and character produces hope. *Romans 5:3–4*

When Christians think about suffering, the words above are often recited. If we are honest, however, we must admit that suffering does not always produce character or hope. Instead suffering may lead to cynicism and despair. People grit their teeth to get through another day. Or they erupt in anger and vengeance.

> If we are honest, however, we must admit that suffering does not always produce character or hope.

What makes the difference? God. The context for these verses is clear. Immediately before writing these words the Apostle Paul says we can rejoice in sufferings because "we rejoice in the hope of the glory of God." Immediately after these verses Paul continues, "Hope does not disappoint us, because God has poured out his love into our hearts by the Holy Spirit whom he has given us." In the preceding chapter, Paul clinches his argument that we can connect with God only by faith in God's love when he affirms, "Against all hope, Abraham in hope believed and so became the father of many nations" (4:18). The God in whom Abraham hoped, as this chapter makes clear, is the God who raised Jesus from death. This is the ground of our hope when we suffer.

Theology of Suffering

Suffering does not automatically improve our character or our hope. Not only sad, beaten-down people bear that out. Escape or sad endurance are the options open to us, according to many philosophers from Stoics to Buddhists to the existentialist Jean-Paul Sartre. Only if God exists and chooses to pour his love into us are we empowered to respond positively to suffering. As we receive God's love, we dare to worship, serve, and even rejoice and pass the love on to others. Then we become channels of love in this hurting world.

In 1935, Italy invaded Ethiopia. At that time there were seventeen baptized believers among the Wallamo people (then known as Wolayta). Although foreign missionaries' home governments advised them to depart, those among the Wallamo chose to stay. By the time they were evicted forcibly two years later, the Wallamo church had grown to forty-eight baptized believers.

When the missionaries returned after the war, they found 10,000 Wallamo Christians. How did this happen? Only the Gospel of Mark and a few booklets had been translated. Most Wallamo were not literate. But little by little the gospel spread. Those who could read taught others, who expressed thanks with gifts of wood, grain, butter, sheep, and field labor. Churches sprang up, famous for their singing. However, because persecution surrounded them, the believers buried their Scripture portions in clay pots or hid them in thatched roofs when they were not reading the books.

Then a man named Wandaro was detained. Because he would not deny Christ, Wandaro was stripped and lashed forty times with a hippopotamus whip in which metal pieces had been imbedded.

Afterwards, an official commanded Wandaro, "Go home and tell your people to bring their big knives. You are going to tear down your new church. Then we will see if you can sing."

The next day, the Christians destroyed their new church and carried all the building material on their heads into town, where it was used to construct a house for the corrupt official.

Wandaro was taken to the marketplace. Five men beat him for several hours, even pulling out some of his beard.

"Who taught you to be so strong? The missionaries are gone," the official taunted.

"But God is still here," Wandaro answered.

When he was returned to the prison, Wandaro was so sore that he could not lie down on his back or on his front. He passed the night on his knees and elbows. When food was brought, he could not eat.

But two weeks later, he had recovered enough to be part of a prison work gang. With other prisoners he pushed a big water barrel up a hill. As he did, he witnessed to the Italian guards alongside.

"Be quiet!" his relatives whispered.

"Why grieve? God has not died yet. He is still with me. It is up to us to witness for the Lord as long as he allows us to be here," Wandaro answered.

For a full year he was held in prison and testified every day. He was such a model prisoner that when the guards wanted to get off duty, they put him in charge.

After his release, the corrupt official commanded Wandaro to bring as many Christians as he could to harvest the official's grain. Wandaro brought one hundred, and they sang all the way.

Not long afterwards, the official fell over backward and died. But the believers continued to multiply by the thousands.[1]

Wandaro is one person in one tribe in one African country, but he represents the vast community of Christians throughout time and space who have rejoiced in suffering because they experienced God's love and therefore dared to hope.

Still, Christian sufferers wonder: Why do the wicked flourish? Why do the innocent agonize? If God is all-powerful, how can he allow this? Is God fair?

Some suffering is due to human sin, even natural disasters like floods. At other times, pain may be a useful warning. But this is not true of all suffering, according to both the story of Job and Jesus' encounter with a blind man (John 9). In the end, we must admit that God is greater than our minds. We know only in part. We cannot contain God within our calculations. What Christians do affirm is the reality of God's presence even as we suffer. In Jesus' life and supremely on the Cross, he entered our suffering. Now the Holy Spirit inside us comforts and strengthens us day by day. Many Christians testify that God gives more grace when the burdens grow greater. Complete answers we do not have, but we do have the presence of God, which is even more powerful than reasons.

> We know only in part. We cannot contain God within our calculations. What Christians do affirm is the reality of God's presence even as we suffer.

Grief Is Not Unspiritual

Although Rizpah was a concubine or sex slave of king Saul, she had two sons and she loved them (2 Sam 3:21). Twice she suffered the risks and agony of childbirth, and twice she forgot the pain when she gazed at the miracle of a new person in her arms. The boys grew to be tall, muscled, capable young men, her joy and her security.

Then, under the next king, tragedy struck. Rizpah's family was connected with the wrong political group. One morning her boys were marched out and hung, their necks broken.

Rizpah was not allowed to bury her boys. The bodies were displayed on a hill as a warning to others. But she spread a mourning cloth on a rock nearby, and there she

---

1   Ray Davis, *Fire on the Mountains: The Story of a Miracle—the Church in Ethiopia* (Cedar Grove, NJ: Sudan Interior Mission, 1980), 119–136.

stayed. From the beginning of the harvest until the rainy season, Rizpah did not let the birds of the air touch her boys' bodies by day or the wild animals by night. When the king heard about it, he relented and gave the young men a proper burial.

Rizpah's epic grief inspires admiration. It is a precursor to the lament howled 1,000 years later when king Herod killed baby boys (Matt 2:18):

> A voice is heard in Ramah,
> Weeping and great mourning,
> Rachel weeping for her children
> And refusing to be comforted
> Because they are no more.

Such grief is not ungodly or unspiritual. When you love, you risk the possibility of pain. Jesus grieved (John 11:35). God himself grieves (Gen 6:6; Ps 78:40; Ps 95:10). Even creation groans (Rom 8:22). Two little books in the Bible, Habakkuk and Lamentations, are among the many Scripture passages that are redolent with sorrow. Mourning like Rizpah's indicates that something is valuable. It shows honor.

And it requires time. Although we Westerners try to get through sorrow quickly, many of us pass through "stages of grief" such as anger, denial, bargaining, withdrawal, and guilt, sometimes cycling through these stages multiple times.

Rituals can help. For example, after the genocide in Rwanda twenty years ago, Christians developed trauma-healing workshops. Here they told stories and listened, knelt to ask forgiveness, nailed momentos of their pain to a cross, burned the momentos and prayed as the ashes wafted upwards, lighted candles, and meditated on scriptural words of hope. Such rituals helped.[2]

The most fundamental grief ritual is a funeral. We should take care not to abbreviate funerals, even though we will discard spiritist components. Rich emotional and sensory and symbolic and communal elements should be present, whether traditional or new. Physical involvement in rituals adds value too, like Holy Communion, or visiting "Stations of the Cross" during the week before Easter, or anointing with oil, or washing feet, or communal meals. Jesus knew the value of the physical, so he touched people when he healed them.

Staying on her rock, Rizpah expressed strength. Lamenting, she was empowered.

> Where there is lament, the believer is able to take initiative with God and so develop ... the ego-strength that is necessary for responsible faith. But where the capacity to initiate lament is absent, one is left only with praise and doxology. God then is omnipotent, always to be praised. The believer is nothing, and can praise or accept guilt uncritically where life with God does

---

2   Miriam Adeney, *Kingdom Without Borders: The Untold Story of Global Christianity* (Downers Grove, IL: InterVarsity Press, 2009), 231–238.

not function properly. The outcome is a "false self" … The absence of lament makes a religion of coercive obedience the only possibility.[3]

Rizpah demonstrated that she was more than an animal or a machine, a producer or consumer, a pawn in a game or a cog in a system. She was a person who loved. She had a voice and demanded a space in which to lift it. As she did, she glorified God who endowed her with dignity even in her pain. Such mourning can be transformative. Some of the world's greatest art has emerged from deep pain.

> "The absence of lament makes a religion of coercive obedience the only possibility."

What to Suffer

Filipino pastor Rico Villanueva heard his people pray about financial problems, sickness, flooding, and straying husbands. Yet their testimonies emphasized victories. Here there seemed to be little place for unanswered prayers. Was this focus on victory biblical? For his doctoral dissertation, Villanueva studied the "Psalms of lament," prayers that arise from situations of despair, such as this passage (Ps 31:10–12):

> My life is consumed by anguish
> And my years by groaning.
> My strength fails because of my affliction
> And my bones grow weak.
> Because of all my enemies
> I am the utter contempt of my neighbors.
> I am a dread to my friends—
> Those who see me on the street flee from me.
> I am forgotten by them as though I were dead.
> I have become like broken pottery.

The balance of joy and sorrow in the Psalms reflects human reality, Villanueva concluded. "My experiences of uncertainty and ambiguity as a Filipino, along with the sense, common among Asians, that life is more cyclical than linear, aided me to see movements between lament and praise."[4]

When we pray such Psalms, we find community with others who have suffered.

In turn, just as we are comforted by this community, so we are called to look outward, to care for others beyond ourselves and our friends. Yes, God is glorified when we ask for help with our personal needs, our messed-up computer, or lack of a parking spot.

---

3   Walter Brueggemann, *The Psalms and the Life of Faith* (Minneapolis, MN: Fortress Press, 1995), 103–4).
4   Federico Villanueva, "The Transforming Power of Lament: Reading the Psalms from a Filipino Context," in *The Gospel in Culture: Contextualization Issues through Asian Eyes*, ed. Melba P. Maggay (Manila: OMF Literature, 2013), 231.

But God also expects us to cry out to him about larger human needs, about poverty and racism, about ISIS and Boko Haram, and about people in crisis in this week's news.

What we grieve matters, Villanueva says. He remembers a standard Western-authored theology textbook in which "there is not even an entry on the word 'injustice' in the subject index. There is one on 'poverty' but only about two pages are devoted to it. In contrast to this, 'predestination' receives more than twenty pages."[5]

Yet Bible themes that interest people in poorer countries include "robbers on the roads, streets full of crippled and sick, the struggle to pay gouging tax and debt collectors, demanding landlords ... imminent national collapse ... personality cults of dictators ... judgments on the rich and haughty ... deliverance from evil."[6] Death itself is a significant human theme, so mystics' spiritual exercises sometimes include meditations on death. Rich or poor, death comes to us all. On a personal level, my parents' deaths changed my understanding of the world.

These larger human realities should cause us to ponder: What am I grieving? Jesus is our model. He is known as the suffering Servant. As he identified with human suffering, so must we. "We cannot love him and yet want to be crowned with roses while he was crowned with thorns," in the words of the desert martyr Charles de Foucauld.[7] We must take up our cross. Spirituality includes being attentive to God's world and to those in need. "The glory of God is a human being fully alive," according to Irenaeus—alive to see and alive to care. Faithfully following Jesus, we enter into the "fellowship of his suffering" (Phil 3:10).

> Jesus is our model. He is known as the suffering Servant. As he identified with human suffering, so must we.

Yet, if suffering is our call, it is never the last word. Suffering is paired with glory, for Jesus and for us. Weeping may endure for a season, but joy will come. In God's time, he will wipe away all tears and will usher in a celebration beyond anything we can imagine. Therefore, even though our projects and our bodies fail, we have hope.

> Yet, if suffering is our call, it is never the last word. Suffering is paired with glory, for Jesus and for us. Weeping may endure for a season, but joy will come.

In my city, Zion Preparatory School has just closed its doors due to a downturn in funding. For thirty years this school served at-risk children. It trained and inspired and networked them and set them on the path to productive, creative lives. Christian African-Americans were prominent among the founders. Now the school is gone. "It's the grieving process. But we had our season,"

---

5   Villanueva, 226.
6   Joel Carpenter, "Back to the Bible: Review of 'The New Faces of Christianity: Believing the Bible in the Global South' by Philip Jenkins," *Books and Culture* (Vol.13, no.3, 2007), 23.
7   Robert Ellsberg, ed. *Charles de Foucauld* (Maryknoll, NY: Orbis Books. 1999), 25.

says Doug Wheeler, a key staff member. Instead of bitterness, he exudes grief, realism, thankfulness, and hope.[8]

Theologian Doug Groothuis speaks the same way about his wife Rebecca's slide into dementia:

> This is my lament and testimony. I lament her losses and the loss to an evangelical world that will no longer benefit from new contributions from her careful thinking and her cogent and lucid writing. But lamentation is the proper response of the soul to the loss of a true good, the recognition of sadness and anger before the face of God…Lament is that element of life under the sun that allows us to hurt before God and even with God. We look up as the tears fall down… And yet I am grateful to the Giver of every good and perfect gift… We lament now. We rejoice later.[9]

Clouds of Witnesses

Youssef and Serena, brother and sister, were raised in a godly Syrian family. Both felt called to the ministry. Youssef now serves in a pastorate. Serena is finishing seminary in Lebanon and her home church has called her to their pulpit. Just recently, however, her cousin was found in his office with his throat cut in the shape of a cross. As a result, the church elders have forbidden Serena to return until things settle down. They still need her sermons, so she writes them out each week and emails them to her uncle. He reads them aloud in the worship services.

Most of Serena's and Youssef's extended family have migrated to Canada. They urge her to follow. Yet she stays in the Middle East. "God has not given me a word for Canada," she says. "God has given me a word for Syria."

Serena and Youssef are part of a "great cloud of witnesses" extending through time:

> Some faced jeers and flogging, while others were chained and
>   put in prison.
> They were stoned, they were sawed in two, they were put to
>   death by the sword.
> They went about in sheepskins and goatskins, destitute,
>   persecuted, and mistreated—
> the world was not worthy of them.
> They wandered in deserts and mountains, and in caves and
>   holes in the ground…

---

8   Sami Edge, "Financial Pressures Force Zion Prep to Shut Its Doors," *Seattle Times* (August 31, 2015), 7.

9   Douglas Groothuis, "Rebecca Merrill Groothuis's Contribution to Biblical Equality: A Personal Testimony and Lament," *Priscilla Papers* (Vol. 29, no. 3, 2015), 5.

We are surrounded by such a great cloud of witnesses.
Hebrews 11:36–12:1

Canon Francis Omondi, writing from Somali ministry in East Africa in August 2015, in a year when so many Christians in his country have been targeted and deliberately murdered by terrorists, says,

> When every indication pointed to terror activities in our region
> how could we possibly carry out Christian mission?
> "Go out in joy, and be led forth with peace!" (Isaiah 55:12)
>
> The joy is not devoid of cries and pleas for mercy and protection.
> We fear, and are under tremendous pressure to give up even
>   our witness.
> We worry that our work over the years will turn to nothing.
>   Can we be joyful?
> SHALOM is how we will be led by our God.
> This is strange in that the tension we live under is not at all peaceful. It is terror!
>
> We often confuse peace with safety, but they are not the same.
> Peace is a great venture. It is a dare to trust God completely.
> Peace requires us to give up our illusions of safety and security,
>   our schemes and plans, in order to rely upon almighty God
>   alone.
> *(Dietrich Bonhoeffer, Finland address to WCC, months before the outbreak of World War II)*
>
> The cloud of terror is still over us as a canopy, yes,
> but battles are not won with weapons but with God.[10]

God makes the difference. With God,

> Suffering produces perseverance,
> perseverance produces character,
> and character produces hope. *Romans 5:3-4*

---

10   Francis Omondi, *Sheepfold Mission Newsletter* (August 2015, 1).

References

Adeney, Miriam. 2009. *Kingdom Without Borders: The Untold Story of Global Christianity.* Downers' Grove, IL: IVP.

Brueggemann, Walter. 1995. *The Psalms and the Life of Faith.* Minneapolis, MN: Fortress Press.

Carpenter, Joel. 2007. "Back to the Bible: Review of 'The New Faces of Christianity: Believing the Bible in the Global South' by Philip Jenkins," *Christianity Today,* Vol 13, No 3.

Davis, Ray. 1980. *Fire on the Mountains: The Story of a Miracle—the Church in Ethiopia.* Cedar Grove, NJ: Sudan Interior Mission.

Edge, Sami. 2015. "Financial Pressures force Zion Prep to Shut Its Doors," *Seattle Times.* August 31.

Ellsberg, Robert, ed. 1999. *Charles de Foucauld.* Maryknoll, NY: Orbis Books.

Groothuis, Douglas. 2015. "Rebecca Merrill Groothuis's Contribution to Biblical Equality: A Personal Testimony and Lament," *Priscilla Papers,* Vol. 29, No.3.

Omondi, Francis. 2015. *Sheepfold Mission Newsletter,* August.

Villanueva, Federico. 2013. "The Transforming Power of Lament: Reading the Psalms from a Filipino Context," in Melba P. Maggay, ed., *The Gospel in Culture: Contextualization Issues through Asian Eyes.* Manila: OMF Literature.

Miriam Adeney (PhD Anthropology) is a professor at Seattle Pacific University, and the author of numerous books, including *Kingdom Without Borders* on global Christianity; *Wealth, Women, and God* on the suffering and service of Christian migrant working women in the Arabian Gulf; *Daughters of Islam: Building Bridges with Muslim Women*; *God's Foreign Policy: How to Help the World's Poor*; and *How to Write: A Christian Writer's Guide.* Miriam began her overseas ministry in the Philippines and continues to return regularly to Southeast Asia. She also has worked in the Middle East, in six countries in Latin America, and three countries in Africa.

Scripture: *Joshua 1:9 ("Have I not commanded you? Be strong and courageous...")*

Resource: *The Good Shepherd,* by Kenneth Bailey (Downers Grove, IL: InterVarsity Press, 2014).

CHAPTER 8

The Journey's Long Obedience

Valdir Steuernagel

Two Addresses but One Direction

There was a mumbling in the air. I had already noticed it the night before without being able to identify what it was and where it came from. As it was occurring again my wife came to me and said, "Listen, she is praying. She is praying for her family, her neighbors, and her friends at the ladies group at church." I felt overwhelmed since "she" was my dying mother.

It all happened a few weeks before my sickly mother actually died. Since she lived in Joinville, a city 120 km away from the place where I live, I had decided to move my home office to her place for a few days in order to be closer to her. That very evening I had spent some time with her, sang a song, and said a prayer before putting her in bed, giving her a good night kiss. But then the mumbling started and I realized she was praying herself into a hopeful night rest. In fact, what I found out later was that she was, so to say, praying herself into God's hands as death was coming closer and closer. She died as she lived, knowing who she was, in whose hands she could trust, and whom she was going to meet.

Her name was Isolde. She lived her whole life in the same neighborhood and knew the *direction* in which she was heading, claiming her kingdom citizenship.

The other address was much more distant. I had to geographically cross Brazil in order to arrive in São Luís do Maranhão, which is located at the very Northeast of the country—a distance of over 3,000 km from the southern city of Curitiba where I live. There I went once I got news that my mother-in-law had died.

Arriving I found out that her body was being viewed at the gymnasium of a Christian seminary, a place that had become a second address to her and her family. There they could host people who were coming in from different places, some traveling overnight as I did, in order to arrive in time for the funeral—a funeral that had to be quick, considering the heat.

Lydia was her name, and as the biblical Lydia, she had opened her house to many different people and had been a witness to Christ in the neighborhood she had moved to fifty years before. She had come from the countryside to the state's capital city where she and her husband found a new place in a poor neighborhood, a kind of "slum home," in order to fulfill a missionary call they had embraced.

As people came in from the neighborhood as well as from distant places, they expressed the desire to honor her because they knew her and were witnesses to the way she had lived. As the faithful wife of an itinerant preacher, a mother to eleven children, and a leader among the women of an emerging Christian denomination, she had witnessed to the Lord's continuous and faithful presence and guidance. Being a continuous host to familiar as well as to strange people who would come to the city to receive medical treatment, for example, she bore witness to what it meant to be a faithful and lifelong follower of Jesus.

> She knew who she was, to whom she belonged, and by whose hands she would be received once her long struggle for life came to a close.

Born on the inlands of one of the poorest states of Brazil and having moved to different places, she had several addresses but *one direction*. She knew who she was, to whom she belonged, and by whose hands she would be received once her long struggle for life came to a close.

At the funerals of both mothers, Isolde and Lydia, I had the privilege to open the Bible at the same page and read a passage that tells of the funeral of a servant of the Lord who had many itinerant addresses but *one direction*. And there it reads:

> Now Samuel died, and all Israel assembled and mourned for him; and they buried him at his home in Ramah. (1 Sam 25:1)

At both occasions, even considering that both congregations were as different as the north is from the south of Brazil, we sang the same and well-known hymn among those surrounding the coffins. It was a song that came to Brazil from as far as Sweden and was translated into Portuguese as well as into English:

> Thanks to God for my Redeemer,
> Thanks for all thou dost provide!
> Thanks for times now but a memory,
> Thanks for Jesus by my side!
> Thanks for pleasant, balmy springtime,
> Thanks for dark and stormy fall!
> Thanks for tears by now forgotten,
> Thanks for peace within my soul!
> Thanks for prayers that thou hast answered,
> Thanks for what thou dost deny!
> Thanks for storms that I have weathered,
> Thanks for all thou dost supply!
> Thanks for pain, and thanks for pleasure,

Thanks for comfort in despair!
Thanks for grace that none can measure,
Thanks for love beyond compare!
Thanks for roses by the wayside,
Thanks for thorns their stems contain!
Thanks for home and thanks for fireside,
Thanks for hope, that sweet refrain!
Thanks for joy and thanks for sorrow,
Thanks for heav'nly peace with thee!
Thanks for hope in the tomorrow,
Thanks through all eternity![1]

A hymn that has come from afar, has found roots in many places, is sung in many voices, yet always points in the same *direction*: "Thanks to God for my Redeemer. Thanks for all thou dost provide!"

You Must Follow Me (John 21:22)

It comes as a surprise as well as a gift: the Bible goes through the tedious trouble of mentioning many names and registering long lists of descendants, going from one generation to another. There is quite some intentionality in mentioning the names of common people and even some who would be qualified as having "questionable backgrounds."

To go through those genealogies can be a boring exercise; speaking for myself, I find it hard to hold my concentration when doing so. But it comes as a surprise that so much attention is given and space is dedicated to such genealogies, even inviting the reader to go through the monotonous exercise of registering the names again and again: "Was the father of… whose mother was… the husband of… of whom was born," and so on.[2] I learned from Eugene Peterson, however, that the biblical genealogies are an insistence on the primacy and continuity of people.[3] Each name is important and they are interconnected in an expression of God's mercy and promises that connect people to each other as they are shaped into God's history.

While genealogies establish a sense of connection and continuity among people and generations, there is no effort to "clean and edit" those lists of names. The genealogy of Jesus is the best example of this, as it includes people "from the outside" and people with the so-mentioned questionable background. Such inclusion is, in fact, an intentional act pointing to the fact that God's nature and action is soteriologically inclusive. Going

---

1   This hymn, *Thanks to God for My Redeemer*, was originally written in Swedish by August Ludvig Storm and was translated into English by Carl E. Backstrom in 1931, while the Portuguese translation was done by Alice Ostergren Denyszczuk.
2   See the genealogy of Jesus in Matthew 1:1–16.
3   Eugene Peterson, "Um Ano com Jesus: Leitura e Meditações Diárias," *Ultimato, Viçosa*, 2015), 14 (my translation).

back to Peterson, we find him stressing that God's act of salvation is inclusive and not exclusive. He points to the fact that those four "outside" names in the genealogy of Jesus are all people who have experienced exploitation, oppression, and/or have been a foreigner.[4] And all four mentioned names there have a place in God's history: Tamar, Rahab, Ruth, and the mother of Salmon, who had been the wife of Uriah (Matt 1:5–6). While it would be worthwhile to further introduce all of those people, it might suffice to register the striking way the mother of Salmon is introduced in this passage. She is still mentioned as "having been the wife of Uriah," even though Salmon had David as his father; and there's no need to remind us how she was brought into his palace and royal chamber.

As we go through the genealogies of yesterday as witnessed in Scripture or as we move into the mission genealogies of our fathers and mothers in the faith we will always encounter the note of surprise, grace, relationality, continuity in peoplehood, and an inclusive invitation to join the caravan of those who have allowed themselves to be called the people-community of the Book, the people-community of the followers of Jesus, the people-community who identify themselves as citizens of God's kingdom.

Furthermore, as we go through those genealogies it is easy to see and important to notice that there is no intention to treat reality nicely, to hide difficulties, or edit wrong decisions and actions. In fact, as we look through Scripture as a whole we become witnesses of the fact that real life, with all its challenges, opportunities, and failures, must be dealt with, the family network must be considered, and a lifelong commitment must be on the table. When God calls Abraham, Moses, Mary, Peter, Augustine, Mother Teresa of Calcutta, to mention a very few names in this strange genealogy, it is nothing less than a call for life that reaches out and captures every one of them. It is, in fact, a call to live and/or to die embraced by it and dive into it, while never changing direction. It is a call to "will the one thing," to use an expression by Kierkegaard, the will to seek first the kingdom of God (Matt 6:33).

> As look through Scripture as a whole we become witnesses of the fact that real life, with all its challenges, opportunities, and failures, must be dealt with, the family network must be considered, and a lifelong commitment must be on the table.

And it is never a call for the other one but a "call for me." It is call that involves "me" for all of life, in spite of anything that takes place around me and in spite of everyone else who is calling upon me. In a striking experience at a sensitive moment, to mention one example, we see this reality come through during a conversation between Jesus and Peter. At a life-defining conversation, at a moment when Jesus is asking about the center of Peter's will and heart, this man gets distracted and points and asks about another disciple who is nearby, only to hear that it was all about *him* and nobody else and nothing else. "Don't loose focus! Keep the direction and stay committed for life," Jesus was telling him with the most serious expression in his face:

---

4   Peterson, *Um Ano com Jesus*, 15.

Peter turned and saw that the disciple whom Jesus loved was following them. (This was the one who had leaned back against Jesus at the supper and had said, "Lord, who is going to betray you?") When Peter saw him, he asked, "Lord, what about him?" Jesus answered, "If I want him to remain alive until I return, what is that to you? You must follow me." (John 21:20–22)

And this Peter did! And he did it for the rest of his life and with his entire life. He did it, according to tradition, until he was martyred for his faith some years later in Rome.

At a moment of reflection about his own pastoral ministry, Peterson speaks about the challenging discovery that his call was not to merely be a "preacher of the gospel" but to be a living expression of it; and this would take his whole and his entire life. He says:

It was not enough that I announce the gospel, explain it, or whip up enthusiasm for it. I wanted it lived—lived in detail, lived on the streets and on the job, lived in the bedrooms and kitchen, lived through cancer and divorce, lived with children and in marriage. Along the way I found that this also meant living it myself, which turned out to be a far more formidable assignment. I realized that this was going to take time. I settled in for the long haul.[5]

"Now Samuel Died" (1 Sam 25:1)

A Man with Many Addresses but Only One Direction

To settle in for the long haul is a fundamental decision. But it is certainly not an easy one. There are no shortcuts in this journey and any attempt to edit it or to try to cover up strange, complicated, and difficult trends in our lives will have us harvesting illusion, sorrow, and shallowness. To settle in for the long haul is an encounter with reality, and the starting point is to stand in front of our own mirror. This journey begins with us and begins on the inside. The long haul is made up of an inside-out journey and is a courageous act, on a daily basis, to commit oneself to walk in the same direction, keeping the same commitment in mind and at heart. It is a journey full of inside and outside demons, so to say, but it is continuously immersed in God's grace. It's a journey nurtured by "bread and wine."

> The long haul is made up of an inside-out journey and is a courageous act, on a daily basis, to commit oneself to walk in the same direction, keeping the same commitment in mind and at heart.

As seen earlier, the Scriptures are not in the cover-up or editing business. Scripture only deals with reality, and like a mirror in front of you it tells you who you are and how you are doing. In fact, the Scriptures can be quite crude when discerning people's life. The

---

5   Eugene H. Peterson, *A Long Obedience in the Same Direction: Discipleship in an Instant Society* (Downers Grove, IL, InterVarsity Press, 2000), 189.

narratives about the different kings of Judah in 2 Chronicles are an example of this. It is said about King Jehoram that after having reigned for eight years, "He passed away, to no one's regret, and was buried in the City of David, but not in the tombs of the kings" (2 Chr 21:20). About his successor, King Ahaziah, it is said that, "He did evil in the eyes of the Lord; and no one from his dynasty followed him" (2 Chr 22:4,9). Later on, when talking about King Uzziah, we learn that, "He did what was right in the eyes of the Lord, just as his father Amaziah had done. He sought God during the days of Zechariah, who instructed him in the fear of God. As long as he sought the Lord, God gave him success" (2 Chr 26:4–5). He became a successful and powerful king—and this became his ruin, as registered in the same book:

> His fame spread far and wide, for he was greatly helped until he became powerful. But after Uzziah became powerful, his pride led to his downfall. He was unfaithful to the Lord his God, and entered the temple of the Lord to burn incense on the altar of incense. (2 Chr 26:15–23)

And he walked away as a leper from that experience.

When going through Scriptures it does not take long to find that no one is free of temptations, struggles, or even downfalls. In fact, there are not many who finished well and certainly no one who did only well throughout his or her life's journey, for, as Paul aptly says, "all have sinned and fall short of the glory of God" (Rom 3:23). However, it is possible to see how different people have experienced God's call and have tried to live by it throughout their lives, sometimes experiencing better times than others, but still trying, hoping and praying to keep the same direction: listening to God and keeping his word, as is said of Samuel, who might be one of the best examples in that regard:

When going through Scriptures it does not take long to find that no one is free of temptations, struggles, or even downfalls.

> The Lord was with Samuel as he grew up, and he let none of Samuel's words fall to the ground. And all Israel from Dan to Beersheba recognized that Samuel was attested as a prophet of the Lord. The Lord continued to appear at Shiloh, and there he revealed himself to Samuel through his word. And Samuel's word came to all Israel (1 Sam 3:19–4:1).

As can be seen throughout the book of 1 Samuel, he had a long life journey as a leader of Israel and played different roles during a time of transition in the history of that emerging nation: he was a prophet, a judge, and a priest to the nation. Still, not everything went well with him. He saw the nation experience a spiritual revival and became confused and stressed when the leaders of the nation looked over the borders and wanted to be a nation like the other ones. He listened to God's voice on a consistent basis, made a special effort to have that word applied to people's lives and the life of the nation, but wasn't able to have the nation live it out on a persistent and even structural basis. He saw what happened to Eli's family but wasn't able to have his own sons follow his own steps, and then saw them behave and become similar to Eli's sons.

Nevertheless, when he died we can see how he lived: faithful to God and surrounded by his people.

Samuel was a man who settled in for the long haul. In fact, he was a man who was born for the long haul. He was the child of a barren woman called Hannah and was prayed into life. He was promised to God before being conceived by a mother who did not waver to fulfill her own promise. He was offered to the Lord in his early childhood, and this his mother promised for his life, while keeping an eye on him throughout his childhood. Early in his life the Lord spoke to him and continued to do so in surprising, exciting, and challenging ways. Even more surprising, however, is the fact that he kept listening to God, obeying his word and honoring his name as he walked his call into reality:

> Samuel continued as Israel's leader all the days of his life. From year to year he went on a circuit from Bethel to Gilgal to Mizpah, judging Israel in all those places. But he always went back to Ramah, where his home was, and there he also held court for Israel. And he built an altar there to the Lord. (1 Sam 7:15–17)

Samuel was a man of different addresses but with one direction, and as such he becomes a model for all of us who call ourselves pilgrims with a heavenly citizenship. And so it was with the Apostle Paul, even if he had a different entrance to this journey and at a different time in his life. But once having heard the Voice and having decided to follow it, the direction was set. And for this reason there is an invitation for us to apply Paul's words to Samuel as well as to many others who have run the race and passed the baton to incoming generations. Paul modeled it to Timothy and called him to keep the direction straight and clear:

> But you, keep your head in all situations, endure hardship, do the work of an evangelist, discharge all the duties of your ministry. For I am already being poured out like a drink offering, and the time for my departure is near. I have fought the good fight, I have finished the race, I have kept the faith. Now there is in store for me the crown of righteousness, which the Lord, the righteous Judge, will award to me on that day—and not only to me, but also to all who have longed for his appearing. (2 Tim 4:5–8)

May It Be to Me (Luke 1:38)

A long journey starts with a beginning. Sometimes it is a small beginning but it is always a key beginning. It is a beginning in which God's revelation meets a listening ear and a hungry heart—a heart that is willing to let God's voice go through its entire existence, with all the questions, fears, and even suspicions that accompany the process. It is a heart that, by the end of that encounter, gladly surrenders entirely to a lifelong journey of obedience. It's a call! A lifelong call that comes in different colors, shapes, and tastes. It is a call that is received in different ways but needs always to give birth to an act of obedience. Revelation calls for obedience, and both, as life partners, are the foundation of a graceful life journey.

We are called to an obedience that moves deeper into intimacy with God, love for neighbor, and participation in the agony of a lost and dying world while being carried by the flavor of God's promise of eternity. Writing to the Colossians Paul points to that life journey while stressing the need and the possibility of moving deeper and deeper into relationship with God and his Word, exercising a profound faith, and never reducing oneself to the beginning. He says it the following way:

> So then, just as you received Christ Jesus as Lord, continue to live your lives in him, rooted and built up in him, strengthened in the faith as you were taught, and overflowing with thankfulness. (Col 2:6–7)

As we come to the end of this "walk" of ours, I call on the person of Mary to keep us company. Her company invites us to the way she began, in a moment of difficulty, and then to the places she is last seen. Her beginning is surrounded by mystery, as revelation always is. The angel arrives, greets her, and entrusts her with a call that means offering her whole life to God; and he leaves her once she responded in a way that always provokes in us a surprised awe: "I am the Lord's servant. May it be to me as you have said" (Luke 1:38). It was a beautiful beginning to be tested many times in the many years to come. At one point the whole family went out to see the son Jesus, only to receive back a puzzling response. In fact, Jesus did not even bother to "go out" to talk to them as they asked of him, and simply asked aloud: "Who are my mother and my brothers?" (Mark 3:33). This was certainly one of those many moments when Mary must have "treasured all these things in her heart" as she had done on other occasions (see Luke 2:19, 52), struggling and praying to understand what was going on and how it all connected to her earlier calling. To establish such a connection is something that needs to be done over and over again, with the note that it might only be done at the "dark night of the soul," to use an expression by Saint John of the Cross. To embrace those "nights" is quite human; yet, they should never have the last word, as they did not have in Mary's life. The last two references to Mary in Scripture take us to find her at the foot of the Cross (John 19:25) and in the bosom of the community of believers as they gathered to pray (Acts 1:14). That is the place to go to and to stay: a place that should not be passed by and a place where all pilgrims of the common journey should meet in order to keep the one direction.

Together with the cloud of witnesses I certainly want to pray too. I pray for me and for my family. I pray for our young evangelical church in this country called Brazil.

We have seen blessing come upon this country where the gospel has been spread out and people have received it in so many ways. Here churches have been planted and ministries been created in a surprising way. But we should be aware that the journey has just started. We need to always keep in mind that we are here "for the long haul" and for a journey of obedience. And even more so, we need to embrace the fact that this journey is made up of one step at a time, for this is how obedience is shaped.

So help us Lord, we pray with thanksgiving!

References

Peterson, Eugene. 2015. Um Ano com Jesus: Leitura e Meditações Diárias. *Ultimato, Viçosa* (my translation).

———. 2000. *A Long Obedience in the Same Direction: Discipleship in an Instant Society*. Downers Grove, IL, InterVarsity Press.

Valdir Steuernagel is married to Silêda Silva, and they have been gifted with four sons. Both are presently pastoring a Lutheran Community in Curitiba, south Brazil. After having ministered with ABU/IFES, pastored a local church, and directed a renewal movement within the Lutheran Church, they served at World Vision International and have now settled into a local ministry with emphasis on spiritual nurture and young leaders. Valdir has a PhD from the Lutheran School of Theology in Chicago and has focused on missiology while publishing in the area of integral mission, especially in Portuguese and Spanish.

Scripture: *Psalm 146 ("Praise the Lord. Praise the Lord, my soul...")*

Resource: *The Sense of the Call*, by Marva J. Dawn (Grand Rapids, MI: Eerdmans, 2006.

Along the Journey

Identifying Issues

CHAPTER 9

Spiritual Formation

The Contours, Ways, and Means of the Journey

Christine Raquel Taylor Warner

Editor's note: this is the first of a two-part series of articles on these two crucial themes that have to do with the process of the transformation of our interior landscape. However, they should be read as a seamless flow.

> Everyone is in a process of spiritual formation. We are being shaped into either the wholeness of the image of Christ or a horribly destructive caricature of that image—destructive not only to ourselves but also to others, for we inflict our brokenness upon them … The direction of our spiritual growth infuses all we do with intimations of either Life or Death. M. Robert Mulholland Jr., *Invitation to a Journey: A Road Map for Spiritual Formation*

From Ashes to Beauty

That's the Story

Clara struggled with sexual brokenness and its consequences for years. Her shattered sense of self due to abandonment and abuse could not be satiated by her numerous outward accomplishments, but rather fueled her strong desires to move against God's ways. In her mind, freedom and wholeness through pursuing Christ was a fantasy that her shredded heart could never hope for. To see her now, with a loving husband and two dear children, living a grounded and fruitful life in community and in her vocation as a writer, one gets the sense that much more than a "tidy" end to a rough story is at stake here, but rather the glorious victory of light over darkness has produced a woman who has about her the fragrance of Christ. Her surrender to Christ is profound; her love for Scripture contagious; her understanding of God as her loving Father transformative; her honest and humble and strong sense of self inspiring; and her rejoicing in the healing power of community and spiritual disciplines instructive. She "looks" like Jesus.

Clara's redemption and healing took years, but anyone who hears her story now is only led to worship of our good and true and beautiful God.

Clara stands as one compelling example of the process of spiritual formation into which all believers are called, the life-long process of being shaped by the Holy Spirit into the likeness of Christ for the sake of others and for the glory of God. The Apostle Paul comments, "We all, with unveiled face, beholding the glory of the Lord, are being transformed into the same image from one degree of glory to another. For this comes from the Lord who is the Spirit." (2 Cor 3:18).

What's the Vision?

Spiritual Formation

Spiritual formation is rooted in our understanding of the gospel and the big story of salvation. When the Triune God created, he created all things "good" and in right relationship with each other. The man and woman were the pinnacle of his creation, made in his image, and in right relationship with God, with themselves, with each other, and with all the rest of creation. The Fall not only damaged each aspect of creation, but also the good and beautiful relationships between them. The work of the Trinity from the Fall on has been to restore God's image in men and women and to heal and repair these relationships. The context for this restoration work is all of life—there is no aspect of life that is outside the reach and scope of the Trinity mending, healing, re-crafting us. Spiritual formation occurs in both the most exquisite and most ordinary circumstances of our lives. Yes, moving worship and powerful sermons shape us Godward, but offering up a mundane workday as a sacrifice of fidelity or allowing diaper changing to be an act of worship or infusing studying for a test with an awareness of God's intimacy—these are the ordinary moments that become sacred and orient and train all of ourselves towards God. We want to shift from merely understanding ourselves as "forgiven sinner" to a bigger vision of being "beloved children of God on a transformational journey that will lead to restoration of the imago Dei and spiritual union."[1] This shift makes all the difference as an inspiring, energizing, and generative vision of the God saturated path ahead, affecting how we view our own lives and how we invite and companion others.

> Spiritual formation occurs in both the most exquisite and most ordinary circumstances of our lives.

---

1   Gary Moon and David Benner, *Spiritual Direction and the Care of Souls* (Downers Grove, IL: InterVarsity Press, 2004), 19.

The Ever Moving Pieces

Two Critical Dynamics

There are two key dynamics that characterize truly biblical and theological spiritual formation. The first is the deepest, truest, and most mysterious dynamic: in order to grow into Christ-likeness, we are invited into participating in the death and resurrection of Christ. In order for the image of God to be restored in us, we are invited to step into a life-long rhythm of regularly entering the mystery of death and resurrection as defined biblically, "unless a seed falls to the ground" (John 12:24). We are to die daily, so that we may be raised to life daily, in order, "that I may know him and the power of his resurrection, and may share his sufferings, becoming like him in his death, that by any means possible I may attain the resurrection from the dead" (Phil 3:10–11). This rhythm involves mystery and grace and obedience, and takes place, on the one hand, in large and dramatic ways such as processing pain and suffering with patient endurance and tenacious hope, allowing God to accompany and transform us through trial. On the other hand, the work of death and resurrection occurs in quiet and small ways such as the choice to avoid name dropping which might get us noticed, the practice of serving in invisible ways, releasing our agenda of productivity for the sake of relationship, and even fighting for hope while struggling with depression. We are likewise shaped as we practice resurrection joy, embrace a Sabbath lifestyle, and reap the rewards of authentic spiritual friendships and community. A robust theology of suffering as well as a theology of joy submerges us into the Eucharistic life of Christ and has real and practical implications for how we press into God and how we live and minister the Eucharistic life in the world.

> In order to grow into Christ-likeness, we are invited into participating in the death and resurrection of Christ.

Complementing this familiar cross-resurrection dynamic of spiritual growth is the less well known rhythm of "dual knowledge." In this second dynamic of spiritual formation we grow in the knowledge of God as we grow in the knowledge of self and vice versa. As we come to know God, we increasingly understand how fearfully and wonderfully we are made by our Creator, how loved we are by our Redeemer, as well as how far short we fall from the glory of God. Likewise, as we come to know ourselves, our strengths, and weaknesses, our beauty and ugliness, our soft-heartedness towards God and our sin, we are then propelled towards our Maker and our Redeemer. We know where to find our thirst slaked and our hunger satisfied. In a life-giving cycle, knowledge of God enhances knowledge of self leading to a deeper knowing of God. The extremes can be instructive, whether it is the "expert" with a head filled exclusively with analytic theology, tragically failing to love and be loved, or the introspective "quester," ever and only pursuing the elusive and unstable "self" who possesses no anchoring in Truth, no grounded relationships. Emerging from a dialectic encounter with God, the

> We grow in the knowledge of God as we grow in the knowledge of self and vice versa.

key character trait in this double-knowledge is humility, the ability to listen humbly to the truth about our lives and in response to humbly entrust ourselves to the Triune God.

> Our wisdom ... consists almost entirely of two parts: the knowledge of God and of ourselves ... no man can survey himself without forthwith turning his thoughts towards the God in whom he lives and moves ... On the other hand, it is evident that man never attains to a true self-knowledge until he has previously contemplated the face of God, and come down after such contemplation to look into himself. *Calvin's Institutes (Book 1)*

As this dual knowledge interacts in and on us, there is discovery and adventure, quietness and passion, rejoicing and lament and repentance. The journey becomes much more than mere obedience and moralism and even healing; it becomes one of living in awe of the mystery and beauty of the human heart engaged in the dance with the divine heart of Love, expressed in the Trinity.

What? A Dancing God?

Knowing the Trinitarian God

Our starting point in the knowledge of God is the self-revealing Trinity whom we are invited to know, fear, and love. According to the church fathers of the fourth century, the Triune God lives in a community of love and mutual indwelling they called "perichoresis," which conveys the divine choreography of a dancing Father, Son, and Holy Spirit. St. Gregory Nazianzus marvels at the Triune God,

> No sooner do I conceive of the One than I am illumined by the splendor of the Three; no sooner do I distinguish them than I am carried back to the One ... When I contemplate the Three together, I see but one torch, and cannot divide or measure out the undivided light.[2]

When we understand God the Father's providential care and fierce but tender love, we are stirred to respond with love. When we know God the Son as the source of our freedom, then we respond by laying down our rebellion and embracing his radical liberty. When we know God the Holy Spirit as comforting, animating, empowering, and companioning us, then we can reciprocate with whole hearts knowing we are not alone.

> When we understand God the Father's providential care and fierce but tender love, we are stirred to respond with love.

---

2   Duncan Reid, *Energies of the Spirit. Trinitarian Models in Eastern Orthodox and Western Theology* (Atlanta: Scholars Press, 1997), 122.

To know God is to know and trust his character. The beautiful diversity of God's character is summed up in his holiness; he is wondrously "other" and to know him as he is is to trust him, to respond with humble reverence, "the fear of the Lord." But might there be core traits that function as clear guideposts for our journey of spiritual transformation? Jerry Bridges argues in *Trusting God* that when we experience a crisis of faith, we struggle to believe one of three fundamental traits of his character, that he is loving, all-powerful, or wise. If we remove any one of this triad, we end up with a frightening, impotent, or capricious god.[3]

In sum, the most important aspect of knowing God is knowing his love for us and how that love then transforms our lives. Our spiritual formation, as we more fully reflect the image of God, will be shaped by how well we know this good and true and beautiful God as well as how well we know the depths to which his love has penetrated and transformed our lives. We become more free, joyful, humble, and intrigued and drawn by this dancing Trinity.

But We Also Need to Know
Our Beautiful and Frightening Selves

In understanding ourselves, our starting point is the image of God, which is stamped on every human being and makes us more beautiful than we can imagine. But things are not the way they are supposed to be. The image of God is terribly, destructively marred. As we understand the ways in which we fall short of the glory of God, we can understand better what the restoration path might look like, what our "yes" to God entails, what must be submitted to the loving work of the Spirit in our lives. We are not only creatures, limited, fragile and made of dust, but we are also fragmented, broken, wounded, sick, sinful, and sinned against. Hence, we must face our dark selves, stand in painful honesty, and allow the Spirit to recraft us into the likeness of Christ. To be free we must name the truth of our shadow selves. Freedom depends on confessing our unhealthy dependencies, our desperate desire to control, our hidden jealousies and insecurities. These confessions, and subsequent lament and mourning (Matt 5), allow the light and love of the Holy Spirit to enter our lives and bring healing.

When we consider the darkness in ourselves and our world, we must address briefly our theology of suffering. In this chapter we have little space to explore this reality in any detail, and even so, immense mystery attends our best understandings of suffering

---

3   Jerry Bridges, *Trusting God* (Colorado Springs: NavPress, 2008), 19.

and the purposes of God. Suffering is a result of the Fall, and all human experience is deeply impacted, from cellular levels of disease, to creation groaning in environmental brokenness, to the evil wrought by human hearts throughout history. For all our pain and unanswered queries, this we do know, that the Triune God entered our suffering himself. He himself grieves over the pain, collecting our every tear in his bottle. And in his unquenchable love he is making all things new. He does this in the world; he does this powerfully and exquisitely in our own lives; one day he will finally accomplish this work throughout all the universe. Knowing this deeply shapes how we live daily.

In joy, surrender, hope, repentance, trust, and awe, we turn from our darkness, from our "false self," to the grace of the God and come to know this Trinitarian Dancer in greater depth and intimacy. We are set free. Knowing him, knowing ourselves—this liberating cycle forms us in the likeness of Christ, the truly human. We become, in a sense, more "human," more alive than ever, able to reflect the glory of our God. Mysteriously, profoundly we are swept up into the death and resurrection of Jesus; we undergo a dying and a crushing, and a rising again to new life, hope, and joy. In love, throughout all of history, the Father, Son, and Spirit are making all things new again. When we say "yes" to this intention of God, to this divine movement, the work of spiritual reformation is launched in us. The glorious imago Dei is being restored.

A Smoking Volcano and an Ant Crossing a Rock

Biblical Creation Spirituality

As we grow in knowing God as our Creator, we also grow in understanding our own creatureliness, our embodied, earthed, material selves living in the frail beauty of the world God made. When we enter into right relationship with creation through our Creator, we, in a sense, come home. We gain humility as we relate to the "humus," the dust from which we come. Beauty and wonder and care characterize our relationship with creation. We notice God's character revealed in creation. Rightly related to the Creator and his creation, we are free to nurture our love for beauty and we are met by God's love in it. Joy and laughter and play are closely related to beauty, and they become prophetic acts of proclaiming the kingdom, of practicing resurrection. Creation and its beauty then matter, not just as a postcard or a screensaver, but as a place where we are invited to live and pay attention, the curve of a child's cheek, a delicious meal of simple goodness, or the moving wonder of a sculpture. In the case of a man named Peter, whose endless work demands overwhelm and deaden him, he finds that cultivating orchids speaks to him of God's care for detail, peace, and beauty and reminds him that the things of the

> Beauty and wonder and care characterize our relationship with creation. We notice God's character revealed in creation.

kingdom are also organic, slow, and yet resilient; orchid cultivating becomes a sacred and holy space. In paying attention, we encounter our Creator and ourselves.

The Ordinary Becomes Sacred
Sacramental Spirituality

Sacramental theology and spirituality follows from right relationship with God and creation. A sacrament is an outward sign of an inward grace or visible symbol of an invisible reality. Hence, the material world becomes a place of encounter with the living God and a context of our spiritual formation. In other words, we do not have to escape reality, the material real world that we live in; it is the very stuff of God's presence in our lives. All of life becomes the stage and place of God's activity. When we expand our understanding that all of creation becomes a context for his voice to be heard, then we can respond to the ordinary, gritty context of our lives with expectation that God is present, that he's revealing himself, that we can encounter him there. This imbues our ordinary living with eternal significance, and our joys and our sufferings both become the places of God's activity. Our job then is to pay attention, to seek him, to glimpse him, and gaze at him. In stark contrast to the paradigm of a celebrity-driven spirituality, the framework of creation-as-sacrament leads us to encounter God among all his creatures, even among and possibly especially so in those typically relegated to the margins, the disabled, the abused, the chronically ill, the mentally shattered. We are to find that surprising hearth of his presence (among the homeless, the brokenhearted, the vulnerable, the poor) and be warmed by it as we see some of his most exquisite work taking place.

> We do not have to escape reality, the material real world that we live in; it is the very stuff of God's presence in our lives. All of life becomes the stage and place of God's activity.

There Are Many Biblical Hearths
Privileged Places and Practices

Our progress into the image of our Lord Jesus emerges from the incarnation and work of atonement; proceeds dialectically in knowing him and knowing ourselves, and is accomplished by the Spirit in the arena of his created order. We can specify elements of this sanctifying process yet further. Historically, the church has recognized particular places and practices that over the centuries offer rich soil for spiritual growth and formation into Christlikeness. Creation and Scripture are powerful places of encounter with God and self, as is authentic Christian community and engaging the broken, vulnerable, and poor of our world as Jesus spoke of in Matthew 25. All places are spaces where we can encounter God, but there are some settings and practices that believers hold as essential to spiritual growth such as community, prayer, Scripture, and mission. Spiritual disciplines of service, worship, silence and solitude, fasting, Sabbath, contemplative prayer, celebration, and confession offer rich soil for spiritual formation. In recent years Protestant believers have incorporated more historic practices of meditation on Scripture, *lectio divina*, pilgrimage, rule of life, and fixed-hour prayer as well as creatively encouraging spiritual disciplines such as play, digital disconnectedness, hospitality, and margin. With as big as creation is and as diverse as humankind is, the variety of ways that God provides to deepen in him are vast. Further supporting all of these spiritual disciplines is the beautiful and generative spiritual discipline is that of spiritual direction.

Discussion Questions

1. Give one example of how knowing some aspect of God might then reveal something about yourself.
2. Give one example of how discovering something about your own heart or story has then turned your gaze to discover something new about God.
3. What spiritual disciplines have been significant in your life as a believer and why? Which have become "dry" and what new spiritual disciplines would you like to explore?
4. What is your experience with silence and solitude? What ways might you engage creation that connects you to God's beauty, joy, freedom, and play?
5. Have you experienced someone else listening attentively to your story with questions that gave you greater insight into God's presence and activity in your life?

References

Bridges, Jerry. 2008. *Trusting God*. Colorado Springs, CO: NavPress.

Moon, Gary and David Benner. 2004. *Spiritual Direction and the Care of Souls*. Downers Grove, IL: InterVarsity Press.

Reid, Duncan. 1997. *Energies of the Spirit. Trinitarian Models in Eastern Orthodox and Western Theology*. Atlanta, GA: Scholars Press.

Born and raised in Guatemala, *Christine Raquel Taylor Warner* witnessed the power and mercy of Jesus Christ in a context of poverty, violence, and civil war. In the United States she has also been involved in campus ministry, urban mission on the Mexican border, and church planting in Austin, Texas. She teaches writing at a small liberal arts university, chairs a denominational task force for biblical justice, is on the supervising faculty of Selah (a spiritual direction training program), and is the director of Lumen: Center for Mission and Spirituality (a ministry for spiritual formation and spiritual direction). Christine lives in Austin, Texas with her husband pastor (Christ Church Anglican) and four children.

Scripture: *Isaiah 30:15 ("In repentance and trust is your salvation...")*

Resource: *Beginning to Pray*, by Anthony Bloom (Mahwah, NJ: Paulist Press, 1970).

CHAPTER 10

Spiritual Direction

Do Not Enter the Soul Unaccompanied

Christine Raquel Taylor Warner

Is God Really Here? Is He Really Near?

As Jesus walked with his disciples on the road to Emmaus, he listened to them talk about the recent experiences in Jerusalem surrounding the death and resurrection of their Messiah. Jesus listened attentively to their stories and asked them questions that led to deeper insight; the result was that the disciples felt a burning in their hearts. They knew that they had encountered and experienced the presence of God. This is the work of spiritual direction, of the spiritual director, who is listening closely to the story of another while also listening closely to the Holy Spirit. Spiritual directors and directees together pay attention to the presence and activity of God in daily life to discern the individual's path towards wholeness and calling.

Defining Christian spiritual direction is crucial given the breadth of the global body of Christ; it is "help given by one believer to another that enables the latter to pay attention to God's personal communication to him or her, to respond to this personally communicating God, to grow in intimacy with this God, and to live out the consequences of that relationship."[1] Spiritual direction is different from counseling, which focuses on a person's history from a therapeutic perspective; it is different from mentoring, which emphasizes acquiring a skill or a competency; it is different from discipleship, which concentrates on the full picture of spiritual growth related to knowledge of Scripture, prayer, service and outreach, and character development. In contrast, spiritual direction is primarily focused on the directee's prayer life and the experience of God's presence in the midst of real, daily living. While there is reference to the directee's history and relationships, skills and competencies, and engagement with all aspects of spiritual growth, those arenas are merely the context for knowing and seeing God in the present, listening to his invitation to respond more deeply to his love.

---

1   William Barry and William Connolly, *The Practice of Spiritual Direction* (New York: Harper Collins, 1982), 8.

Often spiritual direction is referred to as tending to the "care and cure of souls," which includes "healing, sustaining, reconciling, and guiding," seeing the soul as a garden whose health is cultivated for the sake of a lifetime of flourishing.[2] Two other helpful images are those of "midwife to the soul" or "tending the campfire in the wilderness" both which assume that God is already at work and rain-dancing is unnecessary.[3]

In Every Generation and Every Time

Background and History

God's people have always engaged with him experientially in the Old and New Testaments, from Elijah companioning Elisha in supernatural provision (1 Kgs 17–21) and Eli helping Samuel learn God's voice (1 Samuel 3:1–18) to John the Baptist's encounter with God in the desert and subsequently offering his followers specific instructions as a part of their repentance (Luke 3:10–14) and Ananias helping Paul interpret his encounter with Christ (Acts 9:10–19). The desert fathers and mothers as well as the Celtic Christians practiced different forms of spiritual direction. However, the church began to formerly shape this particular mode of listening to God in the fourth century with John Cassian. Cassian, following in the tradition of the desert fathers and mothers, required the younger monks in the monasteries to be under the care of a few older and wise monks; however, in time lay communities began to seek spiritual direction from monks and nuns who offered soul care. This practice was continued by Benedict in the sixth century and then later more fully developed by Ignatius Loyola in the sixteenth century. Loyola articulated values and a framework for spiritual direction that developed into Ignatian spirituality and Ignatian spiritual direction, which includes principles of discernment, individual retreats, retreats in community, spiritual exercises, and emphases practiced in the context of one-on-one spiritual direction. Other salient influencers include Francis of Assisi, Julian of Norwich, Teresa of Avila, John of the Cross, Francis of Sales, Brother Lawrence, and the Anglican Divines such as John Donne and George Herbert.[4]

While the Orthodox and Catholic churches have engaged in spiritual direction for centuries, only recently has the broader Protestant tradition begun paying attention to this spiritual discipline of companioning others in attentiveness towards God. Richard Foster was one of the first to introduce spiritual direction to a broader Protestant and evangelical audience in the 1970s and was considered a lone voice subsequently joined by Dallas Willard's writings in the 1980s; whereas now, several respected Protestant and evangelical seminaries and institutions offer studies and training in spiritual direction.

---

2   Gary Moon and David Benner, *Spiritual Direction and the Care of Souls* (Downers Grove, IL: InterVarsity Press, 2004), 11.
3   Sue Pickering, *Spiritual Direction: A Practical Introduction* (London: Canterbury Press Norwich, 2008), 32.
4   Moon and Benner, 82–83.

Further Up and Further In

Spiritual Direction in a Life

Spiritual direction, as a centuries-old discipline, involves a stillness and a listening that sets aside all distractions, external and internal, in order to pay close attention to the movement of the Spirit in a person's life in a particular moment. Training, spiritual maturity, biblical literacy, emotional and relational health, prophetic words and other factors are important, but they are all set aside as secondary support to being fully present to the sacred "this moment in time" and this person's heart, soul, mind, spirit, and body. Spiritual direction values paying close attention to the present and particular which then elucidates the rest of a person's life and reality. The directee rests in the knowledge that the Holy Spirit uses the material of one moment to speak to all the rest of his or her life. The director trusts that the Spirit is guiding and highlighting what he wants to reveal.

> Spiritual direction, as a centuries-old discipline, involves a stillness and a listening that sets aside all distractions, external and internal, in order to pay close attention to the movement of the Spirit in a person's life in a particular moment.

The director's work is to place the weight of discernment in the micro movements of the moment and not rely primarily on background, training, experience, mentoring tools, discipling, or counseling. Even insight or words of knowledge or wisdom are all submitted to the Spirit and held quietly in prayer, possibly for a later moment, possibly never shared but faithfully brought before the Lord and included in the listening. The work of the director is to set aside distracting ministry tools and even emotional responses so that listening is the focus. Ministry tools and emotional responses are only offered during spiritual direction if the Spirit prompts and guides. The goal is for the directee to listen to God, to hear themselves identify truth and lies, to discern feelings and thoughts, to observe patterns in his or her life, and to see where God is at work in both the mundane and the dramatic. There is a listening to joy and life-giving contexts, but there is also a listening to disappointment or anger with God, to places of pain, issues around sexuality, vulnerability, and abuse, a listening for transitions and crises, barriers, blocks, resistance, signs of isolation, a listening to someone who is grieving and for the "dark night" or the perceived absence of God.[5] All these are brought before the loving gaze of God who is speaking to us "at many times and in various ways" (Heb 1:1) shaping us into his likeness.

Ultimately the experiential objective towards which all spiritual direction leads is that of knowing ourselves beloved of God and walking in the freedom and implications of that love. For example, consider Brenda, an activist, who serves in leadership both in her church and in a non-profit that addresses the alleviation of extreme poverty. The work of spiritual direction has allowed the Holy Spirit to identify her lack of

---

5   Pickering, vi.

trust in God to provide and to address the needs that feel so crushing in her ministry. She has been able to acknowledge her anger at God for allowing so much suffering. In the quiet, she has received the Spirit speaking comfort and hope to her anger and distrust. Through attentive listening, Brenda's spiritual director has helped her engage Scripture about God's love in fresh ways that help train the eyes of her heart to see God's goodness, beauty, and presence in places that had previously only been dark and ugly. Her awareness of God's love for her and others has deepened and has changed the way that she approaches her ministry.

Spiritual direction reminds the minister that an engaged relationship with God, whether in vibrancy or wrestling, is, at the end of the day, both the starting point and the ending point of personal life and ministry life. In spiritual direction the focus is the whole person, a welcome departure from the compartmentalization of reductionistic spiritualities and modern psychology. Spiritual direction takes into account all of Dallas Willard's components for being human: thought (images, concepts, judgments, inferences), feeling (sensations, emotions), choice (will, decision, character), body (action, engagement with physical world), social context (relationship with God and others), and soul (which integrates all components to form life).[6] This whole-person involvement validates the breadth, depth, and mystery of who we are.

What Does it Look Like?

Pragmatics

In our externally and internally noisy world, the silence and quietness of spiritual direction offers a gift that is essential to our knowing God and knowing ourselves, inviting us into Scripture we know but often do not practice such as: "Be still and know that I am God" (Ps 46:10); "In quietness and trust is our strength" (Isa 30:15); "The still small voice of God" (1 Kgs 19:12).

In many ways spiritual direction is an experiential, even at times a mystical encounter with God that is rooted in solid Christian history and tradition and in Scripture. Sadly, in recent history, other mystical religions have adopted the language of "spiritual direction" without a biblical Trinitarian framework, which is focused on listening to the living God in Christ Jesus through the ministry and presence of the Holy Spirit. For this reason, it is critical that someone using the label "spiritual director" has a track record of a life devoted to following Christ, is mature in understanding the rhythms and season of the Christian life, has submitted himself to rigorous training of two to three years of reading the literature in the field, of supervision and internship, of self-examination and discernment of calling, ongoing training, and of living a life under

---

6   Dallas Willard, *Renovation of the Heart: Putting on the Character of Christ* (Colorado Springs, CO: NavPress, 2002), 42.

authority and covering of the Christian spiritual direction community and the local church. Christian spiritual direction is biblical, honors Christian history, is practiced in community, and is offered in service to the body of Christ and the growth of the whole person into Christlikeness.

Practically, spiritual direction is traditionally offered on a once a month basis for an hour at a time. The session often includes silence, Scripture reading, prayer, and other spiritual exercises that are conducive to listening. The assumption is that both director and directee are in constant prayer between sessions, and the session provides a listening attentiveness to that ongoing commitment.

Occasionally, there are seasons that require more frequent meeting, particularly when engaged in more intensive spiritual disciplines or a focus on healing that requires more support. Spiritual direction might also take place in the context of a group or a retreat in addition to one-on-one.

Pastors, missionaries, and those serving in vocational ministry often respond to counseling as a damage control resource, and too often neglect ongoing soul care, maintenance of emotional and relational and spiritual health, and prevention strategies to mitigate burnout and undesirable attrition. Spiritual direction offers a gentle and sustained, yet powerful and profound practice of tending to the garden of the soul, drawing us more deeply into our greatest longing to become like Christ and find ourselves beloved.

Captured by a Dancing God's Love
Conclusion

Spiritual formation and spiritual direction, as one of the many disciplines that form us, are about being captured by the love of the Trinity for each other and for us and for the world. Spiritual formation and spiritual direction are about ordering our loves, directing our loves, cultivating our love, and staying in love with the one who loved us first. This tending of our love for Christ is what shapes us into his likeness and more fully into our God-imagedness. As one spiritual director wrote:

> Nothing is more practical than finding God,
> that is, falling in love in a quite absolute, final way.
> What you are in love with,
> what seizes your imagination,
> will affect everything.
> It will decide
> what gets you out of bed in the morning,

what you will do with your evenings,
how you will spend your weekends,
what you read, who you know,
what breaks your heart,
and what amazes you with joy and gratitude.
Fall in love, stay in love,
and it will decide everything.

(Pedro Arrupe, 1907–1991)

Discussion Questions

1. What are you currently learning about God? What are you currently learning about yourself? How might they interact?
2. How might your ordinary, mundane day change if you were to truly believe that every small act is infused with the presence of God as a meaningful invitation into the rhythm of his death and resurrection?
3. How can you grow in attentiveness to God's presence in your daily routine and relationships?
4. If you were to fully and profoundly believe that you are beloved of God, how might that change how you think and act, especially in difficult circumstances? Consider a current example of a difficult situation and walk out that scenario imagining yourself as fully accepted by God and resting in his love and delight in you.

References

Arrupe, Pedro. 2016. "Fall in Love." *Ignatian Spirituality*. Loyola Press, http://www.ignatianspirituality.com/ignatian-prayer/prayers-by-st-ignatius-and-others/fall-in-love.

Barry, William A. and William J. Connolly. 1982. *The Practice of Spiritual Direction*. New York: Harper Collins.

Demacopoulos, George. 2007. *Five Models of Spiritual Direction in the Early Church*. Notre Dame, IN: University of Notre Dame Press.

Moon, Gary and David Benner. 2004. *Spiritual Direction and the Care of Souls*. Downers Grove, IL: InterVarsity Press.

Pickering, Sue. 2008. S*piritual Direction: A Practical Introduction*. London: Canterbury Press Norwich.

Willard, Dallas. 2002. *Renovation of the Heart: Putting on the Character of Christ*. Colorado Springs, CO: NavPress.

Born and raised in Guatemala, *Christine Raquel Taylor Warner* witnessed the power and mercy of Jesus Christ in a context of poverty, violence, and civil war. In the United States she has also been involved in campus ministry, urban mission on the Mexican border, and church planting in Austin, Texas. She teaches writing at a small liberal arts university, chairs a denominational task force for biblical justice, is on the supervising faculty of Selah (a spiritual direction training program), and is the director of Lumen: Center for Mission and Spirituality (a ministry for spiritual formation and spiritual direction). Christine lives in Austin, Texas with her husband pastor (Christ Church Anglican) and four children.

Scripture: *Isaiah 30:15 ("In repentance and trust is your salvation...")*

Resource: *Beginning to Pray,* by Anthony Bloom (Mahwah, NJ: Paulist Press, 1970).

CHAPTER 11

The Spirituality of Partnerships

Alexandre Araujo

Partnering in missions is one of the major positive developments of the last three or more decades. The core idea is that we can do more together than we can do alone. We can make resources last longer and go farther when we bring them together. And we please God as we live and work in unity (Ps 133).

At first it may seem odd to talk about spirituality and partnerships in the same sentence. Usually we associate partnerships with the practical business of getting things done, while we think of spirituality as referring to disciplines for individual prayer and reflection. Yet from a biblical perspective, partnering can be an expression of our spirituality, as I will seek to explain below.

The Current Context for Missions Partnerships

It is important to understand how mission partnerships have affected the missions movement so that we can speak of partnering as a spiritual walk. What follows is a very brief and incomplete review of the emergence of partnerships as a major component of evangelical missions work. My aim is not to give a full account of the last thirty years of missions but to place the spirituality of partnerships in context.

The pursuit of partnerships came as a breath of fresh air to a missions movement that was individualistic and competitive, in which different denominations and agencies competed for territory, funds, and converts. Strongly influenced by the North American entrepreneurial spirit that projected itself worldwide soon after the end of the second world war, nondenominational mission agencies proliferated, each seeking to establish its distinctive identity and vision. The emergence of competing independent mission agencies was added to the already divided and even conflictive mission work of the various Christian denominations.

While this burst of missions activity from North America and Europe at first made significant inroads into unevangelized areas of the world, it eventually evolved into a crowded field of competing agencies, each in its own way seeking candidates and funds. Contrary to the denominational mission agencies that drew candidates and funds from within their own congregations, independent nondenominational agencies had no direct claim to the candidates and funds from churches. They needed to develop a marketing program to persuade people to invest in their work. This created a competitive marketplace of missions recruiting and fundraising. We found ourselves in this contradictory situation in which the gospel of peace and reconciliation was being propagated by a movement that was competitive and divided.

While much good happened during this period—new fields were opened among previously unreached peoples, churches emerged and grew where they didn't exist before—it soon became clear that we were presenting a disunited face to a needy world. It also became clear that while stimulating creativity in propagation strategies, this competitive and duplicating approach to world evangelization undermined the very thing it sought to offer the world: a new family in Christ in which there was unity around God the Father and loving fellowship among his people.

In this chaotic and competitive missions environment, the Lord inspired some people to promote missions collaboration among mission agencies and churches. By God's grace these dedicated people spearheaded a partnering movement that has permeated large portions of the globe which is now, at least in concept and language, nearly universal in global missions work.

Pragmatic Partnership

The biblical reason for learning to work in partnership is our oneness in Christ that is at the core of the gospel message. But this perspective did not always speak with sufficient force to motivate mission leaders to change minds and structures. They were more responsive to pragmatic arguments that showed how their own agency program would benefit from forming partnerships. Partnerships were seen as optional rather than the obvious way to work as brothers and sisters in God's family. Some might say, "If you can show me that by partnering with you my own vision and goals will be advanced, I will consider partnering. If not, I will continue to do it alone. Otherwise, there is a lost world to win and as a good steward I cannot waste time in trying to agree on how to work together. Nor can I afford to dilute my mission vision and focus to accommodate yours." To break through this individualistic mindset, it was necessary initially to appeal to organizational self-interest—partner because it woks for you.

> The biblical reason for learning to work in partnership is our oneness in Christ that is at the core of the gospel message.

In spite of this initial self-interested motivator, pragmatic partnerships had at least the benefit of getting people together in partnership consultations, training events, and often into some actual partnering experiences. This gave opportunity for believers to meet and discover one another as brothers and sisters in Christ. By appealing to each agency's self interest, promoters of partnerships brought people together to examine practical ways to advance their cause. In that process, people often discovered that their own vision and aims were not that different from the others. In this stage of the partnering movement, the seeds of discovery of our oneness in Christ were planted and often germinated.

But self-serving partnerships did not carry the power to overcome our fears and suspicions of one another. Working together puts pressure on our preferred way of doing things. It requires flexibility and accommodation to different ways of working. In short, partnering exposes our spiritual shortcomings in crucial spiritual qualities such as love, joy, peace, patience, kindness, goodness, faithfulness, gentleness, and self control (Gal 5:22). Different narratives of mission objectives, fear of loss of identity, irritability and impatience with the time spent trying to hear and understand one another, eroded goodwill between partners. No amount of practical partnering principles and skills can by themselves satisfy these anxieties. Instead, partnership trainers and promoters often find themselves acting as pastors and mediators of conflict between brothers and sisters. It became evident that something was missing.

Expanding Our Understanding of Missions

The movement toward mission partnerships exposed some weakness in our understanding of the mission of the church. Western evangelical tradition informed the modern mission movement. This tradition places heavy emphasis on conversion and salvation from eternal damnation. The gospel is often presented as the lifeboat that rescues those who are drowning. This can be a very individualistic message. I am lost and need rescue, so I turn to Jesus for help.

But the gospel is much more than that. In the gospel, God is in Christ reconciling the world to himself (2 Cor 5:19) and gathering together those who were without God in the world, who were not a people, including them into God's people and making them members of God's household. These now belong to God and to one another as one loving family (Eph 2:12,19). The Apostle John, in his first letter, tells us that the reason he proclaims the gospel is so that we might have fellowship with him and other believers and with God the Father and his Son Jesus Christ (1 John 1:1–3). So, the work of missions is the gospel call on all peoples to be reconciled to God and become members of God's household. The missionary is the one who go esout searching for lost brothers and sisters and inviting them back home (Isa 66:18–21).

> Partnering becomes the practical expression of our fellowship in God's household.

As we grow into a loving community where we learn to love God and each other, the idea of working together in missions becomes a natural response to the world's needs. We don't need to be persuaded to partner, because we are increasingly predisposed to spend time together and to help one another. Partnering becomes the default response of loving brothers and sisters when faced with challenges and opportunities. Partnering becomes the practical expression of our fellowship in God's household.

This kind of partnering is prompted by our love for God and one another and offers a great soil for growing the fruit of the Spirit. Practical considerations concerning the specific focus of a partnership are then discussed as among brothers and sisters rather than among competing business executives.

The Spirituality of Partnerships

As previously stated, at first it may seem strange to talk about the spirituality of partnerships. Partnership brings to mind joint action toward a common practical goal, such as a missions project. Spirituality brings to mind private retreat for prayer and reflection.

However, if we follow from the considerations made so far, we can begin to discern how the two concepts come together harmoniously. Let us look at it greater detail.

Spirituality speaks of a person's walk with God in the daily path of life. It speaks of the pursuit of loving fellowship that can be real in the details of living, working, and enjoying human fellowship. In this sense we can see that it is natural to expect such a spiritual walk with God to be real in our partnerships as much as in any other setting.

> Spirituality speaks of a person's walk with God in the daily path of life. It speaks of the pursuit of loving fellowship that can be real in the details of living, working, and enjoying human fellowship.

We add to that the fact that the gospel brings us into fellowship with God and with each other so that, when we find opportunity to work in partnership, we are giving expression to that divine fellowship.

In reality, though, our exposure to partnerships has often been related to the practicality of getting a job done. We see a need and begin to look for the resources to meet that need. In this process we discover that others may have some of the resources we need, and we begin to talk about possibly partnering. Often we see partnering as a work-related activity, and we plan and negotiate our participation at the conference room or the office. We may bring prayer into the process and even consult the Scriptures concerning what we are seeking to do together. But these are often afterthoughts.

If, however, we begin from the reality of our fellowship with God and each other, the partnering discussion begins not at the office but at the dinner table. It is in celebrating our family ties that we find ourselves predisposed to work together. Any cause or need becomes an opportunity to live out our fellowship in practical service to others. At some point we will need to talk about the specific elements of our partnership: we will need to look for consensus around the work to be done, define who has what resources to bring into the task, and many other operational details. But we start with the fact that we already belong to God and to each other in love.

This predisposes us in goodwill toward one another, and the fruit of the Spirit finds fertile ground to grow. Working together tests our love for one another. Our different organizational priorities and work culture may clash. What at the dinner table promised to be a joyful family activity is challenged by the operational details. If the primary motive for partnering is pragmatic, we can easily feel frustrated and choose to break up the arrangement. Or we may become judgmental of the other.

But for us, the fellowship we have around the meal table with the Father and one another is the reality that informs our work together. We often think of a devotional as that time we set aside to meet with the Lord. From this family perspective, devotional is how we live and work all the time. As a sailor who must always be attentive to the wind, we likewise want to be constantly attentive to the wind of the Spirit as we live and work together. So, our partnering, even in its practical operations, functions in fellowship with the Lord and with one another.

Partnering and the Common Goal

Partnering is working together and sharing resources to accomplish a common goal. That means a number of practical things:

1. We need to agree on what that common goal is.
2. We need to determine what resources are needed to achieve that goal.
3. We need to establish who has the resources needed—these will be the active partners.
4. We need to agree as partners on a process of collaboration.

What makes this spiritual partnering is that each of these steps, and all other steps in this process, are discerned together with the Lord. Each practical item is also a devotional item.

In addition, the manner in which we work together is characterized by those spiritual traits of life in God's household. The fruit of the Spirit must be evident, making every "effort to keep the unity of the Spirit through the bond of peace" (Eph 4:3). The goal of the partnership is never more important than the unity of the Spirit in God's household.

> The goal of the partnership is never more important than the unity of the Spirit in God's household.

Tensions will occur in our partnering, but as God's family, we do not shy away from them, rather we work to resolve them with God's help. The task of missions can never be more important than the relationship of the missions family, for it is within the family that we have fellowship with one another and with the Father and with his Son Jesus Christ.

Alexandre (Alex) C. Araujo was born and raised in Brazil, studied at San Jose State University in the USA, and served with the IFES in Portugal from 1970 to 1975 and with a prison ministry in California from 1976 to 1979. During this time he received a Masters in Political Science. From 1979 to 1986, Alex worked for the City of Sunnyvale in California. In 1986, Alex coordinated the first COMIBAM consultation in S. Paulo, Brazil in 1987. After that he served as Director of International Ministries for Partners International. He served for three years with Interdev, and helped found International Partnering Associates (IPA) in 2003. Alex served as International Coordinator of IPA until 2007. He also served as senior partnership consultant for Partners International until 2012. Alex joined United World Mission's Member Care team in March 2012 where currently serves.

Scripture: *Ephesians 2:19 ("Consequently, you are no longer foreigners and aliens...")*

Resource: *The Seeking Heart*, by François Fenelon (Jacksonville, FL: SeedSowers, 1992).

CHAPTER 12

Culture Does Affect Our Spirituality

Observations from the South Pacific

Kirk Franklin

Religion in the South Pacific

Throughout the South Pacific islands, especially in nations such as Papua New Guinea (PNG), the Solomon Islands, and Vanuatu, the practice of traditional religion can be found. It is usually a form of animism that "centers on the accumulation of power through ritual and ... magic."[1] The religion is associated with ancestral spirits such as "disembodied spirits of the dead," nature spirits, and sorcerers—or the priests of animism.[2] There may be malevolent or benevolent spirits, and in both cases they are respected, in the former appeased through traditional ritual and sacrifice.

Into this milieu has come the acceptance of the gospel. Missionaries arrived in the nations of the South Pacific as far back as 1795 when the London Missionary Society sent people to Tahiti. Early missionaries from Tonga brought the gospel to the southern shores of the island of New Guinea, traveling by their deep-sea canoes.[3] Roman Catholic, Seventh Day Adventist, Anglican, and Lutheran missionaries, among others, evangelized the coastal areas of not just New Guinea, but also Vanuatu and the Solomon Islands, then moved into the more mountainous interiors of the islands.[4] Post World War II Christian mission activity in the South Pacific has only increased to the extent that nations such as PNG and Solomon Islands refer to themselves as "Christian" countries with PNG alone counting over one hundred different denominations.[5]

---

1   Kenneth Nehrbass, *Christianity and Animism in Melanesia: Four Approaches to Gospel and Culture* (Pasadena, CA: William Carey Library, 2012), 179.
2   Darryl Whiteman, *Melanesians and Missionaries: An Ethnohistorical Study of Social and Religious Change in the Southwest Pacific* (Eugene, OR: Wipf and Stock Publishers, 2002), 68.
3   See Alan Tippet, *Solomon Islands Christianity: A Study of Growth and Obstruction* (Cambridge: Lutterworth, 1967).
4   See Whiteman, 2002, Tippet 1967, and Johann Fleril, *My Life and God's Mission: Pioneer Missionary and Field Inspector in New Guinea* (Adelaide, Austrailia: Open Book Publishers, 1999).
5   Alexander Wanek, *The State and Its Enemies in Papua New Guinea* (Surrey: Curzon Press, 1996), 307.

Animism has coexisted with Christianity in parts of the Pacific Islands, especially with the "widespread use and knowledge of sorcery."[6] This is often promoted through traditional cults in villages across the islands. The cults employ secret languages and ceremonies. This traditional worldview is usually referred to as *kastam* in PNG's Tok Pisin (one of its national languages) and *kastom* in Bislama (a national language of Vanuatu).[7] *Kastam/kastom* is a religious and cultural connection to people's traditional practices, especially before Christianity came on the scene. While Christian teaching has had some effect in lessening the belief in *kastam/kastom*, "the use and knowledge of [sorcery] is still widespread."[8]

Demographic Overview of the South Pacific

In the South Pacific, 80% of the population are Melanesians (this includes the linguistic group called "Papuans"), 7% are Polynesians, and 5% are Micronesians. The largest nations in the South Pacific with Melanesians, accounting for approximately 95% of each of their total populations, are PNG (over 7 million), Vanuatu (272,000), and the Solomon Islands (523,000). Over 54% of Fijians are Melanesians. Islands with large Polynesian (also called "South Sea Islanders") populations include New Zealand, Tonga, Tahiti, and Samoa. Micronesians call places such as Nauru, Marshall Islands, Guam, and Palau home. Intermarriage and migration between Melanesian, Polynesian, and Micronesian people is common.

Melanesian Spirituality and the Holy Spirit

David Bosch makes the case for openness to theological methods that are different from the prevailing views of how theology should be done.[9] In other words he notes that "the experience of the [global South] as a source of theology must be taken seriously." Since the South Pacific is diverse, my focus is primarily on Melanesia. I have two observations about spirituality from this context:

First, I suggest that the prevailing worldview of many Melanesian Christians has been informed to some degree by animistic cultural perspectives that have been deeply ingrained into local culture. I am not suggesting that Melanesian Christian spirituality is syncretistic, such as a fusion between animism and Christianity, but rather a traditional worldview of the spirit world that has enabled Melanesian Christians to understand the role and movement of the Holy Spirit in a much more dynamic way than parts of the world that have never had an awareness of the spirit world.

---

6   Karl Franklin, *Comments on Sorcery in Papua New Guinea* (http://www.gial.edu/documents/gialens/Vol4-3/Franklin-Comments-on-Sorcery-in-PNG.pdf, 2010), 1.
7   Wanek, 22.
8   Franklin, 3.
9   David Bosch, *Transforming Mission: Paradigm Shifts in the Theology of Mission* (Maryknoll, NY: Orbis Books, 1991), 425–25.

This is where Bosch's observation stated above is helpful. Melanesian Christian spirituality has a contribution to make in wider discussions on spirituality in mission and is worthy of further study. However, it is beyond the scope of this chapter to categorize or systematize Melanesian theology by studying it in such depth. South Pacific theologians are well qualified to add new layers of understanding to Christian spirituality. They are the ones who should lead such a study.

Second, Melanesian Christian spirituality is essentially experiential. It responds to the contexts from which it arises and is located. Holger Jebens gives the example of a "Holy Spirit movement" in the Southern Highlands Province of PNG.[10] It was characterized by lengthy evening prayer meetings where the participants attempted "to enter into direct contact with the Holy Spirit" through a variety of worshipful activities, including hymns, prayers, Bible reading, and "rhythmic hand-clapping" accompanied by encounters of speaking of tongues, "spasms of crying and shaking" and so forth. There were also manifestations of physical healings, the ability to predict the future, and identifying "the sins of others." The methodology of the Holy Spirit movement was passed orally from one set of practitioners to another in much the same way that traditional cult and magical practices were communicated from one group to another. The movement itself often led to divisions between groups with one group accusing the other of various sins and suggesting influence from evil spirits rather than from the Holy Spirit.[11]

The Holy Spirit in Missional Spirituality

Melanesian Christian spirituality has sought to be Holy Spirit led and experienced. In this way it is not unique: We see similar patterns from the outset of Paul and Barnabas' appointment (Acts 13:2). It was the Holy Spirit who identified them as the first missionaries at the church of Antioch, sent them on their way, and guided them. Paul does not appear to have set out with a rigid plan in place to evangelize the region. Rather, the Holy Spirit led him (Acts 16:6). When the Lord prevented Paul from entering Bithynia, the Holy Spirit led Paul to Macedonia instead. Luke stresses that the Holy Spirit guided the mission activity of Paul (Acts 1:8, 13:9, 15:8, 28, 16:6,7; 20:28, 28:25).

These are examples of how the early church was "thrust … outward into [an] 'explosion of joy.'"[12] Over 2,000 years later, one observes that mission, if it is not Holy Spirit breathed, struggles for effectiveness. This is important for the global church to recognize because of its concern about the transformation of people and their communities. For example,

---

10   Holger Jebens, *Pathways to Heaven: Contesting Mainline and Fundamentalist Christianity in Papua New Guinea* (New York: Berghen Books, 2005), 86.

11   Jebens, 86.

12   Timothy Tennet, *Invitation to World Missions* (Grand Rapids, MI: Kregel, 2010), 99.

Sung-wook Hong states that the goal of mission "is to achieve a transformation through the encounter of the gospel with contexts within the power of the Holy Spirit."[13]

Kirsteen Kim notes that the Holy Spirit is already active because "the Christian faith is not imported but emerges out of local experience" as the Holy Spirit is already bringing "local interpretation" into each context.[14] Missional spirituality examines the foundations for mission through discerning the work of the Holy Spirit, discovering what God is doing in the world, and joining with him. The missional Holy Spirit is always seeking to "transform all life-destroying values and systems" wherever they are.[15] Therefore, missional spirituality is "lived in and fuelled by awareness of the *missio Dei* as the Holy Spirit enlivens it."[16]

> Missional spirituality examines the foundations for mission through discerning the work of the Holy Spirit, discovering what God is doing in the world, and joining with him.

There is a transition underway in interpreting mission: it is no longer a group of tasks expected by God to be carried out by his people. Instead, it is the "spontaneous outworking" of the Holy Spirit as he inspires his people to participate in his "life-giving work."[17] God does not need human instrumentality, but "chooses the risky course of partnership," starting with his appointment of the first disciples as his coworkers who held different social and theological positions.[18]

Observations in Melanesia

On some accounts I refer to myself as a Melanesian son. My ancestry is from my US linguist-Bible translator parents who served in PNG. I was born and raised in PNG and grew up in two villages where my parents lived and worked among the East and West Kewa people. Later, I served in PNG as a missionary. Therefore, since birth, I have lived in that nation for nearly twenty-four years. While I have not lived there recently, I have traveled back and forth on numerous occasions, visiting the country on the average of once a year. I consider some of my closest friends to be from PNG. I have also visited, though far less frequently, Vanuatu, Solomon Islands, and New Caledonia.

My associations with Melanesia have at times informed and affected my spirituality. This was most noticeable to me when I lived there as a young adult. I can vividly recall on many occasions being with Melanesian church leaders where many hours

---

13   Sung-wook Hong, *Naming God in Korea: The Case of Protestant Christianity* (Oxford: Regnum, 2008), 33.
14   Kirsteen Kim, *Joining in with the Spirit: Connecting World Church and Local Mission* (London: Epworth, 2009), 47–48.
15   Joosep Keum, ed., *Together Towards Life: Mission and Evangelism in Changing Landscapes with a Practical Guide* (Geneva: WCC. 2013), 29–30.
16   Darryl Balia and Kierstten Kim, eds., *Edinburgh 2010 Volume II: Witnessing to Christ Today* (Oxford: Regnum Books, 2010), 223.
17   Kim, 29–30.
18   Balia and Kim, 128,

were spent in prayer, so much so that we lost track of time. The sick sought us out for prayer and we witnessed miracles of healing. It was an exhilarating time for me, especially as it was happening in the culture in which I grew up. Melanesian Christian spirituality was engaging my heart and making me passionate in new ways about God and what he was doing. It was experiential and I did not stop to consider how my experience was shaping my spirituality until after I left the nation for another assignment in mission.

> Melanesian Christian spirituality was engaging my heart and making me passionate in new ways about God and what he was doing.

When I was in high school in PNG, I personally experienced a Holy Spirit initiated renewal event that impacted people's commitment to Christ and their spirituality. A revival spread across the country, particularly among students. This began at Easter time when a classmate was tragically killed when her motorcycle collided with another vehicle. This shook our school community. A revival started in our school community and spread to a nearby camp of the Tertiary Students Christian Fellowship (TSCF) and from there to around the whole country. There was evidence that the revival had spread to high schools and universities across the country for at least a year.

Years ago I visited New Caledonia, a small French territory in the South Pacific. A group of Melanesians had led an uprising for independence that eventually failed. They had used their black magic to disguise themselves from the French soldiers and carried out raids and ambushes. I met with some of these former rebels who had become Christians after the uprising. While having fellowship over a meal, they shared stories of how their lives had been completely transformed by Christ. Then they sang a hymn they had written which expressed their eternal hope in Christ. As they sang, it felt as though heaven opened to us as we worshiped God on his throne. I have not experienced anything quite like that since.

More recently, I was giving devotional messages with biblical and missiological themes at a retreat of about one hundred PNG Christians who were missionaries among their own people. As I spoke, I followed my notes that I had prepared weeks ahead of time in my home context of Australia on the topic and text that I believed the Lord wanted me to address. However, what transpired during the delivery of the sessions is when I encountered Melanesian spirituality once again, especially in the experiential aspect of the work of the Holy Spirit.

Towards the end of the first session I was giving, I had a growing sense that I was to go "off script"—to detour from what I had prepared and be open to something else. Intuitively I understood this to be the Holy Spirit leading me and that he had a different plan for what should happen next. Without hesitation, I silently prayed for direction. While I prayed, I had the distinct impression that I was to approach one of the PNG leaders in the room. I knew this man and I knew that I could approach him at such short notice. So while the participants were still in their discussion groups, I went to the person and told him that I sensed the Holy Spirit was prompting me to hand the session over to him. I told him that I didn't know what he should say or do but only that I should let him lead. Without hesitation he said he was ready and open to what the Holy Spirit wanted to do. Within a few minutes I handed over to this man and he responded by issuing a call for people to come forward to confess anything sinful in their hearts and lives.

The session I was leading happened to be about accountability and stewardship of financial resources. One of the missionaries came forward and confessed a situation on the misuse of funds; others followed and did the same. There was a great outpouring of the Holy Spirit with people coming forward, weeping and confessing sins, and seeking to be restored in their relationship to each other and to Christ. This went on for over forty-five minutes, well into lunchtime. It was obvious that lunch would just have to wait because the Holy Spirit was doing extraordinary things in people's lives.

As this event was unfolding, I stood to the side of the room to simply be an observer to what the Holy Spirit was orchestrating. It had nothing to do with me, and that was just fine. As I watched I realized that I was witnessing a deep experiential form of spirituality that was affecting individuals who are part of God's mission in PNG. The confessions being made and the resulting restorations would have long-term fruitful consequences for God's kingdom in the nation. This was occurring because I was willing to let go of my plans, listen to the Holy Spirit, and make virtually a last-minute adjustment and handover to someone else.

Thinking that what I had experienced was a once-off occurrence, I returned the next day for the next session. A similar experience happened towards the end of the session where, once again, the Holy Spirit clearly showed me that I must consult the same Melanesian Christian leader that I had the day before. Once again I briefed him quickly at short notice and he again was ready. With the Holy Spirit's enabling, he led a closing session that was a powerful movement of the Holy Spirit. Once more I found myself as the observer watching the Holy Spirit at work in the midst of Melanesian Christians.

Melanesian Spirituality in Mission

In these examples from Melanesia, there is evidence of renewed forms of spirituality. Moving from what was being practiced by the church at the time, there were new or renewed movements of God in his people and an increased hunger for him, all which he used for his mission.

> There were new or renewed movements of God in his people and an increased hunger for him, all which he used for his mission.

I have discussed my observations with some Melanesian Christian leaders from PNG. They seemed intrigued by the Melanesian theology of missional spirituality based upon what I had witnessed and experienced. I summarize it this way: (1) Melanesian Christian spirituality demonstrates complete openness and expectation that the Holy

Spirit will act and move in the hearts and minds of those who are present in various encounters with the Lord; (2) this openness most likely has some of its foundations in the context of the traditional worldview of animism where there was an assumption that the spirit world, whether good or bad, was interacting with people on a daily basis (this is not to suggest syncretism is taking place, but rather signals an awareness of the spirit world); (3) the openness to the activity of the Holy Spirit is intuitive and experiential and it is passed down orally from older and mature Christians to younger ones; (4) the movement of the Holy Spirit generally impacts the participants into a deeper commitment and communion with Christ; and (5) this deeper journey with Christ ultimately impacts Christian expression in Melanesia by its experiential interaction with the Holy Spirit.

Discussion Questions

1. How does animism inform and influence Melanesian spirituality?
2. What role does the Holy Spirit play in Melanesian spirituality?
3. What contribution does Melanesian spirituality make to spirituality in mission from the global South?

References

Balia, Darryl and Kirsteen Kim, eds. 2010. *Edinburgh 2010 Volume II: Witnessing to Christ Today.* Oxford: Regnum Books.

Bosch, David. 1991. *Transforming Mission: Paradigm Shifts in the Theology of Mission.* Maryknoll, NY: Orbis Books.

Fleril, Johann. 1999. *My Life and God's Mission: Pioneer Missionary and Field Inspector in New Guinea.* Adelaide, Austrailia: Open Book Publishers.

Franklin, Karl. 2010. *Comments on Sorcery in Papua New Guinea.* http://www.gial.edu/documents/gialens/Vol4-3/Franklin-Comments-on-Sorcery-in-PNG.pdf

Hong, Sung-wook. 2008. *Naming God in Korea: The Case of Protestant Christianity.* Oxford: Regnum.

Jebens, Holger. 2005. *Pathways to Heaven: Contesting Mainline and Fundamentalist Christianity in Papua New Guinea.* New York: Berghen Books.

Keum, Jooseop, ed. 2013. *Together Towards Life: Mission and Evangelism in Changing Landscapes with a Practical Guide.* Geneva: WCC Publications.

Kim, Kirsteen. 2009. *Joining in with the Spirit: Connecting World Church and Local Mission.* London: Epworth.

Nehrbass, Kenneth. 2012. *Christianity and Animism in Melanesia: Four Approaches to Gospel and Culture*. Pasadena, CA: William Carey Library.

Tennet, Timothy. 2010. *Invitation to World Missions*. Grand Rapids, MI: Kregel.

Tippet, Alan. 2005. *The Deep-sea Canoe: The Story of Third World Missionaries in the South Pacific*. Pasadena, CA: William Carey Library.

————. 1967. *Solomon Islands Christianity: A Study of Growth and Obstruction*. Cambridge: Lutterworth.

Wanek, Alexander. 1996. *The State and Its Enemies in Papua New Guinea*. Surrey: Curzon Press.

Whiteman, Darryl. 2002. *Melanesians and Missionaries: An Ethnohistorical Study of Social and Religious Change in the Southwest Pacific*. Eugene, OR: Wipf and Stock Publishers.

Kirk Franklin, PhD, grew up in Papua New Guinea (PNG), the son of US Bible translators. As an adult, Kirk served in PNG in media-communications, where he met his Australian wife, Christine, and their three children were born there. Since 1991, Kirk and his family have lived in Melbourne where Kirk has held leadership roles with Wycliffe Australia. Since 2008, Kirk has been the Executive Director of the Wycliffe Global Alliance. He has had formal studies in theology, missiology, and leadership from institutions in the US, Australia ,and South Africa. Kirk and Christine are members of Warrandyte Community Church.

Scripture: *Psalm 27:14 ("Wait for the Lord...")*

Resource: *Hearing God: Developing a Conversational Relationship with God*, by Dallas Willard, (Downers Grover, IL: InterVarsity Press, 2012).

CHAPTER 13

Legacy Racism, Living Realities

Benjamin Pillay

A recent article in the Washington Post, "Why Mother Teresa Is Still No Saint to Many of Her Critics," highlights the perception of some for the short-comings of her work.[1] The message is that Christian mission is often called into question over its modus operandi.

It's August 2015 and I'm sitting down to evening tea with a family, not all of whom are believers, when a South African Indian 14-year-old boy asks me the pointed question, "What did Christianity bring?" I shrunk at the instinctive answer that jumped into my mind and knew immediately what the young man had on his mind. I replied by asking him to share his thoughts with me. His immediate reply was "racism."

While many may argue this sounds more like a question of which came first, "the chicken or the egg," the unfortunate reality is that we cannot run away

> We cannot run away from the perception that the great discoveries of new worlds and the accompanying racism which followed are associated with the expansion of Christianity.

from the perception that the great discoveries of new worlds and the accompanying racism which followed are associated with the expansion of Christianity—an experience often viewed as the "civilization" of the natives.

Father Austin Flannery, OP, writes,

> Racial discrimination and racial exploitation are totally at variance with Christianity. Christians, however, have been the most persistent and ruthless offenders in recent centuries. The main reason for this chilling anomaly is that since the commencement of European colonial expansion to the Americas and to Africa the countries of Christian Europe have been faced with massive opportunities for the exploitation of peoples less powerful and technically less advanced than themselves; and they grasped their opportunities.

---

1 Adam Taylor, "Why Mother Teresea Is Still No Saint to Many of Her Critics," *The Washington Post*, (December 18, 2015 and again September 1, 2015).

How eagerly they did so may be gleaned from the blood conquests of the two Americas, the enslavement of the American Indians by Spanish, Portuguese, and British settlers, the virtual annihilation of the North American Indians, and the barbaric African slave trade.

It is only comparatively recently that the majority of Europeans and Americans have begun to see that era of exploitation and mass murder for what it was. In its hey-day, empire building was seen by its beneficiaries as a great and glorious and even benevolent enterprise. Then, as now, self-interest was the most persuasive of arguments.[2]

Dara Strickland writes,

In the 1960s Martin Luther King, Jr. stated that, "Eleven o'clock Sunday morning is the most segregated hour in America." Dr. King was of course speaking of the American church, and racism is still a problem in many American churches today. The truth is as ugly as it is unwelcomed, however, it is a truth that cannot be ignored! While there have been great strides across the "racial divide," there remains some hardcore separatists who would prefer to stick with "their own kind."[3]

There is the controversial Aryan Race Theory which propounds a highly arguable notion as put forward by Aravindan Neelakandan that suggests that,

The Aryan Race Theory is in fact the brainchild of Christian evangelist-scholars, fashioned and tempered in the nineteenth century as a weapon for European expansionism in India. Promulgated to generations of Indian children in British-created schools, it created, like so many other Western creeds and dogmas, social divisions where none had hitherto existed, resulting in jealousy, mistrust, and suspicion among communities where peaceful coexistence had been the norm. This theory, which posits the invasion of ancient India by a white-skinned race (the "Aryans") who conquer an indigenous, dark-skinned population, therefore worked ingeniously with the British divide-and-conquer strategy for rule in India. The theory and its variants continue to be used today by the Vatican and other Christian enterprises in their campaign to "harvest" tribals and other vulnerable communities of Hindus. For these spiritual imperialists, spurious racial theories still hold their divide-and-conquer appeal.[4]

Desmond Tutu made the following statement,

---

2   Father Austin Flannery, OP, "The Christian Churches and Racism (with Special Reference to the Roman Catholic Church," in *The Struggle for Liberation in South Africa and International Solidarity*, ed. ES   Reddy   (http://www.sahistory.org.za/sites/default/files/LIBERATION%20IN%20SOUTH%20 AFRICA-%20UN%20papers,%20full%20book.pdf)

3   http://www.helium.com/items/1116850-racism-still-exist-in-american-churches.

4   Aravindan Neelakandan (Date published: 05/14/2001, posted December 30, 2005.

Thank God I am black. White people will have a lot to answer for at the Last Judgment. (Quoted in the South African newspaper *Argus*, March 19, 1984).

These persons, like many other voices, illustrate the perilous reality represented in the contrast between the discovery of the races and the portrayal of non-whites as requiring a salvation far broader than just of a spiritual nature, but also justifying the schooling of these new ethnicities in the culture of the missionaries. Then either wilfully or inadvertently, new cultural norms, for example in dress or music, are imposed and existing cultural expressions are labeled as being antiquated to the superior cultural expressions of the missionary's culture. This may be more clearly argued by the imposition of Western-style leadership, as opposed to the indigenous leadership of collective culture which is viewed as nondecisive or slow. Perhaps we could have shaken these views in the hundreds of years that have passed, but our practice of mission has often provoked thoughts of racism and or ethnocentricity.

For the purpose of this article, it is worthwhile to note that while the dictionary's definition of racism and ethnicity bare great similarities, the differences are what does not allow them to be used interchangeably or lumped together as some of us may do. The context in which these words appear here will indicate their intended use.

It is crucial to draw the distinction that exists between racism generally and missionary racism. As articulated by many people, this missionary racism is the consideration that white people are superior to everyone else. However, this distinction is not meant to blindly dismiss that racism or ethnocentricity can and does exist between ethnic groups of the same or similar color. Evidence of this can be found, for example, in the Rwandan genocide, the challenges facing North and South Sudan, the Turkish-Kurdish conflict, and many other places.

Racism generally and missionary racism appear to arrive at the same conclusion, albeit from differing hypothesis. Racism generally is entrenched in the belief that characteristics and abilities can be attributed to people on the basis of biological differences. The argument therefore concludes that some groups of people are superior to others.[5] Missionary racism finds its basis in that the difference between races are religious, cultural, and environmental, while some argue that this excludes physical.

> Missionary racism finds its basis in that the difference between races are religious, cultural, and environmental, while some argue that this excludes physical.

The Western mind and culture, in all its advances, is a product of biblical religion. It is a religious, not a racial, product… The culture of the West is not the property of any race or people in its origin. It is biblical. True, much sin is present in Western culture. True, such sin needs to be condemned. But the

---

5   Anup Shah, "Racism" (http://www.globalissues.org/article/165/racism).

mind of the West bears the imprint of the Bible. It is not understandable on any other terms.[6]

This excerpt from a position paper by RJ Rushdoony does well to illustrate the belief in the superiority of Western culture, that culture, as he explains, is the result of religion.

Over the last twenty-five years a great privilege has been afforded me to interact with people from many races, representing many ethnicities. This has also allowed me to be exposed to many expressions of what was and is felt as racism through the work of mission agencies and missionaries engaged with people from all walks of life, expressing salvation and engaging for the salvation all peoples. My thinking is shaped by some of the sentiments expressed by non-whites as they felt the impact of this expressive engagement for their salvation and growth in Christ. Many of my relationships were and are with church leadership, and so the examples may lean more in that direction but also toward everyday encounters.

Much of the experience of racism and or ethnocentricity were experienced in these areas:

- In the manner in which the mission agencies engaged with host country believers
- In the manner in which the mission agencies handled funding
- In the manner in which the mission agencies relate to the church
- In the manner in which the mission agencies drew up and maintained general policy

It is not possible to consider all of the experiences related to this topic, and therefore, I must restrict myself to leading from those sentiments expressed above. I use the term mission agencies in the next section as a generic noun to mean Western or white mission organization or agency. This not intended to complain about Western mission or be accusatory, and it shouldn't be but to serve to remind us of what our actions are perceived to mean and how it makes those, to whom we have come in love, feel. My fear is that we cannot just expect people to "get over it," as was expressed by a renowned American Christian speaker at a gathering of South African Christian leaders, at which the country's president attended for a short while.

The Manner in which Mission Agencies Engage with Host Country Believers

Careful analysis of the focus of mission agencies demonstrates that there is no ministry among white people living in African countries. This lack of foci forces the assumption that white people do not need the spiritual and/or cultural liberation as do their

---

6   R. J. Rushdoony, "The New Racism" (http://americanvision.org/11824/the-new-racism-by-r-j-rushdoony).

indigenous counterparts, or that mission agencies do not view them as a priority. It can also be noted that mission agencies conduct certain activities that are by design meant to exclude indigenous colleagues. This inequality in the valuing of people stems perhaps from a more deeply seated belief reflected in the slow and uneasy approach of the mission agencies to train indigenous leaders, further entrenching ethnocentric values. It begs explanation as to why a mission agency can be in a country for more than ten years and cannot raise indigenous strategic leaders, insisting on being led by expatriates. Often times this insistence is expressed through culturally unacceptable approaches to mission, when leadership will approve or sanction innovative approaches to mission that smack in the face of cultural derision.

> It begs explanation as to why a mission agency can be in a country for more than ten years and cannot raise indigenous strategic leaders, insisting to be led by expatriates.

Another trend that reveals itself in Western mission agencies is the negligent number of sent African American missionaries in proportion to the dominant race being sent. While we may not all agree with this argument, let us consider that we expect people who have been told for decades that only white people can do mission (by policy and practice), compounded by the oppressive socioeconomic effect of racism, to now start believing that they can lead mission.[7] The same could be true of raising indigenous leadership who for years were told, through the appointment of expatriate leaders, that only expatriates have the capacity to lead mission agencies.

Closer to the ground where relationships are expressed and experienced appears to be where the most harm is done. Church leaders feel that they are treated like children, again revealing an expression of a "superiority complex." Missionaries are not viewed as being in a relationship of reciprocity. Constant contention between individualistic and collective practices result in the suppression of indigenous freedom of expression. This is demonstrated in the inequitable expression of hospitality, the frowning upon of missionaries who want to incarnate more than the unspoken norms. Mission agencies have taken deliberate action to dissuade its personnel from getting "too close" to indigenous people, depicting indigenous peoples as opportunistic. One example of this occurs when missionaries return home—they often sell their household items but only offer to host culture people what they fail to sell to their fellow missionaries. (As a dear missionary friend pointed out, a reason for this outcome could be less discriminatory than it appears. Often times a missionary seeks fair price for their belongings and other missionaries are the only ones in a position to purchase.)

7   Vaughn Walston, "Ignite the Passion" *Mission Frontiers* (March–April 2000, https://www.missionfrontiers.org/issue/article/ignite-the-passion; Sarah Eekhoff Zylstra, "Black Churches' Missing Missionaries," *Christianity Today* (April 2013, http://www.christianitytoday.com/ct/2013/april/missing-missionaries.html)/

The alleged absence of genuine love demonstrated by lack of true insertion into a community in all aspects of living further advances the disingenuous motive of mission as characterized in the *Washington Post* article about Mother Teresa, referenced earlier.

I encourage myself as I do you. In the pursuit of doing mission, in expressing our salvation and engaging others for the same, we must do more than our best to ensure that our words and actions are "first, do no harm."[8] It's easy to rationalize our actions and not take responsibility. As a young minister, sitting at a gathering of the who's who of Christian leaders in South Africa, I was pretty chuffed with myself. I did not consider myself a racist because I ate off the same plate and drank out of the same bottle (without first wiping the top bottle), with my black brothers. As I grew, I shamefully realized that I too possessed the capacity to be racist and ethnocentric.

> We must be careful to demonstrate that our mission and vision reveal our stance that all people are reached equally, that socioeconomics do not dictate who needs the gospel or who benefits from our presence.

We must be careful to demonstrate that our mission and vision reveal our stance that all people are reached equally, that socioeconomics do not dictate who needs the gospel or who benefits from our presence. The first act of Jesus was to choose twelve men that would be leaders in his place, not decades later but immediately upon his departure. We must appreciate and value the veracity of indigenous leadership, though it be difficult because we are predisposed to our own cultural imperatives. We can only be better for the ongoing sacrifice we make through the equitable treatment of all, committing ourselves to do no harm.

The Manner in which the Mission Agencies Handle Funding

Funds are another area that leaves both mission agencies and churches reeling from mistrust and doubt. How an organization spends its money is an immediate reflection of their vested interests. Without adequate consultation the allocation of funds can unwittingly result in shaping perceptions that one ethnic beneficiary is more important than another. This can be very dangerous in the polarized sociopolitical society in which we live. Not consulting regarding funds is often the outgrowth of the notion that mission agencies do not owe host culture partners an explanation, premised on the idea of "(our) mission (our) money," or "they only want the money for themselves." The practice further removes the mission and the church away from a spirit of cooperative governance and engages feelings of competing values.

> The allocation of funds can unwittingly result in shaping perceptions that one ethnic beneficiary is more important than another.

---

8   *Primum non nocere.*

At the ground level, I was recently confronted by an old problem in respect of funds raised for a missionary couple, with decades of ministry on a single field, now leaving the place of ministry. I was asked, "Does this mean that the money (for ministry) will always leave once the missionary leaves?" It was a loaded question, and as the conversation continued the many other nuances were unpacked. The discussion was a frightful reminder of paternalistic fallout and the question of whether supporters were really interested in the ministry or only the missionary, or perhaps did the withdrawal of funds indicate a question of trust?

One of my congregation members once said, "Money makes people funny." Perhaps, no other single component has caused more harm in mission agencies as money. Its uses or misuses have initiated feelings of discrimination, nepotism, favoritism, integrity, trust, and more. It would be wise to give careful consideration to the impact of foreign income. We can never run through all the possible scenarios or all the possible outcomes, but history has enough lessons to make us wise if we pay attention. Further, with the introduction of money from the "rest" as opposed to just the West, mission agencies are faced with new challenges about how money is applied and what the desire of this rapidly growing context for their money is.

So much more has to be done to understand these new realities, but so much has already been learned. I can only trust that as we consider the historical lessons we've learned and the new ones being learned that we can minimize the hurt that could be caused by understanding how money should be applied.

The Manner in which Mission Agencies Relate to the Church

Mission is being done independently of the church instead of being characterized by interdependence. Mission agencies are seen as holding the final authority in decision making, a sort of safety net in the event that church partners "mess" it up. This becomes the ideal breeding ground for distrust. The lack of transparency compounded by an unwillingness to communicate leads to suspicion. Complexity is added by the disproportionate amount of documentation required for projects and is viewed as an expression of a lack of trust.

Perhaps this is nothing more than a lack of appreciation by mission agencies for agreements made in a collective context, which is always predicated on trust. Alternatively, it may be that mission agencies need to explain themselves fully in the evolving context of legal requirements for external funding from the various countries they represent in order to provide proof of the bona fide use of the money it receives.

I sadly remember a day when the leadership of a local denomination decided that it no longer wanted missionaries. The independence of the agencies and the attitude of "we're telling you that this is what you should do" had become too much for the local leaders. It would take about ten years before another missionary would serve with this denomination and then it appeared as though the individual missionary's "favored ministry" had to become denominational priorities. I would be the first to defend the passionate plea of the missionary—it was rightly placed, but the approach of encouraging the local church to engage with this need was misplaced. The idea of scolding people into cooperation is just not the appropriate to encourage cooperation. It may be right to assume that mission should be among the priorities of the church, but where the church lives and works and plays there are realities that are different of those of the missionary.

> I believe previously receiving context churches are dissuaded from sending with Western mission agencies because the policies of the mission agencies appear to be uninformed by local context.

Perhaps for these reasons churches are being drawn to doing mission independently of mission agencies. We might want to cite the cost of doing mission with a mission agency as being the sole reason for this, but I cannot find conclusive evidence for this as many non-Western churches are still sending through Western mission agencies. Instead I believe previously receiving context churches are dissuaded from sending with Western mission agencies because the policies of the mission agencies appear to be uninformed by local context. Weak consultation in the formulation of policies leads to feelings of discontent by those who are forced to accept the policies of the mission agencies without choice or input. This in turns forces them to interact with missions in a way predetermined by Western mission agencies.

The encouragement is to work with the church, in its context. As challenging as this may be against the backdrop of what might appear to be abundantly clear to the mission agency, it is essential for us to demonstrate mutual respect in the engagement process. It is also worthwhile to accept that they may know better or have a better way of doing ministry in their own context. What might appear as unconventional and unsustainable might actually be perfectly suitable for that place.

The Manner in which Mission Agencies Handle Matters Pertaining to Property

To define land as it only relates to power would be to diminish and undervalue its significance. Land is indicative of a sense of identity and a sense of being or belonging. Immediately, one recognizes the deep psychological and emotional significance attached to the meaning of land or property to a people; thus, the continuous fight for land world over from the past to the present.

Once we are able to acknowledge this symbol in various cultures, we can understand the contention that arises out of the acquisition, application, and bequeathment of property. Viewing land and or property simply for its value on the balance sheet, an asset to shore up the fiscus, leads to strife between mission agencies and the local church.

We must acknowledge that many relationships between mission agencies and churches have been fractured or completely undone because the mission agencies have had a capitalistic view of land and property and have not seen it in a relational context. I have also witnessed many churches take a less than righteous approach on this matter. I have seen institutions left worried about how they will operate when property is seized by the church because of historical memory. I have also witnessed regret by churches for not seizing opportunities presented by mission agencies for them to take responsibility for property, but instead exploit it for ministry.

Whatever value land and/or property might hold for us, we must acknowledge its significance to the indigenous church. This may constrain us no to treat land or property as we are used to. This approach may be contrary to how we feel, but if we can avoid the land and/or property decisions that have separated mission agencies and church in the past, we must.

Conclusion

One could read this article and immediately react by pointing out the mistakes of the church, its leaders, and peoples, but that would not help any of us.

I believe it is fundamentally important to understand the principles of Paul's teaching in Philippians chapter 2. The incarnation of Jesus has to do with more than just the fulfillment of prophecy. It determines what we see, understand, and realize about ourselves and God. The incarnation opened us up to a reality that communicates God's perfect love and invitation more convincingly than by words alone. I believe that by "becoming like us," he made it possible for us to believe in him for salvation.[9] In other words, he made salvation believable. I am convinced from Peter and Paul's experiences elsewhere that it becomes of paramount importance in cross-cultural ministry that we sacrifice our right to our cultural norms to present an incarnated form of the gospel in ourselves.[10] This does not deny the challenges of such an expectation but exposes the need for as compelling of effort as possible toward that incarnation.

> Though I am free of obligation to anyone, I make myself a slave to everyone, to win as many as possible. (1 Cor 9:19)

"Sacrifice," a word synonymous with mission, is a loaded concept that cannot be explained here but I encourage myself, as I do you, to appreciate its existence in all believers. Sitting at a meeting of multiracial, multiethnic Christian leaders, mission leaders, and missionaries, I heard this being said, "If only missionaries were real people." There was no malice, just honesty. Most didn't even notice.

---

9   Philippians 2:7
10   1 Corinthians 9:22; Galatians 2:11–14; 1 Corinthians 8:9–11

May we take notice. We cannot address the impact of racism in our host cultures if our mission is perceived as racist. Mission must be committed to the evolution of change that will rid it of the policies and practices that cause others to experience "racism." This could make mission agencies vulnerable (financial or otherwise), but I believe it also makes mission agencies relatable and respectable. It reminds me of the great warrior who goes into the king's hut. No matter how great he is, he is bowed low, not looking up as he presents himself to the king. When he leaves, he does so without turning around, but carefully edging backward until he is out the entrance of the hut. Vulnerable but highly honored.

> Mission must be committed to the evolution of change that will rid it of the policies and practices that cause others to experience "racism."

Benjamin Pillay has been preaching and teaching the Bible since he was in eighth grade. He has been the pastor of a local church for close to seventeen years and recently had a second church added to his pastoral responsibilities.

He served as an executive of the Evangelical Church in South Africa for fourteen years until September 2014, spending the latter years as president. He is currently the chairperson of the Council for SIM Southern Africa and also serves on the SIM International Board of Governors. Since January 2014 he has served as the Assistant General Secretary of Evangel Fellowship International.

Scripture: *I Corinthians 2:1–5 ("When I came to you, I did not come with eloquence or human wisdom...")*

Resource: *Perspectives on the World Christian Movement*, edited by Ralph D. Winter and Steven C. Hawthorne (Pasadena, CA: William Carey Library, 1999).

CHAPTER 14

Spirituality and Justice

Abraham (Abey) George

On surveys of religious preference, it is an increasing trend these days to check "none." While it may seem to point to the rise of atheism, that is really not the case. Nearly 70% of the "nones" actually report belief in God or a universal spirit, and 37% describe themselves as "spiritual but not religious."[1] Walk into a bookstore today and one is quite likely to find an overabundance of books and other resources on spirituality or some related topic. "Becoming spiritual" is becoming an increasingly common primary goal in life for people from all walks of life. Spirituality is indeed becoming quite the catchword today, eliciting an intensely positive response among many around the world.

Yet despite its recent prominence, there is much confusion about what the term "spirituality" really means. It may seem the claims of "spiritual but not religious" point to unfamiliarity with religion, but it more likely points to a great dissatisfaction with organized religion and its traditions. Religion is seen as being archaic and dull, and too unbending and concerned largely with beliefs, doctrines, and traditions, as opposed to life-affecting values. There is an increasing recognition of the importance of spirituality to well-being and fulfillment in life.

> It may seem the claims of "spiritual but not religious" point to unfamiliarity with religion, but it more likely points to a great dissatisfaction with organized religion and its traditions.

So, What Is Spirituality?

Describing the term "spirituality" is perhaps a bit like catching water in a sieve. The term is very resistant to a fixed definition because it is used in a range of senses and there are numerous factors that affect its use. People come from a variety of personal backgrounds, they have different personalities, live in different geographical and sociopolitical environments, and belong to a variety of faith and denominational backgrounds—all of these and many other differences affect the way they each perceive and define spirituality. Yet, define, we must!

---

1   Steven Barrie-Anthony, "'Spiritual but Not Religious': A Rising, Misunderstood Voting Bloc," *The Atlantic* (January 14, 2004, http://www.theatlantic.com/politics/archive/2014/01/spiritual-but-not-religious-a-rising -misunderstood-voting-bloc/283000/).

If we understand Christianity to be a system of beliefs and values that affect our way of life, then Christian spirituality refers to the way in which one aims to deepen one's understanding and experience of Christianity. "Christian spirituality concerns the quest for a fulfilled and authentic Christian existence involving the bringing together of the fundamental ideas of Christianity and the whole experience of living on the basis of and within the scope of the Christian faith."[2] Spirituality is then more than just knowing about God or the tenets of the Christian faith. It is, one might argue, about experiencing God and allowing it in turn to transform one's existence towards a more authentic Christian life and thought.

Spirituality then is really about the meeting together of the arc, so to speak, of the biblical narrative with that of one's own life and experiences. The Bible, one might argue, is after all about God's relationship with the world and man's relationship with God brought about through Christ in the Holy Spirit. Viewed this way, it helps us recognize the significance of "narratives" (or stories) in spirituality. It emphasizes the fact that a person's story represents the embodiment of a system of beliefs and values as set forth in the biblical narratives.

> A person's story represents the embodiment of a system of beliefs and values as set forth in the biblical narratives.

Both the Old and the New Testament include narratives which explain how the people of God came into being, and thus they also provide the clearest guidelines for what must constitute their identity as the people of God. These narratives are critical to finding one's identity. Israel drew her identity from the story of her exodus from slavery in Egypt, and the Psalms retold the stories of God's deliverances and provisions. Authentic Christian spirituality today depends similarly on the recognition and acceptance that one is part of the biblical narrative. If Christian spirituality is the embodiment of the beliefs and values of Christianity, the narratives in the Christian Scriptures are then the building blocks of that spirituality.

The Biblical Narrative of Justice

Chapter 2 of the book of Genesis gives us a beautiful picture of what it is that God desires, and in many ways is a picture that constitutes the central arc of the scriptural narrative. The picture here is of a flourishing garden—that the creator God was "satisfied" with, proclaiming it good—of paradise. But this picture is indicative of a lot more than just pleasing aesthetics. It is the perfect embodiment of God's ultimate desire for his creation—Shalom—flourishing, wholeness, delight, and equity.

This indeed is life as God intended it. It is life where man does what he was created to do while being in perfect harmony with God, creation, others, and himself. Of course,

---

2   Alister E McGrath, *Christian Spirituality* (Hoboken, NJ: Wiley-Blackwell, 1999), 2. I have referred extensively to McGrath's excellent primer on spirituality.

the picture is shattered in the following chapter with the introduction of sin and its corrupting influence on creation. The order God had established had been disturbed, and peace had been shattered. And yet, God's desire for restoring shalom is not lost or even deterred. On the contrary, it is, following that brief break, what constitutes the central arc of the rest of the biblical narrative. The ultimate divine plan now is to restore shalom—to set things right.

But what is this shalom God intends through the rest of the Scriptures?

First articulated in the Old Testament poetic and prophetic literature and then expressed again in the New Testament, the idea of shalom places justice prominently at its core. Shalom is present when people live in harmony with God and the rest of creation. But critical to the concept of God's shalom is harmony between human beings. For me and my colleagues, and others like us, who work with victims of violent abuse around the world, this takes on special poignancy.[3]

Shalom, the central narrative of the Christian Scriptures is then intrinsically intertwined with justice, or conversely, with the absence of injustice, of the abuse of power, of exploitation of the weak by the strong.[4]

The Scriptures contain many explicit commands to "do justice" (Mic 6:8) and to "seek justice, defend the oppressed, take up the cause of the fatherless, [and] plead the case of the widow" (Isa 1:17). Yahweh delivered them from oppression in Egypt and now expects them to be liberators as well. The Mosaic

> Jesus did not come to start a religion, but instead to announce a new "kingdom," a new way of life. The *missio Dei*, there can be no doubt, is to bring about shalom.

Law is replete with examples. The prophets echo and reiterate such requirements. The Gospels continue the theme. Jesus did not come to start a religion, but instead to announce a new "kingdom," a new way of life. The *missio Dei*, there can be no doubt, is to bring about shalom:

> To lose the chains of injustice and to untie the cords of the yoke, to set the oppressed free and break every yoke. (Isa 58:6–7)

To be sure, shalom does indeed go beyond justice, and yet there is no shalom without justice.

---

3   Abraham George and Nikki Toyama-Szeto, *God of Justice* (Downers Grove, IL: InterVarsity Press Connect, 2015), 9.
4   Gary Haugen, *Just Courage: God's Great Expedition for the Restless Christian* (Downers Grove, IL: InterVarsity Press, 2008), 46.

Spirituality towards Justice

Justice, and God's heart for the poor and oppressed, is then the beating heart of Christian spirituality. Spirituality opens the door to integrity and empathy, and it causes one to respect the presence and difference of others.[5]

Spirituality's core identity comes from God's divine plan to restore shalom, and the church is God's vehicle to usher in shalom into the brokenness and oppression in the world. For the church to credibly announce that God is God and that his new world has begun, NT Wright reminds us, it has to be "actively involved in seeking justice in the world, both globally and locally, and cheerfully celebrating God's good creation and its rescue from corruption."[6] Without this active interaction with the brokenness around us, our proclamation remains merely a shadow of the glorious gospel we have been tasked with sharing.

> Without this active interaction with the brokenness around us, our proclamation remains merely a shadow of the glorious gospel we have been tasked with sharing.

It is important to note also that spirituality is not detached from the physical world, nor is it only about the personal relationship with God. It is embedded within community and the maze of relationships within it. We as individual Christians are in turn embedded within these communities, and therefore what affects the community affects us, and vice versa. So justice has more "community" aspect to it than "individual." Put differently, justice is not only about the rewarding of the good and the punishment of the bad. Rather, justice happens when shalom in the community is restored, when all relationships are set right and are thriving, when orphans and widows are cared for and protected, when those abused and oppressed are rescued and restored.

Christian spirituality must then naturally lead to an agency of transformation in this broken and hurting world. If it does, it will become an unmistakable part of the process of God birthing his shalom in this world.

References

George, Abraham and Nikki Toyama-Szeto. 2015. *God of Justice*. Downers Grove, IL: InterVarsity Press Connect.

Haugen, Gary A. 2008. *Just Courage: God's Great Expedition for the Restless Christian*. Downers Grove, IL: InterVarsity Press Books.

McGrath, Alister. 1999. *Christian Spirituality*. Hoboken, NJ: Wiley-Blackwell.

---

5   J. O'Donohue, *Eternal Echoes: Exploring Our Hunger to Belong* (Auckland, NZ: Bantam, 1998), 108–109.
6   N. T. Wright, *Surprised by Hope: Rethinking Heaven, the Resurrection, and the Mission of the Church* (New York: Harper Collins, 2008), 227.

O'Donohue, J. 1998. *Eternal Echoes: Exploring Our Hunger to Belong*. Auckland, New Zealand: Bantam.

Wright, N.T. 2008. *Surprised by Hope: Rethinking Heaven, the Resurrection, and the Mission of the Church*. New York: Harper Collins.

Abraham (Abey) George serves as the Director of International Church Mobilization with the International Justice Mission. IJM is a human rights agency that secures justice for victims of slavery, sexual exploitation, and other forms of violent oppression. He seeks to strengthen the community and civic factors that promote functioning public justice systems around the world. He earned his ThM in Historical Theology in 1999 from Trinity Theological College, Singapore, and is the coauthor of *God of Justice* (Inter Varsity Press, 2015).

Scripture: *Philippians 2:5–8*, The Message ("Think of yourselves the way Christ Jesus thought of himself…"

Resource: *The Divine Conspiracy: Rediscovering Our Hidden Life in God*, by Dallas Willard (New York: Harper Collins, 1997).

CHAPTER 15

How to Discern the Will of God

David Tai-Woong Lee

As I take a good look at my spiritual journey, a desire for knowing the will of God and my spiritual growth were interrelated; the closer I walked with God on my spiritual journey and gained spiritual maturity, the more my desire to know the will of God for my life also grew. There were times when I followed step by step the formulas that some of the spiritual giants had presented. These giants included George Mueller, Hudson Taylor, G Christian-Weiss, and FB Meyer, to name a few. They unanimously recommended taking the following preparatory steps: that I make sure I have surrendered my life to the Lord and that I am willing to obey him at all cost.[1] The rest of the formula usually includes the following: reliance on the Word of God, prayer for guidance, paying close attention to the situation to watch for any signs of God's leading (including Providence), and eagerly seeking to understand where the Holy Spirit is leading in the particular matter in which I was trying to determine his will.[2] During the final step in this process, I would make a decision based upon all of the information that I had gained on the matter. Then I would wait for any signs, particularly the sign of feeling peace in my heart.[3]

This process can be repeated several times, depending on how important the subject for which I am seeking his will. One time I repeated this kind of process ten times, trying to determine whether the girl that I was dating would be someone that I should marry because I felt that I could not afford to make a wrong decision knowing that it could have tremendous effect on my entire life. I think it was during the tenth time through the process that the Holy Spirit seemed to speak to me, "David, you don't want to marry her?" Since then, I have never doubted his will on this matter. We have been married for forty-four years, and it has been forty-seven years since I asked the Lord to show me his will for our marriage. I have never been happier and more grateful knowing that it was according to God's will that we were to get married.

---

1   G Christian Weiss, *The Perfect Will of God* (Chicago: Moody Press, 1950), 41–72; FB Meyer, *The Secret of Guidance* (Chicago: Moody Press, n.d.), 9–12.

2   Weiss, 73–99.

3   Weiss, 100–101.

Perhaps the readers' experience in determining the will of God may be different than what I have described using my life journey as a case study. Nonetheless, it is possible to know the will of God on our lives. How we determine the will of God in our lives will not be uniform. For one thing, we can not put God in a box. Strictly speaking, no amount of formulas could guarantee us knowing the will of God. He is God whom we cannot control by any sacrifices, nor even good works that we do to please him. In the final analysis, it is he who will determine what must be his will for our lives and our surroundings. But he is not impersonal, unimpressed, nor stone-hearted. He cares for us. He loves us. He is our Father. What earthly parents would not like to let their children know what their children want to know and do? How much more our heavenly Father would like to let his children know what they need to know and do!

God's Ultimate Purpose: How It Affects Knowing His Will for Our Lives

When I was still a baby in Christ after being converted at the age of twenty-two, my main concern for many years was on the immediate issues that I faced. Discerning the will of God during this period inevitably focused on what I wanted and how it would affect my life and my near relationships, such as my family, my job, and my friends. Over the years these immediate concerns have often been superseded by larger issues, such as kingdom matters, the church, ministry and missions, and organizations I was a part of.

> Over the years these immediate concerns have often been superseded by larger issues, such as kingdom matters, the church, ministry and missions, and organizations I was a part of.

As I began to study the Bible, I began to see how God leads his people and the church as well as his people in missions towards his goal. One aspect of his purpose on us as people of God is as follows:

> For God knows his people in advance and he chose them to become like his Son, so that his Son would be the firstborn, with many brothers and sisters. And having chosen them, he called them to come to him. And he gave them right standing with himself, and he promised them his glory. (Romans 8:29–30, NLT)

On whatever matter that I am seeking his will, the answer will ultimately depend on how it will be in accord with this purpose of God on our lives. This principle can be expanded to include what the whole Bible says about the ultimate purpose of our lives and what God expects us to be and do as people of God. In a nutshell, this is like becoming real actors and actresses in a "divine-theo-drama." Vanhoozer has put this aspect as follows in his book: "Indeed at the heart of the biblical action is the relationship, and the conflict, between two freedoms: human and divine. Conflict arises only when human beings refuse to play their parts."[4]

There are certain rules and guides that these actors and actresses adhere to as they play their positions. Knowing these rules by which they act can only be correctly known by getting familiar with the contents of the Bible, in the case of Christians. Sad to say though, when ordinary Christians talk about finding the will of God, they usually gloss over this aspect and jump right into the microlevel of what an individual could do and be. We need to put a greater emphasis on the macrolevel as one grows more toward being a disciple of Christ. Note the following comments:

> [There is] no more urgent task for Christians today than to engage in living truthfully with others before God. He [Vanhoozer] details how doctrine [culturally appropriate expression of what the Bible says about the will of God for the church and an individual in general—*my addition and emphasis*] serves the church the theater of the gospel by directing individuals and congregations to participate in the drama of what God is doing to renew all things in Jesus Christ.[5]

It is this aspect that we need to reinforce as we try to discern the will of God on whatever matters that we are seeking after.

The Corporate Life of the Church: How It Aids Knowing His Will on Our Lives

It was fortunate that some of the delegates from the West in the 2010 Lausanne III Congress held in Cape Town expressed appreciation as well as renewed emphasis on the corporate life of the church. The Christianity that the Western missionary spread since the modern missionary movement began in the eighteenth century tends to stress the value of the individual confession of the faith. The community life of the church received less attention. Most of the books dealing with finding the will of God naturally did not put enough emphasis on the role of the corporate body.[6] This is contrary to biblical teaching. Both the Old Testament and the New Testament taught on the corporate nature of the people of God. The life of individual Christian is likened to parts of human body in the Pauline epistles (1 Cor 12:12–30). There was a lively interaction between the members resulting in spiritual growth. It was the sharing

---

4   Kevin Vanhoozer, *The Drama of Doctrine: A Canonical Linguistical Approach to Christian Theology* (Louisville, KT: John Knox Press, 2006), 49.
5   An excerpt from the editorial review of the same book, *The Thoughtful Christian* blog (https://www.thethoughtfulchristian.com/Products/0664223273/the-drama-of-doctrine.aspx)
6   This is true of the most of the books on finding will of God both old and new alike (Meyer, Weiss, Friezen, Steffen and Douglass—see reference section). Sitter is an exception. He mentions how the community had helped him find God's will at a crucial time of his life; Gerald Sitter, *The Will of God as a Way of Life* (Korean Scripture Union Press, 2013), 61–67.

of lives and spiritual gifts that brought nurture and edification to each member (1 Cor 12:4–11). They shared common visions and concerns as they were taught by the apostles and prayed with one mind and heart. They knew exactly what they were called to do and be as they shared their lives together (Acts 2:42–47). These could be repeated over and over in the lives of the corporate body of the church throughout ages.

Most modern churches have lost this corporate sharing of lives as well as spiritual gifts and ministry to each other in a "body life" (1 Cor 12:1–30, 14:26–33). The mindset of "some with gifts of teaching, some with gifts of prophecy, some with gifts of leadership, and some with gifts of hospitality" could help each in finding the will of God. If the church prayed for each other as one mind in this corporate context it would become much easier for each to find the will of God, both for the whole body as well as for individuals.

> If the church prayed for each other as one mind in this corporate context it would become much easier for each to find the will of God, both for the whole body as well as for individuals.

As one grows deeper in spirituality, the greater concern will be to know his will for the world and his church, such as how to fulfill that purpose of God and be the kind of people that God wants them to be. Less emphasis will be on finding the will of God for private matters. We find the Lord praying to know the Father's will and confessing how he has succeeded in following the will of the Father as he faced his final days on earth (Matt 26:39, 42; John 19:30). We find the same pattern in the life of the apostles. They seemed to be less concerned about finding his will on personal level. Instead, finding God's will for the people of God as corporate body was more often the case in the New Testament (Eph 3:1–6, 2 Cor 1:1). Modern Christians may have weakened this perspective in finding the will of God. Instead, they have focused more on personal matters at the cost of the kingdom and the corporate body of the church. We need to reclaim these areas as we find the will of God on our lives.

Finding the Will of God: Practical Implications

The Role of Scripture

At least two aspects could be said in regards to the role that Scripture plays in finding the will of God. While reading the Scripture, God could show some sign(s) on a particular matter in which we are seeking his will. This happens often in my life. God puts in my mind what to do as I read his Word. Another way is to reveal a specific passage of Scripture through which one finds the answer. The first is the indirect way that God helps us to find the will of God on the particular theme we are seeking to find. The other is a direct way that God speaks to our heart through his Word.

For many years I prayed for God to show me how to be wiser as a leader. One day in a retreat God seemed to point right at a passage from Proverbs (1:7). I felt that God was so close to me that I could not refrain from weeping, unable to express my feeling any other manner.[7] I remained in an almost prostrate position for a long time, unable to take my mind off the passage. He taught me that day that the greatest wisdom is to fear him. My life afterward was never the same; for he showed me his will for my life regarding becoming a wiser person. This is simply one personal experience where the Bible was used to show me the will of God. There are untold numbers of ways God uses the Bible to show his will on whatever question we are trying to find an answer to. The unchanging proposition in finding the will of God is that God does speak to us personally through his Word.

The Role of Prayer

Finding the will of God without prayer is unthinkable. Even things that seem so clear to our mind as to where God is seeming to lead us, we still need to pray that God would show us his will. How much more should we pray when we do not know the will of God on a particular subject? There were times that I had to pray a whole year to confirm his will on my life. I was an electrical engineer employed by a prestigious Korean Power Company while at the same time serving as a leader in an indigenous student ministry known as the JOY Mission. God seemed to speak to me for some time to let go of my secular job and become a full-time minister of that organization. Having grown up on almost poverty level and having to support my family as well as earn my own way in school since the age of ten, it was unthinkable to let go of my job. It was all the more difficult as I had been married only one year and needed to support my new family. I remember praying to receive a concrete answer from the Lord for almost a year. I would leave home thinking that I would submit my resignation that day, only to return home unchanged. Finally I prayed, "God, you need to pick me up and take me out of that company as I am unable by my own strength." In a short while on a certain Christmas Eve, our company caught fire, and our office, which was on the thirteenth and fourteenth floor of the Dae Yun Gak building, burned to ashes, killing more than 160 people. Not all answers to prayer will be that dramatic, but it is unthinkable for me to know the will of God without prayer. Honestly, I do not want to know his will if I have not prayed, for fear that I might err.

> Finding the will of God without prayer is unthinkable.

The Role of Reason and Spiritual Discernment

There can be at least two opposite poles in a continuum in regards to using our reason. One is that as long as we are in accord with God's broader will as prescribed in the Bible and follow a certain number of principles, we are given a range of freedom to choose out of many equally right ways. In this case, right decision-making plays an

---

7   Korean Christians generally cry or weep when they are deeply touched by the Holy Spirit, whether convicted or blessed; while Western Christians seem to laugh instead, according to my experience in the US.

important role in finding God's will.[8] The opposite end of the continuum emphasizes that finding the will of God requires that one must depend more on God's initiative. This camp usually emphasizes more on completely surrendering one's will and letting God take the initiative.[9] Numerous Korean pastors' practices on how to find the will of God at one time fell on this end of the continuum along with Weiss. The Korean pastors often went to the mountains to pray for many days and nights with fasting until they found the will of God for what they were seeking his answer. Currently this tradition is seldom practiced with the creeping secularization among the church leaders and pastors in even among Korean churches. Important decisions are usually made in board meetings.

Our reason is imperfect, stained by the fall of mankind. Nevertheless, God still allows us to use our reason and knowledge as we make important decisions.[10] In seeking the will of God, it is inevitable that we use reason to discern the following: Is the subject at hand in accordance with what Scripture says? Is it contradictory to what is already known by the common understanding of academic community? The most important thing, however, is that it is not contradictory to what the Bible says and the teachings of the church. The following are some of the additional things that require attention: Has there been prayer seeking the leading of the Holy Spirit? Have some of the mature Christian leaders been consulted and given positive feedback on the matter? Although it could indicate both ways, open doors usually mean a positive sign. Finally, is there peace in one's heart as the final decision is adopted? If the answers to these tests are positive, it would be safe to conclude that God is pleased with the decision we made. Although this is not meant to be a formula, if one can test one's decision a number of times and sense the leading of God in the same direction, it may be safe to proceed with what has been found to be the will of God. In all this, one needs to exercise spiritual discernment.

> Our reason is imperfect, stained by the fall of mankind. Nevertheless, God still allows us to use our reason and knowledge as we make important decisions.

---

8   MacArthur argues that if one is "saved, Spirit-filled, sanctified, submissive, and suffering," God's Word makes all this clear." "Do whatever you want! (emphasis his)." John MacArthur, *Found: God's Will* (Colorado Springs, CO: David C. Cook Book (Kindle Edition), 2012), 75. MacArthur, 67; Tom Steffen and Lois Mckinney Douglas, *Encountering Missionary Life and Work: Preparing for Intercultural Ministry* (Grand Rapids, MI: Baker, 2008), 48–50; Gary Friesen and Rabin Maxson, *Decision Making and the Will of God: A Biblical Alternative to the Traditional View* (Portland, OR: Multnomah (Kindle Edition), 1988/2014), 244–55.

9   Weiss, 34–40.

10   At one end of the continuum is G. Christian Weiss who plays down our own decision-making and emphasizes more of God's role. The opposite end of the continuum are Friesen and MacArthur. The rest of the older writers on this theme agree about using their own decision-making ability more carefully. These include FB Myer and George Mueller from Bristol, England. More recent writers such as Sitter would also fall towards Friesen. My own position would be leaning toward Myer and Mueller. Do use a decision-making process, yet depend much on God's guidance.

The Role of Practice in Discerning the Will of God

As we deepen our daily walk with God in our lives, we will be able to know better when it is the Lord saying, "Yes, you are on the right track, go ahead!" It is likened to an intimate relationship between a husband and wife. As they become more intimate and their relationship deepens, there will be a common understanding on certain matters without saying anything. They will be able to know some things by instinct. Likewise, as we have a deeper relationship with the Lord we will know whether it is of the Lord saying, "This is the right way, go on ahead." It will still take faith to act upon what we think to be the will of God. It is when we finally take a step forward by faith and there is still peace in our hearts that we will feel confident it is the will of God after all.

In the early years of my spiritual journey, I actually practiced how to know the will of God on certain matters. I began with less important things. I would go to the market and try to discern the will of God whether to buy certain items. I would go through step by step and finally make a decision either to buy or not. I searched my heart to hear what the Holy Spirit was saying with his still small voice. I did this to get used to how I would feel when there is peace in my heart so that when I have to discern his will on more important matters in my life's journey I would not err. Result? I honestly cannot say that these practices made it easier to discern his will when I had to make more important decisions in my life. Nevertheless, it has helped me in the long run, as this practice has helped me to be better sensitized to his leading.

Conclusion

I began with a personal experience in seeking the will of God by way of introduction. Two broader contexts on how God acts that we must be aware of have been mentioned. They are the wider purpose of God in our lives and the corporate life of the church. Furthermore, some areas that need to be considered in discerning the will of God have been mentioned. On the basis of these, an attempt will be made to put all these in one composite diagram so that novices, as well as those who are more experienced in finding the will of God, will both benefit.

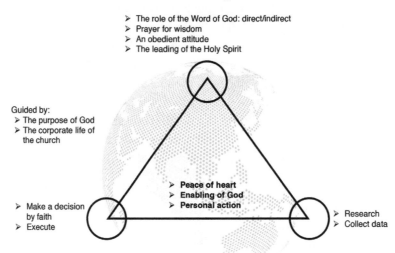

The Process of Finding the Will of God

> The role of the Word of God: direct/indirect
> Prayer for wisdom
> An obedient attitude
> The leading of the Holy Spirit

Guided by:
> The purpose of God
> The corporate life of
  the church

> **Peace of heart**
> **Enabling of God**
> **Personal action**

> Make a decision
  by faith
> Execute

> Research
> Collect data

Although I have tried to give a concrete picture, finding the will of God cannot be a mere formula. We will never be able to fathom the way in which God acts; even in showing his will in our lives. For this reason, it will be closer to the truth to say that finding the will of God is an art rather than like solving a mathematical problem. Nevertheless, looking back at my personal journey in regards to finding his will, there were no mistakes in his guidance in all the ways of my life. This is not saying in any way that I was able to find his perfect will each time. But it is his leading that is perfect for all his children in all the days of their lives from the times of the Bible throughout the history of the church.

Although I have tried to give a concrete picture, finding the will of God cannot be a mere formula.

Thus, as imperfect as we may feel in our efforts to find his will, we will continue to walk with him in faith knowing that we will ultimately be guided by his Word, the Triune God, and the church in whatever areas that we are seeking his will. For, he is our great Shepherd and Guide who will take us to the final destination without failure. In the meantime, he will let us know his will as we walk close to him and listen to him continually. Amen.

References

Friesen, Gary and Rabin Maxson. 1988/2004. *Decision Making and the Will of God: A Biblical Alternative to the Traditional View.* Portland, OR: Multnomah (Kindle Edition).

Macarthur, John. 2012. *Found: God's Will.* Colorado Springs, CO: David C. Cook Book (Kindle Edition).

Meyer, FB. N.d. *The Secret of Guidance*. Chicago, IL: Moody Press.

Steffen, Tom and Lois Mckinney Douglas. 2008. *Encountering Missionary Life and Work: Preparing for Intercultural Ministry*. Grand Rapids, MI: Baker.

Sitter, Gerald L. 2013. [Korean Translated Version]. 『하나님의 뜻』 [*The Will of God as a Way of Life*]. 성서유니온[Korean Scripture Union Press].

Vanhoozer, Kevin J. 2006. *The Drama of Doctrine: A Canonical Linguistical Approach to Christian Theology*. Louisville, KY: John Knox Press.

Weiss, G Christian. 1950. *The Perfect Will of God*. Chicago, IL: Moody Press.

Dr. David Tai-Woong Lee lived without knowing Jesus until 1962. He met Jesus at JOY Mission, where he served and became their first Director (1962–1979). He began theological training at the Southern Baptist Theological Seminary and completed this MDiv and DMiss at Trinity Evangelical Divinity School. He was the founding director of Global Missionary Training Center (1986–2007) and the Chairman of the World Evangelical Alliance, Mission Commission (1994–2002). Currently he serves as the associate pastor at Yoido Baptist Church and the Director of Global Leadership Focus—an arm of Global Missionary Fellowship (GMTC). His wife, Hun-Bock Song taught Family Life at GMTC, and they have two sons, Young-Min(his wife KiJu, daughter Duhee) and Kyoung-Min. He has published *Korean Missions: Theory and Practice* (Joy Publisher) and *Training Disciples* (Tyrannus Publisher). He has further contributed to world missions by writing various articles, published both nationally and internationally.

Scripture: *Proverbs 3 ("My son, do not forget my teaching, but keep my commands in your heart...")*

Resource: *The Kingdom Life: A Practical Theology of Discipleship and Spiritual Formation*, by Alan Andrews, ed. (Carol Stream, IL: Navpress, 2010).

CHAPTER 16

Embracing the Invitation to Brokenness and Deconstruction

Yvonne Christine DeAcutis Taylor

Then Jesus said to his disciples, "If any of you wants to be my follower, you must turn from your selfish ways, take up your cross, and follow me." (Matthew 16:24)

So Jesus asked the twelve apostles, "Do you want to leave me too?" (John 6:67)

A grain of wheat must fall into the ground and die. (John 12:24)

Let the inquiring Christian trample underfoot every slippery trick of his deceitful heart... the ancient curse will not go out painlessly; the tough, old miser within us will not lie down and die in obedience to our commands. He must be torn out of our heart like a plant from the soil; he must be extracted in agony and blood like a tooth from the jaw. He must be expelled from our soul by violence... and we shall need to steel ourselves against his piteous begging, to recognize it as springing out of self-pity, one of the most reprehensible sins of the human heart. If we would indeed know God in growing intimacy, we must go this way of renunciation. (A.W. Tozer, "The Blessedness of Possessing Nothing," in *The Pursuit of God*)

Framing Our Thoughts

I come to the writing of this chapter with mixed feelings. There are so many wonderful resources available nowadays drawing on the historic wisdom of the mystics and saints of old, as well as current-day writers, to help us along the path of discipleship and costly devotion to Christ. On the other hand, there may be those who have not had the time or opportunity to study these resources or perhaps be exposed to this deep-time wisdom because of the constraints of the particular stream of Christianity that has shaped them. Others have been left vulnerable because their paradigm of spirituality has not taught them nor prepared them for these aspects of brokenness and deconstruction as part of the lifelong journey in Christ.

So, I set out not to cover these themes exhaustively nor as one who has "arrived" spiritually. Rather I hope to share just a few of the insights gained and lessons learned along the way in my own journey of following Christ. I have been shaped by the beauty and mystery of high liturgical Anglicanism, by the biblical and gospel-shaped discipleship of evangelicalism, and by the vitality of the glad embrace of the Holy Spirit and a practicing supernaturalism of the Charismatic movement. I will share a little later something of my own experience with these themes.

Defining the Terms

First, what is this "invitation to brokenness and deconstruction"? What is it about and where does it come from? We are all familiar with Scriptures that allude to carrying a cross (Matt 10:38), to know Christ in his sufferings (Phil 3:10), to persevere through suffering (Heb 12:7), to "die" in order to bear fruit (John 12:24), to submit to God's discipline that we might share in his holiness (Heb 12:10b or Rev 3:10).

Holy Scripture is clear that salvation and the promise of eternal life through Jesus Christ is but the beginning of a long journey towards sanctification and transformation. The entrenched power and disfigurement of the fallen Self Life (i.e., "old self" or "old man" of Romans 6:6) will only be dismantled as we embrace the invitation to brokenness and deconstruction. In the end, there is no other way. Yet everything in us resists and flees from this reality. Can there not be a softer, easier way? In the context of this article, "brokenness" focuses not so much on the trials and tribulations that assault us all by living in this fallen world, but rather on the means that God allows at certain points in our journey to address entrenched sin/False Self systems that can only be rooted out as Tozer describes in the quote at the beginning of this chapter. "Deconstruction" speaks of the process whereby God dismantles those systems to move us towards freedom and marked transformation into the likeness of Christ.

> The entrenched power and disfigurement of the fallen Self Life (i.e., "old self" or "old man" of Romans 6:6) will only be dismantled as we embrace the invitation to brokenness and deconstruction.

Engaging Our Topic

Each age of Christian history is replete with the wisdom and sayings of those faithful disciples who have persevered along the path that has the shadow of the Cross over it. They have expressed the call to transformative holiness in varied and compelling ways:

> Thomas Merton: "Be careful if you are thinking of making friends with the Holy Spirit, because he is going to ask you die."

> Sirach 2: "If you wish to live a spiritual life, prepare yourself for an ordeal, since gold is tested in fire, and the chosen one in the furnace of humiliation."

The Divine Game of Penzanski: "Arthur and I put out the fire once more. Sparks whirled. 'Man is born to trouble,' he quoted from Job, 'as the sparks fly upwards.' 'Meaning what about God?' I challenged him. He did not hesitate. 'Meaning God is not soft. If he thinks a person needs to go through something in order to carve more glory out of him or her, he'll do it. He might weep; but he will do it.'"

The serious and devoted follower of Christ comes to realize that the baptismal pattern of death followed by resurrection will be repeated many times throughout our life.

Yet we are constantly bombarded by the siren voices of the world system and the crafty lies of dark spirits to turn from this path. As eager followers of Christ, we set out on our journeys with passion and high hopes. As missionaries, we desire to extend his kingdom, bring him glory, and see many brought to salvation. However, we find that weariness, battered hopes, unanswered prayers, and heart-breaking life experiences threaten to derail us. We begin to find ourselves in fierce landscapes marked by the silence of God, and we are tempted to despair or bitterness or a rebellion against our circumstances.

> As missionaries, we desire to extend his kingdom, bring him glory, and see many brought to salvation. However, we find that weariness, battered hopes, unanswered prayers, and heart-breaking life experiences threaten to derail us.

These are the seasons when we must return again and again to the foundational words of Christ and surrender to his call to follow him through the fires to the glory beyond.

As one who has known and followed Christ since childhood and served in ministry/ mission for some fifty years, I have seen many people begin the journey; but, sadly, over time, a significant number fall by the wayside. Others may manage to sustain a measure of faith, but have lost hope or simply choose to remain stuck in a holding pattern. Some resist the invitation to see themselves accurately and honestly (i.e., true self-knowledge) and refuse to face the hidden addictions that God wants to bring out into the light (things like the drive for power, control, significance, fame, pleasing others to a fault, to be where the action is, to make our mark in the world, for placing ministry opportunities and travel over marriage and family, etc.). CS Lewis aptly describes this as "the sweet poison of a false infinite." Through reading, study, and listening to those coming to me for spiritual wisdom, I realize that this matter of understanding the call to brokenness and deconstruction is critical if one is to persevere and finish well.

Once we grasp that brokenness and deconstruction of the False Self are gifts given to us to set us free and bring about the transformation we long for, we can then embrace them and humbly submit to the Holy Spirit's pruning and tempering work in us. However, because these "gifts" are so painful and require great courage and strength, we need wise and faithful spiritual mentors and companions to help us persist and not give up.

Two Helpful Constructs

There are many paradigms or constructs across the streams of Christianity that help us better understand how God uses these "tools" to call forth our True Selves that he saw and intended for us when he created us. One construct that I learned about through my own study and reading and have found very helpful for myself as well as others who have come to me for spiritual counsel is the following. The narrative goes something like this:

When we are born into the world, we find from the beginning that it is a dangerous and threatening place. Subconsciously and often unawares, we begin to construct internal systems to protect ourselves physically, emotionally, psychologically, and spiritually. We all need these systems to cope and to thrive as our life unfolds. This is true even within the best of families and home backgrounds as well as the more wounded family systems.

God mercifully allows us to keep these survival systems in place throughout childhood and youth and even into young adulthood. But in the end these systems are inadequate and flawed, for they constitute the systems of the False Self. God's ultimate aim is to set us free from enslavement to our False Selves and gradually, steadily transform us into our True Selves. And this is where God's "deconstruction" process begins in the life of the believer. However, this is the work of a lifetime. He knows that we are "frail and but dust" and can only handle so much at any given time. So, in his vast wisdom, he deals with us according to our capacity. As a loving Father, God will not test us beyond that which we can bear (Isa 42:3a; 1 Cor 10:13 ESV; Ps 51:17 ESV)

> The sacrifices of God are a broken spirit; A broken and a contrite heart, O God, You will not despise, *Psalm 51:17*
>
> No temptation has overtaken you but such as is common to man; and God is faithful, who will not allow you to be tempted beyond your ability, but with the temptation will provide the way of escape also, so that you will be able to endure it. *1 Cor 10:13*
>
> A bruised reed he will not break, and a smoldering wick he will not snuff out. *Isaiah 42:3a*

A second concept that I came across and have found helpful is that in the early stages of our life the call is, "I must increase, so that Christ in me may increase." This is when we are discovering who we are and our unique, God-designed, individuated identity vis a vis others. We are developing our gifts and talents and sense of place in the wider world. However, the time arrives when our loving Father draws near to ask if we will willingly accept his call to brokenness and the deconstruction of the False Self systems. This is when we must shift into, "I must decrease so that Christ can increase." The False Self begins to be dismantled (i.e., deconstructed) so our truest, deepest Self can emerge and be set free.

Generally speaking, God's invitation into this process doesn't begin until young adulthood at the earliest. For many the process doesn't begin in earnest until midlife or later. Periodically, God draws near to ask us if we are ready to say "yes" to the next stage of deconstruction. We are free to say "yes" or "no." And this is where the battle between the old, False Self and God's wooing is engaged. Over the years I have seen those who turn from the invitation and simply continue on as before due to pride or fear or resistance. They continue to circle, sometimes for years, around the base of the "mountains"(as described in Hannah Hurnard's *Hinds Feet on High Places*), more comfortable with an earlier stage of spiritual formation than the fearful unknowns of the journey "deeper in and higher up" (*The Last Battle*, CS Lewis)

For others of us, we manage to muster enough courage to say "yes" because our hunger for greater intimacy with the Lord and for freedom from our old self is greater than our fear. Our False Self systems have begun to break down and we are ready to deal with the junk in our lives. We are finally ready to grapple with our broken family systems, our subconscious addictions, our self-inflicted wounds, and those wounds inflicted against us. And like the character Much Afraid in *Hinds Feet*, we surrender to the Lord's appointing of "Sorrow and Suffering" as our companions for the journey. Sadly, there are streams within Christianity that fail to teach about these aspects of our journey with Christ; and many disciples are left to circle around the lower reaches of the mountains, not knowing or desiring to embrace Christ's call to transformational holiness. And this can sometimes lead to some eventually foundering and breaking up on the shoals of adversity.

> Many disciples are left to circle around the lower reaches of the mountains, not knowing or desiring to embrace Christ's call to transformational holiness.

When we look at Scripture, we see vivid examples of God's transforming work in the lives of his servants through brokenness and deconstruction. A study of the lives of people like Joseph, Moses, and David helps us see God's pattern wherein he firmly yet faithfully breaks and then shapes these men through many "wilderness" years before they are ready to step fully into the destiny he has created for them. Certainly the annals of missionary history are replete and overflowing with examples of those who were transformed by the suffering, loss, and sorrow they experienced. These heroes of the faith were shaped by a rigorous, cross-centered spirituality that enabled them to accept and persevere through the fiery trials God sent their way in the process of being shaped into the likeness of Christ.

From My Own Narrative

My earliest memory of an encounter with God was when I was about five. It happened in the middle of a high Anglican Eucharistic service at our church when all the beauty, mystery, and majesty happening around me suddenly transformed into a mystical encounter with God. He was revealing himself to me and was giving me a glimpse of the beauty realm where he dwells. It was so powerful that I felt an intense love and desire for him that marked me from that moment on. I knew he was real and that Christ was the Savior of the world. Later, at seven, through a neighbor's Child Evangelism Good News Club I came to understand and embrace Christ as my personal Savior. At sixteen my family started attending a Bible-teaching, gospel church where I began the lifelong journey of discipleship and entrusting my whole life to his lordship.

The journey has been both glorious and incredibly costly. When he said we needed to take up our cross and follow him, he meant it. But once having glimpsed his glory and beauty, there was no turning back. In the ensuing years I began to experience his calls to brokenness and deconstruction that he was initiating. The writings on the deeper life by saints like Andrew Murray and AW Tozer, Amy Carmichael, Oswald Chambers, Paul Billheimer, and many others laid the groundwork to help me navigate the cross-bearing experiences as I found the courage to say "yes."

Without question it has been the merciful grace of God that brought me through each testing without falling away. When I was forty-five, the Lord called me into the fierce landscape of "the dark night of the soul," something unknown to me and never mentioned or taught up to that point within the circles in which we moved. The Lord had been preparing me, however, through reading the great classics and writings of evangelical, Catholic, Anglican, Celtic Christian, and Eastern Orthodox saints and mystics. Without this preparation and orientation, I would have floundered and gotten lost without any understanding of what was happening. I recall reading in Richard Foster's *Celebration of Discipline*,

> What should we do during such a time of inward affliction? First, disregard the advice of well-meaning friends to snap out of it. They do not understand what is occurring. Our age is so ignorant of such things that I do not recommend that you even talk about these matters. Above all, do not try to explain or justify… God is your justifier. Rest your case with him… hold in your heart a deep, inner, listening silence—and there be still until the work of solitude is done.

The fierce landscape of the "dark night" was so intense that there were moments when I didn't know if I would survive the pain. But by that point in the journey, I knew that there was no alternative but to cling fiercely to Jesus, even when I couldn't perceive his presence. God sent me to "sit at the feet" of saints from past ages who themselves had written of their experiences in the "wilderness," in the "desert," in the rocky outcroppings of remote islands, in self-imposed exile where they encountered God as a consuming fire who dwells in inapproachable Light. They became soul companions for the journey whom God used to instruct and help me through this particular testing into which he had called me. And Richard Foster was right. There were few who understood and some who were offended or uneasy when I tried to describe that journey. Thankfully, I had a loving, supportive husband and children who gave me space during this challenging time. The Lord told me, "Don't try to 'fix this.' Don't medicate. Stay present and drink this cup." I thank God for those saints who understood the contours of that landscape

> The Lord told me, "Don't try to 'fix this.' Don't medicate. Stay present and drink this cup."

through whose writings I could find insight. The Lover of my soul, in his time, brought me through, back out into the Light and consolation of his presence.

Drawing to a Close

God has unlimited and diverse ways to deal with each of us according to who we are. Each person's journey is unique. Yet there are commonalities that run through all narratives of the journey towards transformational holiness. These commonalities help us to not feel alone and to find comfort and draw inspiration from the wisdom and experience of others. Our journeys are both individual and communal at the same time. And those journeys are marked by his invitation into brokenness and deconstruction. Many of us have stories to tell of this fierce love of the God who, "If he thinks a person needs to go through something in order to carve more glory out of him or her, he'll do it. He might weep; but he will do it" (Penzanski). Someday we will see him face to face and find that, indeed, it was worth it all.

I close with the well-known sonnet by John Donne, "Batter my heart, Three-Person'd God" that speaks eloquently of the struggle between the False Self that resists God's working in the life of the soul and the True Self that longs above all else to be set free and transformed, no matter the cost:

> Batter my heart, three-person'd God, for you
> As yet but knock, breathe, shine, and seek to mend;
> That I may rise and stand, o'erthrow me, and bend
> Your force to break, blow, burn, and make me new.
> I, like an usurp'd town to another due,
> Labor to admit you, but oh, to no end;
> Reason, your viceroy in me, me should defend,
> But is captiv'd, and proves weak or untrue.
> Yet dearly I love you, and would be lov'd fain,
> But am betroth'd unto your enemy;
> Divorce me, untie or break that knot again,
> Take me to you, imprison me, for I,
> Except you enthrall me, never shall be free,
> Nor ever chaste, except you ravish me.

References

Hurrnard, Hannah. [1953] 1979. *Hinds Feet in High Places*. Carol Stream, IL: Tyndale.

Lewis, CS. [1956] 2013. *The Last Battle*. New York: Harper Collins.

Tozer, AW. [1948] 2013. *The Pursuit of God*. Bloomington, MN: Bethany House Publishers.

Yvonne Christine DeAcutis Taylor has served together with her husband in cross-cultural mission since 1967. Her university degree is in the liberal arts and music. She is a classical musician and a long-time student of Christian spirituality in the various historic streams of Christianity. God's calling on her in ministry includes spiritual formation and spiritual direction/mentoring, as well as dedicated intercession. Additional areas of study and specific ministry are Church history and Celtic Christianity.

Scripture: *Hebrews 12:1–13 ("Therefore, since we are surrounded by such a great cloud of witnesses…")*

Resource: *Don't Waste Your Sorrows: New Insight Into God's Eternal Purpose for Each Christian in the Midst of Life's Greatest Adversities*, by Paul E. Billheimer (Bloomington, MN: Bethany House Publishers, 1977).

CHAPTER 17

Spirituality and Planning

The Walk by Faith Continuum

Rodolfo "Rudy" Giron

Defining the Issues

Regretfully, many think of spirituality as an antithesis of planning. Either they spiritualized their religious practices at the expense of good planning, or they are so well-planned that there is no room for spirituality. Finding a balance between these two divinely inclusive elements will be the key to doing God´s work.

Commonly, planning is thought to be unspiritual, but doing things with much prayer and under the leading of the Spirit—that is spiritual. Until recently, labeling planning as unspiritual has been common in a large portion of the body of Christ. Although education and ecclesiastical development have smothered that mentality, there still are segments of the church that will sacrifice good planning under the excuse of being spiritual. On the other hand, there are those segments of the church who believe that everything has to be carefully planned because "God is a God of order." No room is left for the leading of the Spirit because it is argued that it may lead to confusion and disorder.

Regretfully, those two extreme views mislead toward a dichotomized view of God's work. Planning is seen as the antithesis of spirituality, something completely unscriptural and impractical. More worrisome is the fact that those two elements are linked to conflicting ecclesiastical traditions that prevent a necessary balance between spirituality and planning.

Some questions are here raised. Are there any biblical bases for us to understand how spirituality and planning relate each other? Can we be spiritual but at the same time be very careful in planning and executing things in our daily life and ministry? Can we avoid a pure human process of planning, leaving no room for spirituality when it comes to doing God's work? Can we avoid an overemphasis on spirituality at the expense of careful planning? Answering those questions will affirm that there is no conflict between a carefully planned and professionally executed work and a deep, serious, and profound spiritual process that allows the Holy Spirit's intervention at any level of our human activities. The key may be in a proper balance that willingly surrenders all plans and activities to God.

A Brief Literature Review

As we briefly examine available literature on the subject, we find that there is not much literature that extensively relates to the topics of spirituality and planning.[1] Furthermore, the issue of planning and spirituality is centered on matters related to the personality and the way of life of individuals. Erick Klein, in an article titled *Can Planning Be a Spiritual Practice?* sees planning as the "practice of actively embodying the truth of who you are and allowing life to guide you."[2] Spirituality, on the other hand, is something that takes into consideration the "now" and does not dichotomize between the now and the future. Interestingly, Klein considers that those who live in the now generally experience more satisfaction in what they do because they live in the present and do not worry too much about the future.

As Klein compares two approaches to life, one based on meditation and the other on planning, he writes:

- Can you focus on your breath and still achieve your goals?
- Can you rest in the "now" and still reserve the aisle seat on your next flight?
- What's the connection between planning and being in the present moment?

The connection between planning and being present depends on your level of consciousness.

When your awareness is on the surface of the mind, being in the now and planning are incompatible. By surface mind, I mean the level of consciousness that organizes your world into fixed, dualistic, either/or categories.

The surface mind is dualistic.

To this polarized, surface consciousness life appears as a battlefield of light/dark, good/bad; a tension-filled experience defined by either-or struggle. From the perspective of surface consciousness:

- Either you're planning or you're in the now.
- Either you're up or you're down.
- Either you're winning or you're losing. (see footnote 2)

---

1   Michael Anhorn, *Spirituality and Planning in a Diverse World* (unpublished dissertation in partial fulfillment of a Master of Arts/Planning, Vancouver, BC: School of Community and Regional Planning. The Univesity of British Columbia, 2005), ii.

2   Eirck Klein, "Can Planning Be a Spiritual Practice? (http://www.elephantjournal.com/2013/12/can-planning-be-a-spiritual-practice/, December 2013).

In a very insightful paper on urbanization, planning, and spirituality for a sustainable world, two Indian students discuss the matter that urban planning fails to "integrate the human interior dimensions such as identity, emotions, relatedness, psyche, and spirituality" in the planning process. They argue that,

> Inner and outer transformation is a central aspect of most spiritual practices, especially if envisaged within a practical notion of spirituality that is concerned with changing one's everyday attitudes and behavior. Intrinsic of this perspective is a type of spirituality clearly rooted "in-this-world" practicing conscious action in the quotidian world situated in the "here-and-now."[3]

In this brief literature analysis, we notice that the emphasis, when speaking of spirituality, is placed on the inner being, and on the "here-and-now." It has to do with the reality of a daily life that is based on the values, attitudes, and behavior of the individual. On the other hand, planning has to do with the rational being who is concerned with the future. It is something based on facts, data, information, and measurable elements that are implicit in any human activity that will achieve efficiency and effectiveness.

As we mentioned earlier, there is a constant dichotomization of spirituality and planning. A proper balance based on biblical data may show that for God, the action of his Spirit never conflicts or dichotomizes with his immaculate and perfectly planned activity. At creation the Spirit and the Word are mysteriously enmeshed to produce a perfect universe where God´s Spirit brings order, balance, and beauty.

> For God, the action of his Spirit never conflicts or dichotomizes with his immaculate and perfectly planned activity.

A Biblical Perspective on Spirituality and Planning

God's Providence Is Profoundly Spiritual

The first question that we need to ask is if there any biblical basis for understanding how spirituality and planning relate to each other. Of course, there is no better place to start than at creation. In Genesis 1:2 we see chaos, but in the midst of that chaos, the Spirit of God brings order. The product is God´s creation that more and more puzzles scientists and forces them to advocate all kind of theories. The idea is to find a logical explanation as to how the immeasurable macro and micro universe is so logically balanced, while at the same time so profoundly mysterious and mystical. Although the Genesis 1 language of creation is not scientific, we see how logically God planned the creation of all that exists. There is no conflict between his Spirit and the creative

---

3   Christoph Woiwode and Sathish Selvakumar, "Urbanization, Planing, and Spirituality for a Sustainable World" (Paper AISSQ-14 SUBMISSION 18, *Since and Spiritual Quest,* 2014), 5.

planned activity of his Word. It shows a progressive logic where things are created to sustain the next stage of creation. Spirit and Word interact dynamically as they create all that exists.

From creation we learn that we cannot pretend to do God's work depending solely on our human logic and planning. At the same time, we cannot pretend to discard God's order from all we do because of an overemphasized spirituality. There is an entanglement of God's spiritual activity and his divine order as expressed in his providence. That providence brings to us the assurance that everything is in his control and his plans are perfect for us. Such assurance is given to us by the agency of the Spirit through the Word of God. Holding a balance between those two elements makes us powerful and unstoppable. The biblical declaration that, "Nothing is impossible for God," or "Nothing is too difficult for him," becomes a reality as we properly relate spirituality and planning.

Furthermore, we all understand that God has a plan for all his creatures. It is unconceivable to think that something is left out of God's control. Not even the most minimum detail is left to venture. In fact, our security in him relays in our knowledge that he controls even the number of hairs we have on our head (Matt 10:30). Even circumstantial situations, apparently out of his control, are brought to work in favor of those who love him (Rom 8:26).

As we recreate our minds contemplating God's plan of salvation for humanity, we marvel as we see how the Divine Providence works so perfectly in history to bring salvation to humanity. From the promise of the protoevangelium of Genesis 3:15 to the calling of an old man, Abraham, married to a barren woman, comes the formation of a nation to become his people. They are the people of the Book and the people of the Savior. From those people the Savior of the world will come and will show God's perfect plan of salvation. Nothing is left to improvisation.

Another notable example of God's plan is seen in the Joseph narrative. His dreams, his brothers' rejection, his sufferings, his tribulations, and finally his rise to power in Egypt, shows how God providentially—meaning in a perfectly planned way—works his way to save Israel from destruction. Eventually, after four centuries, he raises up Moses as the liberator and founder of the nation of Israel, the nation that will be the people of the Book and the people of the Savior.

Moses' vision and mission are related to his spiritual experience at Sinai that affected him profoundly.

There is nothing left to improvisation. Everything is carefully and meticulously planned. Nevertheless, from those individuals chosen by God to fulfill his perfect plan we see a profound spiritual dependency on God. They knew they were fulfilling God´s mission, as impossible it may seem. For instance, Moses' vision and mission are related to his spiritual experience at Sinai that affected him profoundly. The wonders and miracles performed by him in Egypt and the desert are the result of that experience at Sinai. He combined all his training and professional formation received in Egypt with his encounter with God. He recognized that he was incapable, but his vision (revelation) of who God was made him able to do things that surpassed all conceivable human possibilities.

The Walk by Faith Continuum

A second question may be, can we be spiritual and at the same time be very careful to plan and execute things in our daily life and ministry? Paul tells us in 1 Corinthians 5:7 that "we walk by faith and not by sight." What does Paul mean by "walking by faith and not by sight"? Does he mean that walking by faith is spiritual and walking by sight is a planned experience? Looking at the context, Paul is talking about our human existence where we are absent from God but present in the earthly body. That reality makes us sojourners on this earth—sojourners who are challenged to face our humanity embedded in a faith that is based solely on our belief and trust in God's Word. It never excludes the possibility of a carefully planned life. On the contrary, in that same letter Paul shows the church that things have to be done in order and that each member of Christ´s body has a function. As the body works together, perfectly synchronized, so we should also strive to walk a life that is carefully planned but profoundly dependent on God. Such a life is lived in the assurance of the presence of the Holy Spirit that leads us to fulfill God´s plan. We cannot and should not ignore the fact that we are on this earth, subject to all the human elements and experiences; but we live that human life indwelled by the power of the Holy Spirit who leads us, by way of the Scriptures, as we sojourn.

Paul upholds both our human existence and our spiritual existence as a continuum where we are sustained by faith. A good example of that kind of life is shown in Acts 16. Paul planned his journeys carefully, but when it was necessary, he surrendered his plans to the guidance of the Holy Spirit. Europe would not be evangelized in God´s time if Paul did not allow God´s spiritual leading. His willingness to change plans and his knowledge of God's voice made him able to follow the leading of the Holy Spirit who took him to Macedonia. There he established the first European church.

> It takes an attitude of surrender and obedience to God's spiritual leading in order to effectively and efficiently fulfill his mission.

We may summarize that it takes an attitude of surrender and obedience to God's spiritual leading in order to effectively and efficiently fulfill his mission. Walking by faith is walking under God's providential plan. Such a plan will never lead us to confusion, but it will lead us to success.

Walking by Planning and Not by Faith

The third question we need to deal with is, can we avoid a pure human process of planning leaving no room for spirituality when it comes to doing God's work? From a biblical standpoint it is clear that human nature tends to reject God's plan and guidance and establish its own plan and will.

One of the best examples of human pride and at the same time of human capability for well-planned projects is found in Genesis 11. The narrative of the Babel tower shows that God intervened in order to stop something that would not have otherwise been stopped. It was a project well-planned and well-executed. It showed all the marks of a perfectly planned activity, thus God had to come and disrupt such a great human enterprise. Nothing was left for the endeavor to fail. The vision and mission were well articulated: "Come, let's build a great city for ourselves with a tower that reaches into the sky. This will make us famous and keep us from being scattered all over the world," (v 4, NLT). Strategies and methods were also innovative and creative: "Let's make bricks and harden them with fire," (v 3, NLT). (In this region bricks were used instead of stone, and tar was used for mortar.) The human resources were so well-integrated and well-managed that God himself recognizes it when he says, "The people are united, and they all speak the same language," (v 6, NLT). He has to intervene because he knows that unity of purpose and clear communication are the key to succeed in any endeavor, "After this, nothing they set out to do will be impossible for them! Come, let's go down and confuse the people with different languages. (Verses 6b and 7, NLT)."

The question arises, why did God stop such a great project? The scope of this essay is not theological, nevertheless, we may say that Babel represents the human pride and effort that opposes God's will and tries to rise up to God's level. Humans are always challenging God's will with their wisdom and pride. God is left out of the plan and humans take control. Does that sound familiar to you? The question of spirituality and planning takes another turn. It becomes a matter of pretending to play god as we do his work. The result is God's rejection of human pride and the consequent disapproval and failure of any enterprise.

Spirituality is a necessary component of everything we do. There is no way to do God's work effectively and fruitfully if we try to do it without the leading of his Spirit. Fundamental to fulfill God's mission are well-planned projects where vision, mission, strategies, methods, and human resources are carefully considered, but they may come to failure when we leave out the leading of the Spirit. There is nothing more powerful and effective in fulfilling God's mission than doing things well-planned and well-prayed for.

> There is no way to do God's work effectively and fruitfully if we try to do it without the leading of his Spirit.

On a practical note, how many times we have seen great projects being laid out? The funding is there because the project is presented with excellence. Every element is carefully planned and considered, but in the end the project fails. Those who fund the project wonder, where did we miss it? How did we fund a failed project? The dreamers and visionaries as well as the executors are wondering, were did we fail? Everything was thought of carefully, why then did we fail? As we search deeply on those failed project we find that the simple answer is leadership pride, or perhaps leadership stubbornness, or perhaps leadership lack of common sense and wisdom. Probably the failure is due to a poor team culture, or perhaps assumptions that were made without sufficient prayer, reflection, and submission to God. Perhaps it is the combination of all of the above elements. In a simple word, it is a project humanly speaking well-planned but poorly supported spiritually. Once again, balance is the key.

My People Are Destroyed from Lack of Knowledge

According to Hosea, the reason for Israel's destruction as a nation was the lack of knowledge of the Word of God. It was not just a lack of intellectual knowledge, but in the Hebrew sense, it was also a lack of intimacy with God. That lack of knowledge produced chaos, and chaos is the epitome of disorder. Israel was a nation that had always been inconsistent in its standing before God. If they suffered they prayed to God for mercy and would "repent" before him. But the next day, once their "now-here" situation was solved, they returned to their spiritual inconsistencies. Such an attitude showed lack of purpose and goals for their life as a nation. Usually that kind of situation results from a lack of clear leadership, both spiritual and political. Emotionalism and enthusiasm without proper planning lead to chaos, and chaos leads to destruction.

> Emotionalism and enthusiasm without proper planning leads to chaos and chaos leads to destruction.

The question is, can we avoid an overemphasis on spirituality at the expense of careful planning? How many times in circles where spirituality is overemphasized the lack of knowledge drives people to failure? Enthusiasm does not make up for efficiency. A very conspicuous passage in 1 Corinthians 14:15 serves as a good example of the balance between over-spirituality and order: "So what shall I do? I will pray with my spirit, but I will also pray with my understanding; I will sing with my spirit, but I will also sing with my understanding." The context of the passage is clearly pnuemathologic and is related to corporate worship in the body of Christ. Paul is instructing the Corinthian church to exercise their spiritual gifts in and orderly manner so that their worship to God will also be meaningful to those experiencing it. That means combining the leading of the Spirit but also the intellectual capacity of the believer. The passage though, referring to spiritual order in the corporate worship of the church, is also useful to illustrate the tendency to be enthusiastic at the expenses of order, where planning and execution in an orderly manner should be exercised.

On the practical side, how many times we have seen the failure of great spiritual enterprises due to overenthusiastic attitudes? Great ministries and ministers have failed because things are not properly planned and executed. Culture has do a lot with that. Some northern cultures will be less enthusiastic and more brain oriented. They will have a more rational approach to their religious, spiritual, and liturgical experience. The Southern cultures, on the contrary, tend to be more oriented to spontaneity and improvisation in their religious approach. The here and now experience will be immensely rewarding, but it will be inconsistent in their daily life. That will eventually produce spiritual weaknesses and failure.

The question then is, can we live a balanced life where spirituality and planning are dichotomized? Based on what we have examined the answer is yes. We can live a balanced life where we plan and execute following the example of a Provident God that is never taken by surprise because nothing escapes his perfect plan. At the same time, following the example of those biblical leaders, we surrender our knowledge and abilities to the leading of the Spirit. We crucify our ego and surrender our pride before Christ. In humbleness and sincerity, we put control of our lives and projects in his hands. Many times it is not easy to do so, it is not pleasant, it is not convenient, it is not productive, but it is for sure, it is the most important element to success when doing and fulfilling God´s mission.

Spirituality and planning should always intermingle in our lives and projects so that God's name will be known as we fulfill his mission.

Discussion Questions

1. Are there any other biblical examples you find to aid in understanding how spirituality and planning relate to each other?
2. Can you make a list of things you consider spiritual and things you consider rational and subject to planning?
3. Do you see the differences and relatedness of those things you listed above?
4. In your religious experience, are you more rationally oriented or more spiritually oriented? Where do you see balance in your life when it comes to spirituality and planning?

References

Anhorn, Michael Robert. 2005. *Spirituality and Planning in a Diverse World.* Unpublished dissertation in partial fulfillment of a Master of Arts/Planning. School of Community and Regional Planning. The University of British Columbia.

Klein, Erick. 2013. "Can Planning Be a Spiritual Practice?" (http://www.elephantjournal.com/2013/12/can-planning-be-a-spiritual-practice/, December 2013).

Woiwode, Christoph and Selvakumar, Sathish. 2014. "Urbanization, Planning, and Spirituality for a Sustainable World." Paper AISSQ-14 SUBMISSION 18, *Since and Spiritual Quest.*

Rodolfo "Rudy" Girón is a Guatemalan with US citizenship. Since 2008 he and his wife Alma have served as missionaries in Malaga, Spain where he leads IIbET (The Ibero-American Institute of Intercultural Studies) and Vision 2020 Project whose purpose is to establish UNIbE (The IberoAmerican European University). He is an architect with a MDiv and a DMin degree. For eight years he was the President of COMIBAM and later he served as a missionary to Russia where he founded the Eurasian Theological Seminary in Moscow. Upon returning to the USA, he served his denomination Church of God (Cleveland, TN) leading the Hispanic Educational Ministries in the USA.

Scripture: *Philippians 2:5–9 ("In your relationships with one another, have the same mindset as Christ Jesus…")*

Resource: *A Tale of Three Kings*, by Gene Edwards (Carol Stream, IL: Tyndale House Publishers. Kindle Edition, 1980/1992).

CHAPTER 18

Spirituality…It's about Renewing Minds

Ellen Alexander

We were planning to set out driving the next day from Chennai to Bangalore at 9:30 am when my father-in-law announced that it wasn't an auspicious time to leave the house. My father-in-law is from an Orthodox Christian background: the Syrian Christian community in South India trace their Christian heritage back to Thomas the Apostle. We told him we believed that God is the Lord of our time and every hour in it, prayed, and left at 9:30 am. When we got home my husband said, "I was driving a little extra carefully, I did want us to get home without a scratch so that Dad will see that it is God who protects and cares for us, and that he is Lord of Time."

What happens to our spirituality—to centuries of heritage, years of going to church, hearing, and reading Scripture and praying—all of which seem to be expressions of a Christian spirituality? It seems then to be possible to combine these expressions of Christian spirituality without a "renewing of the mind," or change of worldview as envisaged in the New Testament. In Romans (12:1, 2) Paul links our worship to the renewing of our minds. (We need to take note that worship here is not merely that part of the service when the leader comes and announces, "Let's now worship the Lord," and we sing, songs/hymns or choruses of worship for 10–30 minutes.) Paul here is talking about worship as being the offering of our bodies in sacrifice and service. Worship is certainly one of the more tangible evident expressions of our spirituality.

Christian spirituality must go deeper and change (even turn upside-down) our beliefs and worldviews. Only when our tangible or intangible expressions of Christian spirituality have deep roots in a continually renewed mind can they really bring glory to God or make sense to our fellow human beings. Unfortunately in our discipleship we often stop at the expression without getting to the root. The expressions of our spirituality need to become the unconscious choices and behavior rooted in our worldview.

> Only when our tangible or intangible expressions of Christian spirituality have deep roots in a continually renewed mind can they really bring glory to God or make sense to our fellow human beings.

Being from India I feel the need to define spirituality, for we have various traditions and expressions of spirituality that are not Christian and even contradictory to Christian spirituality. We mushroom spiritual gurus in our backyard! So, I would like to qualify the expression by using the term "Christian spirituality."

The Fall has fragmented our world, our relationships, and did not spare our minds. So we are able to live comfortably in compartments of neatly packed boxes, naively deeming that what we believe in our spiritual box is watertight and must not or cannot affect what we believe in or about the political or social or psychological or supernatural box and vice versa.

It is possible in Hinduism to believe in bad gods and good demons, which is in fact a contradiction in terms. A mind that is not being continually transformed and renewed has watertight compartments that can even contradict each other. And so it is possible to believe in a sovereign God and say we trust him and pray to him and yet believe that the bad stars or evil spirits can control our lives and destiny. Or to believe that God is creator, the one who created the sun and the stars—but then lock that belief tightly away in a "spiritual" compartment, compelling one to go to the stars or astrology to consult for a good time before a journey or beginning a project.

Or take another example, yoga, which is popularly practiced around the world as a simple art of meditation and physical exercise, is actually a spiritual expression—a practice with the ultimate goal of being in complete control of the mind in order to negate the mind so that the individual mind (the person meditating) is immersed or submerged in the cosmic mind (Brahma or god).

I don't want to judge those who think they can get on an escalator and not move up the ladder. But I do want to consider the two different worldviews held here.

One is a worldview where the creator and the creature are one and same, in essence like the fire and the spark, a worldview where enlightenment is the knowledge that "I am god" and therefore the possibility of merging of the individual soul and cosmic soul.

The other worldview comes from Genesis where the creator is eternal, absolute, and distinct from humans, the two can never merge into one, and the very first temptation was, "Your eyes will be opened and you will be like gods" (Gen 3:4). It is the very aspiration or desire to be god that led to the fall of humankind.

> The renewing of the mind then is not just checking to see if my behavior is spiritual or not—but going further to ask what kind of a worldview it springs from and reflects.

The renewing of the mind then is not just checking to see if my behavior is spiritual or not—but going further to ask what kind of a worldview it springs from and reflects. It would then be not about just picking texts to suit our behavior but working out a framework. It's not even about principles and values, but building a strong deep foundation of our understanding of God, his creation and revelation, human beings and our fall, redemption, and eschatology. Not as self-contained chapters in a book or bricks in a foundation, but colors that merge and blend into each other as landscape from a wide angle lens. A worldview that's wholistic, integrated, and biblical.

Renewing our mind calls us to become aware of what is in our minds, to become aware of our existing worldviews which are formed from the earliest days of our childhood and have been influenced by family, peers, culture, religious traditions, education, and media and then allowing them to be critically appraised and changed by the Spirit.

From this foundation springs our behavior and expressions of spirituality.

Ellen Alexander served with Interserve in various capacities that included as the Chair of the Governing Body of Interserve India, Member of the International Council of Interserve International, Director of Ministry Development, Training and Resources, Interserve International, and finally Director of Member Care for Interserve India. Ellen started her ministry involvement as a staff worker for Union of Evangelical Students in India (UESI) and later as a lecturer teaching undergraduate students Indian Religions, Culture, and Civilizations. She had discipled hundreds of university students in voluntary ministry roles. Along with her husband Vijay she had a ministry of an open home excelling in the gift of hospitality and mentoring through a home Bible study group. They have a married daughter Arpana and an adult son Ashish. She was a people's person, a friend to all, loved to travel, enjoyed creation, and lived life to the fullest until she passed into glory on 31st October 2015.

Scripture: *Psalm 121 ("I lift my eyes to the mountains, where does my help come from?...")*

Resource: *Paul and the Faithfulness of God*, by NT Wright (Minneapolis, MN: Fortress Press, 2013).

CHAPTER 19

The Spirituality of Professional Skills and Business

Peter Shaukat

This short and surely inadequate article on the place of professional and business skills in spirituality and mission is essentially a plea for Christ-followers to demonstrate and proclaim a wholistic gospel and to pursue authentic whole-life discipleship. In many respects, it reflects one element of my own pilgrimage in mission, which might be described as a long pursuit of an answer to the question: "How do we integrate our Christian faith with our vocational talents and training in a life committed to the global mission enterprise of the Father, Son, and Holy Spirit?"

My journey thus far is still for me most memorably crystallized when, as a young engineer-in-training experiencing the breakout of Jesus in my personal world, I approached a mission agency leader with the question: "What should I do to serve Christ globally?" The answer I received then was to go to seminary for four years and then come back and see him. His answer may just possibly (but probably quite remotely) have had to do with his perception that perhaps I had certain "ministry gifts" needing development. However, with the passage of more than four decades since that conversation, I am inclined to believe that it had more to do with a pervasive, dichotomous, sacred-secular worldview rooted in Greek Platonic (and Buddhist/Hindu) thought than with the biblical, integrated notions of shalom, holiness, and service. Since then, by God's grace, through observing the modeling of Christ's virtues in the lives of hundreds of fellow-travelers, imbibing five decades of studying Scripture on a personal devotional level, embracing divinely appointed circumstances, and following personally chosen pathways on five continents, some progress in answering that question first posed in the 1970s is slowly being made.

Having set the stage so readers will know where this layman with a background in engineering, education, and business is coming from, I propose to address the issue at hand under the following three broad categories: hazarding a comment on the global and ecclesiastical context of our time, offering a rough and ready theology of work, and outlining a few suggested essentials of a working spirituality with a missional worldview for the professional or business person.

Our Global and Ecclesiastical Context

Our times are profoundly influenced by global economic factors, to a degree perhaps never before seen in history, on account of sheer numerical size and geographic scope and our digital age with its rapid democratization of information to the masses. From the anarchic and disparate "Occupy Movement" to the trigger point of the so-called "Arab Spring," in which a young Tunisian selling vegetables from an unauthorized push-cart set himself on fire in frustration at the insurmountable challenges of eking out a simple living for his family, across the world protest movements which have their roots in a disenchantment with status quo economic systems. It is worth noting that these systems are interconnected with and have an impact upon multiple professional disciplines and that they are constructed, developed, and led by professional and business people. It is also disconcerting to realize that we are all, everyone, involved in some manner or other in the very marketplaces we find, by turns, enthralling and galling—whether we be producers or consumers, buyers, or sellers.

> Our times are profoundly influenced by global economic factors, to a degree perhaps never before seen in history, on account of sheer numerical.

The World Economic Forum, in its Insight Report on Global Risks in 2015, cites the following as the five most likely risks in our world: interstate conflict, extreme weather events, failure of national governance, state collapse or crisis, and unemployment or underemployment. In terms of impact there is not necessarily a direct correlation risk to risk; nevertheless, interstate conflict, the failure to adapt to climate change, and unemployment or unemployment are in the top ten.[1] Jim Clifton, Chairman and CEO of Gallup, in a similar vein writes that "a global jobs war is coming," because what everyone in the world wants is a good job. The breakdown of families, municipalities, and countries is directly and progressively linked to the masses of unemployed and underemployed. Gallup reckons that the world presently has a shortfall of some one to two billion good jobs.

What is immediately evident is that all of these risks reflect the dark side of the human spiritual condition to some degree or other, and conversely, require remarkable and diverse professional and business skills to mitigate and overcome. If one believes that peace-making flows from the very wellspring of genuine spirituality, then surely anything that contributes to the diminishing of jobs-related conflict and brings dignified employment in redemptive relationship settings qualifies as a Himalayan peak of mission endeavor.

In the light of this context, the questions "What is our mission?" and "How do we live our spirituality?" are pressing ones which cannot be ignored. I propose that the most relevant spirituality is the most practical and that the mission of the people of God

---

1   The full report can be found at http://opim.wharton.upenn.edu/risk/library/Global_Risks_2015.pdf.

must certainly include participation in the kind of issues cited above. It has always been thus.

This leads us to a brief consideration of our ecclesiastical context. Traveling on the London Underground, one cannot miss the incessant audio and visual warnings to "Mind the Gap"—the dangerous space between train and platform, which apparently leads to hundreds of serious injuries every year. A similar, deadly gap exists in the church. It is the gap between "full-time ministry" and everything else. It is the gulf between "those called into ministry" and those who "pay and pray" for these ministries. It is the chasm of ignorance and misunderstanding of what the professional and business world entails that leaves so many searching for any nurturing relevance at all in so much of the churches' teaching, hymnology, and programs. Decades of informal polling on the question in dozens of countries turn up the same result: most Christians have never heard a message on work in their life, the vast majority of business people have never been explicitly confirmed in their calling into business as a ministry, and for reasons still largely inexplicable to me, troubling numbers of Christians leave professions of significant relevance to serve in the church.

> A deadly gap exists in the church. It is the gap between "full-time ministry" and everything else.

A young man in his thirties recently confided to me that he had felt a "reluctance to enter business due to concern about mission drift" and that nothing had been offered to him as a Christian disciple to disabuse him of that feeling. Another now retired businessman recently come to Christ acknowledged that he could not connect Sunday to Monday and that he was therefore essentially resigned to living a sort of schizophrenic spirituality. The lingering legacy of the "social vs. evangelical gospel" war, to the extent that it continues to influence the landscape of the global church, in some cases with renewed animation, is an issue which must be resolved.

Addressing this issue, Os Hillman states that the church has a major task before it of "rethinking Jesus." He writes:

> Of Jesus' 132 public appearances, 122 were in the marketplace. Of 52 parables Jesus told, 45 had a workplace context. Jesus spent his adult life as a carpenter until age 30 before he went into a preaching ministry in the workplace. And 54% of Jesus' reported teaching ministry arose out of issues posed by others in the scope of daily life experience. Saint Bonaventure said, "His doing nothing 'wonderful' (his first thirty years) was in itself a kind of wonder."

We live in a world characterized by widespread protest, with many objects of complaint—multinational business, globalization, the widening gap between the rich and the poor, and a host of other issues. Some acts of agitation are more legitimate than others; all are tinged with the reality of sinful human nature. One of these demonstrations of discontent, the so-called "Occupy Movement," got its name from the "Occupy Wall Street" rally which began on September 11, 2011 in New York City as a protest against the financial industry's perceived rapacious and unethical behavior, and bloomed into a larger global movement directed against rising social and economic inequality.

It may come as a surprise to our protesting world and to those who claim to be followers of Christ to discover that it was Jesus in fact who was (and is) the true Founder of the "Occupy Movement." For in his enduring words recorded in Matthew we are told to "occupy until he comes"—and to do so with justice, mercy, and humility. The context of his words (and in fact an alternate rendering of them being to "make money") is a clear trumpet call to the church to embrace the missional spirituality of the professions, including, notably, the missional calling to business. We must take note of the fact that there can be no "wealth redistribution" for example, without "wealth creation" in the first place, and it is intrinsic to the nature and practice of business to create wealth. It is intriguing to contemplate that a full embrace of all that Jesus said, did, was, and is may enable us to find more common ground with more of our fellow man, including protestors we might not naturally identify with, than we at first imagined!

Towards a Practical Theology of Work

At an early stage in my journey, I encountered the writings of Elton Trueblood. He wrote that the First Reformation brought the Word of God to the people of God. How gloriously true, as the previously unattainable Scriptures came at great cost via translation from one language to another to the global body of Christ, and consequently nurtured the spirituality of generations. On the other hand, how provocative is Trueblood's further declaration that the church is now on the cusp of a Second Reformation—even more far-reaching—that will bring the work of God to the people of God. It is this thought which connects our ecclesiastical context with the urgent need to construct a robust, applied theology of work.

Let it be noted straight away that by "work" I do not mean paid employment alone. Economists have estimated that the variety of tasks skillfully brought to bear in the vocation of homemaking, for example, might, in each family, amount to a quarter of a million dollars a year were they to be monetarily compensated. Similarly, the role of volunteerism as a vital element of the civil contract that binds our societies together is of incalculable value.

The Puritans referred to work as that social place where we can exercise the gifts God has given us in the service of others. Clearly this applies to the professions. More narrowly applied to business, Pope John Paul II wrote: "The purpose of a business firm is not simply to make a profit, but is to be found in its very existence as a community of persons who in various ways are endeavoring to satisfy their basic needs, and who form a particular group at the service of the whole of society." It seems to me that this is a more uplifting and helpful statement in shaping our practical spirituality and motivating our engagement in the missional task of solving real-world problems than recalling the medieval statement that unbridled greed is the "dung of the devil" and applying it to the problems of capitalism in the present day. A workable spirituality must have hope, and cannot afford as its driving force ambivalence at best and antipathy at worst. From a practical theological standpoint, spirituality is serving my neighbor through the skills, talents, and opportunities God has given me.

> From a practical theological standpoint, spirituality is serving my neighbor through the skills, talents, and opportunities God has given me.

Not only do we as followers of Christ need to reformat our thinking about work, but to do so will represent a strategically important witness and service to the not-yet worshiper of Jesus as Lord. Robert L. Kahn, in an article entitled "On the Meaning of Work," from the *Journal of Occupational Medicine* and quoted in "The Fabric of this World" by Hardy reveals the following fascinating picture of the typical paradoxical view of work held by most: "A nationwide survey of a cross-section of [the population] found that although the vast majority defined work as necessary, done for the sake of money and in itself unenjoyable, over three-fourths would continue working even if they were to receive enough money to live comfortably for the rest of their lives!"[2] We cannot stand the tedium and emptiness of work—yet to be unemployed carries a stigma we cannot bear. Many prepare for years for their chosen profession, and yet spend but moments thinking about its spiritual significance. The professional or business context is where we meet most people in our lives most often, and from which we draw a large sense of our identity, yet how isolated and divisive a place it can be.

Three biblical themes are central to building a practical theology of work and connecting that theology to applied, missional spirituality.

Work is Worship

The first great theme is that work is worship. God himself works; indeed, before we meet him in any other capacity we meet him as worker (Gen 1:1). We are created to work, not cursed to work (Gen 1:28; 2:15, 19). The curse of Eden is that the human race has the knowledge potential to do all things but that it has been cut off from the spiritual wisdom needed to know if, why, and how it should. It is the curse of having capacity and capability without the spirituality to reflect truly on the thing. Having been made in the image of God and having that image renewed in Christ, as he is, so we are meant to reflect and grow into his likeness. The biblical term "Avodah" is the transliteration of the Hebrew word both for worship and work. The root word means to work or to serve. One easily recognizes the connection to "vocation" and the logically related concept of "occupation." The first and greatest commandment to love the Lord our God with all our heart, soul, mind, and strength is in the first instance the locus of any understanding of our spirituality. But for anyone who loves their profession of art, business, education, engineering, entertainment, forestry, journalism, law, medicine,

---

2   Robert Kahn, Robert, "On the Meaning of Work," *Journal of Occupational Medicine* (16(11):716-719, November 1974); Lee Hardy, *The Fabric of this World* (Grand Rapids, MI: Eerdemans, 1990).

music, politics, waste-management, and any number of other professions—in whatever alphabet—engaging in these, as unto God, to the service of my fellow man, with all my heart, soul, mind and strength is my reasonable service/worship.

If this be true, we must vigorously reject the "sacred-secular/clergy-laity/Sunday-weekday" division which tends to dominate our thinking in the church.

Work is Ministry

The second great theme is that work is ministry and its corollary is that we (all of us) are a kingdom of priests, that we (all of us) are saints, and that to all of us, as saints, has been given "the work of the ministry." In the great missional task for which Jesus prepared his disciples he declared that through their practical spirituality, people would see their works and give glory to their Father in Heaven (Matt 5:13–16) This is but an ideological continuation of the ancient words of Moses that our skills are given and blessed by God (Ex 31:1–6, 35:30–36.1, Deut 33:11). We have already seen that the opportunities to serve our world in some of its most pressing needs can only be delivered by the brilliant, creative, wholistic application of professional and business skills. The challenge is whether or not we see our work as the means to our paycheck or the means by which our spirituality is predominantly brought to the world.

> The challenge is whether or not we see our work as the means to our paycheck or the means by which our spirituality is predominantly brought to the world.

In the context of a theology of work, business carries with it some unique challenges and opportunities, which deserve far greater treatment than can be given here. Three are worth mentioning. The first is the connection between a theology of work and a theology of creation or "enterprise"—bringing into being that which was not. In this calling the business person is uniquely bearing the image of God. The second is the connection, for the business person, between a theology of work and a theology of wealth. It is uniquely the role of business enterprise to create wealth—and this is, according to Moses, a gift given by God, one which carries risk, and one for which the business practitioner is accountable to God. For those oriented towards a dogma of wealth redistribution, it is an uncomfortable fact that this cannot be done without wealth creation in the first place. The third unique challenge and opportunity rests in the notion of job-creation. Business people carry a particular "divine DNA" to create livelihoods—opportunities to till, to steward, to subdue—for others. It is worth reflecting on the modern-day scourge of unemployment and its equivalence to the leprosy of ancient times. That which was so profound an opportunity for Holy Spirit imbued mission as Jesus touched the leper, made him clean, and allowed him to reenter the mainstream of society, is for business people in our day, to rescue the unemployed with the social marginalization, atrophying of skills, and demoralizing dependency upon the goodwill of others that increases with every prolongation of being without work.

If this be true, we are all (not just the modern-day Luthers among us) participants in this Second Reformation.

Work Submits to the Lordship of Christ

The third great theme has to do with the lordship of Christ. Paul's exhortation to take all our thoughts captive to Christ is most typically and narrowly applied to issues of human sexuality and relational interactions. But its remit—because he is Lord of all or not Lord at all—is all-encompassing. It extends to the thoughts engineers, marketers, financial planners, managers, and executives of a modern-day automotive company think about their product and its environmental claims. It includes the purchasing decisions we make regarding our latest iPhones. It applies to the notions managers and unions entertain one about the other. And so on. There is no territory Christ does not lay claim to. There is no human discipline he does not understand.

A brilliant young woman, a declared Christian engaged in genetic research, admitted that on Monday morning when she put on her lab coat and entered the laboratory she "left Jesus outside." Why would that be? Was she indeed not a Christian? We're not in a position to judge. More worryingly, might it suggest that Jesus actually prefers to stay outside the genetics lab because it's too complex inside with technical and ethical dilemmas? I think not, since in the beginning was the Word, and all things were made by that Word—including DNA—and it was that Word which became flesh and dwelt among us. It seems to me, therefore, that our sole remaining option for genuine spirituality on the missional frontlines of our world is to repent of our ungodly retreat and to embrace the lordship of Christ in every domain.

Closely related to the theme of the lordship of Christ is the forgiveness of Christ. The difficulty of getting down into the dirt and grime of the world's various professional spheres and the grey zones of ambiguity that continually harass the business person unless met with the antidote of a profoundly held and practiced "liturgy of forgiveness" will simply be too much for most. It will lead either to withdrawal—leaving the world in ignorance of Jesus as Lord—or to mindless carelessness and hardening of the conscience—leaving the world to wander in its cynicism, even while it yearns for an answer.

If this be true, then we must follow the injunction that in all we do, we do so with the purpose and in the way he would do that same thing, to bring glory to Christ. This theology is pastoral, prophetic, and apostolic.

Essentials of a Working Spirituality

The first essential is to embrace the incarnation of Christ. Specifically, devotionally, prayerfully to remember and internalize the fact that Jesus walks the Holy Land of your country, your marketplace, your professional sphere through you. You are his hands and feet. You are his mind and word. You are a channel of his redemption and restoration. His promise that we would do greater works than he did in Palestine is surely supported by his promise to be with us and evidenced by the work and witness of practising Christians in every profession, especially in places where it's still highly unlikely that the majority have ever seen a Christian engineer, teacher, or businessman.

The second essential is to live a life of integration recognizing that your work—paid or not—is your primary ministry. Take up your profession and the full armor of God and fight the good fight. You will be wounded, but he will bind your wounds, increasingly using your brothers and sisters in Christ who perceive what you perceive. Indeed, God gives us multiple spheres of ministry—in our families, neighborhoods, churches, etc.,—but for most of us who spend the majority of our time in the place of our professional vocation or business calling this will be the dominant point of sustained, transformational witness. If the gospel works there, it will work anywhere. If it doesn't, the implications are distressing in the extreme.

The third essential is to strive to be people of integrity—being who we say we are. Derived from the Latin adjective "integer" meaning whole or complete, integrity implies a spirituality and mission that are internally consistent and authentic. This is of particular significance for those who take their professional or business skills into cross-cultural mission settings, particularly where access to so-called "closed countries" is problematic for religious workers. When the driving force behind being deployed as a "professional" is access to a visa, but the day to day sustained engagement in that declared profession is not in evidence, integrity breaks down. The "professional" no longer exists. Achieving an inner sense of wholeness in which the practitioner bases their work on the fundamentals of a theology of work, on the pursuit of a living spirituality and upon a missional passion that all would become like them as a follower of Jesus is not an easy or automatic outcome. But it is the worthy goal.

The fourth essential is to live with intentionality. Mission is not accidental. Spirituality must be cultivated, albeit in a wide variety of ways. Our calling is to be and to make disciples. Our professions are not just a means to an end, but are a sacred stewardship in their own right and become a significant context in which our own and others' spiritual formation takes place, if we will spend the time to reflect upon them in that light. Our mission is not simply to coast or to spend our lives in the safe harbor of a career, being carried along by external forces over which we have no control and in which we take no interest. To live excellently in our profession—creatively, ethically—is costly. Similarly, to receive the praise of men for a noble business career but to do nothing in regards to making disciples of all nations is a life poorly invested.

> Mission is not accidental.

In conclusion, the remark has been attributed to Thomas Edison, famously known as the inventor of the electric light bulb and the founder of General Electric: "Opportunity is missed by most people because it is dressed in overalls and looks like work." To which we would add, so too is spirituality dressed!

References

Hardy, Lee. 1990. *The Fabric of this World*. Grand Rapids, MI: Eerdmans.

Kahn, Robert L. 1974. On the Meaning of Work. *Journal of Occupational Medicine*. 16(11):716-19.

Peter Shaukat was born and raised in Toronto, Canada. With a professional background in chemical engineering, education, and business, he is cofounder and CEO of a global investment fund which has invested in dozens of kingdom-focused companies across the Arab world and Asia. Having served in cross-cultural mission for over forty years on six continents, Peter has given leadership to a variety of for-profit and not-for-profit entities, including a satellite television media company in the Arab world, a maternal mortality reduction program in Africa, an engineering company in South Asia, and major international mission agencies.

Scripture: *Colossians 1:18 ("And he is the head of the body...")*

Resource: *The Economist* (London).

CHAPTER 20

Engaging the Arts in God's Mission

Katie Hoogerheide and Robin Harris

Reliving the pain, I (Katie) angled my brown pencil into the lower left corner of the paper in front of me. Adding an extra touch of pressure to create a dark blob representing the place of deepest sorrow, I lifted my pencil and thought about the traumatic moment I was processing—a brief exchange in middle school that had sunk its tentacles deep into my emotions and thought patterns, thereby impacting my understanding and experience of God as well. That time had been painful, but looking at the rest of the clean white paper spread before me, I realized with acute clarity that God had brought abundant life and beauty beyond the heartache. I had gone on to have full and rich high school and college years and now enjoyed adulthood with overall satisfaction. I began to recognize that the painful event of so long ago had actually been a decisive moment in my life, the moment in which God freed me from the inclination to conform to the expectations of peer pressure. I drew a butterfly rising from the dark spot—hope and life birthed in sorrow. Clearly evident in the drawing before me, God had been present, intentional in redeeming my pain for his purposes and his glory.

Arts give us another way of knowing. By accessing the raw, gutsy, visceral thoughts and feelings of our lives, arts depict with startling concreteness the complex intersection of our inner world with the context around us—past, present, and anticipated. Artistic representations have the capacity to reframe our world, providing fresh perspective and potentially rescuing our experiences from the chaotic and overwhelming to something we can understand with increased clarity. For me, a traumatic moment so many years ago, although historically and factually real, was now relegated to a brown blob, and only a blob, on a harmless piece of paper. In effect, this transaction had stripped a past event of its power to pervade my present life.

> Arts give us another way of knowing.

Arts and the Kingdom

In examining this capacity of the arts to project a world from within an artist, philosopher Nicholas Wolterstorff postulates an innate human desire for concreteness that creates a drive to engage the arts in order to be able to see and experience those things that otherwise must be held solely in the mind and heart.[1] This dynamic renders the arts a powerful form of communication in the hands of anyone whose desires focus primarily on the strengthening and expanding of God's kingdom. As Wolterstorff so elegantly states, "The kingdom of God is not escape from our earthly condition; it is that state in which men acknowledge God's sovereignty and carry out their creaturely responsibilities."[2] Therefore, "Since we are now called to be God's agents in his cause of renewal, of whose ultimate success he has assured us, art now gains new significance. Art can serve as instrument in our struggle to overcome the fallenness of our existence, while also, in the delight which it affords, anticipating the shalom which awaits us."[3]

Viewing the arts as an effective means toward spiritual renewal informs the potential incorporation of the arts in two equally important but also imminently practical dimensions for anyone engaged in mission. On a more introspective level, each mission worker approaches the field with a singular array of weaknesses, limitations, challenging circumstances, and other broken aspects of personal life. This very human practitioner will find that the arts offer an extraordinary capacity to bring inner thoughts and emotions to the surface, where these murky mysteries can fall under the Light and Truth of the Maker. The Creator thus employs the very creativity he placed in all humans, made in his image, to raise the depths of their spirits to a place of concreteness and processing toward increased clarity, whether people are actively creating or simply benefiting from others' creations. In this way the arts serve to strengthen mission workers' spirituality, their connection with the one on whom they depend—the one who has called them and the one who will empower them to persevere, running the course and bearing fruit in the kingdom.[4]

In addition to needing this personal connection with God, however, those with a heart for mission desire to bring all those they encounter into contact with the one who can touch them, save them, and heal them, thereby restoring them to completeness, the shalom of the kingdom. Toward this end, the mission worker can employ the arts to reach out to others, thereby aiding them in accessing the deep places of their hearts and minds.

> The mission worker can employ the arts to reach out to others, thereby aiding them in accessing the deep places of their hearts and minds.

With God's blessing, this approach can break down intellectual and emotional barriers, thus bringing the inner being to a place of increased openness to experiencing God's presence and internalizing his truth, love, and justice.

1   Nicholas Wolterstorff, *Art in Action* (Grand Rapids:, MI Eerdmans, 1980), 145.
2   Wolsterhoff, 84.
3   Wolsterhoff, 84. See Wolterstorff's more extensive treatment of the place of shalom and joy in the Christian's life and their interaction with the arts (78–83).
4   We identify with Sittser's understanding of spirituality as "What it means to seek, know and experience God." Gerald Sittser, *Water From a Deep Well: Christian Spirituality from Early Martyrs to Modern Missionaries* (Downers Grove, IL: InterVarsity Press, 2007), 18.

Motivated by this need all over the world, Brian Schrag (2013a) structures his practical guidebook for engaging the arts in mission, *Creating Local Arts Together: A Manual to Help Communities Reach Their Kingdom Goals*, around specific "goals that could indicate that the kingdom of God is thriving in a community."[5] The following three possible applications for using the arts toward the restoration of both individuals and communities stem loosely from his suggested six categories of valuable kingdom intentions.

Inner Healing

As already suggested by my (Katie's) story of finding emotional healing through processing a difficult event by means of drawing, artistic communication can affect our minds and hearts in a way that helps people find inner healing. From addressing a mission worker's past hurts, including field-based trauma, to coming alongside people's lives turned upside down by chronic illness, to attending to children's incomprehensible losses in war and displacement, the arts provide a powerful means to guide people in seeing and knowing their world differently. Used effectively, the arts allow such survivors to process, share, and express their pain in a way that reduces their suffering and begins to lead them toward a sense of inward resolution. The resulting increase in inner peace may also lead to benefits such as reconciliation with others, an enhanced enjoyment of rest and play, and a strengthened emotional solidity and stability, providing a healthy foundation for ministry to others.

In *Anatomy of the Soul*, medical doctor Curt Thompson provides insights into some of the neuroscience involved in emotionally and mentally challenging circumstances. He shows how the more logical, linear, analytical, cognitive-based, and past/future-oriented aspects of the brain may fail to integrate with the more holistic, intuitive, trust-based, emotion-generating, present-oriented dimensions of the brain system. This state of "disintegration," as Thompson names it, creates emotional and mental discomfort resulting in a wide range of feelings, from simply feeling unsettled to feeling traumatized. While Thompson focuses primarily on stories, especially the autobiographical narrative, as well as several other word and attention-based exercises for purposes of seeking healing, he also recommends engaging other arts to the same end:

> Nowhere does the power and grace of interpersonal neurobiology speak more eloquently than in and through the arts. For it is drama, painting, music, sculpture, poetry, and dance (to name but a few) that activate the resonance circuits of the right hemisphere and weave a deeply felt sense of meaning into

---

5   Brian Schrag, *Creating Local Arts Together: A Manual to Help Communities Reach Their Kingdom Goals*, ed. James R. Krabill (Pasadena, CA: William Carey Library, 2013a), 24.

the more logical tapestry of the left brain. As such, the arts have the potential to facilitate the integration of our minds.[6]

Bethany Haley Williams tapped into this potential for integration as she came alongside children in Africa who had experienced unspeakable trauma through war. As the children drew their sorrow and pain on one handkerchief, and their hopeful dreams on another, they produced "a tangible, color-filled storyboard to help them find the words that seem to leave us in times of deep trauma."[7] Sharing their stories of grief often unlocked emotions held back for years, and when the children wept into their handkerchiefs, "the stories drawn on their handkerchiefs with markers began to blend with their tears and became, in many ways, a rainbow of pain, hope, and healing on cloth."[8] This healing, in turn, seemed to open their hearts to peace, forgiveness, and the courage to move forward and help others.

> This healing, in turn, seemed to open their hearts to peace, forgiveness, and the courage to move forward and help others.

Williams' work lends additional support to Thompson's observation that "thoughtfully crafted art…bypasses our carefully designed mental roadblocks, often revealing pain and awakening us to wonder."[9]

Recognizing the importance of the arts as well as the vital necessity of approaching each people group according to its particular sociocultural context, the Trauma Healing Institute has developed a program, including the book *Healing the Wounds of Trauma: How the Church Can Help* and other facilitation materials, to guide cross-cultural workers in supporting others through trauma healing.[10] Their approach includes artistic activities such as "skit writing and performing, writing and sharing personal laments, composing and sharing songs, [and] art exercises."[11] In an effort to integrate use of the arts even more extensively, the Center for Excellence in World Arts at GIAL in Dallas, Texas (USA) currently offers a distinctive graduate level, faith-based, cross-culturally focused trauma healing course that incorporates the use of multiple artistic domains in trauma healing. Cathy Malchiodi's *Expressive Art Therapies* provides another valuable resource, presenting the history, theoretical grounding, methodologies, and applications,

---

6   Curt Thompson, *Anatomy of the Soul: Surprising Connections between Neuroscience and Spiritual Practices That can Transform Your Life and Relationships* (Carol Stream, IL: Tyndale, 2010), 260.

7   Bethany Haley Williams, *The Color of Grace: How One Woman's Brokenness Brought Healing and Hope to Child Survivors of War* (New York: Simon & Schuster, 2015), 104.

8   Haley Williams, 174.

9   Haley Williams, 261. For example, Haley Williams describes the children's coming to understand that God could turn evil to good and that they could serve as peace ambassadors for their country (171). She also describes various ways the children reached out to others, including performing reconciliation dramas in the places they had suffered, dreaming of becoming a psychiatric doctor in order to help others, or writing songs and directing a choir for orphaned children (235–239).

10   http://thi.americanbible.org/.

11   Patricia Miersma, "A Review of 'Healing the Wounds of Trauma,'" in *Sorrow and Blood: Christian Mission in Contexts of Suffering, Persecution, and Martyrdom*, William D. Taylor, Antonia van der Meer, and Reg Reimer, eds. (Pasadena, CA: William Carey, 2012), 460.

including case studies, of seven different types of art therapy as well as the integrated arts approach of expressive therapy.[12]

Identity

Matters of identity often surface as areas of the human heart which could benefit from expression through the arts for wholeness and healing. Cross-cultural workers may struggle with navigating the many changes required by incarnational living. Likewise, many whom they serve may suffer marginalization by a dominant society, whether this status stems from the use of a nondominant language and culture, adherence to a variant religious or political viewpoint, or espousal of a practice that effectively relegates them to the fringes of society. In these and similar cases, a solid sense of identity will prove essential to furthering inner healing. The arts provide additional avenues for this strengthening of identity.

> The arts provide additional avenues for this strengthening of identity.

Perhaps most significantly, engagement with the arts in highly visible venues and with the approval of the key gatekeepers for those contexts often has a profound impact on increasing status and recognition for the group or individual whose cultural arts are being celebrated. For example, playing a song from a minority group as part of the regular programming on a respected radio station, or showing a local dance on national television will automatically raise awareness and visibility as well as subtly assigning increased validity to the work in the eyes of both the dominant culture and the members of the minority group themselves. Arts facilitators can play a key role in finding local talent in marginalized communities, encouraging the production and refinement of their artistic creations, and assisting artists by strategizing with them appropriate ways to present their work in significant public spaces.[13]

Carrying this idea further, Michelle Petersen deftly applies three principles from the field of developing local languages to the expansion of local arts.[14] In addition to status development or the presentation of arts in important domains of use, she speaks of corpus development, the production of a large and varied body of artistic works that appeal to a wide range of intended audiences and are presented in a variety of forms, such as live performances or recordings on various media. Completely intertwined and interdependent with these first two aspects, acquisition development emphasizes the need to increase the number of participants in the arts by getting these new artistic works into the hands of the people, interesting them in engaging with the arts, and drawing them into participating in the further production of these art forms. The

---

12   Cathy Malchiodi, ed., *Expressive Therapies* (New York: The Guilford Press, 2005).
13   See Schrag, 2013a.
14   Petersen's work (forthcoming at www.artsandchristianfaith.org) is drawn from Robert Cooper, *Language Planning and Social Change* (Cambridge: Cambridge University Press, 1989). 99–163.

rise or fall of any of these three elements, status, corpus, or acquisition development, strengthens or weakens the overall presence of the arts in that particular context.

Undergirding all these considerations, however, remains the reality that lasting fulfillment and peace with one's identity ultimately rests in strong spiritual roots. Only people who know that the efficacy of the blood of Jesus Christ applies independently of culture or any other aspect of identity can even potentially enjoy in deep measure the stability and security of a grounded hope in God alone. Regretfully, living for years under the shadow of another prevailing culture may create the feeling that their own perspectives carry no value, and therefore their personal, culturally influenced expressions of worship will also not prove adequate for the Lord. As a result, an essential component of serving such hurting communities includes validating the culture by teaching about the glorious presence of diverse languages, arts, and other cultural elements within the kingdom of God.[15] Coming to understand the value and intrinsic beauty of their own arts can, in turn, give people the inner strength and stability to risk expressing themselves in this manner, thereby freeing them to worship God with heart, soul, and mind.

> Coming to understand the value and intrinsic beauty of their own arts can in turn give people the inner strength and stability to risk expressing themselves in this manner, thereby freeing them to worship God with heart, soul, and mind.

Integrating Scripture into Life

Without question, a relationship with God himself has proven throughout history and across cultures to be the bedrock of both inner healing and security in identity, and one of the most powerful means he has given to inform and strengthen this relationship is Scripture. The struggling cross-cultural worker can find comfort, insight, correction, and guidance in God's Word. As biblical principles become interwoven with one's character, they in turn inform one's prayers, conversations, decisions, and the ability to persevere with trust and patience in the mandate God has given every believer to serve others.

One of the core ways of serving others includes introducing them to the living God and getting his Word into a form they can understand and remember. Just as translating Scripture into the local language makes the Word more accessible to a given linguistic community, so uniting those concepts with local art forms brings the Word even closer to their daily experiences. As Roberta King states about music, artistic renditions serve as "an essential integrator of life," "a key means of communication," and a

---

15   For further reading, see (1) Adeney (2009), who references the beautiful image of a "kaleidoscope of cultures" (417, 422); (2) Farhadian (2007), who explores the implications for Christian worship as both a universal/global and culturally particular/local phenomenon; and (3) Cherry (2010), who notes that singing worship songs from other traditions enlarges our understanding of God: "All cultures have unique perspectives of God's story, none of which is complete on its own" (172).

"life-processor."[16] Speaking more broadly, Schrag observes that "artistic communication is embedded in culture and so touches many important aspects of a society"—for example, by heightening the impact of messages, communicating on emotional and experiential as well as cognitive levels, and increasing a sense of unity and identity within a community.[17]

The arts can serve as a powerful vehicle for integrating Scripture into any life pattern, whether individual or communal. Corporately, a body of believers may build up a body of Scripture-based songs, dances, or other artistic expressions for worshiping God. Whether used corporately or individually, artistic forms prove especially helpful for internalizing Scripture. To this day, I (Robin), although fluent in Russian, can remember word-for-word only those Russian Bible verses that my husband set to music. In fact, because people tend to recall artistic renditions of biblical words and principles far more easily than propositional statements, familiarity with a body of biblically-based, culturally appropriate works of art allows them to incorporate these concepts far more often into their daily lives. For example, they may draw from these creations in times of personal prayer, Bible study, meditation, or even in times of difficulty or conflict, such as solving an argument with a neighbor or making an important decision.

> The arts can serve as a powerful vehicle for integrating Scripture into any life pattern, whether individual or communal.

Hill and Hill provide several simple chapters for guiding people in learning to express Scripture through music, drama, and the visual arts.[18] Their chapter on music also includes material supporting the suitability of local instruments or song-writing styles, thus touching on a concern voiced around the world and across the ages—what makes for an appropriate contextualization of art forms? How far is too far? While much has been written on this topic, John Piper provides perhaps the most important overarching consideration when he observes that Jesus stripped the Old Testament concept of worship "of its last vestiges of localized and outward connotations."[19] As a result, as mission takes us out to the nations, "outward forms of worship will vary drastically, but the inner reality of treasuring Christ in spirit and truth is common ground."[20] Of course, the practical considerations in walking the fine line between syncretism and contextualization remain. Addressing this issue, Hiebert suggests pursuing "critical contextualization" through the careful exegesis of both the local culture and of Scripture,

---

16   Roberta King, "Musical bridges in Christian communication: Lessons for the church," in *Worship and Mission for the Global Church: An Ethnodoxology Handbook*, ed. James R. Krabill (Pasadena, CA: William Carey Library., 2013), 115.

17   Schrag, 2013a, 51.

18   Harriet Hill and Margaret Hill, *Translating the Bible into Action* (Carlisle: Piquant Editions, 2008), 199–228.

19   John Piper, "The Missional Impulse Toward Incarnational Worship in the New Testament," in *Worship and Mission for the Global Church: An Ethnodoxology Handbook*, ed. James R. Krabill (Pasadena, CA: William Carey Library., 2013), 99.

20   Piper, 102.

thus allowing for a deep understanding of both the local situation and the original intention of God's Word before attempting to apply the principles of the latter to the present circumstances.[21] Such a conscientious pursuit of truth will free a community to flourish under the nurturing, healing, and strengthening presence of the Scriptures as woven by the arts throughout the many aspects of their lives.

Arts and You

Beyond the areas of inner healing, identity, and the integration of Scripture, the arts have proven invaluable in a wide variety of other applications, including community development, children's education, adult literacy, and many other approaches to working toward social justice and spiritual freedom. Additional possibilities for the regular and effective application of the arts in the life of the cross-cultural worker, both personally and in outreach, are bound only by limitations of awareness or confidence. A growing number of faith-based training programs provide cross-cultural workers with guidance in discerning and responding to situations ripe for benefit from engaging a wide range of arts.[22] A network for arts in mission, the International Council of Ethnodoxologists (ICE), works with the Arts in Mission Task Force of the WEA Mission Commission to provide significant printed and media resources as well as both electronic and face-to-face opportunities to connect with others interested in facilitating artistic expression in cross-cultural contexts.[23]

The stories we've shared in this chapter, each of which happened in the daily contexts of our own lives, demonstrate how naturally the arts can serve the kingdom. No one need exert a large amount of effort—I (Robin) internalized my husband's Scripture songs simply by singing them and hearing them sung by the rest of the family. No one need have an exceptional amount of raw or developed talent—I (Katie) am no visual artist and often have people tell me they're glad I share my "folk art" so that others can see that "anyone at any level" can process life through art! No one need have an extraordinary measure of creativity—the imagination provided to each person by our Maker will prove more than adequate to connect one's inner and outer perceptions through the arts. Regardless of exertion, talent, or ingenuity, art simply provides another way of knowing, a way of seeing the world from another angle or connecting with others on another level. No matter how small an artistic influence may seem, be open. Encourage awareness and use of the arts in yourself and those around you. Arts

---

21   Paula Hiebert, *Anthropological Insights for Missionaries* (Grand Rapids:, MI Baker Book House Co., 1986), 171–91.

22   See, for example, All Nations Christian College (http://www.allnations.ac.uk/); Center for Excellence in World Arts at GIAL (www.gial.edu/cewa); and Payap University (http://ic.payap.ac.th/graduate/linguistics/certificate-ethnoarts.php). Programs focusing primarily on ethnomusicology can be found at Fuller Theological Seminary (www.fuller.edu), Liberty University (www.liberty.edu), Moody Bible Institute (www.moody.edu), and Oral Roberts University (www.oru.edu).

23   Explore ICE resources at http://www.worldofworship.org/.

have served, are serving, and will continue to serve the kingdom well. They can serve you in God's mission, too.

References

Adeney, Miriam. 2009. "Is God Colorblind or Colorful? The Gospel, Globalization and Ethnicity." In *Perspectives on the World Christian Movement: A Reader*, 415-422. Pasadena, CA: William Carey Library.

Cherry, Constance M. 2010. *The Worship Architect: A Blueprint for Designing Culturally Relevant and Biblically Faithful Services*. Grand Rapids, MI: Baker Academic.

Farhadian, Charles E. 2007. *Christian Worship Worldwide: Expanding Horizons, Deepening Practices*. Grand Rapids, MI: Eerdmans.

Haley Williams, Bethany. 2015. *The Color of Grace: How One Woman's Brokenness Brought Healing and Hope to Child Survivors of War*. New York: Simon and Schuster.

Hiebert, Paul G. 1986. *Anthropological Insights for Missionaries*. Grand Rapids, MI: Baker Book House Co.

Hill, Harriet, and Margaret Hill. 2008. *Translating the Bible into Action*. Carlisle: Piquant Editions.

Hill, Harriet, Margaret Hill, Richard Bagge, and Pat Miersma. 2013. *Healing the Wounds of Trauma: How the Church Can Help*. New York: American Bible Society.

King, Roberta R. 2013. "Musical Bridges in Christian Communication: Lessons for the Church." In *Worship and Mission for the Global Church: An Ethnodoxology Handbook*, 110–118. Ed. James R. Krabill, Frank Fortunato, Robin P. Harris, and Brian Schrag. Pasadena, CA: William Carey Library.

Malchiodi, Cathy A., Ed. 2005. *Expressive Therapies*. New York: The Guilford Press.

Miersma, Patricia. 2012. "A Review of 'Healing the Wounds of Trauma.'" In *Sorrow and Blood: Christian Mission in Contexts of Suffering, Persecution, and Martyrdom*, 459-461. Ed. William D. Taylor, Antonia van der Meer, and Reg Reimer. Pasadena, CA: William Carey.

Piper, John. 2013. "The Missional Impulse toward Incarnational Worship in the New Testament." In *Worship and Mission for the Global Church: An Ethnodoxology Handbook*, 96-102. Ed. James R. Krabill, Frank Fortunato, Robin P. Harris, and Brian Schrag. Pasadena, CA: William Carey Library.

Schrag, Brian. 2013a. *Creating Local Arts Together: A Manual to Help Communities Reach their Kingdom Goals.* Ed. James R. Krabill. Pasadena, CA: William Carey Library.

———. 2013b. "Ethnoartistic Cocreation in the Kingdom of God." In *Worship and Mission for the Global Church: An Ethnodoxology Handbook*, 49–56. Ed. James R. Krabill,.Frank Fortunato, Robin P. Harris, and Brian Schrag. Pasadena, CA: William Carey Library.

Sittser, Gerald L. 2007. *Water from a Deep Well: Christian Spirituality from Early Martyrs to Modern Missionaries.* Downers Grove, IL: InterVarsity Press.

Thompson, Curt. 2010. *Anatomy of the Soul: Surprising Connections between Neuroscience and Spiritual Practices That Can Transform Your Life and Relationships.* Carol Stream, IL: Tyndale House Publishers.

Wolterstorff, Nicholas. 1980. *Art in Action.* Grand Rapids, MI: Eerdmans.

Robin Harris, PhD, is president of the International Council of Ethnodoxologists (ICE) and director of the Center for Excellence in World Arts in Dallas, Texas. She served for decades in cross-cultural ministry—including ten years in northern Russia—and helped to launch the Arts in Mission Task Force of the WEA Mission Commission. Her publications include coediting the award-winning *Worship and Mission for the Global Church: An Ethnodoxology Handbook* (William Carey Library, 2013) and a forthcoming volume through University of Illinois Press, *Death and Rebirth in Siberia: The Olonkho Epic.*

Scripture: *2 Corinthians 12:9 ("But he said to me, "My grace is sufficient for you…")*

Resource: *Spiritual Friendship*, by Aelred of Rievaulx, ed. Marsha L. Dutton, trans. Lawrence C. Braceland (Collegeville, MN: Cistercian Publications, 2010).

Katie Hoogerheide serves as associate director of the Center for Excellence in World Arts in Dallas, Texas. The overseas experiences particularly influencing her work include time spent living, working, and traveling in Europe, the Middle East, and South Africa. In addition, she draws from work and graduate studies in organ performance, ethnoarts, linguistics, and pedagogy. A member of the International Council of Ethnodoxologists, she also works as associate editor for the Global Forum on Arts and Christian Faith.

Scripture: *Isaiah 41.10-20* ESV ("Fear not, for I am with you…")

Resource: *Always Enough: God's Miraculous Provision among the Poorest Children on Earth*, by Rolland and Heidi Baker (Grand Rapids, MI: Chosen Books, Baker Book House, 2003).

CHAPTER 21

Stages of Spiritual Development

A Story and a Model on the Journey

William D. Taylor

Starting with a Sober Word

"God is in the business of creating holy people and saints, but the path to these inevitably flows through deconstruction and suffering." My wife, Yvonne, spoke that to me while discussing the content of this chapter. As we believer-servants embrace the very long journey—at times it is frustratingly difficult and at times our hearts celebrate in high places, and at other times we make our way along, somehow. But we have to be willing to commit to the long-term, the pilgrimage route. Thankfully, this journey is made in community, and we trust this book introduces you to a new and global community of those who have walked through the stages of spiritual development.

A True Story

He's now a veteran cross-cultural servant, a scarred elder with the track record of a life-long journey of thoughtful yet passionate commitment and obedience to the mission of God—that complex yet clear assignment of the Trinitarian God for sending and transforming mission. He made mistakes, and I know most of them all too well, having observed his journey over a long pilgrimage.

But how did he start off in missions, and how did his journey work out with his gifted and equally committed younger wife?

He recalls being shaped by missionary songs and choruses (many of them deeply emotional, focusing on desperate and dark global needs and untold millions and what it would mean to be sent to labor unrewarded, to serve unpaid, unknown, unheralded, and more) and a focus on the second coming of Jesus. Missionary slogans were the bread and milk of local churches. The missionary messages focused on one aspect of the Great Commission—proclamation-evangelism. It was GO! Yet there were personal opportunities to make a difference. There were promised rewards here and There. He, and later she (for he married well) were willing to pay the price. As his artist wife said in her high school senior year, "I'll do anything, go anywhere, pay any price in obedience to my Lord. And if that means with you, then it's with you."

They met at a Christian camp, where he was on staff and she a camper (five years age difference!). A move from Chicago to Dallas allowed him to attend, coincidentally, her church; and soon he became the unpaid youth pastor. The rest happened naturally! Their early joint commitment was shaped by the joint reading of Elizabeth Elliot's writings of the Ecuadorian martyrs. To them, the journals of Jim Elliot were dreams that could be re-realized by successive generations if they were radical enough. And they thought they were, though nobody could ever reach the heights of the legendary Jim and Elizabeth Elliot. Significantly, his mentor for nearly fifty years was Elizabeth's own younger brother, David.

Their theological and mission training was substantive and extensive, laying a foundation to prepare them for a life of cross-cultural mission, evangelism, leadership development, and church planting. He had come from an evangelical, mission-minded family. A life in "missions" was normal to him. Not she. Her background was non-gospel, liturgical-sacramental … until her mother came to faith in a women's Bible study and she led the family to an evangelical Presbyterian church. He was an activist; she a classically-trained pianist with a very strong analytical left brain orientation and a love for the liberal arts.

They were sent out by their agency and their local church, fulfilled a year of intense language school, and started into the dreams. Having been shaped by three years on IVCF staff, he was at that time heavily influenced by strategic planning and measurable goal-setting. They soon found themselves thrust into the challenges of cross-cultural adaptation, each from a different perspective. His Spanish was fluent, but she learned with the caliber of a classical pianist engaging a new sonata—slowly and thoroughly. He plunged right in and soon was busy with ministry opportunities, even travel, while she struggled to learn the culture, gain language fluency, and begin the task of building cross-cultural relationships.

Once settled into their permanent assignment he found himself caught up right away in a myriad of ministries and responsibilities often requiring his absence from home while she struggled to find her own place and identity in the new subculture in which she found herself, along with being a new mother far from family and friends. He had assumed she would minister right alongside him in "his" ministry—following a pattern he had seen in the missionary subculture he had grown up in—but it soon became apparent that was not her calling. One night it all came to a head when she told him he needed to stop and have a serious conversation addressing these issues or she would be taking a break with the baby back home in Texas until he could pause long enough for them to talk things through. Needless to say, he canceled his appointments for a week and they talked. A lot! It required the hard work of honest communication and adaptation of expectations, but in time they learned how and where they would minister together in the same arena and where they would find their divergent roles and areas of interest. And he learned to slow down and trim back his over-committed schedule.

Meanwhile, other stuff began to hit the fan. Conflict and differences with field mission leaders began to emerge, in part due to toxic leadership, to the point that a crisis moment came. The dreams with which he had come to the field were slowly shattering and coming apart. One night it dawned on him that he was a live candidate for missionary attrition (though not a term used in those years). It was a time of breaking and crushing with confusion regarding the will of God that had seemed so clear at first. But late one night there was a knock on the door. God had sent an "angel" in the guise of a beloved mentor who surprisingly showed up from the States with a word of wisdom, encouragement, and clarity from the Lord.

Additionally, his wife's discernment of what was happening suggested that God was repositioning them and opening a door for them to recoup and to be renewed and built back up. That gracious door of relocation for a few years meant he was able to return under new leadership where he flourished and saw God's hand of blessing for many years. Attrition routed by the mercy of God!

And those were just the early years. There were many, many more testings and trials to come. Times when the Holy One seemed hidden and silent and life and circumstances made no sense. But over the years he learned that the living God was inviting him into a different kind of faith journey than he had heard about, one that would often be wrapped in mystery but ever drawing him steadily "deeper in and higher up" into the presence of God. That journey would not be straightforward and readily comprehensible with the path lit up by stadium lights. No, it would be a cross-shadowed journey with the Triune God-on-mission who dwells in inapproachable light.

> The story raises a set of key questions: First, what kind of spirituality drives-attracts-takes-motivates people into cross-cultural mission? Second, what happens to them in the middle—a long season—when "stuff happens?"

The story raises a set of key questions: First, what kind of spirituality drives-attracts-takes-motivates people into cross-cultural mission? Second, what happens to them in the middle—a long season—when "stuff happens?" They are shaken, broken, sifted, challenged to change or adjust their spirituality, to grow theologically. Perhaps they deny the reality of the hard stuff happening to them, and they ignore the fact that these experiences may actually be an invitation into a deeper walk with the living God. What if these realities turn out to be an invitation into brokenness and deconstruction that will prepare them for the next stages of our journey? Finally, what kind of spirituality carries us in the later laps of this journey?

What I propose to do with you, our reader, is engage with some reflections on the stages of spiritual development that we are invited into by the living Spirit of God. I will share personally while also pointing you to some other sources and resources. My starting caveat: I write this having just celebrated my seventy-sixth birthday, thankful to God for the gift of life and my journey with him. I also write with gratitude for my rich marriage of fifty years, for my wife and best friend, Yvonne, and for our relationship. All have powerfully shaped me.

A Transition

First, a word on "stages." I know this term sounds almost mechanical and artificial, as if life were predictable periods of time and the Holy Spirit locks us into an artificial template. The concept seems to imply less freedom for God to intervene supernaturally. I get that. But at my age now, having observed hundreds of other fellow-believers and having read much on the spiritual journey, I do sense the value of seeing our spiritual journey as flowing stages. Each story is unique, each person has a singular narrative of the journey into Christ, and yes, each of us is "surrounded by a great cloud of witnesses;" no, neither Jesus nor the apostles taught it this way. Yet, the language of stages does not have to be mechanical nor identically replicated in us all.

> Having observed hundreds of other fellow-believers and having read much on the spiritual journey, I do sense the value of seeing our spiritual journey as flowing stages.

Much of what Fowler describes makes sense to me. So follow along and see if these stages connect with your own pilgrimage of faith.[1]

James Fowler's *Stages of Faith*

I first heard of Fowler's model or paradigm (his seminal book was published in 1981) when Yvonne and I served in 1996 as visiting tutors at All Nations Christian College in the UK. Fowler's language and categories were new to me, but they resonated with many areas of my own journey. Clearly it does not fit all of us, and the model is just that: a model.

What I will do in this chapter is primarily use Fowler's own words (I limit this recitation to the core six stages and not his futuristic 7th one).[2] After each stage, I pose questions for your thoughtful reflection.

The well known American psychiatrist and best-selling writer Scott Peck has attempted to simplify Fowler in this fashion. We have no space to develop his thinking so I simply

---

1   James Fowler, *Stages of Faith: The Psychology of Human Development and the Quest for Meaning* (New York: Harper One, 1995 [1981]).

2   https://www.integrallife.com/node/40372

point you to the site: http://www.psychologycharts.com/james-fowler-stages-of-faith. html. A head's up: Peck's thinking may seem far-fetched for some of you and your own experience, but consider spiritual elements that take place in non-Christian contexts, whether secular or new age, or of other religious systems. Try to engage, and feel free to disagree with elements of the narrative as I do.

Stage 0: Primal Faith

If we start with infancy—the time from birth to two years—we have what we call undifferentiated faith. It's a time before language and conceptual thought are possible. The infant is forming a basic sense of trust, of being at home in the world. The infant is also forming what I call pre-images of God or the Holy, and of the kind of world we live in. On this foundation of basic trust or mistrust is built all that comes later in terms of faith. Future religious experience will either have to confirm or reground that basic trust. (Fowler)

- In what way does this stage reflect your own life or the life of family and friends?
- In what ways did this stage shape or prepare your later decision for mission service?

Stage 1: Intuitive-Projective Faith

The first stage we call intuitive/projective faith. It characterizes the child of two to six or seven. It's a changing, growing, and dynamic faith. It's marked by the rise of imagination. The child doesn't have the kind of logic that makes possible or necessary the questioning of perceptions or fantasies. Therefore the child's mind is "religiously pregnant," one might say. It is striking how many times in our interviews we find that experiences and images that occur and take form before the child is six have powerful and long-lasting effects on the life of faith, both positive and negative. (Fowler)

- In what way does this stage reflect your own life or the life of family and friends?
- In what ways did this stage shape or prepare your later decision for mission service?

Stage 2: Mythic-Literal Faith

The second stage we call mythic/literal faith. Here the child develops a way of dealing with the world and making meaning that now criticizes and evaluates the previous stage of imagination and fantasy. The gift of this stage is narrative. The child now can really form and re-tell powerful stories that grasp his or her experiences of meaning. There is a quality of literalness about this. The child is not yet ready to step outside the stories and reflect upon their meanings. The child takes symbols and myths at pretty much face value, though they may touch or move him or her at a deeper level. (Fowler)

- In what way does this stage reflect your own life or the life of family and friends?
- In what ways did this stage shape perhaps an early decision for mission service?

Stage 3: Synthetic-Conventional Faith

There is a third stage we call synthetic/conventional faith which typically has its rise beginning around age twelve or thirteen. It's marked by the beginning of what Piaget calls formal operational thinking. That simply means that we now can think about our own thinking. It's a time when a person is typically concerned about forming an identity and is deeply concerned about the evaluations and feedback from significant other people in his or her life. We call this a synthetic/conventional stage; synthetic, not in the sense that it's artificial, but in the sense that it's a pulling together of one's valued images and values, the pulling together of a sense of self or identity. (Fowler)

- In what way does this stage reflect your own life, or the life of family and friends?
- In what ways did this stage shape or modify your understanding of God, mission, and mission service?

Stage 4: Individuative-Reflective Faith

Stage Four, for those who develop it, is a time in which the person is pushed out of, or steps out of, the circle of interpersonal relationships that have sustained his life to that point. Now comes the burden of reflecting upon the self as separate from the groups and the shared world that defines one's life. I sometimes quote Santayana who said that we don't know who discovered water but we know it wasn't fish. The person in Stage Three is like the fish sustained by the water. To enter Stage Four means to spring out of the fish tank and to begin to reflect upon the water. Many people don't complete this transition but get caught between three and four. The transition to Stage Four can begin as early as seventeen, but it's usually not completed until the mid-twenties, and often doesn't even begin until around twenty. It comes most naturally in young adulthood. Some people, however, don't make the transition until their late thirties. It becomes a more traumatic thing then, because they have already built an adult life. Their relationships have to be reworked in light of the stage change. (Fowler)

- In what way does this stage reflect your own life or the life of family and friends?
- At what point in your journey did you begin to reflect, and perhaps to doubt? What did you do with your doubts?

Stage 5: Conjunctive Faith

Sometime around thirty-five or forty or beyond some people undergo a change to what we call conjunctive faith, which is a kind of midlife way of being in faith. What Stage Four works so hard to get clear and clean in terms of boundaries and identity, Stage Five makes more permeable and more porous. As one moves into Stage Five one begins to recognize that the conscious self is not all there is of me. I have an unconscious. Much of my behavior and response to things is shaped by dimensions of self that I'm not fully aware of. There is a deepened readiness for a relationship to God that includes God's mystery and unavailability and strangeness as well as God's closeness and clarity. (Fowler)

- In what way does this stage reflect your own life or the life of family and friends?
- In the second part of this discussion we will deal with wounding and the Wall. How does this stage address that?

Stage 6: Universalizing Faith

Some few persons we find move into Stage Six, which we call universalizing faith. In a sense I think we can describe this stage as one in which persons begin radically to live as though what Christians and Jews call the "kingdom of God" were already a fact. I don't want to confine it to Christian and Jewish images of the kingdom. It's more than that. I'm saying these people experience a shift from the self as the center of experience. Now their center becomes a participation in God or ultimate reality. There's a reversal of figure and ground. They're at home with what I call a commonwealth of being. (Fowler)

- In what way does this stage reflect your own life or the life of family and friends?
- Do you sense that in some ways you have been able to move into this stage? Why yes or no?

Pause to Reflect

We draw to a partial conclusion the first discussion of this journey of the stages. My desire is that you will have engaged with Fowler's thinking while thoughtfully making connections to your own journey or that of family, friends, and colleagues. We next move to study two evangelical models and then bring these observations to an end.

Reference

Fowler, James. [1981] 1995. *Stages of Faith: The Psychology of Human Development and the Quest for Meaning.* New York: Harper One.

William D. Taylor was born and raised in Latin America (dual nationality—Costa Rica and USA). His studies include Dip (Moody Bible Institute), BA (University of North Texas), ThM (Dallas Theological Seminary); PhD (University of Texas—Austin). He has served in global mission for fifty years in diverse capacities. He lived in Latin America for thirty years, including seventeen at CAM International at Seminario Teológico Centroamericano. From 1986–2006 he was Executive Director of the Mission Commission of World Evangelical Alliance, now MC Senior Mentor. As president of TaylorGlobalConsult (2011), Bill now invests his life in selective mentoring-apprenticing-life coaching, consulting, writing, teaching and speaking—local and global. He is married to Yvonne, a native Texan, and together they have three Guatemala-born children and seven grandchildren.

Scripture: *Luke 4: 14–21 ("Then Jesus returned to Galilee, filled with the Holy Spirit's power...")* and *2 Corinthians 1:3–7 (NLT) ("All praise to God...")*

Resource: *Water from a Deep Well: Christian Spirituality from Early Martyrs to Modern Missionaries*, by Gerald L. Sittser (Downers Grove, IL: InterVarsity Press, 2007).

CHAPTER 22

Stages of Spiritual Development

Models and Applications for the Journey

William D. Taylor

We continue our conversation to examine two helpful evangelical models that frame the spiritual journey as stages. Remember that these stages are generalizations. Nobody fits all of them with precision. We are human, after all, and not robots. So we may find ourselves looping back and forth in order to make sense of our lives.

Our First Evangelical Model of Faith-Life Development:

Robert Hicks' *Six Stages of Manhood*

In late 1990 a wise Austin, TX friend gave me the book *The Masculine Journey: Understanding the Six Stages of Manhood* by Robert Hicks at a critical moment in my life.[1] My wife and I were facing a complex and protracted transition beginning with a move in 1985 from Latin America to Trinity Evangelical Divinity School for one year, then to four years in Arkansas, and finally Austin, Texas in mid-1990. I was in the middle of a paralyzing desert season, and Yvonne was simultaneously battling through the "dark night of the soul." Going full steam in my work with the WEA Mission Commission, we were witnessing the development of a unique community of global leaders in Christian mission. On the exterior, I was at the top of my game. But my inner life was drying up; I was on life support, my relationship with God was not working. Because of the move from Latin America we had to start all over again with a new church, new community, new friends, new culture, new geography, new everything. I

---

1   Robert Hicks, *The Masculine Journey: Understanding the Six Stages of Manhood* (Carol Stream, IL: Navpress, 1993).

continued to work out of my home office. The worst was that I could not help Yvonne get out of her "depression."

The book arrived just in time and made sense of my own experience. I was the wounded warrior of Stage Four. I recommend this model for our male readers, knowing it has brought help and clarity to many others. A word to my sisters, married or not, this may help you understand the men in your own lives.

Stage 1: Creational Male, Adam, the Noble Savage

This stage returns us to Genesis 1–2 and the creation of man, "Adam," with woman coming later as "Adamah" (though this generative term will apply to both male and female). Hicks says, "The word depicts mankind at the most base level of flesh, blood, and dirt. It suggests what we really are as humans and men."[2] The four stage markers are: we are created for relationship, with dignity, with creational mortality, and with creational savagery in soul, will, heart, body. "The savagery of the soul should not surprise us as men. Though we are made in God's image and are creational—that is, possessing great capabilities for good—we are also free to pursue unholy courses and to become the most evil of men."[3] Only the living God can save us from ourselves.

Stage 2: Phallic (Sexual) Male, Zakar, the Mysterious Taskmaster

This second Hebrew word marking the masculine journey, zakar, undeniably identifies the male by his sexual physiology. "In other words, the Scriptures root male identity and sexuality firmly in anatomy, rather than in psychology or sociology."[4] Later, "The entirety of the Scriptures reflect the simple twofold division of the entire human and animal kingdom into male (zakar) and female (neqevah)."[5]

Its potential is for great good and great evil; we need only ponder history with uncontrolled male sexuality. But it is equally an invitation to worship as fully male in every way, not androgynous nor emasculated. Perhaps for this reason Jewish male babies were to be circumcised, a constant visual and physical reminder of that covenant relationship with Jehovah. The male is male, for good, procreation, and love as well as for dangerous fantasy, violence, and evil.

---

2   Hicks, 32.
3   Hicks, 41.
4   Hicks, 48.
5   Hicks, 49.

Stage 3: The Warrior, Gibbor, the Glorious Hero

> Of the various Hebrew words associated with the concept of maleness, the word for warrior, gibbor, is often used and most striking. It stands unapologetically through the biblical text as one of the primary stages on the male journey.[6]

Insightfully and significantly, much literature and film, whether "true" narrative, fantasy, or computer generated graphic, presents the warrior male. Yes, history, and now film, are marked with women warriors also.

Significantly, many families are returning to rites of passage for our teenage boys. Last year I was honored to participate in one of these celebrations for my oldest grandson, Brendan Warner. We had six grown men, models, friends, and family as the "tested warriors" and mentors. Each one spoke words of manly wisdom and blessing. One of Brendan's tasks was to hunt and shoot a buck (an elderly one that needed to be culled) in the hunter-provider mold. He was becoming a man.

In my own life and ministry I clearly identify my warrior years primarily in the early season in Guatemala. I gave it my all; I plunged into cross-cultural surviving and thriving, into preaching, teaching, mastering Spanish, and discipling with all my creativity, heart, and strength. I was a warrior—strong, energetic, visionary, eager to accomplish much for God and his kingdom. As a young visionary, I found myself in conflict with some of the older missionaries who were sometimes threatened or simply didn't like change. Needless to say, it was a learning experience for me. Along the way I became a wounded warrior and paid a price in those first eighteen years of my public ministry. And thus we transition to the next season.

Stage 4: The Wounded Male, Enosh, the Painful Incongruency

By this stage the warrior has hit "the Wall." He has fought battles for God and mission, for family and integrity, for change and progress, for good and for self. This is distinct from the wounds we carry from early childhood through young manhood, wounds from personal brokenness, broken family systems, or inflicted on us by others.

> Wounding is part of creation, even essential in the making of the adult.

The enosh concept here is critical. Wounding is part of creation, even essential in the making of the adult. The prophetic voices foretold that our Messiah himself would be wounded, then executed. Plants are pruned back to produce better fruit.

> This Hebrew expression for the word man describes his mortality, calamity, frailty, and fears… It is most often used in the book of Job, which records the

---

6   Hicks, 76.

extreme violence and emotional wounding that the loss of life, property, health, and wealth did to one undeserving of such.[7]

In my striving in Guatemala I brought some of the wounds on myself, but others were inflicted on me. After leaving Latin America, other wounds came as a result of the wrenching transition from a beloved Guatemala to a foreign culture which I did not love, i.e., the USA.

By 1990, in Austin, in the middle of my wounding and desert years and Yvonne's prolonged "dark night of the soul," I found a Christian counselor who himself was a third culture person and understood some of the issues of our journey. Yvonne and I went to him so he could help her in her anguish. But to my astonishment, he first turned on me, having the audacity to think that I needed help! This was his penetrating question: "Bill, are you pleased with the fact that God has brought you to the USA?" My retort was, "No, of course not." Then he plunged the sword, "Ah, in other words, God made a mistake in bringing you to the USA." Checkmated, I was devastated. Then he finished me off, "If you are not able to thank God that he brought you to the USA, he will not be able to release you into the fullness of your future."

That watershed conversation led to an extended season of healing of internal wounds dating far back to the way I was parented—loving but passive, present but distant—as well as the woundings of life and ministry.

The wounded season had left me in grief—bleeding, uncertain, weakened, and at times desperate. Ironically, Yvonne, in the depths of her darkness, was able to speak deep truth to me. Her words one day were hard. "Bill, you are very gifted (I agreed!), but you need to go deeper into God. Gifting and service to God are good, but God is calling you to the next level of intimacy with him."

> Our response to the wounding season determines whether we can engage the next stage.

Our response to the wounding season determines whether we can engage the next stage. Not everyone chooses to do so wisely, willing to pay the price. And they remain stuck here.

Stage 5: The Mature Man, 'Ish, the Reborn Ruler

Hicks: "Maturity springs only from adversity." How painfully true. His book was given to me in the memorable transition out of woundedness into what I wanted above all else for it to be, leading to maturity, and even beyond that.

> The usage of 'ish speaks not only of man but also of God, especially where God is portrayed as the husband of his people (Hosea). However, the most important element about 'ish is its apparent reference to the adult male. 'Ish is always in contrast to the Hebrew terms yeled (young man), na'ar (youth), and

7   Hicks, 103.

zaqen (old man)… In other words, 'ish is the mature man, the man who has been resurrected from the wounds of life and has a new perspective on the meaning of life and manhood because of that pain. This man knows who he is and is known for his attributes.[8]

Hicks richly develops this theme. This stage generally marks the man who out of wounding, leads with gifting and compassion, with skill and sensitivity. I know of too many men whose leadership was marked by their unresolved wounds or toxic qualities. They are gifted but destructive leaders. The mature man is different; for God has tested, purified, remade, and relaunched the mature man into a new kind of servanthood and possible leadership.

This stage can and should mark the man until his death, though there is one more intriguing season of our lives.

Stage 6: The Sage, Zaqen, the Fulfilled Man

Zaqen is also found in close proximity with its synonym seb, which means "to be gray or old." Thus, Samuel is "old and gray" (1 Sam 12:2) as is Abraham (Gen 15:15). Throughout the Old Testament the zaqen also represents various social groups… This elder then is far removed from our modern concepts of the retired, uninvolved senior citizen. Instead, his focus is on the social community to which he belongs, either holding office or representing the various groups he values.[9]

It's not realistic that all mature men will transition into sage. It is best that we not call ourselves that unless others have truly named us. But perhaps there is a new kind of elder calling, gifting, investment in life, ministry, and above all, people—family, grandchildren, church community, broader outreach into global mission and servanthood.

In societies that worship at the altar of youth, the Bible invites the people of God to value the gray-headed elders, some of whom are to become sages. I find myself in the latter laps of my race and have been challenged to do two things: divest myself of titles and positions and invest wisdom into the younger. God has called me to do this with my grandchildren as well as to mentor younger believers in the marketplace and ministry.

> In societies that worship at the altar of youth, the Bible invites the people of God to value the gray-headed elders, some of whom are to become sages.

I want to be a zaqen, living a unique kind of fulfillment as I come to the foothills of that range that I shall not cross.

---

8   Hicks, 123–24.
9   Hicks, 151–52.

Our Second Evangelical Model of Faith-Life Development:

Hagberg and Guelich's *The Critical Journey: Stages in the Life of Faith*

This thoughtful work emerges out of the crucible of wounding and maturity of its writers. It is not a new book (1995, 2004) and that is one reason I appreciate it. It is a tested template. *The Critical Journey* exclusively focuses on the seasons of our faith life. We find parallels in Fowler's "Stages of Faith" development, but now we have a purely Christian discussion. As we have stated earlier, the literature on Christian spirituality as applied to mission in general and especially cross-cultural mission is scarce; therefore we must make the applications. Hagberg and Guelich "have chosen to speak of spirituality ultimately as the way in which we live out our response to God. Unless we find this personal, transformational meaning in its fullest sense, the struggle for wholeness will remain unresolved."[10]

Thankfully, we speak of the journey where both process and destination have equal value. "Journey" is our prime metaphor for this book on spirituality and mission: "A long trip with no strict timetable, ...traveling companions" amongst other descriptors.[11] They help us with clarifying diagrams and connective transitions between chapters.

> Thankfully, we speak of the journey where both process and destination have equal value.

The authors' graphic puts "Stages of Faith" in a central circle, and radiating from it the six stages: 1) recognition of God; 2) life of discipleship; 3) productive life; 4) journey inward; [the Wall]; 5) journey outward, 6) life of love. The Wall is not a stage but a reality that gobsmacks (British slang for "astonishes") us all. It parallels Hick's "season of wounding," but in this case the Wall emerges in different places along the journey. In a sense we never leave it permanently.

Stage 1: The Recognition of God

(This) is where we all begin the journey of faith. We may experience it during early childhood or as adults who come for the first time to recognize the reality of the presence of Someone who stands behind it all. Regardless of our age, however, it seems true that most begin the journey in a childlike way. We come to it with an innocence, a freshness, that is seldom ever again as vivid or vital.[12]

10   Janet Hagberg and Robert A. Guelich, *The Critical Journey: Stages in the Life of Faith* (Salem, WI: Sheffield Publishing Company; [1995] 2004), 3.
11   Hagberg and Guelich, 5.
12   Hagberg and Guelich, 33.

Refreshingly, they place this stage either at different places in the journey, but always at the intersection of that first-flush relationship with God in Christ. This season is marked by a sense of awe and need, by a natural awareness, greater meaning in life and innocence.

One of their ongoing motifs is the "cage," of getting stuck in any of the stages. The cage can be used of God, but the believer must work out of the cage in order to mature. They provide markers for what life looks like when caged at each stage.

However, even if this stage takes place in adulthood, it is never wise to release new believers into longer-term cross-cultural ministry. What works best here is the first of a series of shorter-term service projects, where life and faith are tested, and most importantly, where the person matures as a believer in Jesus.

Stage 2: The Life of Discipleship

> This stage is best characterized as a time of learning and belonging... Stage 2 frees us to explore, to learn, to quest, to absorb, to put into place our set of beliefs or faith principles. In this stage we learn the most about God as perceived by others we respect and trust. We are apprentices.[13]

Here we separate meaning from belonging, we find answers in a cause or a leader and we establish a sense of rightness and security.

But we can also find ourselves caged in this stage: we can become rigid in our system, it's us against them and worse. In the transition into Stage 3 we begin to individuate from the crowd, to take risks, to discover our uniqueness and gifting as contributors, and we seek responsibility.

Stage 3: The Productive Life

> (This season) is best described as the "doing" stage. It is the period of time when we most consciously find ourselves working for God. In fact, our faith is characterized as just that, working for God or being in God's service. Having gone through the apprenticeship period... we are ready to do it on our own.... Having been given to and having received so much from our association with others, the time of reciprocity has come. It is now our turn to give in return.[14]

This is when many of us move towards longer-term cross-cultural work. We have been blessed and want to be a blessing. We have been challenged regarding global needs, spiritual and physical, from gospel transformation to justice issues, to the least-reached rural peoples or the inner cities. We have gone to student and young adult global mission conferences. We have taken courses like the Perspectives on the World

---

13 Hagberg and Guelich, 53.
14 Hagberg and Guelich, 73.

Christian Movement. Now it is time to get on with it, do our basic training for mission, get basic testing for responsibility, servanthood, and character. We have reached some spiritual goals. It's time!

All these are good, but the cage can trap us if we are excessively zealous. We can become self-centered and exhausted and primarily focused on outward performance without development of the inward life.

But obviously this is a season linked to the full journey and we begin the transition to the next step as we seek wisdom and guidance from mature leaders and mentors.

Stage 4: The Journey Inward

(This stage) is aptly described by its title, for it is a deep and very personal inward journey. It almost always comes as an unsettling experience yet results in healing for those who continue through it. Until now, our journey has had an external dimension to it. Our life of faith was more visible, more outwardly oriented, even though things certainly were happening inside us. But the focus fell more on the outside, the community of faith, nature, leadership, the display and use of the Spirit's gifts, belonging, and productivity.[15]

This stage may be marked by a destabilizing life or faith crisis; we encounter too many uncertainties on the journey. While we pursue God with integrity, it does not get easier to do so, for God slips out of the boxes. The theological and spiritual assumptions that drove us begin to falter at the edges and may implode in the core. We question our faith, period!

> While we pursue God with integrity, it does not get easier to do so, for God slips out of the boxes.

The cages here include perpetual questions and the absence of movement to resolutions, or not seeking wisdom and prayer from the mature ones. We self-immobilize, and perhaps we begin to discern our false self. Here we grapple with a new understanding of God, of the Holy Spirit, of Jesus the Christ.

It is perhaps in this stage that we come close to, or smack into the Wall. And this is the most critical season—never short nor easy in our journey.

Stage 4 Continued: The Wall

Aptly termed, the Wall describes the Spirit's invitation to deconstruction of the false self into the true self, as developed in Yvonne Taylor's chapter. The Wall also reminds us of the wounded warrior and the response to the wounding that determines the rest of the journey.

---

15   Hagberg and Guelich, 93.

We cannot go around, under, or over the Wall; if we will move forward we must go through the Wall. We must not attempt to go through the Wall by ourselves; it takes wise colleagues, family, friends, insightful shepherds, and counselors; it takes a community that understands the Wall and walks beside those breaking through it. It leads to healing of systemic family and personal wounds. The healing may come supernaturally quick, though in most cases it will be gradual but sure.

In my own experience when people hit the Wall or are invited into the deconstruction of the false self there is often denial or resistance—institutional or personal. Some drive the piles deeper into their own theology and spirituality. But others are nurtured by different streams and grow in new theological and spirituality understandings. Non-charismatics move into a stronger life of the Spirit; some become empowered evangelicals—that midpoint between cessationism of the gifts and the full charismatic stance. Some find it necessary to move out of their institutional community or mission agency or church. This means they must be willing to ask God for new friends and community, for some of the previous community cannot walk the new journey with them. But if they search God will open a new community of faith and spirituality, of being and doing church.

The Wall hits some through illness, perhaps permanently changing their capacity to work, and for others it a terminal disease. Having witnessed my own parents slip into dementia and Alzheimers, I ask myself, "Where is God in this picture? What is really happening inside this person I know and love?" It's not easy.

In other cases, the attack is openly demonic and this requires a very specific and gifted set of colleagues and deliverance to help the person walk through the Wall.

A final thought on the Wall. This testing brings out the best or the worst in us. When God invites us into the pathway of brokenness, he will not force it upon us, but rather gives us a choice. If we say "no," he might not remove his general blessing, but we will not be what we could have been in his original purpose of growth through suffering and facing the Wall. Only when we submit in humility to the deconstruction and reconstruction will we be the woman or man God wants us to be.

> Only when we submit in humility to the deconstruction and reconstruction will we be the woman or man God wants us to be.

Stage 5: The Journey Outward

We cannot enter this season without having gone through the Wall and the season has its particular cages. But this stage:

> Is the next step after rediscovering God and accepting love. Now we surrender to God's will to fully direct our lives, but with our eyes wide open, aware but unafraid of the consequences. Once parts of the deep, excruciating inward journey have been experienced, the natural outcome is to venture outside of

one's self-centeredness and back into the active world with a new sense of fulfillment.[16]

Here we encounter a new sense of God's acceptance, a new sense of calling/vocation and ministry, our focus is on others and hopefully we are marked by a new sense of stillness of the inner person. The cages are there, and tricky as ever, for we can lose focus or appear to be out of touch with reality and practical life. Yet we want to move on, not striving but seeing God in all of our life. We are engaging the deeper sense of God's calling/vocation in our lives, regardless of where he places us.

Stage 6: The Life of Love

At this stage we reflect God to others in the world more clearly and consistently than we ever thought possible. We let our lights shine in such a way that God is given the credit and the thanks. In many ways, at this stage we represent an extension of Stage 5. Yet the characteristics of Stage 5 are more complete, just as Stage 3 represents a more confident, fuller version of Stage 2.[17]

I find this stage similar to Hicks' "mature" category. It could be relatively easy to boast about having arrived at this stage, and that's a deadly cage. However, we want to live in total obedience to the Triune God on mission; we want to be orthodox Christians; we want to be marked by wisdom because of wounding and perceptive understanding; we want to be truly compassionate towards others while not losing our sense of justice; we surely want to live a correctly-detached life. And yes, this stage does have its cages, for we can neglect ourselves and apparently waste our lives.

> We must remain open to the ongoing work of the Spirit, giving constant room for growth and change, searching always for the "deeper-in" path.

One cage to the life of love is the temptation to become jaded, pessimistic, overly critical, passive, resorting to reductionisms or even cynicism. Rather, we must remain open to the ongoing work of the Spirit, giving constant room for growth and change, searching always for the "deeper-in" path.

The rest of this insightful book focuses on the reality and need of us living all 6 stages of the spiritual journey, including the Wall. In my own experience the Wall has shown up a number of times, and the older I get the less easy it is to go through. We will loop back to enjoy, or struggle with, aspects of earlier stages as we cycle and circle through them in singular ways. The book concludes with very helpful exercises as we pilgrimage through our journey.

---

16 Hagberg and Guelich, 133.
17 Hagberg and Guelich, 152.

Drawing the Chapter to a Close

I return to some of my thoughts on the introduction to this book and a simple tristage model of the journey.

First, what kind of spirituality gets us into cross-cultural ministry? We remember those experiences, theologies, seminars, dramas, songs, sermons, courses, short-term trips, shorter study courses, or major mission events. For others it was simply a quiet but life-changing encounter with the God on mission. Yet for others, it was a marriage to a particular person who definitely was headed into mission.

Second, what happens sooner or later when "stuff happens," when our most fundamental beliefs and passions are tested, when we are cut to the bone, when we bleed in silence (or in public), when God ever so clearly does not conform to what we expected? In other words, when we have "hit the proverbial Wall."

How shall we then live and what shall we do? Will we dig deeper into our theology and spirituality? Will we seek God-resources in other Christian streams and reflections on spirituality? Might some be tempted to abandon faith or go dormant and passive? Will we deny or stuff our crisis? Will we fluctuate from one spirituality or theological extreme to another?

How we respond to God reshaping us for the journey is crucial, for this will be the longest season of these three.

How we respond to God reshaping us for the journey is crucial, for this will be the longest season of these three.

Third, for those of us who are in the latter laps of our journey, what spirituality will carry us to the very end of life? How will we resolve the pain of unanswered prayer, of unfulfilled labor, of broken family, of children whose faith crisis leads them far from Christ? How do we grapple with the relatively "unfair" Christian experience, where some families seem to consistently get the happy cards of life and others are dealt the tough ones? When I begin to fail physically or mentally will I hold fast to the essentials of the Christian faith?

The overarching themes of this book reveal that Christian spirituality in the context of world mission is a challenge, never neat. Due to its inherent worldview and cultural, linguistic, geographic, and different religious dimensions, mission service is an incredibly complex reality, a journey both personal and communal. We will never "arrive" spiritually until we "permanently change our address" and go home.

Do you remember the third-person narrative at the start of this discussion of the stages? Yes, it revealed my own personal faith narrative for those years. As we finish editorial work on this manuscript, I have reached my seventy-sixth year. My battles have to do with the latter laps of the faith marathon. I am still on the journey and want to walk it with patience and courage, in faith, and in community. I want to finish well.

I conclude with the final words of Henri Nouwen in his 1990, pregnant small book, *In the Name of Jesus*. His challenge to Christian leadership is singular and has significantly impacted my own life and spiritual pilgrimage.

> I leave you with the image of the leader with outstretched hands, who chooses a life of downward mobility. It is the image of the praying leader, the vulnerable leader, and the trusting leader. May that image fill your hearts with hope, courage, and confidence as you anticipate the next century.[18]

References

Hagberg, Janet and Robert A. Guelich. [1995] 2004. *The Critical Journey: Stages in the Life of Faith*. Salem, WI: Sheffield Publishing Company.

Hicks, Robert. 1993. *The Masculine Journey: Understanding the Six Stages of Manhood*. Carol Stream, IL: Navpress.

Nouwen, Henri. 1992. *In the Name of Jesus*. New York: The Crossroad Publishing Company.

William D. Taylor was born and raised in Latin America (dual nationality—Costa Rica and USA). His studies include Dip (Moody Bible Institute), BA (University of North Texas), ThM (Dallas Theological Seminary); PhD (University of Texas—Austin). He has served in global mission for fifty years in diverse capacities. He lived in Latin America for thirty years, including seventeen at CAM International at Seminario Teológico Centroamericano. From 1986–2006 he was Executive Director of the Mission Commission of World Evangelical Alliance, now MC Senior Mentor. As president of TaylorGlobalConsult (2011), Bill now invests his life in selective mentoring-apprenticing-life coaching, consulting, writing, teaching and speaking—local and global. He is married to Yvonne, a native Texan, and together they have three Guatemala-born children and seven grandchildren.

Scripture: *Luke 4: 14–21 ("Then Jesus returned to Galilee, filled with the Holy Spirit's power...") and 2 Corinthians 1:3–7 (NLT) ("All praise to God...")*

Resource: *Water from a Deep Well: Christian Spirituality from Early Martyrs to Modern Missionaries*, by Gerald L. Sittser (Downers Grove, IL: InterVarsity Press, 2007).

---

18   Henri Nouwen, *In the Name of Jesus* (New York: The Crossroad Publishing Company, 1992), 173.

Along the Journey

Discerning Organizational Spiritualities

Issues and Case Studies

CHAPTER 23

Organizational Spirituality

Paul Bendor-Samuel

Growing Awareness

Whether in the world of business, the church, or mission agencies, there is a growing interest in organizational spirituality. The business world is driven by the pragmatic question, "Does paying attention to organizational spirituality make a difference to organizational performance and profits?" Eve Poole, in a literature review, suggests a tentative "yes."[1] Spirituality is understood by Poole as a "meaning-making" construct that gives people a sense of purpose. It includes "meaning, wholeness, integrity, interconnectedness, creativity, ethics and transformation."[2] Spirituality is important for building the kind of organizational environment that brings the best out of the workforce.

However inadequate this definition of spirituality might be and however limited the motivation for exploring it, we genuinely affirm the importance of these elements. If some in the business world are tentatively bringing business to spirituality, as Christians we should humbly confess our own slowness in bring spirituality to business. How encouraging, then, to see a movement in many parts of the global church to recognize the lordship of Christ in the world of work. Recovering a biblical understanding of work and marketplace ministry, including business as mission, are aspects of a broad interest in organizational spirituality in the church.

There is more to organizational spirituality than recovering a biblical worldview of work. The word "organization" is commonly understood to simply mean "a group of people who work together in an organized way for a shared purpose" (*Cambridge English Online Dictionary*). However, our understanding of organizational dynamics

---

1   Eve Poole, "Organizational Spirituality—A Literature Review," *Journal of Business Ethics* (2009), 577–588.
2   Eve Poole, "Organizational Spirituality—Away with the Fairies?" *The Ashridge Journal* (Autumn 2006), 32.

is largely shaped by a business model or institutions like schools and hospitals. While we affirm that their primary identity lies elsewhere, churches and mission agencies function as organizations. Leaders in church and mission agencies must wrestle with the degree to which their organizational life reflects biblical spiritualties. This reflection is urgently needed. Some are so disillusioned by their perception of mission agencies that they look for alternatives they believe are radically different.[3]

Many in cross-cultural mission recognize the extent to which we have adopted a secular organizational worldview, with its self-confident dependence on strategies, statistics and visible measures of success: so-called "mission-by-management."[4] Our hearts cry out for a better way. We recognize the instinctive individualism that characterizes so much mission practice, both personal and organizational. We long for authentic community and collaboration. Whatever the organizational arrangements, this is what lies at the heart of Christian organizational spirituality.

The Heart of the Matter

As individual followers of Jesus, our spirituality flows out of and is defined by our relationship with God. In the gospel of John, chapters 13–17, Jesus prepares his disciples for life after the cross. He wants them to thrive. So Jesus teaches deeply and clearly about the community of the Trinity; their oneness, their mutual submission, their love and intimacy. Then he makes the stunning statement, "If anyone loves me, he will obey my teaching. My Father will love him and we will come to him and make our home with him" (John 14:23). Just as the Father and Son are one, we are now invited to share in that oneness through the Holy Spirit. All true spirituality flows from this relationship of intimacy with the Father and Son through the enduring presence of the Spirit.

> As individual followers of Jesus, our spirituality flows out of and is defined by our relationship with God.

Jesus states that there is a condition for experiencing this intimacy and new identity: love for God expressed in obedience to his teaching. "If you love me you will obey my teaching" (John 14:23; 15:10). What is it we are to obey? "A new command I give you: love one another. As I have loved you, so you must love one another" (John 13:34; 15:12).

It follows, then, that there is no Christian spirituality without community. To be authentic, our personal spirituality has to be lived out in community. This, we suggest, is the basis for organizational spirituality; our communal expression of intimacy with the community of the Trinity; Father, Son, and Spirit.

---

3   For example, Scott Bessenker, ed., *Living Mission: The Vision and Voices of New Friars* (Downers Grover, IL: InterVarsity Press, 2010).

4   Samuel Escobar, "Evangelical Missiology: Peering into the Future," in *Global Missiology for the Twenty-first Century*, ed. William D Taylor (Grand Rapids, MI: Baker Academic, 2000), 109.

Through the community of the Trinity, God has given his people a template for growing an authentic organizational spirituality. Relational, mutual, engaged, with shared responsibilities, supportive, submitted; the Trinity provides a rich model for how Christian community is expected to function. Much has been written about the Trinity and mission recently, but we have more work in applying this to Christian organizational dynamics.

> Relational, mutual, engaged, with shared responsibilities, supportive, submitted; the Trinity provides a rich model for how Christian community is expected to function.

In our globalized but fractured world, we know how powerfully social, political, and religious movements and leaders use ethnicity as a primary identity marker. Shockingly, Paul states that because of the cross, God has changed our ethnicity, bring us into a common citizenship as the people of God (Eph 2:19–22). Our identity "in Christ" is primary. All other identity markers are now secondary. As disciples of Jesus we are no longer defined primarily by the usual identity markers of gender, ethnicity, or social status but by relationship with God (Gal 3:28; Col 3:11; 1 Cor 12:13).

The issue of identity is critical in the development of Christian organizational spirituality. In a changed church and world context, many mission organizations are suffering an identity crisis: who are we and where do we belong? We suggest that the use of the term "parachurch" has been particularly damaging in this regard. It may be that the term was intended as simply a role descriptor: those who come alongside local churches to assist them in their participation in the mission of God. Instead, the term has become an identity descriptor, suggesting that mission agencies are something other than the church. This is untrue and deeply misleading. Mission agencies are not local churches but they are a legitimate and important expression of the body of Christ. The mission agency's core identity is nothing less than a spiritual community "in Christ."

The term "parachurch" has perhaps encouraged Christian organizations, consciously or unconsciously, to seek an organizational identity outside of a relationship with Christ. We suggest it is time to abandon the use of the term parachurch and find alternatives that affirm an identity as the people of God in mission. In Interserve, the mission agency my wife and I have worked with for twenty-five years, we have adopted the term "spiritual community."

Organizational Spirituality and Theories of Organizational Development

Having established that the essential identity of the Christian organization is a spiritual community "in Christ," modeled to us by relationships within the Trinity, we will now explore the dynamics of organizational spirituality further. At once this raises the question of approach. How do we examine and understand what shapes our organizations? To what degree, if any, can we draw on insights and tools produced by various schools of organizational development?

In Interserve, as we worked on our first values statement a few years ago, I asked myself how essential it really was, given that the organization was already over 150 years old. Indeed, the now popular term "organizational culture" only started to be used in the 1970s as North American businesses attempted to understand why Japanese firms had higher productivity and better product quality.[5] Answers were found in the cohesive, tribal culture of firms that facilitated both innovation and deep commitment in workers.

Most organizational development theories do not explicitly refer to our relationship with God as the cornerstone of personal and corporate life. In that sense they can be said to be secular. The exclusion of the divine leads to a reduced understanding of organizational life. When management theories are applied uncritically they have disastrous effects on individual and communal life and in our ability to participate faithfully in God's mission.

When Jesus begins to teach on the dynamics of kingdom life in Matthew 5–7, the Beatitudes begin: "happy are the poor in spirit, for theirs is the kingdom of heaven" (Matt 5:3). Poverty of spirit is brokenness and emptiness. In humility we recognize our complete dependence on God. By contrast, the subtle whisper of management techniques says, "with the right mission, values, and vision statements, the right strategies and enough finance and people we can overcome the problems and succeed in mission." This cancerous independence grows unseen, stripping our muscles, rotting our bones, and draining the spiritual life of our organizations until we have reduced mission to a task to be accomplished.

Considerable reflection has been given to the way Western secular culture has infiltrated church and mission and we need to continue the reflection. Yet none of us live beyond the influence of our surrounding culture. It is critical that each part of the global mission movement reflect on the ways in which their own cultures have distorted their practice of mission and organizational spirituality.

> It is critical that each part of the global mission movement reflect on the ways in which their own cultures have distorted their practice of mission and organizational spirituality.

Despite the dangers of an uncritical adoption of organizational development and management techniques, there is definitely a place for using them with discernment. All truth belongs to God and comes from him. We therefore suggest that there is much to be gained by a critical use of organizational development tools.

---

5   Mike Wall, *Understanding the Values of Christian Organizations: A Case Study of Across (1972–2005) Using the Organizational Culture Theory of Edgar Schein* (unpublished PhD thesis, 2015), 29.

Edgar Schein has developed a helpful diagnostic process.[6] He demonstrates that the espoused values of an organization may not reflect the real values that are driving organizational behavior and culture. For example, an organization may state that one of its values is dependence on God. In practice, it may in fact rely on a strategic planning process that allows very little place for spiritual discernment, ambiguity, or change of direction under the wind of the Spirit. Schein's diagnostic approach does not directly reference God. Nor does it recognize the source of our values and beliefs. But it does provide leaders with a tool for systemically diagnosing the real values and beliefs in their organization.

What Shapes Mission Organizational Spirituality?

Richard Foster, in his book *Streams of Living Water*, identified six main spiritual streams through church history, demonstrating that authentic biblical spirituality varies across time and culture. They are the contemplative, the holiness, the charismatic, social justice, evangelical, and incarnational streams. Christian organizations share the same core identity in Christ as the life-giving source. I suggest three other influences that shape organizational spirituality are worth noting.

Founders, Leaders, and Followers

A while ago I was invited to participate in the long-term strategic planning conference of a mission agency. As an outsider, it was striking how the vision, priorities, and commitments of the founders continued to shape the spirituality and missiology of the agency over one hundred years later. Founders have an enduring influence on the organizational spirituality of a community and this may be especially so in mission agencies.

Founders are generally strong, determined individuals. Interserve was founded by a woman and for one hundred years was a women-only organization. Lady Jane Kinnaird, devout, passionate, and influential, has never been thought of in celebrity terms. Nonetheless, the values that she brought continue to mark our organizational spirituality, reflected in inclusivity, service, humility, collaboration, and wholism.

Subsequent leaders also exert significant influence on organizational spirituality. They do this particularly through the modeling of their lives, what they choose to pay

---

6   Edgar Schein is a respected leader and researcher in the field of organizational development. His book *Organizational Culture and Leadership, 4th edition,* 2010, has been highly influential. For an in depth study of Schein's approach applied to a Christian organization I am indebted to Dr. Mike Wall for access to his PhD thesis that is cited above.

attention to, and the kind of people they appoint to positions of influence.[7] A leader who is focused primarily on strategy and measurable outcomes will likely grow a task-focused spirituality. One who focuses primarily on spiritual disciplines and personal discipleship is more likely to foster a more reflective organizational spirituality.

Again, an example may help: Between 2011–14, Interserve underwent an organization-wide reflective missiological process called "Building the Next Generation." The international board and leadership recognized that in a rapidly changing mission landscape, the organization needed to reflect again on our understanding and practice of mission. Through times of corporate worship and prayer, papers, conferences, and group discussions the whole organization was given the opportunity to participate. The result was not simply a revised purpose statement but a new organizational vocabulary focusing on church, discipleship, and community. This is turn is beginning to shape the way we follow Christ together—our organizational spirituality.

Prevailing Christian Culture

Mission agencies bring together people from different local churches. Agency spirituality is therefore impacted by the spirituality of the churches and denominations of its members. Dominant church worldviews of the resourcing churches have always affected mission agencies. For example, in the 1950s and 60s Interserve developed an organizational structure of autonomous national entities. This choice reflected the post-colonial church view (itself a reflection of prevailing secular culture) that centralized direction was to be avoided. Fifty years later this worldview was so deeply built into the spirituality of the organization that it threatened fragmentation. The negative effects of this part of organizational spirituality had to be confronted and radical restructuring performed. The example illustrates how an appropriate organizational response at one point in time may become a hindrance in the future.

We know from the experience of the past thirty years that cultural inclusivity requires organizations to practice great flexibility in all kinds of policy areas, particularly with personnel and finances. This calls to mind the oft-quoted phrase, "In essentials unity, in non-essentials liberty, in all things charity."[8] The development of a culturally inclusive organization provides a glorious opportunity to dig down and uncover the core beliefs and values that shape an organization's spirituality and ensure that these remain the essentials. No surprise then that a SIL International and Wycliffe Bible Translators International working group on building multicultural teams concluded:

---

7   Schein identifies six primary and six secondary ways in which leaders shape organizational culture. Schein's primary and secondary mechanisms for influencing organizational culture work this way—primary mechanisms can be done on their own—secondary mechanisms only work "if they are consistent with the primary mechanisms" (Schein, 236, 250).

8   Often wrongly attributed to St Augustine, it first appeared in the early seventeenth century during at time of religious wars in Europe (see http://www.ligonier.org/learn/articles/essentials-unity-non-essentials-liberty-all-things/.)

As we have thought and prayed and strained toward our goal, it has become increasingly clear that training in how to adapt to and work in a multicultural environment is important, but spiritual growth is key to successfully incorporating that training into one's attitudes and behaviors... Immersion in the written Word and fellowship with the living Word will develop in us a Christ-like humility and courage to enable us to serve one another in multicultural partnerships and make disciples of all nations.[9]

> The bedrock of Christian organizational spirituality is our shared identity in Christ.

This underlines what we have already stressed, that the bedrock of Christian organizational spirituality is our shared identity in Christ.

Missional Context

Secular culture, leaders, church culture: these all influence the spirituality of an organization. So too does the context in which mission is being undertaken. The context may be defined by geography. Work in the Middle East or Afghanistan is very different from Latin America or sub-Saharan Africa. For decades Interserve has worked in creative access countries where professional work is almost the only way to minister. This has influenced organizational spirituality, contributing to a very strong belief that work offered to God is ministry and not simply a platform for evangelism or church planting.

The mission context may also be defined by ministry focus. For example, we would expect a mission agency focused on supporting the persecuted church to demonstrate an organizational spirituality that embraces suffering and places a high value on intercessory prayer. Sometimes ministry focus can subtly undermine healthy organizational spirituality. One leader shared that having spent many years working for a Christian organization focused on poverty reduction, they joined another agency. The person noticed the difference between being involved in an organization where poverty reduction was the central focus compared to an organization where knowing and listening to Christ is the central focus.

The example raises the question: How do we grow and sustain healthy organizational spirituality?

Growing Healthy Organizational Spirituality

First, we affirm again that there is no single, authentic organizational spirituality. We rejoice in healthy diversity arising from organizations faithfully following Christ in their specific calling and context. At the same time, from our experience we propose a

---

9   Internal Wycliffe Bible Translators International and SIL International report: *Healthy Multicultural Team Initiative. Report to Global Leadership* (November 2006).

number of elements that contribute to healthy organizational spirituality in mission at this point in history. Space permits only a brief mention of these elements.

Renewed Focus on Christ at the Center

We began this chapter with the affirmation that Christian organizational spirituality finds its source in our relationship with Christ and shared identity as his people. This reality must be lifted from the depths of unspoken assumption and given expression in every fiber, tissue, and connection within the organizational body. Leaders carry a huge responsibility to ensure that Christ remains the head and life-giving center of organizational life.

Ruth Haley Barton, in her outstanding book *Pursuing God's Will Together*, considers that the primary responsibility of leaders is to discern God's purposes for their community.[10] She provides a practical approach for corporate discernment. The strength of her approach arises from her insistence that the leaders' personal relationship with Christ is the non-negotiable foundation to corporate discernment. Leaders need to learn to listen to God through various spiritual disciplines and especially the practices of solitude and silence. They must experience personal submission to the will of the Father through stillness, waiting, and the "prayer of indifference" through which they are able to say, "Nevertheless Father, not my will but yours be done."

This approach to decision-making does not deny the use of intellect. Indeed, Haley Barton points out that part of the process of discernment is the gathering of all necessary information. The difference is that information becomes a tool rather than the driver in decision-making. It is possible to practice this approach in boards, leadership teams, and large communal gatherings. The results are life-giving. Dependence on God brings freedom. The poor in spirit do inherit the kingdom of God.

Commitment to Spiritual Community

Keeping Christ at the center in our organizations requires a commitment to deepening personal relationships in community. Leadership teams cannot practice spiritual discernment without a commitment to practicing community. Authentic organizational spirituality requires integrity, vulnerability, mutual support, and accountability in the whole community. This is a particular challenge to the modern mission movement, birthed and nourished by pioneers for whom individualism has been a badge of honor.

> Authentic organizational spirituality requires integrity, vulnerability, mutual support, and accountability in the whole community.

---

10   I don't know a better book designed to help leaders grow in their corporate practice of spiritual discernment. Ruth Haley Barton, *Pursuing God's Will Together* (Downers Grove, IL: InterVarsity Press, 2012).

It is time to realign our practice of mission and recover missional community not just for a few but for the mainstream in mission. Investment in our own community is not a distraction to mission. Jesus told us that the most powerful testimony to his lordship is the unity of his people. The ultimate goal of God's mission is the reintegration of all things in heaven and on earth under Jesus as Lord (Eph 1:10). We must practice mission in a way that is consistent with the end goal, and that means mission in community. Mission today continues to require individual faith, courage, determination, and perseverance. Healthy organizational spirituality nurtures these things in community.

As seen above, leadership has a critical element in shaping spiritual community. The pioneering individualism that attracts robust cross-cultural workers can carry with it at best a suspicion of leaders and at worst a spirituality that is toxic to leadership. Mission agencies need to examine this area of organizational spirituality and recover biblical attitudes and behaviors in leadership and followership. This has a critical impact on our ability to engage in mission. Unless we understand and exercise appropriate authority within our communities we will struggle to exercise spiritual authority in spiritual warfare.

Embrace Servanthood and Suffering

Service and suffering are marks of discipleship in any age. However, the context of mission today requires us to embrace both in our organizational spirituality.

The growth of the church in even the most difficult of contexts means that more than ever the cross-cultural mission movement today is called to model servanthood. Increasingly the question for the cross-cultural worker is not, "How can I develop my ministry here?" but "How can I enable the local body of Christ to engage more faithfully in God's mission here?" To grow workers with this mindset requires an organizational culture that models service.

> The question for the cross-cultural worker is not, "How can I develop my ministry here?" but "How can I enable the local body of Christ to engage more faithfully in God's mission here?"

Ministry in a context of suffering is the norm in most of Asia, the Middle East, and large parts of Africa. Organizations working in such contexts need to develop an organizational spirituality that theologically understands the place of suffering and pastorally supports those facing it.

Ruthless Practice of a Kingdom-first Mindset

Despite significant advances over the past twenty years in building ministry partnerships, the default approach to mission remains individual agencies, and now churches, going it alone. Jim Plueddemann has pointed out that this approach is like each town sending its own little army into battle in time of war.[11] Yet evangelicals still behave as if their personal call is unique and no one else gets missiology and mission quite as well as their group. One result of the phenomenal increase in the number of agencies and churches in mission is that most work in splendid isolation.

We suggest that an appeal to collaboration must be based on a deeper set of beliefs than simply the potential gains in efficiency and effectiveness. Mission today must nurture an organizational spirituality that flows from our oneness in Christ and the nature of God's mission. The individualistic model of mission places us in competition with each other—for people, money, the best stories, success, and more. A kingdom mindset is reflected in humility, mutual submission, and a desire to serve each other's organizations. This will require nothing short of a conversion experience for most of us.

> A kingdom mindset is reflected in humility, mutual submission, and a desire to serve each other's organizations.

Conclusion

The mainstream Protestant missionary movement faces a crisis, a moment of threat and opportunity. There is a weariness with the way we have organized ourselves in the global North. Many in the global South cannot and do not want to follow the same tired systems and processes. Wherever the church is fragile it faces growing opposition and hostility. Political instability, war, suspicion of NGOs, fierce ethnocentrism—the challenges to cross-cultural mission are immense. Yet these threats provide us with bright opportunity. Humbled, we can renounce dependence on our own wisdom, techniques, and resources. We can turn to the Lord and seek him. There we will experience fresh ways in which the lordship of Christ is expressed among us. From this living water we will discover authentic organizational, communal spirituality and become a channel of life for those he places us among. What an opportunity!

Discussion Questions

Regarding your organization:

1. What are the main characteristics of organizational spirituality laid down by the founder? How have these been strengthened or changed by subsequent leaders?
2. What external realities (society and church culture, widely held missiological beliefs, context where you are serving in mission) have the most impact on your current organizational spirituality?
3. Take the three values that most fully express your organization's stated spirituality. What behaviors in the organization reflect these values? What behaviors are not

---

11   *International Bulletin of Missionary Research* (October, 1999), 158.

in keeping with the values? From your assessment of organizational behavior, what do you think people really believe is important? What steps might you and others take to grow the kind of organizational spirituality you desire?

References

Barton, Ruth Haley. 2012. *Pursuing God's Will Together.* Downers Grover, IL: InterVarsity Press.

Escobar, Samuel. 2000. "Evangelical Missiology: Peering into the Future." In *Global Missiology for the Twenty-first Century.* Ed. William D. Taylor. Grand Rapids, MI: Baker Academic.

Foster, Richard J. 1998. *Streams of Living Water.* New York: Harper Collins.

Poole, Eve. 2006. "Organizational Spirituality—Away with the Fairies?" *The Ashridge Journal.* Autumn.

———. 2009. "Organizational Spirituality—A Literature Review." *Journal of Business Ethics,* 84:577–588.

Wall, Mike. 2015. *Understanding the Values of Christian Organizations: A Case Study of Across (1972–2005) Using the Organizational Culture Theory of Edgar Schein.* Unpublished PhD thesis.

Paul Bendor-Samuel grew up in Latin America and West Africa, studied medicine in Wales and has worked with Interserve since 1990. Paul, Liz and their four boys spent twelve years in North Africa where he practiced primary health care and community development. They saw the Lord establish the church once again after more than a millennium. Paul then led Interserve International for twelve years. In 2016 he was seconded to the Oxford Centre for Mission Studies as Executive Director. He is passionate about helping individuals and organizations live out their identity in Christ.

Scripture: *Ephesians 1:9–10 ("He made known to us the mystery of his will...")*

Resource: *Developing Intimacy with God,* by Alex B Aronis (Manila: Union Church of Manila, 2002).

CHAPTER 24

Case Studies

China Inland Mission
Not Repaying Evil With Evil

Patrick Fung, OMF (Singapore)

Hudson Taylor was recuperating in Switzerland when the unimaginable "Boxer Uprising" erupted in China. William Cooper, one of the China Inland Mission missionaries, became one of the early martyrs. On July 1, 1900 he and others were tied together and led out to execution. All were beheaded and their bodies exposed overnight before being thrown into a common graveyard outside Baoding.[1] Eight days later forty-seven missionaries were massacred in Taiyuan. All told, 189 missionaries were killed; 126 in Shanxi, 22 in Mongolia, 19 in Hebei, 11 in Zhejiang, and 11 in Shandong, Hubei, Henan, Beijing, and Shanghai. The China Inland Mission lost 58 missionaries and 21 children. More than 200 Chinese Christians were martyred. This is part of what became known as the "Boxer Uprising."

When news reached Hudson Taylor in Switzerland, he was devastated. He said, "I cannot read; I cannot think; I cannot even pray; but I can trust." At the end of the year, he started writing letters to the victims' families. Dixon Edward Hoste was appointed Acting General Director in January 1901.

In February 1901, a letter was sent by J. W. Stevenson, the China Director at that time, to all missionaries of the China Inland Mission. In the letter he said,

> The subject of compensation for loss of life or property at the hands of the Chinese was brought before us some time ago, in connection with the massacre in Ch'li-cheo. After long and careful consideration, [and in consultation] with

---

1 *Biographical Dictionary of Chinese Christianity*, OMF International, *Christ Alone: A Pictorial Presentation of Hudson Taylor's Life and Legacy* (Hong Kong: OMFHK, 2005), 109.

Mr. Taylor for his judgment as we wish to acquaint you with his views in respect to it, that the opinion of the China Council is "TO CLAIM NOTHING"… we hold on trust for God's work. In respect to claiming compensation, whether for loss of life, injury to persons, or loss of property, whether private or helping to the Mission, [Mr. Taylor] considers such action to be contrary to the Purpose and Principles of the China Inland Mission and is, therefore, to be avoided. In regard to accepting compensation for private properties when offered, whilst he feels that each of us must prayerfully decide for his or herself… as a rule, it would be wiser not to accept compensation in view of the effect which such acceptance would have upon the native Christians. [2]

Following discussion with colleagues, a decision was reached by Dixon E. Hoste, the Acting General Director, that the China Inland Mission would neither claim nor accept any compensation, even if offered. The Chinese authority was dumbfounded.

On October 11, 1901, the governor of Shanxi ordered that placards to be displayed in schools, government buildings, and wherever the CIM had worked and suffered, throughout Shanxi. They read:

The Mission, in rebuilding these churches with its own funds, aims in so doing to fulfill the command of the Savior of the world, that all men should love their neighbors as themselves, and is unwilling to lay any heavy pecuniary burden on the traders or on the poor. I, the Governor, find… that the chief work of the Christian religion is in all places to exhort men to live virtuously. From the time of their entrance into China, Christian missionaries have given medicine gratuitously to the sick.

Jesus, in his instructions, inculcates forbearance and forgiveness and all desire for revenge is discouraged. Mr. Hoste [CIM] is able to carry out these principles to the full; this mode of action deserves the fullest approval.

> They did not repay evil with evil nor insult with insult, but with blessing because to this they were called so that the Chinese may inherit blessings in Christ

I charge you all, gentry, scholars, army, and people, those of you who are fathers to exhort your sons, and those who are elder sons, to exhort your younger brothers, to bear in mind the example of Pastor Hoste (CIM), who is able to forbear and forgive as taught by Jesus to do so. [3]

In the next few years, the number of China Inland Mission missionaries in Henan, Shanxi, and other provinces continued to grow and the work further developed. They did not repay evil with evil nor insult with insult but with blessing, because to this they were called so that the Chinese may inherit blessings in Christ (1 Pet 3:9).

---

2   Archive Material at OMF International IHQ Singapore.
3   *China's Millions* (1902), 33, 36.

Patrick Fung is the General Director of OMF International, formerly the China Inland Mission. He and his wife, Jennie, previously served in a Muslim context in South Asia. Patrick was one of the plenary speakers for the Cape Town 2010 Third Lausanne Congress on World Evangelization. He was the Bible expositor for Urbana 2015.   Patrick also serves on the International Board of the Lausanne Movement and Langham Partnership.

Scripture: *Acts 13:36 a ("Now when David had served God's purpose in his own generation, he fell asleep")*

Resource: *Finishing Our Course with Joy,* by JI Packer (Wheaton, IL: Crossway Publishing, 2014).

Assemblies of God World Missions

Greg Mundis

Assemblies of God World Missions is committed to practicing spiritual disciplines and to the development of personal and spiritual formation. A key element of our spiritual formation is understanding that Christ "did not come to be served, but to serve" (Matt 20:28). Nothing emphasizes this more than the fact that God became flesh and dwelt among us.

Christ's incarnation has great similarities to what we as a missionary family are doing by learning a new language, adapting to a new culture, and integrating into a society that is not our own. Sometimes the strain and stress of this process can cause difficulties in our personal lives, our families, and our relationships with others. If we can adjust our thinking and attitudes to emulate Christ, who made himself of no reputation as he took on human flesh as a baby and became completely dependent on others, then in our human flesh we will take on more of his godliness as we adjust to new languages, cultures, and societies.

Our commitment to organizational spirituality encompasses seven additional core values that integrate with the spiritual formation described above. Taken together, the eight values are:

- Biblical Understanding of the Church
- Team Concept
- Indigenous Principles and Partnership
- Proclamation to Unreached
- Cultural Understanding
- Holistic Missions
- Spiritual Formation
- Spirit Empowerment

Along with our mission statement (Reach, Plant, Train, Serve), these values should be a part of our identity as missionaries.

Every one of these values points back to Christ, who modeled them perfectly for all who would follow him in life practice and missions commitment. Christ's biblical understanding was absolute. He created a team of disciples who changed the world. He related to Jews and Samaritans and Gentiles, the rich and poor, lepers and the blind—all in a manner that connected indigenously with their life experiences. Of course, the Savior boldly proclaimed the kingdom to the unreached, had absolute cultural understanding of the humanity he had created and ministered to every corner of human need holistically. Everything Christ accomplished was an outgrowth of his own spiritual formation and empowerment built upon his communion with the Father and anointing by the Spirit.

To measure our biblical understanding of the church's mission, we must use the founder and head of the church, Jesus Christ, as our plumb line. Jesus, on the night of his betrayal and subsequent arrest, prayed to his Father: "As you sent me into the world, I have sent them into the world" (John 17:18). Three days later, on the evening of his resurrection from the dead, he said to his disciples, "As the Father has sent me, I am sending you" (John 20:21).

Assemblies of God World Missions' commitment to practicing spiritual disciplines and to the development of personal and spiritual formation effectively empowers participants to carry out Jesus'

> Assemblies of God World Missions' commitment to practicing spiritual disciplines and to the development of personal and spiritual formation effectively empowers participants to carry out Jesus' primary goal for his followers—to send them to continue the work he was sent to do!

primary goal for his followers—to send them to continue the work he was sent to do! He "came to seek and to save what was lost" (Luke 19:10). He identified with humanity so that he could reach humanity with the good news. As the individual members of the larger Assemblies of God missionary family emulate the Savior and exercise their spiritual gifts in a manner unique to each of their life experiences and specific callings, we will move forward into the twenty-first century as a compelling Great Commission force for worldwide witness.

Dr. Greg Mundis is Executive Director, Assemblies of God World Missions. Greg provides leadership for 2,778 AG missionaries and associates. In 1980 Greg and his wife Sandie were appointed as missionaries to Austria where Greg cofounded an international church and served as area director for Central Europe. Greg was selected as regional director for the Europe Region in 1998 and served there until 2011, when he was elected as AGWM executive director. Greg, alongside the AGWM Executive Committee, is focusing on the future by emphasizing global partnerships, the suffering church, and unreached people groups.

Scripture: *Mark 10:45 ("For even the Son of Man did not come to be served…")*

Resources: *Emotionally Healthy Spiritually: Unleash a Revolution in Your Life in Christ,* by Peter Scazzero (Nashville, TN: Thomas Nelson, 2006).

Embracing Brokenness: How God Refines Us Through Life's Disappointments, by Alan Nelson (Carol Stream, IL: NavPress, 2002).

YWAM East Asia

Harry Hoffmann

Youth With a Mission (YWAM) was founded in 1960 by Loren and Darleen Cunningham (USA), confronting and filling two major gaps in the global mission movement at that time. The first gap was about young people. In the mid-twentieth century young people were not considered candidates for missions. The second gap was about the "all" and "every." The achievability and the fulfillment of the Great Commission to "Go into all the world and preach the gospel to every creature" (Mark 16:15 NKJV) was something new.

YWAMs spirituality is greatly influenced by its passion to make a difference confronting these two gaps. The following examples highlight a few of the unique spiritual aspects of YWAM:

Young People Can Hear His Voice

YWAM believes that every person has the ability to hear God's voice. The practice of hearing God's voice is encouraged in every YWAM team on a daily basis for the sake of personal as well as team and cooperate encouragement and guidance. Therefore, everyone's relationship with God and contribution to the team—no matter the age, gender, race, or culture—is valued, affirmed, and treated equally. Processing questions like: "What did God speak to me today?" "What did I learn about him today?" and "What part of God's character did I get to know better today?" are part of every YWAM'ers daily life.

Intimate Relationship with God, Prayer, and Worship

Knowing God, intimacy with God, knowing his character, his ways, seeking his counsel, and (out of intimate relationship with him) obeying his instructions is the red thread in every YWAM team and every YWAM training school. The Discipleship Training School (DTS), which is YWAM's foundational entry-level school, seeks to bring individuals into a more intimate relationship with God. The practice of daily praise and worship of the Lamb of God are important parts of building that intimacy. By teaching and encouraging daily intercessory prayer and spiritual warfare, YWAM also emphasizes the realities of the spiritual world. "How does God see you?" and "What has God done in your life over the last year" are questions often asked in YWAM circles.

Community

YWAM teams throughout the world live in communities called YWAM bases. Living and working together, serving one another, and daily corporate worship and intercession are important YWAM values. The goal of every YWAM base is to be a relationship-oriented and God-centered community. The desire is to minimize the need for structure and rules by leading lives of transparency, humility, and open communication. One aspect of this is the importance of families—fathers, mothers, and children all sharing a call to missions and contributing in unique and complementary ways. YWAM families on the mission field often say: "We are a family in ministry," to express their calling as a family rather than as individuals. A typical YWAM question when making major decisions is: "Have you prayed about this with your YWAM base, your leaders, and your family?"

> A typical YWAM question when making major decisions is: "Have you prayed about this with your YWAM base, your leaders, and your family?"

Every Person Has a Unique Calling

The DTS as well as many other YWAM training schools give an opportunity to discover one's passions and one's part in God's purposes for the world. Being a Christian is not primarily about behavior, and being a missionary is not merely a job or a profession. Based on Scripture YWAM believes that every person on earth was designed with a unique call of God on their lives. This design includes one's personality, spiritual gifts, passions, desires, experiences, identity, and more. Helping every person to explore this design combined with hearing his voice and building intimacy with God both individually as well as corporately is part YWAM's core values. A typical YWAM question is: "What is God calling you to accomplish for his kingdom?"

Cocreating with God

Championing young people's individual callings has brought YWAM to lead out apostolically to birth fresh, entrepreneurial initiatives. The emphasis on the creator God and our human capacity to cocreate with God based on our unique design calls young and old YWAMers around the world to a lifestyle of pioneering, doing, and encouraging others to do new things in new ways in order to accomplish Great Commission goals. "If you could do the impossible for his kingdom, what would that look like?" is a question YWAMers are encouraged to examine.

In order to give as much space as possible to pioneering and cocreating with God, YWAM is not centrally controlled by a few leaders in a head office. Instead YWAM is broadly structured and decentralized, with operating locations linked together by relationship, shared values, and accountability to international elders. Because of this, YWAM is often referred to as a "Tribe," a "Movement," or a "Family" rather than a mission organization.

International Flavor

YWAM is international like no other mission organization. The focus on the "all's" and "every's" of the Great Commission encourages every person to go everywhere and every tribe and nation to become a missionary sending tribe and nation as led by God's Spirit. YWAM operates in more than 1,100 locations in over 180 countries with a staff of over 18,000. Regional and global YWAM conferences and the experience of worshiping, interceding, and fellowshiping together with many cultures is something one never forgets.

Jehovah-Jireh, God Who Provides

YWAM is a volunteer organization and workers are called to practice a life of dependence upon God for financial provision, both corporately and individually. All YWAM staff are self-supported and no one receives a salary. This daily dependence upon God draws YWAMers closer towards knowing God, hearing his voice, prayer and intercession, community and relationship. Testimonies of how Jehovah Jireh has revealed himself in the most miraculous ways are part of every YWAMers life.

A lot more can be said about the spirituality of YWAM. As values and principles unique to YWAM are lived out, the spiritual expressions and experiences are many.

To know God and to make him known is YWAMs slogan that undergirds everything. Giving young (and old) people from every tribe and nation the freedom in the Spirit to hear and obey God in a cocreative way, advancing God's missional purposes, and living healthy, loving relationships under God's lordship, guided by his word, makes YWAM an expression of aspects of God's character that were attractive in the 1960s and still attractive today.

Harry Hoffmann (Germany) finished his Masters in Chinese Studies in Berlin, 1995, after which he and his family were accepted to join an orphanage ministry in China. Shortly after that his member care ministry journey began. Today, drawing from over twenty years experience in China and Thailand; father of three Third Culture Kids; husband of a counselor, social entrepreneur, leader, and teacher; conflict mediator and member of various boards, the red thread in his life is a calling to start and help start new ministries as well as consult with ministries in crisis. Harry founded and co-founded several member care centers and he leads the work of the WEA Mission Commission Global Member Care Network.

Scripture: *Joshua 24:15, ("Choose for yourselves this day…"); Luke 10:1–2 (After these things the Lord appointed seventy others also…")*

Resource: "Stephanas: A New Testament Example of Frontier Member Care," by S. J. Ellis, *International Journal of Frontier Missions* (12:171–175, 1995).

WEC

Susan Sutton

Subsaharan Africa. A team gathers from various parts of the country for their annual conference. Confusion, dejection, frustration. They have just heard news that sets back a major hope the team has held for over a year. They believed God was leading them to buy a specific property for ministry purposes in a strategic city. They had a sense that this was God's vision and they were following his lead. They had also put in a lot of hard work, praying and negotiating through an extremely complicated cultural and legal system of family ownership. Some team members had even prayer-walked around the property several times, declaring God's Word and claiming the land for Christ's use. And now the door was closed. The owners were selling to someone else.

Had they misunderstood God? They were keenly aware that this was a possibility. They were also inclined to spend time discussing the news and complaining about the culture, which would have been satisfying in a way, but was not what was needed. They needed instead to talk with God and hear from him. Setting aside the planned agenda the leaders declared a time of fasting and prayer. The next two days were filled with worship, prayer, listening to God, and sharing with each other. By the end, the team sensed God saying the land was still theirs. They left the conference believing God was going to come through despite a closed door.

The following week, an African coworker excitedly gave the latest news, "I don't know why, but the owners just said they're not going to sell to the other group. The land is still available!"

They knew why—God's purposes cannot be stopped by the decisions of man. The team continued to pray, trusting God for further negotiations. Holding to WEC's policy of not openly appealing for funds, they also prayed and trusted for finances for the purchase of the property. A year later the land was purchased and building had begun. A core principle of WEC was affirmed when faith took the risk of practice: "We believe in… the power of God to supply every need in every situation, so that his work is not determined by circumstances but rather by the 'great and precious promises' in his Word."

> "We believe in… the power of God to supply every need in every situation, so that his work is not determined by circumstances but rather by the 'great and precious promises' in his Word."

C. T. Studd, the founder of WEC, was deeply influenced by men of faith in his time, especially Hudson Taylor and George Mueller. Inspired by their examples, Studd held a passionate belief that God is worthy of our deepest trust. This view of God's worthiness not only of our trust but our lives shaped WEC's beginnings in the early twentieth century. WEC was also shaped in its early years by teachings on deeper life in Christ, affirming that our outward, visible life is only as strong as our inner, hidden life in Christ. Holiness of life, fellowship, and sacrifice joined faith as foundational pillars of WEC. To some observers in the early days, WEC seemed too radical in its brand of faith, too inflexible in its call to discipleship, and too irresponsible in the willingness to sacrifice, but these principles were rooted in a genuine desire to honor Christ, to take God at his Word, and to live as his disciples while seeking to make disciples. It was and still is recognized that living out these principles is possible only through an indwelling Christ and the transforming work of the Holy Spirit.

As a multicultural, multidenominational, multigenerational, not to mention obviously human fellowship today we are keenly aware of our weaknesses. Inspiring principles on paper are one thing. Living them out in the daily realities of team and ministry are another. We are aware, too, that organizational structures and patterns of functioning as a mission may need to change as the world changes, but a core truth remains: "Christ is the head of WEC International. We live as his servants and are committed to seek his will all aspects of life and service." Two former International Directors for WEC have stated it well: "The life of the mission depends on the spirituality of the membership" (Evan Davies) and, "Our advance (for God's kingdom) will mean lonely places, dangers, difficulties. It will only be possible with a deepening spiritual life" (Dieter Kuhl).

Susan Sutton and her husband, Louis, have served with WEC International for thirty years. For thirteen years they were in church-planting and medical ministries in northeastern Chad, followed by seven years in Pennsylvania as the directors of WEC-USA. They currently serve as WEC's International Directors and live in Singapore. Susan's passion, apart from God's restoration of the world he created, is spiritual formation and life in Christ. Susan is the author of books on the deeper life in Christ including *A Quiet Center, A Sure Path, Vision of the Deep*, and *Designer Living*.

Scripture: *John 15:1–9 ("I am the true vine..."); Galatians 2:20 ("I have been crucified with Christ..."), 4:19 ("...until Christ is formed in you")*

Resources: *Strengthening the Soul of Your Leadership: Seeking God in the Crucible of Ministry*, by Ruth Haley Barton (Downers Grover, Il: IVP Books, 2008). *Living in Christ's Presence: Final Words on Heaven and the Kingdom of God*, by Dallas Willard and John Ortberg (Downers Grover, Il: IVP Books, 2014).

SIM

Geoffrey W. Hahn with Joshua Bogunjoko

Each community of believers has its unique characteristics and ethos, whether that community is a local church or an international mission organization. Spiritual vitality is essential to SIM and its kingdom effectiveness, and SIM's ministries flow out of this spiritual health. Two areas of particular spiritual focus for SIM are prayer and diversity.

SIM came into existence by prayer. The histories of the missions that form today's SIM are rooted in the prayers of men and women petitioning God for the lost. "I feel that God is calling us into a ministry which will reach all races of South Africa," wrote Mrs. Osborn to her friend Mr. Walton. "My special burden at present is for the Africans." After a time of prayer, Mr. Walton's response was, "Oh loose my tongue that I may tell, with burning words, to sinners lost, that thou didst come to seek and save, to purchase them

> The histories of the missions that form today's SIM are rooted in the prayers of men and women petitioning God for the lost.

at such cost." Out of this, the Cape General Mission was founded in 1889 by Martha Osborn, Spencer Walton, and Andrew Murray, which later became Africa Evangelical Fellowship and then SIM.

Similar stories of the founding of SIM's work in other continents reveal a priority on prayer. Through prayer, God moved the hearts of SIM's founders to consider the plight of those who were then living and dying without the gospel. Since these beginnings in North America, Europe, Africa, Asia, and Latin America, SIM has continued resolutely "by prayer." Today SIM is emboldened by the same confidence that its pioneers had in the God who answers prayer. SIM remains prayerfully dependent on God as the mission crosses barriers to proclaim the crucified and risen Christ and express his love in communities where he is least known. God draws SIM's workers together for prayer, unites them in prayer, and emboldens them to go out by prayer.

Diversity is a second core component of SIM's spiritual heritage and vitality. From its beginnings, the mission has been composed of multicultural teams. Rowland Bingham (English-born Canadian), Walter Gowans (Scottish-born Canadian), and Thomas Kent (American) were the first three missionaries to venture out with SIM. Over time other mission organizations that originated in Australia, South Africa, New Zealand, and the United Kingdom merged with SIM. Today, SIM's more than 4,000 active workers represent about 70 nationalities. SIM's multicultural, multiskilled teams serve among diverse people groups on every continent except Antarctica!

The diversity of gifts and cultures are critical to SIM's spiritual vitality as colleagues from around the world journey together for Christ's kingdom. The tremendous variety of gifts, skills, cultures, and perspectives at work in the mission strengthens its strategies, enriches its ministries, and displays God's love for the nations.

As SIM teams composed of Ethiopians and Ecuadorians, Canadians and Koreans, Argentinians and Australians serve together, they express a living testimony of God's transforming grace that brings unity amidst diversity. In dependence on God, by prayer, SIM models and celebrates what is to come, a multitude "from every nation, tribe, people, and language, standing... in front of the Lamb."

Dr. Joshua Bogunjoko commenced a five-year term as the International Director of SIM in June 2013. SIM is an organization founded over a century ago that promotes missions work in over seventy countries worldwide. Dr. Bogunjoko's life in Christ began with prayer in his bedroom during high school. Despite a desire to major in engineering, he surrendered to the Lord's direction to study medicine at the University of Port Harcourt. As a student, he was an active leader in the Nigerian Fellowship of Evangelical Students (NIFES). Dr. Bogunjoko graduated in 1988 and went on to complete his residency in family medicine at a mission hospital in Jos, Nigeria. He later served at the SIM Hospital in Galmi, Niger with his wife and colleague Dr. Joanna Bogunjoko, eventually becoming both the Chief Medical Officer and hospital director. Dr. and Dr. Bogunjoko are currently based in Fort Mill, SC with their children Jochebed and Joel.

Scripture: *Psalm 67:1-2 ("God be merciful to us and bless us...")*

Resources: *Why Revival Tarries*, by Leonard Ravenhill (Bloomington, MN: Bethany House, 2004). *Discipline: The Glad Surrender*, by Elizabeth Elliott (Ada, MI: Revell, 2006).

Geoffrey W. Hahn accepted Christ at a young age, and God called him to missions when he was a teenager on a short-term medical mission trip. He completed his BA at Wheaton College, M.Div. at Trinity Evangelical Divinity School, and doctorate at Denver Seminary, with a thesis on cross-cultural partnerships. Geoffrey and his wife, Fiona, have two young adult sons. They served in pastoral roles in Chicago area churches and as SIM missionaries in rural and urban settings in Ecuador. In mission leadership Geoffrey has served as a country and area director, and on SIM's International Leadership Team as Director of Ministry Development and currently as a Deputy International Director. Geoffrey seeks to empower others for effective ministry responses to the ever-changing ministry settings and realities in our world.

Scripture: *Micah 6:8* ("He has shown you, O Man what is good...")

Resource: *The Brothers Karamazov,* Fyodor Dostoevsky.

EMS of ECWA

Simon Yako

What Is EMS?

Evangelical Mission Society (EMS) is the product of Sudan Interior Mission (SIM); it was formerly known as the African Mission Society (AMS) of SIM which changed when Sudan was preparing for independence. The sense of nationalism prevailed at that time and the church was not left out; hence the formation of AMS was an exciting part of the change that was taking place.[4] AMS was then changed to EMS in June 1964 in order to avoid confusion with another organization in the country bearing the same acronym.

EMS is a mission organization with its foundation based on the Great Commission that says, "Go into all the world and preach the good news to all creation" (Mark 16:15–16 cf Matt 28:19).

What Is the Spirituality Behind the Formation of EMS?

It is pertinent here to mention that Mrs. Margaret Gowans contributed immensely to the birth of SIM. As an active leader of the women of St. James Square Presbyterian Church of Toronto, Canada, she was disposed to mission activities. Her zeal moved her to pray for the Sudan—then a region in North Africa, south of the Sahara and Libyan deserts, extending from the Atlantic to the Red Sea—which she considered as one of the neglected mission fields of the world. It is on record that this woman passed on her vision and burden for the Sudan to her son Walter.[5] Her passion and commitment for mission infected her children. First her daughter, Miss Annie Gowans, went to China as a missionary. Next her son, Mr. Walter Gowans, not only developed an interest for mission but was burdened to take the gospel to the Sudan region. He died within his first year of reaching Africa but stayed committed to the mission of bringing the gospel to Sudan.

Like a fire burning in her bosom Mrs. Gowan could not keep silent and shared her burden to as many as were willing to listen. She is also credited with sharing the burden of reaching the Sudan with Rowland Bingham, which challenged him and opened his spiritual eyes to see the great need that moved him to the Sudan mission field. Her

---

4   Panya Baba, *A Vision Received, A Vision Passed On: The History of EMS of ECWA 1948–1998* (Nigeria: Gajofa Venture Ltd, 2014), 61.

5   Yusuf Turaki, *An Introduction to the History of SIM/ECWA in Nigeria 1893 – 1983* (Jos, Nigeria: Challenge Press, 1993), 41.

contribution facilitated the founding of SIM (later EMS). She preferred to have her son die in the mission field than having him at home disobeying the Lord.

The spirituality behind the foundation of EMS of ECWA is the burden to do God's will rather than to make a name or acquire material wealth. There were great sacrifices made for the souls of those perishing in darkness. It is written, "The people walking in darkness have seen a great light; on those living in the land of the shadow of death a light has dawned" (Isa 9:2). It is not physical darkness that this passage is referring to, but spiritual, as it affects the deliverance of humanity from the bondage of Satan that has holds the people of the world captive. It was this spirituality that encompassed a true devotion to Christ among the poor and downtrodden and was the formation of EMS.

> The spirituality behind the foundation of EMS of ECWA is the burden to do God's will rather than to make a name or acquire material wealth. There were great sacrifices made for the souls of those perishing in darkness.

As a mission body it is our responsibility to be obedient to Christ's mandate; our lives reflect what we say to men and the power of the Holy Spirit convinces and convicts men of sin to repent. When the Bible says he who wins a soul is wise, it is not talking about the wisdom of this world but the wisdom of God, which is made available through the power of the Holy Spirit.

Has EMS Maintained the Dream of the Founding Fathers?

As a faith-based organization, EMS raises funds through the support of individuals and organizations that have passion for mission as partners in the Lord's Vineyard. The maxim on which the EMS operates is, "Go in Faith, Prayer, and Action." We are not only presenting the message in word, but in kindness and action, reaching people through building schools, clinics, wells, and reaching out to displaced people and less privileged people, like widows and orphans.

EMS continues the spirituality that it was founded upon as more than 1,600 missionaries continue its work. Missionaries are spread across the nation, past the boundaries into Nigeria, and beyond. The pioneer missionaries that founded SIM came from Canada, the USA, and the UK; today EMS missionaries take the same gospel back to these countries and other parts of the world.

Conclusion

Spirituality and mission are inseparable because spiritual fruit is expected in one's life by allowing the Word of God to saturate every aspect of our behavior. The manifestation of spirituality is realized by our sharing that hope which is within our heart. The abiding of Jesus within our lives is not true unless it is visible to those who are in our environments. This is the focus of EMS until Christ comes again.

Simon Yako is the present director of EMS of ECWA. He is married to Ruth Yako and has three children. He is a former and present missionary, still working in the vineyard as he has for over thirty-one years. He and his wife served the Lord as missionaries since 1985 in various fields in Nigeria and Togo. He was also the former Northwest EMS regional coordinator and foreign missions coordinator. He is passionate about training missionaries and global missions.

Scripture: *Philippians 4:13 ("I can do all things through Christ who strengthens me")*

Resources: *A Vision Received: A Vision Passed On*, by Panya Baba (Jos, Nigeria: Africa Christian Textbooks, 2009).

History of SIM/ECWA 1893-1993, by Yusufu Turaki (published by Y. Turaki, 1993).

Global Missionary Fellowship

Steve Sang-Cheol Moon

The basic perspective in this case study is that God's words shape and mold not only the personal spirituality of a leader but also the spirituality of his or her organization. That has been the case with David Tai-Woong Lee who was the founding chairman of the Global Missionary Fellowship(GMF) based in Seoul, Korea.

> God's words shape and mold not only the personal spirituality of a leader but also the spirituality of his or her organization.

GMF was founded in 1987 by David Tai-Woong Lee and several other Korean church leaders to send Korean missionaries overseas. It now has 764 member missionaries who are working in 55 countries as of March 2015. GMF is an umbrella organization and also a legal body composed of three sending arms, three training centers, one research institute, an arm for missionary kids' education, and a legal department.

In response to my request to share the key Bible verses that impacted his spirituality and guided his ministry, Dr. Lee pointed to five Bible passages: Ephesians 4:11–13, Philippians 2:5–8, Philippians 4:4–9, 2 Peter 1:1–7, and 1 Peter 2:1–9. The key points in the passages explain the connection between his personal spirituality and the organizational spirituality and culture of GMF.

Lee highlighted the leadership role of maturing and equipping God's people for the work of ministry through the passage in Ephesians 4:11–13. As a result of this emphasis, a number of leaders and specialists as well as field missionaries grew under his leadership. GMF spirituality values people and the growth of their gifts.

What does it mean to follow the example of Christ Jesus' condescension and sacrifice in our lives? The practical challenge from Philippians 2:5–8, according to Lee, can be summarized as disclaiming our rights, lowering ourselves, and being obedient to God. Lee is always thankful for his colleagues' sacrificial commitment that motivates them to work behind the scenes.

From Philippians 4:4–9, Lee emphasizes the importance of spiritual joy, balance in personality, recognition of God's rule, and prayer. These elements of spirituality have been pursued in the community of GMF, especially at the Global Missionary Training Center(GMTC) which is one of its training arms. Every ministry division of GMF starts a communal prayer time at noon that lasts about one hour every day of the week.

2 Peter 1:1–7 is meaningful to Lee in terms of the maturation of spirituality. The passage explains the growth model of spirituality. Lee has heavily emphasized the importance of continual growth, showing a good example of diligent readership and eagerness to

learn. His encouragement and advice for younger leaders have been an important factor that shaped a learning environment of GMF.

1 Peter 2:1–9 posits the identity of God's people who are called to grow into salvation. This aspect of his spiritual emphasis resonates well with GMF's commitment to kingdom perspective and partnership. GMF's training centers have served other missionary sending agencies widely by welcoming their members in the programs.

Dong-hwa Kim, the new executive director and CEO of GMF, thinks that GMF needs to reflect the holistic aspect of mission more on its spiritual atmosphere while affirming its spiritual heritage. Kim draws a biblical foundation for his position from Matthew 9:35 and other passages.

It is God who colored the spirituality of GMF through David Tai-Woong Lee and other leaders. The name of the Lord is to be praised. Amen.

Steve Sang-Cheol Moon is Executive Director of the Korea Research Institute for Misions in Seoul, South Korea. He is the author of the *Korean Missionary Movement: Dynamics and Trends 1988–2013* (William Carey Library, 2016). He is married to Hee-Joo Yoo with two grown children.

Scripture: *Mark 8:34–35 ("Whoever wants to be my disciple...")*

Resource: *John Calvin, Institutes of the Christian Religion,* ed. John T. McNeill (Philadelphia: The Westminster Press, 1960).

Operation Mobilisation

Viv Thomas

Operation Mobilisation was founded in the late 1950s and emerged out of the North American Cultural Revolution that happened in the 1960s. It reflected the gift of a powerfully driven leader (George Verwer), American culture, and the social revolution taking place at that time. All three streams fed into the spirituality of OM in its early days.

Right at the heart of OM's spirituality was a brand of conservative evangelicalism which echoed the early Billy Graham. George Verwer had come to faith at a Billy Graham meeting. OM was Bible-based, direct, and an early adopter of any media that could get the message of the gospel out to as many people as possible. One of George Verwer's big ideas was that everyone should have the opportunity hear the gospel once. The activistic spirituality of evangelicalism in general, (and George Verwer's personality in particular), his distinctive theology of "redeeming the time," and a genuine passion for the lost drove the organization along in the power of the Holy Spirit. The primary prayer model was intercession. Nights of prayer were common and the style was focused on God answering particular prayers articulated in those meetings.

Alongside this was a desire for "spiritual revolution" through a "revolution of love." The 1960s was an age of social revolution with students dropping out of college, the emergence of black power, drug experimentation, the feminist movement, and the hippy culture of "peace and love." OM rode the waves of social revolution along with peace and love. Connected with this was a call to forsake all and follow Christ. It was a radical theme which called people to a simple lifestyle—to not be entangled by the world but to focus instead on the gospel spreading around the world. The military metaphor shaped much of OM's thinking. OM's name has military roots and there was an emphasis on personal discipline and duty.

The world has changed, so has OM. Sixty years later other themes have emerged, radically changing the organization's spirituality. As OM has engaged the world, so it has absorbed different emphases and practices; at its heart, OM is a pragmatic organization. Moving from the dominance of Western Enlightenment, rationalistic thinking towards the more ecstatic, fluid, and holistic models of the Middle East, Latin America, Africa, and Asia have been decisive in the spiritual development of OM. A widespread embrace of holistic ministries has brought the themes of justice and social transformation right to the front of the organization's imagination.

Perhaps the greatest change in OM's spirituality has been its response to the charismatic/Pentecostal movement. Half a billion of the world's population identify themselves as being Pentecostal and/or charismatic. Having emerged from a primary influence of the Christian Brethren in its early days, OM now finds itself with many identifying themselves loosely with charismatic theology or charismatic styles of worship and encounters with God. At its core, there is still a conservative evangelical theology shaping its spirituality, but styles of music, praise, and prayer often look charismatic. The supremacy of Scripture and the reality of spiritual warfare have always been a huge part of OM's spirituality. Conservative, Pentecostal, and charismatic come together around these themes in their various ways. Genuinely international teams embrace genuinely diverse styles of worship in multiple nations around the world.

More recently, another wave has developed shaping the organization's spirituality and this comes from another side of the church which has an emphasis on contemplation. It is not uncommon for leaders in OM to have spiritual retreats, practice meditative readings of Scripture, and practice silence in a desire to grow deeper with God. The values and sensibilities of the so-called "millennials" are helping to drive this emphasis.

> It is not uncommon for leaders in OM to have spiritual retreats, practice meditative readings of Scripture, and practice silence in a desire to grow deeper with God

As the organization has developed so has its marketing, donor development, strategic thinking, and communications systems. Perhaps the greatest danger facing OM in the shaping of its spiritual life into the future is in trusting these valid management systems too much and then accidentally cultivating a thin and unsatisfying spirituality that looks effective, but no longer inspires succeeding generations as the spiritual revolution of the 1960s certainly did. For now, OM is a glorious melting pot of worship styles and traditions, all seeking to glorify God in the holistic ministry of his Word throughout the nations.

Viv Thomas is the founder of Formation (www.formation.org.uk). He loves football (soccer), theater, movies, sport of most kinds, seeing people grow, eating healthy food, riding his bike around London; walking along the River Thames and spending time with his wife. He is an Associate International Director for OM International and continues to travel the world seeking to see leaders grow. He is an ordained Anglican; a lecturer; a mentor; spiritual director; organizational consultant and writer. He has written *Future Leader, Second Choice, Paper Boys*, *The Spectacular Ordinary Life,* and *The Spectacular Ordinary Organization* (the latter can be downloaded free from the above site). Viv has a PhD from King's College, London where his research focused on Christian leadership in relation to the Trinity.

Scripture: *Psalm 27* ("The Lord is my light and my salvation—whom shall I fear?...")

Resource: *In the name of Jesus,* by Henri Nowuen (New York: The Crossroad Publishing Company, 1989).

Pueblos Musulmanes Internacional

Allan Matamoros

PMI (Pueblos Musulmanes Internacional) is a Latin American mission society focused on serving and reaching out to the Muslim world with the gospel through the efforts of Spanish and Portuguese speaking churches.

PMI was born during the 1980s in a time of remarkable evangelical growth in our continent. Proyecto Magreb—our first official name—was greatly influenced by the missionary winds of the newly formed Iberoamerican Missionary Movement (Comibam).

Since our inception there have been two concepts that have moved our spirituality as a mission. The first is a holistic/integral understanding of missions, and the second is Jesus's incarnational model. These have shaped our convictions, life, and praxis in our journey through different Muslim settings around the world. These expressions have been lived by a community composed of twenty-one Latin-American nationalities and a few dozen of denominations and evangelical expressions.

> Since our inception there have been two concepts that have moved our spirituality as a mission. The first is a holistic/integral understanding of missions, and the second is Jesus's incarnational model.

An Integral Missional Community

In Latin America, until a few years ago, some of our evangelical churches and communities lived with the tendency of being disconnected from the outside world. The evangelical presence in several parts of this side of the world was perceived, and lived, as rather isolated, without strong connections to the extensive and deep difficulties in which our neighbors, cities, and countries were living. In that context the contribution of brothers and leaders such as Samuel Escobar and Rene Padilla helped us to express our faith in such a way that the whole gospel would be a blessing to the whole person; to show the gospel through our whole lives, deeds, and words. This impacted the ecclesiological life of many congregations throughout the Spanish and Portuguese speaking world. In addition this thinking deeply impressed the missional practices of PMI, a relatively young mission society in a journey to every nation.

Our passion has been to pursue being "integral" in our understanding of the physical needs of our Muslim neighbors. These are the people that we love; the people that we want to serve in the name of the Lord Jesus. As with many other missional communities, we have understood that our service to these people, through water well projects, development initiatives for women, medical work, and care for the children are more than just excuses to get a long-term residential visa or tools for evangelism, but rather, and above all, a vital expression of the values and message of the kingdom and a transparent and selfless way to show the unconditional love of the Father.

Our pursuit is to be integral in our church planting efforts and to avoid the dichotomist temptation of separating the "saint from the profane." Our mission statement says, "PMI exists to cooperate with the evangelical church of Latin America in the task of establishing, extending, and respectfully supporting the Church of Jesus Christ among Muslims through an integral missional approach."

Finally, we pursue an integral understanding of the spiritual realms, living and proclaiming our passion, love, and devotion for God, the ruler of the universe and beloved Father who is attracting every nation to himself for his glory. At the same time we aim to proclaim through our lives, words, and deeds that every language, nation, and spiritual dominion sooner or later will be pledging loyalty to Christ, the servant king and his kingdom.

> At the same time we aim to proclaim through our lives, words, and deeds that every language, nation, and spiritual dominion sooner or later will be pledging loyalty to Christ, the servant king and his kingdom.

An Incarnational Body

Our passion is to express the values of our community imitating the example of Jesus as part of our holistic understanding—the example he gave of denying himself in order to be one among us (Phil 2). The first step for a new PMI worker coming to serve in a Muslim nation is not renting a house, buying appliances, or starting a life, but rather immersing his/her life with the people he or she is called to serve and living with Muslim families for that initial season. Living with them, understanding the culture and worldview from within has proven throughout the years to be a way to incarnate ourselves on the field and leave a deep mark of a long-term commitment among our neighbors.

In that regards we understand that our incarnational journey in the Muslim world is going to bring joy, but not without doses of suffering and pain. This approach has proven, however, to be the way of the Calvary and a way to be companions of the Messiah in our common journey and path to the nations.

Allan Matamoros (Costa Rica) lives in the Middle East with his wife Patricia and his teenage children. Allan has served Latin American missionary agencies for the last twenty-five years deploying church planting and holistic missional teams in the Muslim World. He has served as the Director of FEDEMEC (The Costa Rican Evangelical Missions Federation), member of the COMIBAM executive team, Chairman of Vision 5:9, and as the International Director of PMI (Pueblos Musulmanes Internacional). Recently Allan served as one of the URBANA 2015 speakers and Middle East and North Africa Director for PARTNERS International.

Scripture: *Philippians 2:1–11 ("Therefore if you have any encouragement from being united with Christ...")*

Resources: *The Emotionally Healthy Leader: How Transforming Your Inner Life Will Deeply Transform Your Church, Team, and the World*, by Peter Scazzero (Grand Rapids, MI: Zondervan, 2015).

In the Name of Jesus: Reflections on Christian Leadership, by Henri Nouwen (New York: The Crossroad Publishing Company, 1989).

Friends Missionary Prayer Band—India

Simon Ponniah

Time and again in history God has raised people movements as missions for his purpose. Friends Missionary Prayer Band (FMPB) is one such mission movement God raised in the land of India in the 1950s. It was formed in an era of emerging missions, making multiple ripples of spiritual revival in the church—wave after wave of realization for the responsibility to the unreached nation. It was formed in a crucial moment when the nationalist government decided not to encourage any more of foreign missions and missionaries (ref: Nayogi commission).

FMPB emerged as a prayer movement initially through passion for the unreached Indian millions. Revival came among the local churches as a new spirituality in South India took place, then moved to other parts of the country. Vibrant change in the life of individuals and local church communities appeared as an indigenous spirituality swept across the church. There were a number of evangelistic initiatives with local church teams going around doing gospel work, sharing the good news of the Lord Jesus Christ. A renouncing of the pleasure of being comfortable, choosing a lifestyle of holy living, and sacrificial giving were components of kingdom culture that were spontaneously evident. They were locally united and became a stream of evangelistic movement.

Vacation Bible School (VBS) had just finished and volunteers from VBS began to be called VBS friends. They wanted to have an ongoing ministry with the local churches and outreach to the nearby regions, proclaiming the good news of the gospel by word and deed.

Our VBS friends who had been praying for the nation with their undying passion started reaching out wherever they pleased as a prayer group. One such outreach effort to Periyamalai, a hilly place then in Dharmapuri district of Tamil Nadu, became the first mission station. The South India Bible Seminary students and teachers with their holiness tradition had influence with this movement, and this seminary had a Missionary Prayer Band, a student body group involved in evangelism. The Missionary Prayer Band had been involved in evangelistic work on the weekends, then on Mondays the community had come back, reported the work, and prayed over it. On Fridays they prepared their work for the weekend and prayed over it. From these weekend trips the VBS friends adopted the word "Friends" and added it to "Missionary Prayer Band" to create the new name now known as FMPB. It was registered as a society in 1968 with the government.

The spiritual journey of this movement embraced an ascetic lifestyle along with daring faith in taking up the difficult task of evangelism in difficult situations and rather tough communities. It was felt this was a calling of mission. Further, the indigenous nature of zeal, passion, prayer, sacrifice, renewal, and daring obedience were seen as a mark of spirituality. The following five decades have seen these prayer bands become reflective practitioners of mission. In the 1960s the FMPB became a missionary sending movement, in the 1970s it became a church planting movement, in the 1980s a wholistic mission movement, and in 2000s these movements combined to become people reaching people with transformation as a focus. In 2010, church integration was a focus, and it started collaborating with church and all mass movements of people. This has initiated a massive initiative towards a 2020 focus of impacting the nation as a whole.

> The spiritual journey of this movement embraced an ascetic lifestyle along with daring faith in taking up the difficult task of evangelism in difficult situations and rather tough communities.

Today in 2016 FMPB has raised 1,100 cross-cultural missionaries, 1,700 evangelists from the local regions serving 300 people groups in about 200 districts to have saturation evangelism, 16 Bible translation projects, numerous adult literacy programs, 264 transformation packages in communities, child care, leadership development, training with theology and contextualization along systematic theology. In another 200 districts mission mobilization was done by serving the churches engaged in God's mission. Bishop Leslie Newbegin commented that the mission emulated the initiative of God the Holy Spirit, as he alone would initiate such a newness in the life of people. This has resulted in 7,000 first generation congregations with 70,000 disciples involved in training and taking their gospel to their neighbor groups and to form church bodies/dioceses/synods/conferences to empower the local leadership and the congregations to be integrated with national church bodies. Bishop Stephen Neil claimed this movement as God's wonder of this era and he was instrumental in shaping the mission vibrancy in its grassroots.

By then the spirituality called "simple lifestyle" shaped into a wartime mode of living was adopted as part of discipleship among all ranks and files of missionaries and among volunteers. This contextual lifestyle model imparted a sense of urgency for the proclamation of the gospel in attempting the big task of mission to the nation and expecting a great turnaround to happen in the lives of the people.

Now, the mission thrust is brought back to the center stage of the local churches for their teaching ministry. The cooperative efforts make complimentary situations of unity and solidarity in mission. The dialogue of biblical discipleship and a progressive missional thrust has been a challenge with the reality of poverty, need for justice, environment of ecology, and the new challenge of green energy as part of progressive, inclusive mission. Dr. Ralph Winter commented that this is a movement of God unique in the way of handling world mission in the context of poverty with a sense of prayer and sacrifice. The journey goes on learning from one level to the next level in God's mission.

Simon Ponniah started his mission journey with Friends Missionary Prayer Band (FMPB) as media missionary and a student volunteer in the seventies. Having been nurtured by the Evangelical Union, he was active with the local church for the prayer group and youth work before joining as a long term missionary. He completed his theological training in Union Biblical Seminary and later completed the Masters in Communication with Gurukul Lutehern Theological College and is currently completing a doctoral research thesis with the Senate of Serampore. He has been involved in church mission mobilization in North East India, Middle East, Europe and North America. He recently retired as the General Secretary of FMPB in 2016 and is now assigned to facilitate, mentor, and coach the emerging leadership. He is married to Rubella who is a youth worker and who continues to serve as resource teammate. Both are blessed with a son and daughter who are serving as professionals in the corporate world.

Scripture: *Luke 24:47 ("And repentance for the forgiveness of sins will be preached in his name to all nations...")*

Resource: *Knowing God*, by J I Packer (Downers Grove, IL: InterVarsity Press, 2011).

Mizo Movement, North East India

L N Tluanga

Mizo literally means hill people, and they live in Mizoram which is sandwiched between Myanmar to the east and south and Bangladesh to the west, the southernmost state among the seven North East India states. It covers a hilly area of 21,087 square kilometers with a population of 1,091,014 (2011 census) and a very pleasant climate.[6]

Church Planting in Mizoram

Christian missionaries came to Mizoram in the last decade of the nineteenth century and they began preaching the simple gospel message with emphasis on "faith in Jesus" and "deliverance from the power of evil spirits." The first missionary who set foot on Mizoram soil was Rev. William Williams, a Welsh missionary who came in 1891. Nearly three years later, two English missionaries, Rev. FW Savidge and Rev. JH Lorrain, sent by the Arthington Aborigines Mission arrived. By God's providence and intervention, the early missionaries agreed between themselves that the Welsh Calvinistic Presbyterian missionaries would plant Presbyterian churches in the north, and English missionaries would plant Baptist churches in the south of Mizoram. This arrangement continued for many years with excellent relationships and cooperation between them such that any Presbyterian church member who happened to migrate to the south for any reason automatically became a Baptist church member and vice versa. This unity was unique in Mizoram and many Christian workers who came to Mizoram for ministry considered this a miracle!

This unity was unique in Mizoram and many Christian workers who came to Mizoram for ministry considered this a miracle!

Church Growth through Revivals

God in his mercy and grace visited the Mizo church with a series of revivals with the result that within fifty years of the coming of the first missionaries, practically all Mizos claimed to have become Christians! The revival fires spread equally to both North and South Mizoram. The first revival came in the year 1906 as a result and outcome of the great Welsh revival of 1904, which ignited the Khasi church planted by the Welsh Mission. A group of ten church members—seven from the north and three from the south—traveled on foot to Mairang village, Khasi hills (now Meghalaya) in the hope of receiving the revival fire from them. But nothing happened to them as they had anticipated and they started home rather disappointed and dejected, even quarreling among themselves as they went back. But before reaching Aizawl, they stopped to offer

---

6   "Destination that Delights" (colorful publicity folder; Govt. of Mizoram, November 2008).

a short prayer of thanksgiving at Chaltlang village. First one prayed, then another and then another until the very last of the ten prayed. One member Zathanga remarked, "While the first of us was praying I was aware of a streak of flame very high above us. And, as each one prayed in turn, the flame descended lower and lower, and as the last one prayed, it disappeared. I am sure it went inside us."[7] The revival fire came upon them five days later (Monday, April 9, 1906) when they were saying farewell to the three members from south; "But as they sang the usual farewell hymn, 'God be with you till we meet again,' something mysterious happened. The hymn was repeated time and time again and so too with other hymns. An ecstasy possessed the congregation as others came to join them... The missionaries were in tears."[8] The hallmark of this first revival was conviction of sin—many lay prostrate on the floor confessing their sins and pleading for God's mercy and forgiveness. "Believers were confirmed in their faith and a considerable number of non-believers were converted."[9] The second revival came in April 1913 "which was more powerful than that of 1906" with emphasis on the second coming of Christ.[10] The third revival occurred simultaneously on July 26, 1919 in three villages, one in the north and two in the south. "The emphasis was on the Cross and sufferings of Christ, revealing the love of God for man and demanding the corollary of brotherly love and Christian affection."[11] It is not easy to pinpoint the exact date of the arrival of the fourth revival, usually regarded as beginning in 1933 and continuing for a number of years with emphasis on the work and gifts of the Holy Spirit. Some of us can count future revivals—the fifth occurring from 1958 and continuing till 1966, the sixth starting in 1984 and continuing, the seventh from 1989 into the early 90s, and the eighth starting in Kelkang village in 2013 and continuing and spreading unabated in 2015 all over Mizoram. In *Amazing Mizo Missions*, the author, analyzing the first four revivals in Mizoram, concluded their impacts as (a) creating mission awareness; (b) affirming the missionary call; (c) bringing commitment for mission.[12]

> The hallmark of this first revival was conviction of sin—many lay prostrate on the floor confessing their sins and pleading for God's mercy and forgiveness.

Mizo Mission Movements

The Mizo Presbyterian church was strongly mission oriented from its infancy, so much so that within about ten years of its existence in 1910, "Three boys, Vanzika, Savawma, and Thangchhingpuia, students in Aizawl, went to Senvawn, Manipur" to preach the gospel. "Then in 1911 Mr. Hrangvunga of Bunghmun village in western Mizoram traveled to Tripura because of his burden for the lost souls there. In 1913, Mr. Upa

7   Merion J. Lloyd, *History of the Church in Mizoram (Harvest in the Hills)* (Aizawl: Synod Publication Board, 1991), 90, 94.
8   Lloyd, 95.
9   Lloyd, 96.
10   Lloyd, 162.
11   Lloyd, 191.
12   S Nengzakhup, *Amazing Mizo Missions* (Bangalore : SAIACS Press, 1999), 27–29.

Thianga, later Rev. Thianga, migrated to Haflong for the sake of the gospel. Another early volunteer, Mr. R Dala, an ordained elder of Mission Veng church, Aizawl, migrated in 1913 to Manipur to preach the gospel."[13]

The Synod Mission Board of the Mizo Presbyterian church reports in 2015 that it has 2,497 missionaries working within India and abroad with a mission fund of more than $8 million US dollars. The Baptist Church of Mizoram has 1,118 missionaries with a mission fund of over $2.5 million US dollars (2015). Thirteen other churches in Mizoram have between them 1,446 missionaries; and there are eleven parachurch bodies in Mizoram sending out a total of 343 missionaries between them. The total number of all missionaries sent out from Mizoram by the churches and parachurch groups adds up to 5,404. It must be noted here that the number is constantly increasing as the sending bodies are in the process of recruiting more missionaries on a continual basis. It is reported that the number has increased by four already after the data was collected early in July 2015.

It may be pointed out here that the above figure works out as one missionary for every 200 inhabitants of Mizoram state, irrespective of whether they are Christians or not. It must be noted that the number of missionaries keeps increasing at a constant rate. Despite these encouraging number of missionaries sent out from Mizoram, it must be realized that in view of the great need for the evangelization of India and the world our (Mizo) contribution may not even amount to "a drop in the bucket" in the wider world mission scenario!

References (Mizo)

Baba, Panya. 2014. *A Vision Received, A Vision Passed On: The History of EMS of ECWA 1948–1998*. Nigeria: Gajofa Venture Ltd.

"Destination that Delights." 2008. Publicity folder: Govt. of Mizoram.

Lloyd, J. Merion. 1991. *History of the Church in Mizoram (Harvest in the Hills)*. Aizawl: Synod Publication Board.

Nengzakhup, S. 1999. *Amazing Mizo Missions*. Bangalore: SAIACS Press.

OMF International. 2005. *Christ Alone: A Pictorial Presentation of Hudson Taylor's Life and Legacy*. Hong Kong: OMFHK.

Synod Mission Board. 2015. "A Brief Report of the Mizoram Synod Mission Board." Unpublished, Aizawl, Mizoram: Synod Mission Board.

---

13   Nengzakhup, 5.

Tluanga, Upa Dr L. N. 2011. "Hlimna aiin Tharna—a thupui zawk lo vem ni?" In Article 100, *Thlan Chhuah: Kristian Tlangau Centenary Project*. Aizawl: Synod Literature and Publication Board.

Turaki, Yusuf. 1993. *An Introduction to the History of SIM/ECWA in Nigeria 1893–1983*. Jos, Nigeria: Challenge Press.

L N Tluanga was born in Mizoram, North East India. He obtained MSc from Calcutta University, PhD from Gauhwati University and worked as Lecturer in Colleges/University and then as Mizoram Director of Education for a total of twenty years. In response to God's call, he left the Government role and served first as a missionary teacher then as Secretary for Education in the Kiribati Protestant Church, Central Pacific for seven years; then for ten years as Staff Consultant, Evangelical Teachers' Fellowship of India and Executive Secretary, Interserve India based in New Delhi in the nineties. Three books edited by him and published are *Teacher's Challenge* (1989), *Teacher Speaks* (1995) and *The Making of a Christian Teacher* (1998).

Scripture: *Luke 1:74–75 ("To rescue us from the hand of our enemies,and to enable us to serve him without fear…"), John 15:16, 1 Corinthians 15:58, 2 Corinthians 4:17–18*

Resource: *The Christian's Secret of a Happy Life,* by Hannah Whitall Smith (Brooklyn, NY: Brownstone Books, 2009).

Along the
Journey

Preparing and Engaging

CHAPTER 25

Spirituality and the Missionary Call

Bruce Dipple

Several decades ago, the mission agency SIM published a brochure with the title, *The Missionary Call: What to Do if You Don't Have One.* This brochure was so in demand that it had to be reprinted more than any other SIM brochure of the era.

In *Too Valuable To Lose*, global research on missionary attrition indicated that the lack of an adequate sense of call was the second highest cause of attrition amongst missionaries from newer sending countries.[1]

Subsequent research on missionary retention reported in *Worth Keeping* also highlighted the significant relationship between a clear calling and continuation in missionary service.[2] But the editors of the report went on to point out that all the responses were made without any attempt to define the concept of a call. This highlights a common problem. In so much of the literature and in so many mission-oriented sermons, the reality and appropriateness of the concept of a missionary call is simply assumed.

It is clear from all that has been said and written that the concept of a missionary call is an important one for many people. The term and the concept are worthy of reflection, particularly as they are often linked with spiritual maturity. Indeed, one pastor of a multicultural church explained in a personal conversation that, "If a missionary shares the details of their specific missionary call with the church, the congregation

> Is it valid to link the idea of a missionary call with the depth of our spirituality?

perceives them as more spiritual than a missionary who does not have the experience of such a call." Is it valid to link the idea of a missionary call with the depth of our spirituality?

---

1   William D. Taylor, *Too Valuable To Lose* (Pasadena CA: William Carey Library, 1997), 94.
2   Rob Hay, et al, *Worth Keeping* (Pasadena CA: William Carey Library, 2007), 93–95.

What Is the Origin of the Term?

Some years ago, the personal papers of a deceased missionary were returned to his agency by non-Christian relatives who were not sure what to do with them. Among those materials were two papers written by mission leaders in the 1930s. Both of the papers referred to the necessity of a missionary call, and both of them referred to passages in Isaiah 6, Jeremiah 1, and Ezekiel 1.

Closer inspection, however, revealed that neither writer actually referred to the text of these passages, but rather to the headings inserted in their particular translation of the Bible—The Call of Isaiah, The Call of Jeremiah, etc. Those particular headings appear less frequently today, but they are clearly one source for our usage of the term "call" with regard to Christian ministry.

More recently, a theological student presented an essay on missionary motivation which made reference to the missionary call. The essay traced the use of the term through the history of the English language. It linked its present Christian usage to the early nineteenth century practice of describing work that entailed a significant level of personal sacrifice as a "calling." It was applied to doctors and nurses, as well as to clergy, and by extension, missionaries.

Still others see the term originating with the testimony of Paul, who described himself as "called to be an apostle." This personal statement of Paul with regard to his apostleship and authoritative role in the church is seen as establishing a pattern for others involved in ministry.

Perhaps all of the above contribute to the emergence of the term "missionary call" in the English language. It is certainly true that the term has been used widely for many years in the mission context. But it is also valid to ask if every user of the term is actually using it to convey the same meaning.

What Is Meant by the Term?

Many cross-cultural workers today make reference to their missionary call. But what exactly are they seeking to convey when they use the term? What ideas or experiences are being included in the term?

A few years ago, a group of students in an Australian mission training center were given the assignment of speaking to every missionary visiting the institution who used the term "missionary call" or something similar in their presentation. They were to ask them to explain in more detail what they meant when they used the term. The students found that the responses related to one of three areas: to an assurance of God's presence in the whole decision-making and preparation process; to the knowledge that God's Word was the source of their conviction and motivation for what they were doing; or to a spiritual experience that gave them a sense of divine authority in their ministry.

The group of students summarized all the explanations as meaning, "God is in this with me!" And any Christian involved in ministry would surely agree with the necessity of having this level of assurance of God's involvement in their life. But … is "missionary call" the appropriate and most useful term to use to describe this assurance of God's involvement? Would it not be clearer and more beneficial for everyone if we described exactly what we meant, rather than using an insider term that might actually be a source of confusion or misdirection for some growing Christians?

> Is "missionary call" the appropriate and most useful term to use to describe this assurance of God's involvement?

Some Christians do not feel it necessary to consider involvement in cross-cultural ministry because "I have not received a call." Some Christians moving into ministry who receive advice that is contrary to their existing plans will press ahead and ignore that advice with the assertion that "God called me." In other words, it does not take much for the "missionary call" idea to become an excuse, rather than a motivation.

Similarly, a claim to have a missionary call can easily provoke some Christians to put that missionary on a spiritual pedestal and instill a sense of never being able to be like them. Many of the early missionary biographies are written in such a way that they portray the missionary as a spiritual giant, for whom the "call" was a fundamental aspect of their great spirituality. So perhaps, from a communication perspective, it would be more helpful to explain what is being meant, rather than using the term and assuming our audience understands the intended meaning.

What Input Does the Bible Give Us?

Some forty years ago, missiologist J Herbert Kane suggested, "The term 'missionary call' should never have been coined. It is not scriptural and therefore can be harmful."[3] Is his comment justified? There is general consensus that the primary use of "call" in Scripture relates to God's calling of people to himself in the context of salvation and to people calling on his name. Walter McConnell commented that "the Bible never specifically mentions a call to missions. Most of the calls mentioned in Scripture entreat people either to begin or to live out the Christian life, not to engage in particular forms of Christian service. These two aspects of calling—to salvation and to ethical living—are brought together in Ephesians 4:1 where Paul urges his readers 'to live a life worthy of the calling you have received.'"[4]

The term "call" is used twice in the New Testament in the context of service—Acts 13:2 and Acts 16:10. Neither case, however, refers to the subjective experience of the

---

3   J. Herbert Kane, *Understanding Christian Mission* (Grand Rapids MI: Baker, 1974), 41.
4   Walter McConnell, "The Missionary Call: A Biblical and Practical Appraisal," *Evangelical Missions Quarterly* (43:2, 2007) 210–217.

individual being the deciding factor concerning their involvement in ministry. In Acts 13:2, while some personal awareness of God's purpose for them may well be indicated by the phrase "to which I have called them," the central emphasis is on the involvement of the local church at Antioch in sending off Paul and Barnabas. With Acts 16:10, although Paul was the one who had the vision, it is the whole group who discussed the vision and determined its meaning—"we got ready... concluding that God had called us." In each example, there is a strong emphasis on the corporate aspect. And that corporate aspect can easily be left in the shadows when the emphasis is placed on the necessity of a personal and subjective "call" as the basis for moving out in ministry.

What About Spirituality and the Corporate Aspect?

Our topic indicated that we are exploring the relationship between spirituality and the missionary call. Spirituality can be defined in many different ways, depending on the context of the discussion. For the purpose of this discussion, spirituality is understood as speaking of a deep and developing relationship with God that draws us towards an increasing measure of conformity to his image (2 Cor 3:18). It is the experience of transformation at the hand of God such that elements of his nature and purpose become visible in our lives—the fruit of the Spirit's presence and ministry (Gal 5:22). It is a transformation that finds the framework for its expression in the redeemed body of Christ, God's alternate community in the world. It is the pathway of godliness, of the Spirit's work in our life as we become more like Jesus—more like him in:

> Spirituality is understood as speaking of a deep and developing relationship with God that draws us towards an increasing measure of conformity to his image (2 Cor 3:18).

- Our understanding of the mind of God (Rom 12:2)
- Our relationships in the body of Christ (John 13:34–35)
- Our view of the world (John 3:16–17)
- Our servant attitude (Phil 2:5–7)
- Our desire to walk in obedience (John 14:23–24, 15:9–12)
- Our ministry in the world to which he has sent us (John 17:18)

The concept of the missionary call is often portrayed as a step along that pathway of godliness. But does the concept serve us well? Or is it captive to the individualistic nature of Western culture? Does it separate the issue of our personal direction in life from our understanding of what it means to be living in unity within the body of Christ (Rom 12:3–5)? "There is no Christian spirituality without community. No community, no spirituality. Our personal spirituality is lived out in community."[5]

---

5   Paul Bendor-Samuel, "Organizational Spirituality: A Journey in Growing," *Connections* (8.1:23, 2009), 23.

What Are the Implications for a Local Church?

If we read again those passages mentioned above in Isaiah 6, Jeremiah 1, etc., we will soon find that the focus of activity is with God as sender. Have a look at Isaiah 6:8, Jeremiah 1:7, Ezekiel 2:3, as well as Exodus 3:10, and you will see that they all speak of God sending his servant to a particular ministry. We also see in the Gospels that the fact of being sent was very significant to Jesus. He frequently refers to the Father as the one who sent him (Luke 4:43, John 6:38–39, 8:16–18, 15:21, 16:5, etc.). He also linked that same awareness of being sent with the ministry of his disciples (Matt 9:38, Mark 3:14).

As Jesus speaks to his Father in John 17, he refers on several occasions to two groups of people. The first group are "those you have given me," with the second being "the world" out of which they came. Jesus speaks of the relationship between those he has been given and the world from which they came in 17:14–19, including the statement "As you sent me into the world, I have sent them into the world" (17:18). All those the Father has given him are sent into the world. And he goes on in verse 20 to make it clear that all future believers are included in his thinking as he speaks of sending "them" into the world.

What did Jesus have in mind as he spoke of sending his followers into the world? His use of the phrase "As you sent me" indicates that we will find our understanding in considering the key aspects of Jesus himself being sent by the Father. Even a quick reading of those places in the Gospels where Jesus speaks of himself being sent gives us the key topics of authority, purpose, global perspective, and message. These key areas give the agenda for the church, global and local, to consider its role as God's sent community in the world.

In Jesus' teaching here, we do not have certain individuals being given the command to go, but the whole group is being given the identity of "sent." The body of Christ is portrayed as a sent body. Flowing from that, in Acts 13:1–3 we have the picture of a local church expressing its "sentness" by sending some of its key people to minister elsewhere. This sending role of the local church is also exercised when Paul and Silas are "commended by the brothers to the grace of the Lord" in Acts 15:40 and "the brothers at Lystra and Iconium spoke well of" Timothy in Acts 16:2. There is no individualistic, subjective missionary call as the single motivation of the individuals here—rather it is the body of Christ, guided by the Spirit, expressing its identity as God's sent people in the world. It is a picture of the body that Paul reflects in his comment, "And how can anyone preach unless they are sent?"

> There is no individualistic, subjective missionary call as the single motivation of the individuals here—rather it is the body of Christ, guided by the Spirit, expressing its identity as God's sent people in the world.

This biblical concept of a sent body of Christ makes a further contribution to the way we view participation in mission. It challenges the here/there, local/global dichotomy that infects so much thinking concerning our missional responsibility. Being sent is part of the nature of the church. Being sent can, therefore, be expressed in many different ways that do not have to be validated by geography, by financial need, by a particular title, or by a special missionary call.

Christ has called us all to himself for his grace gift of salvation, and as his transformed people he sends us into the world outside of his redeemed community. This argues against the cross-cultural gospel worker serving in a distant land being put on a spiritual pedestal. It affirms that the Christian with a disciplined prayer life that intentionally embraces the world is expressing the sent nature of the church of which they are a part. And those who do go to distant lands are an expression of the nature of the local church as a sent body—their ministry far away becomes an extension of the ministry of their local church. This in turn impacts the life of the local church. No longer are they restricted to "send away, pay, and pray." Even when the expertise of a mission agency is being used, the ownership by the church increases, the sense of it being "our ministry" grows, their interest in the people being reached develops—what can we do "through" our missionaries replaces the common question of what can we do "for" our missionaries.

The Missionary Call and Spirituality?

Every Christian who has been reconciled to God in Christ has also been given a ministry of reconciliation (2 Cor 5:18). It is a part of who we are in Christ. It is now part of our new nature. And whatever form our involvement takes in that reconciliation ministry, it is essential that every Christian has the assurance of God's presence and of the Spirit's enabling in their ministry. And that assurance is founded on God's Word to us as members of his alternate community in the world. Yet that same Word also makes it clear that there will always be diversity in the way God deals with his children in giving us that assurance which he promises.

> Every Christian who has been reconciled to God in Christ has also been given a ministry of reconciliation (2 Cor 5:18). It is a part of who we are in Christ.

As we confront the topic of this chapter, there are certain things that we can affirm. We can affirm that all of life walked in harmony and relationship with the Triune God is spiritual. It is a spiritual experience to know that God is with me, to know that the Holy Spirit will guide me into all truth and empower me as a member of God's people in the world, to know who I am as part of God's community in the world. We can also affirm that the realm of the spiritual may embrace an element of the mystical while insisting that our diversity of personality, culture, and religious background prevents that mystical experience from ever becoming mandatory for every Christian.

We also need to affirm that there is no biblical demand or obligation for a spiritual or mystical experience that is labeled as a "missionary call." With the term "missionary" now frequently inappropriate as a description of Christians moving out into the world with gospel intent, and the importance of the biblical term "call" with regard to our salvation, it is definitely time for greater clarity as we testify to the way God has led and taught us obedience along the steps of the long journey.

Spirituality finds its foundation in God calling us to himself; it finds its development in the spiritual growth fuelled by the ministry of the Spirit and the Word; it finds its fulfillment in obedient participation in God's alternate community expressing its sent nature in the world.

Discussion Questions

1. Use a concordance or search facility to identify every occurrence of "sent" or "send" in John's gospel. Read each one in its context and write down what each one teaches you about Jesus' thinking about the Father, himself, and his disciples. Then write a paragraph setting out the implications for you and for your local church of what you have learned.
2. With a map of the Mediterranean Sea region in New Testament times in front of you, read 1 Thessalonians 1:2–10. Note how Paul describes the breadth of their impact for the gospel. What links can you observe between their witness and the words of Christ in Acts 1:8? To what degree is this same pattern identifiable in your local church? What steps could be taken to develop further your church's ministry to the world beyond its doors?
3. Assume you are responsible in your local church for a discipleship group for young adults. Outline an 8–10 step process (reading, prayer, activity, etc.) that you would propose to a member(s) of the group who expresses interest in possibly becoming involved in full-time ministry somewhere in the world.

References

Bendor-Samuel, Paul. 2009. "Organizational Spirituality: A Journey in Growing." *Connections*. 8.1:23.

Hay, Rob, et al. 2007. *Worth Keeping*. Pasadena CA: William Carey Library.

Kane, J. Herbert. 1974. *Understanding Christian Mission*. Grand Rapids MI: Baker.

McConnell, Walter. 2007. "The Missionary Call: A Biblical and Practical Appraisal." *Evangelical Missions Quarterly*. 43:2.

Taylor, William D. 1997. *Too Valuable To Lose*. Pasadena CA: William Carey Library.

Bruce Dipple served as a church planter and pastor in Australia, Bible College Principal in Niger, SIM Director for Australia/East Asia, and mission lecturer at Sydney Missionary and Bible College (SMBC). He continues in semiretirement as a research supervisor at SMBC, as adjunct faculty in the Asia doctoral program of Grace Theological Seminary Indiana, as Pastor for Education and Global Focus at his home church in Sydney, and consults with local churches on the integrated development of their global mission programs. Bruce and his wife, Sylvia, live in Waterfall, Australia.

Scripture: *Hebrews 10:19-25 ("Therefore, brothers and sisters, since we have confidence to enter the Most Holy Place by the blood of Jesus…")*

Resource: *The Perfect Saviour*, ed. by Jonathan Griffiths (Downers Grove, IL: InterVarsity Press, 2012).

CHAPTER 26

Teaching and Learning to Nurture Spirituality

Ruth Wall

Praxis in the Classroom

For nearly a decade (2006–2015) I lived at All Nations Christian College in the UK, training adults from around the world for cross-cultural life and ministry. Walking alongside several hundred men and women has greatly impacted my own spirituality and given a greater appreciation of how spiritual maturity may be fostered. The classroom can be a context of praxis and transformation, but it concerns me that the classroom (and the pulpit) is too easily reduced to a place for the transmission of information rather than a space for transformation. Over years I have explored how spirituality might be fostered and discovered adult educational theories of transformative learning have something of value to offer spiritual formation.[1]

This chapter is for those who are concerned to understand how to nurture and develop spirituality in others and offers five theoretically informed themes that have been tested practically in the classroom. These themes are not new and may be recognized in the writing of others. For example, in his paper "Missionary Training and Spirituality" Robert Brynjolfson includes intentionality and integration as themes for nurturing spiritual formation.[2]

Before addressing how we nurture spirituality we need to be clear about what we mean by spiritual maturity.

---

1   Ruth Wall, *Preparing Adults for Crossing Cultures: A Study of a Transformative Learning Approach to Christian Mission Training* (PhD Thesis UCL Institute of Education, London, 2015).
2   Rob Brynjolfson, *Missionary Training and Spirituality: Spiritual Formation in Theological Education* (https://www.oikoumene.org, 2009).

What Is Spiritual Maturity?

Earlier chapters of this book have addressed the question, "What does Christian spiritual maturity look like?" Christian spirituality is expressed in being rooted in Christ and related to the body of Christ. Christian spirituality is a transformed identity that is no longer "apart from Christ" (Eph 2:12) but is reconciled to God and renewed by God's Spirit, rooted in Christ and part of the body of Christ where, "together with all the saints" (Eph 3:18) we share a corporate longing to know Christ more and be filled with God.

Spirituality is demonstrated in radical obedience to all that Jesus taught and is evidenced by lasting fruit. Spirituality creates a hunger for the gifts of the Spirit in order to be empowered for service in the church and in the world.

This is spirituality that is both mystical and earthy; it involves our thinking, attitudes, will, emotions, choices, motivation, actions, and relationships. It is "whole person spirituality," a spirituality of our head, heart, and hands. Christian spirituality affects—and transforms—every sphere of our life in the world.

> Christian spirituality affects—and transforms—every sphere of our life in the world.

Five Characteristics of Training to Nurture Spiritual Maturity

With this holistic perspective of Christian spirituality in mind let us consider how spirituality may be nurtured. These ideas are not an exhaustive set of teaching and learning principles but rather guiding principles that have been well tested and offered to stimulate your own reflection and guide your practice.

The five guiding themes for fostering spirituality overlap and are interrelated but are described separately in order to help consider the place of each in fostering spirituality. When present, these five themes work synergistically with each one enhancing and enabling the others.

Five themes for fostering spirituality are:

1. Intentional
2. Holistic
3. Relational
4. Integrated
5. Reproducible

Intentional

Learning that Is Intentional about Spiritual Formation

Spiritual maturity is the essence of Christian discipleship, not an optional add-on. Therefore spiritual formation needs to be expressed as the heart of any discipleship training. All other learning goals are subsidiary to, and shaped by, the goal of spiritual maturity.

> Spiritual maturity is the essence of Christian discipleship, not an optional add-on.

Why is intentionality so important? Educators and learners give attention to the parts of learning that they are intentional about. An unexamined assumption of educators may be the successful transfer of the formal curriculum to the student. The educator's intention is to develop students with knowledge of the subject. Transmission largely involves the cognitive skills of remembering, understanding, and applying, and hopefully will also include analyzing, evaluating, and synthesizing, and the extent that the transfer of knowledge is achieved is measured by some kind of assessment at the end.[3] But, if spiritual maturity is the heart of learning then educators need to be intentional about teaching and learning that goes beyond the transfer of knowledge to also nurture other aspects of spiritual development.

Educators also need to anticipate that they will be growing spiritually as they teach and as they learn with and from the students. If the educator has no expectation of growing spiritually then how can they lead students to grow?

Practical Suggestions to Promote Intentionality

- **Be explicit.** Make the intention to foster spiritual growth explicit.

    Write the goal of spiritual formation into course descriptions, module outlines, course materials, learning tasks, and assessment methods.

    Speak about spiritual formation from the start of the course.

    Give spirituality space and attention in various ways, e.g., incorporate different kinds of prayer and use a variety of participatory approaches (debates, presentations, and collaborative assignments) that challenge attitudes and relational skills alongside the cognitive dimension.

    Employ creative and artistic forms to help bring to life the cognitive dimension and to inspire wonder and worship and to foster joy.

---

3   Benjamin Bloom, *Taxonomy of Educational Objectives, Handbook 1: Cognitive Domain* (Addison Wesley Publishing Company, 1956). LW Anderson and David Krathwohl, eds. *A Taxonomy for Learning, Teaching, and Assessing: A Revision of Bloom's Taxonomy of Educational Objectives* (New York: Longman, 2001).

- **Be bidirectional**. Spiritual growth is a bidirectional process between educator and student and between student and student.

  Enable learners to identify their own spiritual goals and share these in appropriate ways with their tutor and their peers.

  Be open to learning from the experiences, faith, and wisdom of the students. It is in a shared sense of pilgrimage that spirituality is fostered.

  Be careful to notice what God is doing among you as you learn together.

- **Develop rituals.** Allow rituals to emerge that will help foster spirituality, e.g., ritualized beginnings and endings of class can help aspects of spirituality (hospitality, caring, honesty, faith, etc.) to be noticed and shared.

  Inviting students to open in prayer or taking a moment of silent reflection at the end of a class creates space for the Holy Spirit to work in our hearts and minds.

  Encourage each cohort of students to develop their own rituals in ways that are dynamic and uniquely express the community.

Holistic

Learning that Engages and Transforms the Whole Person

Spiritual maturity involves the whole person so it follows that training will need to involve the whole person. We need to have a whole person perspective of learning.

To conceptualize the process of learning imagine a triple-helix or three-stranded rope. The three strands can be identified but are inseparable. In the same way learning involves an integration of three processes. There is a cognitive process that involves our thinking and understanding; an affective process that involves our attitudes, feelings, and motivations; and a social process that involves our relationship with the experience or subject, with our self, and with others. These three inseparable dimensions combine in the process we call "learning."[4]

> A whole person perspective of learning understands the inseparable nature of these three dimensions—thinking-feeling-relating.

Helping people learn requires addressing how people think, how people feel, and how they relate. We can call this the head-heart-hands or whole person view of learning.

A whole person perspective of learning understands the inseparable nature of these three dimensions—thinking-feeling-relating. All three dimensions are recognized

---

4   Knud Illeris, *How We Learn* (Oxford: Routledge, 2007).

whether the context of learning is formal (classroom), non-formal (workplace or church), or informal (coffee shop or home).

We already noted that much learning in the classroom involves the transfer of knowledge that is then tested. At its best transfer learning is assimilation or learning by addition and this has its place. But transfer learning at its worst is a "banking system" that may be "non-learning" because it lacks any critical thinking or ownership by the student.[5] Transferring knowledge may provide students with what to think but it does not teach how to think.

When Jesus trained his disciples he could not prepare them for every situation they would face or give them every tool to meet every challenge ahead. Instead, Jesus equipped his disciples for ministry through a change in their DNA. This is transformation. They were led through a process of transformation in their identity, worldview, attitudes, and relationships.

Nurturing spiritual maturity requires challenging our "taken for granted" ways of thinking, habitual attitudes, and ways of relating to one another so that we "conform to the image of his Son" (Rom 8:29). Developing new ways of thinking, feeling, and relating is sometimes an uncomfortable process!

How is transformation fostered? Three core processes are critical reflection, dialogue, and action: critical reflection on our own assumptions, attitudes, and ways of doing things, learning from and with others through dialogue, and taking transformative action are all steps in a process of transformation.

This kind of holistic learning calls for a radical renewal in our planning and training designs. We need to renew the classroom so that it becomes a space for learning in community, and renew the curriculum so that students learn the processes of reflection, dialogue, and action.

Balia and Kim express this kind of whole-person learning as the vision for theological and mission education that educates:

> the ear to hear God's word and the cry of God's people;
> the heart to heed and respond to suffering;
> the tongue to speak to both weary and arrogant;
> the hands to work with the lowly;
> the mind to reflect on the good news of the gospel;
> the will to respond to God's call;

---

5   Paulo Freire used the term "banking system" to critique the traditional education system where knowledge is transferred from educator to student without any critical thinking; Paulo Freire, *Pedagogy of the Oppressed* (New York: Bloomsbury Academic, 1968). Peter Jarvis identifies three kinds of "non-learning"; presumption (things you already understand), non-consideration (things you do not relate to) and rejection (things you do not want to learn); Peter Jarvis, *Paradoxes of Learning: On Becoming an Individual in Society* (Hoboken, NJ: Wiley and Sons, 1992).

the spirit to wait on God in prayer, to struggle, and to be silent,
    to intercede for the church and the world;
the body to be the temple of the Holy Spirit.[6]

When we see people as whole and not simply as thinkers, important as thinking is, transformation is possible. Whole person learning involves the Spirit and the mind, the thinking and the feeling, the individual and the social.

Involving the whole person in learning requires different approaches to teaching.

Practical Suggestions for Encouraging Holistic Learning

- **Learning tasks.** Use a variety of learning tasks that build critical reflection, dialogue, and application of learning. Learning tasks can be varied and creative such as group work, debates, reading, reflective journals, simulations, seminars, lectures, field visits, practical tasks, case studies, and role plays.

- **Assessments.** Use a variety of assessments to promote holistic learning as well as test learning. Alongside the traditional assessment methods (essays, exams) incorporate collaborative assignments (e.g., group project with presentation). Assessment can include different elements including presentation, reflective journaling, reports (verbal or written) on practical assignments, reading logs, or short answer responses to questions that encourage reflection and application.

- **Research.** Incorporate research whatever level or length of study. Engaging students in different kinds of inquiry builds a sense of ownership in the learning process.

  Teachers may "steal" the learning from students by always providing the answer so use inductive methods as well as deductive methods that invite the student to be involved in discovery.

- **Share discoveries.** Give time for students to share their discoveries with one another in different ways (e.g., testimonies, stories, short reports and presentations, summary power point slides, or visual aids.) Sharing can be done via email, Facebook, or other social media as well as during class time.

- **Recognize and handle emotions.** Encourage communication that goes beyond sharing ideas. Allow students to make emotional and spiritual connections with each other through telling their stories and expressing their feelings as well as their thinking.

  Allow space for sharing. Learn to listen to one another.

---

6   Daryl Balia, and Kirsteen Kim, eds, *Witnessing to Christ Today* (Oxford: Regnum, 2010), 153.

Create opportunities for prayer.

Transformation is often an uncomfortable process that may involve strong emotions.

Disequilibrium is created through critical reflection and students may be resistant to learn when their emotions are negative. Educators need to recognize and acknowledge when emotions are stirred and handle emotions with respect and care so that learners are supported and enabled to examine what is underlying the feelings so that they can work through the process of learning.

Relational

Learning that Is Embedded in Community

Learning is a social, relational process and promoting transformative learning focuses on developing reciprocal relationships of learning. Taylor and Snyder (2012) reviewed the education literature on transformative learning and found that "in every review of transformative learning, the role of relationships has been identified as being significant in the process of transformation."[7]

> Learning is a social, relational process and promoting transformative learning focuses on developing reciprocal relationships of learning.

A learning community is a group of people who learn with and from one another. A great deal of lip service is paid to the idea of "learning community," but the authentic practice of fostering a learning community requires a transformed pedagogy. A learning community may be found in various contexts including residential colleges, online forums, workplace, church, community, and the home. The direct benefits of learning communities include sharing, synergy and better scholarship, as well as connecting and nurturing personal and spiritual transformation.

Learning communities have more than a sound educational basis; they are shaped by biblical and theological concepts. Humans are made in the image of a Triune God who reveals to us the nature of community in which each participates in serving the other, and the whole is an expression of agape-love. This is the design for all human relationships and therefore, it is no wonder that community is the place for deep spiritual nurture and development.

---

7   Edward Taylor and Melissa Synder, "A Critical Review of Research on Transformative Learning Theory, 2006–2010," in *The Handbook of Transformative Learning*, eds. Taylor, Cranton, and Associates (Hoboken, NJ: Jossey-Bass, 2012) 37–55.

Practical Suggestions for Fostering A Learning Community

- **Hospitality**. Find ways to express hospitality in the classroom. From the first encounter educators need to show openness and acceptance to each member of the class. A short pre-course questionnaire can help educators to begin to know their students so that students immediately feel welcomed. As relationships develop students are made to feel safe by handling questions sensitively, recognizing goals, and encouraging good listening to one another.

- **Membership**. Think creatively about how to establish a sense of membership or belonging (e.g., through adopting a group name, establishing class rituals, sharing goals and learning experiences together).

- **Trust.** Trust is like the glue needed to bond the community together. Openness, acceptance, and belonging require trust and also develop trust. Trust can flourish where there are appropriate structures, boundaries, and leadership.

- **Reciprocity.** Learning communities are built on the principle of reciprocity where all members of the community recognize they have something to give and something to receive. Allow time to recognize hopes and gifts and allow opportunities to exercise these gifts.

- **Cocreate the learning space.** The learning environment itself can contribute to the flourishing of relationships when it reflects the learning and lives of the group members. Be creative in allowing the learning space to reflect the cultures, stories, and learning of the students.

- **Connections.** Make space for sharing our lives. Look for ways outside and inside the classroom to make meaningful connections (e.g., celebrations and times of lament are critical opportunities to form strong (and often lifelong) relationships).

Integrated

Learning that Integrates Spiritual Formation with Other Aspects of the Curriculum and with Every Sphere of Life

Learning is strengthened by integrating or connecting one piece of learning to another. Integration helps memory because the more connections we make the better we can remember things. Integration also encourages better understanding and the ability to apply what we have understood to new contexts. Spiritual maturity is fostered as we connect and integrate our identity in Christ with every sphere of life.

Fostering spirituality means making all kinds of connections. For example, integrating:

- Ideas and knowledge with practical application and action
- What is learned from one class/place with what is learned in another
- Learning about spirituality with other aspects of the curriculum
- Knowledge with experience
- The head (ideas and actions) with the heart (emotions and attitudes) and the hand (relationships)

Theological educator Perry Shaw's handbook for "Integrative Learning" offers many practical ideas.[8]

Integration also means recognizing and intentionally using all of the curriculum. That means giving time to the formal curriculum with all its written learning objectives and the implicit or "hidden curriculum" with crucial aspects of spirituality such as developing biblical values, godly attitudes, and right relationships. It is the hidden curriculum that is remembered when all the words are forgotten!

Shaw offers a list of practical ways to use the hidden curriculum, including;

- Strengthen mentoring and spiritual direction
- Establish accountability groups
- Require journaling
- Emphasize practical ministry needs
- De-emphasize grades
- Integrate theory and practice
- Integrate the syllabus
- Recognize the centrality of mission to the curriculum
- Nurture spirituality in the classroom
- Challenge students to live in obedience to the theology they study
- Emphasize practical, critical reflection[9]

Practical Suggestions for Integration

- **Connect teaching with leaners' experiences.** Find out about the learners as individuals—understand their contexts, experiences, questions, and goals so that the content of the learning is connected (and relevant) to the learners' lives and goals. A precourse questionnaire is one useful way to discover who the learners are and how to integrate the course content with the learners' aspirations and questions.

- **Use the whole curriculum.** Intentionally and explicitly employ the written, formal content and the informal, implicit, unwritten values, attitudes, and relationships of learning. Give attention to all the learning—noticing the hidden curriculum

---

8   Perry Shaw, *Transforming Theological Education: A Practical Handbook for Integrative Learning* (Carlisle, UK: Langham Global Library, 2014).

9   Perry Shaw, "The Hidden and Null Curriculum. Training to Failure, Training to Success: The Hidden Curriculum of Seminary Education," *The Theological Educator 1 (2)* (Online, 2006), 43-51.

such as developing right attitudes, fostering spirituality in the classroom, and building healthy, collaborative relationships of learning.

- **Make spiritual formation a thread through all the learning.** Identify key themes of spirituality that run through (cross cutting) the whole course and notice as the learning occurs (e.g., identity deeply rooted in Christ, developing holy habits (spiritual disciplines), standing firm in faith, recognizing and using the gifts of the Spirit, showing openness and hospitality to others, being obedient to the ethical demands of God's Word, etc.) Notice when these themes appear in the class—whether in the formal content of the teaching or in the informal interactions. Stop and reflect on the learning so that the whole learning community is encouraged to integrate spiritual development with all aspects of learning.

Reproducibility

Learning Spiritual Maturity through Demonstration and Action

One of the most challenging aspects of promoting spirituality in others is that spirituality is caught as well as taught. Therefore, educators need to model what it means to be growing in spiritual maturity. "Text-people" not only text books are needed![10] Role modeling is best understood in the example of Jesus. He demonstrated what he wanted his disciples to learn, then sent them out to practice. After they returned and he had debriefed them he continued to demonstrate what it meant to be obedient to God, even to death. After his resurrection Jesus commissioned them to go and be witnesses to all they had seen and heard (Luke 24:48). Jesus modeled each lesson so that the disciples were able to go and do the same. In John's account Jesus commissioned them with, "As the Father has sent me so I am sending you" (John 20:21). The disciples were to reproduce what they had been taught.

This is hugely challenging if we take it seriously. Living alongside others in such a way that they can observe and learn from how we relate to God, to others, and to ourself. This requires humility (that flows from knowing who we are in Christ—fallen yet redeemed and renewed) and a constant reliance on God's Spirit.

Paul wrote, "Whatever you have learned or received or heard from me, or seen in me—put it into practice" (Phil 4:9). Paul, Silas, and Timothy could say,

> Our gospel came to you not simply with words but also with power, with the Holy Spirit, and deep conviction. You know how we lived among you for your sake. You became imitators of us and of the Lord." (1 Thes 1:5–6a)

---

10   AJ Heschel, "The Spirit of Jewish Education," *Journal of Jewish Education*, 24(2), 1953.

The capacity of the educator to be open, to be a learner, to be a practitioner, to offer hospitality in the classroom so that others feel welcome, to build reciprocal relationships, and to walk humbly dependent on God's Spirit is crucial for spiritual formation.

The opportunity for learners to practice what has been modeled is also crucial. This was the pattern of training for Jesus disciples. Watch, practice, learn more, practice more—even after Pentecost, empowered with God's Spirit, they continued learning and practicing/doing.

> Renewed thinking, attitudes, and relationships need to be put into practice. It is a vain hope to imagine that we can learn spiritual maturity passively.

Renewed thinking, attitudes, and relationships need to be put into practice. It is a vain hope to imagine that we can learn spiritual maturity passively. Each lesson needs to be applied here and now.

Practical Suggestions for Modeling and Action

- **Prayer as a lifestyle**. Paul writes, "And pray in the Spirit on all occasions with all kinds of prayers and requests. With this in mind, be alert and always keep on praying for all the Lord's people" (Eph 6:18). This kind of prayer is more than keeping a regular prayer time. It is learning to live in communion with God. It is an attitude, an approach to life, a way of being, a lifestyle.

  What should we pray for? We should first be worshipers whose prayer expresses awe and reverence of God. Out of an attitude of worship and thanksgiving flows intercession. Praying for the learners, asking God to be present in the learning, asking for the wisdom to be silent and the wisdom to speak in a way that will connect with the learners, for relationships that glorify Christ, and for the power of the Holy Spirit to transform lives.

- **Critical reflection as a habit.** Firsthand experience is useful but unless experiences have been processed through critical reflection and dialogue they may not be of great benefit to others. Educators who habitually critically reflect upon their experiences model lifelong learning to others and encourage fellow pilgrims to do the work of reflection.

- **Make learning practical.** Find ways for students to engage practically in the learning. Build in application and set practical assignments when possible.

  Enable students to identify and practice skills and competencies that will remain with them at the end of class.

  Start each class sharing experiences and lessons learned as they put ideas into practice.

Summary

This chapter has set out a range of practical approaches to teaching and learning that nurture spiritual formation. Spiritual maturity is an important goal for all disciples of Jesus Christ but it doesn't happen without intention, addressing the whole person, being rooted in community, connecting spirituality with the whole of life and learning, and seeing spirituality modeled in others so that it can be practiced and reproduced.

For those involved in teaching adults a starting place for nurturing spiritual maturity is designing and delivering learning that adopts these five themes; intentional, holistic, relational, integrated, and reproducible.

Discussion Questions

1. How does our worldview influence our understanding of spiritual maturity?
2. In what ways does theological and mission training need to be renewed so that spiritual maturity may be nurtured?
3. What barriers may prevent educators adopting each theme in this chapter—intentional, holistic, relational, integrated, and reproducible learning? What steps can be taken to overcome each barrier you identify?

References

Anderson, LW, and David Krathwohl eds. 2001. *A Taxonomy for Learning, Teaching, and Assessing: A Revision of Bloom's Taxonomy of Educational Objectives*. New York: Longman.

Balia, Daryl and Kirsteen Kim, eds. 2010. *Witnessing to Christ Today*. Oxford: Regnum.

Bloom, Benjamin. 1956. *Taxonomy of Educational Objectives, Handbook 1: Cognitive Domain*. Boston, MA: Addison Wesley Publishing Company.

Brynjolfson, Rob. 2009. *Missionary Training and Spirituality: Spiritual Formation in Theological Education*. https://www.oikoumene.org.

Freire, Paulo. 1968. *Pedagogy of the Oppressed*. New York: Bloomsbury Academic.

Heschel, AJ. 1953. "The Spirit of Jewish Education." *Journal of Jewish Education*, 24(2).

Illeris, Knud. 2007. *How We Learn*. Oxford: Routledge.

Jarvis, Peter. 1992. *Paradoxes of Learning: On Becoming an Individual in Society*. Hoboken, NJ: Wiley and Sons.

Shaw, Perry. 2006. The Hidden and Null Curriculum. Training to Failure, Training to Success: The Hidden Curriculum of Seminary Education. [Online] *The Theological Educator.* 1 (2).

———. 2014. *Transforming Theological Education: A Practical Handbook for Integrative Learning.* Carlisle, UK: Langham Global Library.

Taylor, Edward and Melissa Synder. 2012. A Critical Review of Research on Transformative Learning Theory, 2006–2010. In *The Handbook of Transformative Learning.* Eds. Taylor, Cranton, and Associates. Hoboken, NJ: Jossey-Bass.

Wall, Ruth. 2015. *Preparing Adults for Crossing Cultures: A Study of a Transformative Learning Approach to Christian Mission Training.* PhD Thesis UCL Institute of Education, London.

Ruth Wall is passionate about learning and discipleship and for more than twenty years has worked as an educator in Africa and as a tutor at All Nations Christian College, UK. Her specialty is in developing and delivering holistic and transformative mission training. Her PhD from London's Institute of Education is titled, "Preparing Adults for Crossing Cultures: A Study of a Transformative Learning Approach to Christian Mission Training." Ruth chairs the International Mission Training Network (IMTN), a network of the WEA-Mission Commission, which facilitates a global conversation about mission training.

Scripture: *Matthew 11:28-30* ("Come to me, all you who are weary and burdened, and I will give you rest")

Resource: *A Celebration of Discipline,* by Richard Foster (New York: Harper Collins, 1978)

CHAPTER 27

Grappling with the Invisible Evil Powers

Margaretha Adiwardana

In 1990, at a missionary training center in India, I met a couple of Americans. They were to teach "Spiritual Warfare" for a few days within the eight-month course that was for Indian pastors, wives, and single workers coming from several states and going out to different unreached people groups of the country. I was curious to find out why Americans were teaching spiritual warfare to Indians, some of whom were from Hindu backgrounds. The couple told their story: they had just graduated from a seminary in the US when they went as missionaries to the city where I was born (in West Java, Indonesia). They were happy to be able to rent a beautiful house for a very low price, but at night they would hear footsteps although there was no one else in the house, doors opening and closing, feet above the ground, and other strange things. They were at a loss to understand what was happening. Finally they found out that no one dared to live in the house and that it used to belong to the mightiest dukun (healer). Having never learned about the phenomena, they studied all they could find to understand and looked it up in the Bible. In the end they became experts about the unseen powers, teaching to new missionaries in India.

The leader of the largest denomination in East Timor told about the beginning of evangelism in the country. She was married to a Portuguese missionary. They went to the island of Atauro where they were received by a group of the most powerful witches in East Timor. They were served something to drink. As they prayed before drinking, the glasses in their hands exploded. The witches later told the couple that the drink they served was poison powerful enough to kill immediately. Seeing that the couple served a mighty God, they allowed them to share their message. Today over eighty percent of the population of the island of Atauro is Christian and many church workers come from this island.

As young girl in a church youth group in Indonesia, we were told that one of the girls quite active in leading worship unknowingly had stepped on the burial ground of a local holy man. She became possessed from sunset till dawn. Our pastor prayed but with no result. Her mother prayed and was beaten by the girl. We went to pray for her. I sat on her bed next to her while she was talking and smiling normally. But then the sun began to set. I was not aware of it. She gripped my hand forcefully and asked me to pray for her. In the middle of the sentence her voice changed to a man's voice and she became violent. We prayed but she continued being possessed for several days in the evenings till dawn. Only when our pastor started to fast did the demon leave her, serving as a reminder of the kind of demons which can only be cast away by prayer and fasting (Matt 17:21: Mark 9:29).

Animism is a belief in supernatural beings and powers which permeate the universe and a belief that all objects contain anima, life—including water, stones, wood, trees. The worldview of an animist is holistic, where unseen powers and beings live in interaction, the unseen powerful and influencing the daily lives of human beings. Some people have special gifts to communicate with the unseen powers. These powers enable them to heal, to exorcise, to hurt people indirectly, to curse or to prevent and avoid curses, or to bring blessings such as riches. Underneath their world religions, animism is often at the back of the minds of many people around the world, handed down from generation to generation through stories, myths, and mostly "traditional" practices used to solve daily life problems where science fails as a solution.

Where former beliefs and practices were not eliminated when people embraced a world religion, animism continues to be the solution of their "here and now" problems.

Where there is no discipleship in studying the application of biblical principles to former practices by a newly convert to Christ, one will continue to hold to the former animist worldview. We need to learn to find out people's felt needs, desires, fears, hopes, and expectations as well as their perceptions, because if no solution is given as an alternative to the old ways, people in their need will resort to what they think works.

> We need to learn to find out people's felt needs, desires, fears, hopes, and expectations as well as their perceptions, because if no solution is given as an alternative to the old ways, people in their need will resort to what they think works.

In some cultures where there have been a mixture of several dominating religions in the course of their histories, more than one belief can form their worldview. An example is the Brazilian culture where there is a mixture of peoples and cultures: the Portuguese settled in Brazil propagating Roman Catholicism; they met the American Indians with their animistic beliefs and traditions; then African slaves brought their religions, beliefs, and practices. The result is a heterogeneous people with a mixture of beliefs and traditional practices. Jim Chew's explanation in *When You Cross Cultures,* describes the Brazilian ideology, worldview, and beliefs as per the below pyramid.[1] When Brazilians need to solve daily life problems many go to a spiritist medium or African-beliefs practician, or practice the so-called "sympathy" of indigenous origin as magical solutions. This is "Folk Roman Catholic," the syncretistic practice of a world religion mixed with former

1   Jim Chew, *When You Cross Cultures* (Carol Stream, IL: NavPress, 1984); Paul Hiebert and Daniel Shaw, "The Power and the Glory: A Working Manuscript," *The International Journal of Frontier Missiology* (www.ijfm.org/PDFs_IJFM/12_3_PDFs/08_Shaw.pd, 1992), 10.

tribal or primary beliefs. The anismistic views is a form to escape from suffering—to overcome evil in the world.[2]

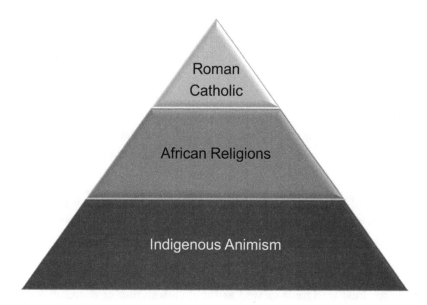

Demons and unseen powers are mentioned in the Bible not only in the Old Testament but in the New Testament as well. A scientific mind has difficulty in believing, much less understanding, what is not seen and cannot be explained. Thus, this unseen reality and how to deal with it is often not taught in the seminaries, even though a great many people around the world hold the worldview. We need to understand these beliefs and seek a biblical perspective to address them in evangelism and discipleship so that all of our minds can be transformed and become Christ-like.

In several parts of the world, these are age-long practices. Even some Westerners, through the adoption of Eastern philosophies, engage in such practices. Thus, there is the need to respond to unseen powers with biblical teaching.

Spiritual Warfare: Who, What, and How to Engage

The most known verses in the Bible on spiritual warfare are in Ephesians 6:10–20.

There have been many ideas expressed about spiritual warfare. It is necessary to understand from the Bible and from his letter to the Ephesians that Paul refers frequently to spiritual warfare in his context as a missionary.

---

2   Gailyn Van Rheenen, *Communicating Christ in Animistic Contexts* (Grand Rapids, MI: Baker, 1991), 304.

To understand against whom, what is it all about and how to engage in the warfare, we turn to the biblical text in Ephesians.

Who

Verse 11 warns us to take stand against "the schemes of the devil." The devil, diabolos, is explained by his deeds: to slander; to accuse; to divide; to sow strife; to reject; to describe falsely; to cheat.[3]

Verse 12, "We do not wrestle against flesh and blood, but against the rulers, against the authorities, against the cosmic powers over this present darkness, against the spiritual forces of evil in the heavenly places." The unseen powers are the spiritual forces of evil in the heavenly places.

Further, Ephesians 2:2 mentions the prince of the power of the air. John 12:31 refers to the ruler of this world. Matthew 25:41 speaks about the devil and his angels.

What

Sometimes spiritual warfare is viewed as the manifestation of exorcism and demonic possession. In the Bible we find many occurrences which explain current practices, not only among tribal animistic peoples but also among those with New Age beliefs and practices derived from the beliefs.

Human beings, with their worries for the future, have turned to divination to prevent bad luck. Acts 16:16–18 mentions the spirit of divination in the slave girl in Philippi. Divination is a practice of old times, mentioned in in the Old Testament, e.g., Ezekiel 21:21 and Hosea 4:12.

Magic, manipulating the invisible powers for one's own interest, for healing, riches, well-being, or to harm other people is practiced in many Africa and Asian countries, as well in the West with the revival of old practices.

The magicians of Pharaoh's court copied some of the ten plagues brought by Moses to the Egyptians.

Acts 13:6–12 describes Elymas in Cyprus, the magician and "false prophet," whose intention was "seeking to turn away the proconsul from the faith." Magic practices used as the solution for daily life problems turns people away from the real faith which relies on God. Witchcraft has studies and arts, as seen in Acts 19:18–19 when books on magic arts and practices were burned.

---

3   Lothar Coenen and Colin Brown, *Dicionário Internacional de Teologia do Novo Testamento* (São Paulo, Vida Nova, 2000), 378–79.

How

Spirits are expelled not by some Christian ritual, but by the authority which Christ has given to his disciples.[4]

The spiritual gift of discernment distinguishes between spirits (1 Cor 12:10). The evil one can imitate miracles.

Spiritual Warfare and Mission

In the missionary life of the Apostle Paul, there were other kinds of spiritual warfare which formed the greater part of struggles in mission.

1. Diseases: Satan's messenger = "thorn in the flesh" (2 Cor 12:7). Several commentators conclude this could be a disease Paul suffered from. Illnesses, infirmities, and diseases are sometimes mentioned as the work of the devil, i.e., Luke 13:16, "Satan has kept bound" and Acts 10:38, "Healing all who were under the power of the devil."
2. Blocking the mission journey: "Again and again... Satan blocked our way," (1 Thess 2:18). More than once Paul was hindered from going to Thessalonica, though several times he wanted to. In Matthew 16:23 when Peter tried to prevent Jesus from going to Jerusalem to die, Jesus rebuked him as "Satan... a stumbling block."
3. "False prophets, deceitful workers:" (2 Cor 11:13–14), "For Satan himself masquerades as an angel of light." Many today are teaching false doctrines and cultivating sects and individual worship.
4. Temptation (1 Thess 3:5): Paul was afraid that the Thessalonians were tempted, that "in some way the tempter might have tempted you and that our efforts might have been useless."The traps of the devil are to take men captive to do his will among the communities of believers which were planted by missionaries (2 Tim 2:26). They "fall into the devil's trap"(1 Tim 3:7), making the labor of the missionaries in vain.
5. All kinds of danger: 2 Corinthians 11:23–27 describes danger in journeys (rivers, bandits, cities, deserts, sea); from men (countrymen, Gentiles, false brothers, prison); hardships in ministry (labor, toil, hunger and thirst, without food); emotional (concern for all churches and pressures); and danger of death.

Thus verse 13 of Ephesians 6 warns us to put on the armor from God in order to be able to stand our ground against "the evil day," and after having done everything, to continue standing. The evil day would be the day of the greatest temptation to deny the Lord and fall into the devil's scheme and trap, to not be able to resist temptations.[5]

---

4   David Burnett, *Unearthly Powers: A Christian Perspective on Primal and Folk Religion* (London: MARC, 1988) 263.

5   Russell Shedd, *Bíblia Vida Nova* (São Paulo, Vida Nova, 1988), footnote 234.

The description of the full armor explains what is involved in spiritual warfare: The "belt of truth" in verse 14, Jesus is the truth against all lies; the "breastplate of righteousness," Jesus is our justice, we have been justified against all accusations of the enemy while living a righteous life. The "shoes for your feet, having put on the readiness given by the gospel of peace" (v 15) are sharing the gospel going to all peoples, in peace with God, in peace with men. The "shield of faith" (v 16) is used so that whatever the situation, our faith assures us that God loves us, nothing can separate us from him, and he will never forsake us; it is faith for all circumstances in things we have not seen yet. Our shield is a living faith, confident in the promises and the power of God "which will extinguish all the flaming darts of the evil one." The darts are lies, evil thoughts against others, doubts, blasphemous thoughts, desires to sin.[6]

> Our shield is a living faith, confident in the promises and the power of God "which will extinguish all the flaming darts of the evil one."

In the missionary life, these darts may appear in the form of depression or thoughts that we cannot do what is needed in the face of pressures to adapt and to be successful in the mission field. They may be doubts about whether we are really called when there are no fruits in our ministry as yet. They may be darts of mistrust or dissension among team members (e.g., Phil 4:2, the disagreement among coworkers such as Euodia and Syntyche), mistrust among missionaries, with the local Christians, or with leaders. Darts could be seeing coworkers or friends love the world too much like Demas, cause harm like Alexander, or desert you (2 Tim 4:9–16).

Against such attacks to the mind there is the need to put on "the helmet of salvation," (v 17). We must not just defend, but also attack with "the sword of the Spirit," as Jesus did when he was tempted: "It is written" (Matt 4:4–7). We are to know well the truth given by the Spirit, the written Word of God, the Word who was since the beginning, Jesus himself.

The Word is the base, the judge, the direction, the authority, and the truth with which to confront and to judge all kind of lies, facts, doctrines, thoughts; it is the guidance for direction, personal and spiritual experiences, sentiments, attitudes, teachings, and counsel.

The Key to Be Engaged in Spiritual Warfare Is the Word, Jesus, and Prayer

"Pray," (v 18), to talk with God, "in the Spirit" in accordance with guidance from the Spirit of God who knows the mind of God, in accordance with the will of God.

---

6   Warren Wiersbe, *Be Rich, Ephesians* (https://books.google.com.br/books?id=7E2l4hIKFPYC&pg=PA163&hl=pt-BR&source=gbs_toc_r&cad=3#v=onepage&q&f=false), 169.

Pray "on all occasions,"never ceasing, tirelessly, making known "all kinds of prayers and requests."

Praying ceaselessly according to the Spirit makes us alert, aware of all things happening around us. There is the need to be always informed about such situations which are potentially dangerous, as a soldier in battle. With this in mind, "always keep on praying for all the saints," not just for ourselves, but for all missionaries, the church, the believers, those who are in prison, those who suffer. "Always" praying is a hard task—it requires perseverance when we have not yet seen the answer.

Paul himself asked for prayers that he would be bold to preach the mystery of the gospel as he should, and that despite being in chains because of preaching he should be fearless (Eph 6:19). In Romans 15:30–33 he asked the church in Rome to join him in his struggle by praying for him that he might be rescued from the unbelievers (the rebels) in Judaea, that his service in Jerusalem would be acceptable by all saints, and that he would be able to come to them with joy so as to be refreshed together. In Colossians 4:3 he asked for prayer that the door would be opened for his message so he might proclaim the mystery of Christ, even in chains. In 2 Thessalonians 3:1–3 he asked for prayer for the rapid spread and the honor of the gospel, for him and those with him to be delivered from wicked and evil men, the faithless. He reminds us that "the Lord is faithful, he will protect you from the evil one." Paul was confident in God that the church in Thessalonica was doing and would continue to do the things commanded, and he asked the Lord to direct their hearts towards God's love in Christ's perseverance.

To Overcome Spiritual Warfare by Testimony

As the warfare is against the evil one, to overcome there is a hint of martyrdom, to persevere in giving testimony, not loving this life "so much as to shrink from death" by the blood of the Lamb who has overcome. The devil is filled with fury because he knows that his time is short (Rev 12:7–12).

The contexts of most of the least reached people groups are of situations which involve risk for the missionaries, mostly persecution and harassment. But also at any time anywhere, for any reason violent conflicts can occur—political, national, ideological, personal power, social-economic-cultural, tribal, and racial. Poverty in its extreme level causes a high infant mortality, precarious hygiene, and lack of health services. Cultural shock is bound to happen while learning a new language and in the process of cultural adaptation. Then relational problems arise—loneliness and privations, homesickness and longings—while at the same time there arises a confrontation of animism or of Hinduism, Buddhism, Islam, Atheism, New Age, secularism, all ranges of Spiritism, and Occultism. Spiritual warfare enhances the problems, the evil one enlarges these problems with lies and depressive thoughts.

Missionaries need to be prepared by spiritual discipline and practice to walk with God. They must learn to analyze the beliefs and practices in the culture in order to discern the worldview underneath the world religions, which may be influenced by animistic beliefs, enhanced by lies, and will deviate from the truth. They need to seek the biblical principles which can confront the spiritual phenomena and underlying beliefs. Then they can study together with the community how to conform to biblical principles, bringing new believers to a transformation to the mind of Christ.

We are in the midst of a spiritual warfare involving body, mind, and spirit, but our position is of the one attacking the gates of Hades and of prevailing over it (Matt 16:18).

Discussion Questions

1. Among the people you are working with, what kinds of spiritual warfare manifestation do you encounter and what would be some underlying beliefs?
2. What is more critical, to confront the visible manifestation of evil or the deceitful thoughts planted in the mind?

References

Burnett, David. 1988. *Unearthly Powers: A Christian Perspective on Primal and Folk Religion*. London: MARC.

Chew, Jim. 1984. *When You Cross Cultures*. Carol Stream, IL: NavPress.

Coenen, Lothar and Colin Brown. 2000. *Dicionário Internacional de Teologia do Novo Testamento*. São Paulo: Vida Nova.

Hiebert, Paul G. and Daniel R. Shaw. 1992 *The Power and the Glory: A Working Manuscript*. www.ijfm.org/PDFs_IJFM/12_3_PDFs/08_Shaw.pdf.

Rheenen, Gailyn Van. 1991. *Communicating Christ in Animistic Contexts*. Grand Rapids, MI: Baker.

Shedd, Russell P., ed. 1988. *Bíblia Vida Nova*. São Paulo: Vida Nova.

Wiersbe, Warren W., *Be Rich, Ephesians*. https://books.google.com.br/books?id=7E2 l4hIKFPYC&pg=PA163&hl=pt-BR&source=gbs_toc_r&cad=3#v=onepage&q &f=false.

Margaretha Adiwardana is Indonesian-Chinese, living for the last forty-six years in Brazil. She has a BTh in Missiology from São Paulo Baptist Seminary and MCS from Discipleship Training Center in Singapore. She has served as a cross-cultural missionary trainer at several mission schools and agencies, planter and pastor of an Indonesian church in Brazil, founder-CEO of Associação Missão Esperança (AME)—in integral community development in post-disaster communities strengthening the local churches suffering from poverty and discrimination, founder-coordinator of Rede SOS Global—a Brazilian network for integral disaster relief, and an associate of Missions Commission of the WEA.

Scripture: *2 Corinthians 1:3–5 ("Praise be to the God and Father of our Lord Jesus Christ...")*

Resource: *Communicating Christ in Animistic Contexts*, by Gailyn Van Rheenen (Grand Rapids, MI: Baker, 1991).

CHAPTER 28

Risk along the Journey

Individual, Church, Agency

Geoffrey W. Hahn

Should I leave my family, friends, and church to serve people in a city renowned for its severe air pollution? How will my health be affected over the years? The people to whom God has called me are antagonistic toward the gospel; what does that mean for how they will treat me? As we recognize that people are living and dying without hearing God's good news and being discipled, we are drawn to serve cross-culturally to share the gospel and see God transform lives. As missionaries, responding to God's guidance in our lives often takes us to places of service that introduce significant risks to us. Those risks may be physical, psychosocial, spiritual, or any combination of the three. Joshua Bogunjoko, International Director for SIM, expresses that, "We are aware that the least reached are often in places that are spiritually, physically, politically, and environmentally challenging. A right perspective on risk and suffering are essential for our current and future workers."

With the growing diversity of the global missions movement, the subject of risk perception and risk management is increasingly complex to navigate. So it is prudent to reflect together on the theological principles of risk that guide us as followers of Christ. With this in mind, a diverse working group was formed by SIM to produce a paper, "A Theological Reflection on Risk," from which I will quote the eleven theological principles presented and provide illustrations for these as we consider risk as part of the spiritual journey of mission.[1] While the principles apply to extreme risk and crisis scenarios, I have sought to provide examples that are more commonplace in the missionary experience. Many of the applications of the principles come from my own spiritual journey, not because it has involved more risk than others', but with the hope

---

1   The working group included Mark Brooks (USA), Worku Hailemariam (Ethiopia), Abi Hunt (Nigeria), Tohru Inoue (South Sudan), Phill Marshall (Australia), David Park (South Korea), Carlos Pinto (Peru), Teo Popa (Romania), and Nancy Writebol (USA). It was cochaired by Helen Heron (UK), SIM International Personnel Director and Gary Corwin (USA), SIM Missiologist. The first nine principles are adapted with minor changes from "Theological Bases for Our Team's Response to Crisis Situations," an unpublished paper, n.d. by Karen Shaw and R. Weymouth. They are borrowed with permission and gratitude.

that these illustrations might prompt you to think of personal applications for the path that God has set before you.

1. We affirm Jesus' teaching that internal motivation is more important than external action. We affirm that true believers may differ on interpreting and responding to risk, and that each should be convinced in his or her own mind and allow others the same dignity.

    [Matthew 6:1–8; Matthew 7:1–5; Romans 14:1–15:7; 1 Corinthians 4:1–5; 2 Timothy 4:16]

    Therefore, we will not be critical of one another, especially regarding differing choices that individuals or families may make in crisis situations. We will assume in others the best motives.

In serving on a ministry team, there will be times when members of the team will differ in their risk analysis, even when the situation is not one of crisis. For example, my wife and I responded to God's leading in going to an unreached, rural community. There was a critical point in our mission journey when we were ready to make exploratory trips into an unreached region in order to help determine exactly where God would have us relocate. An experienced missionary on the team was adamantly opposed to our trips, much less moving there, because of the region's renowned hostility toward the gospel. This senior missionary had our safety in mind, and in his risk analysis, the risks were too great.

As one with a higher tolerance for risk-taking, it was difficult for me to understand why my senior colleague was so risk adverse. While my wife and I were willing to submit to his wisdom, we could not ignore God's evident calling in our lives to serve him in an unreached area. In the end we compromised—we did not move out to the unreached area during our first term, but ended up moving to the most resistant of the communities in our second term. God worked through this to establish a new ministry initiative. And God worked through our colleague's lower tolerance for risk to establish a launching point for sending future missionaries out into the unreached areas (which continues to function as such today). God used both of our approaches to risk to accomplish his purposes.

> God used both of our approaches to risk to accomplish his purposes.

It can be tempting to judge one another in such circumstances. Those leaning toward the lower risk option may be tempted to judge the other as being reckless. Those leaning toward the higher risk option may judge the other as lacking faith. In such scenarios, we need to be gracious when there are legitimate differences of opinion regarding the risk assessment, as we each strive to walk in obedience to God's specific call on our lives.

2.   We serve a caring and faithful God; therefore we affirm that our security is based ultimately in God's providence rather than on our circumstances. We are to fear God, not people.

[Joshua 1:6–9; 1 Samuel 17:45–47; Psalm 20:7; Psalm 33:16–22; Psalm 34:6–10; Psalm 91; Proverbs 21:30–31; Isaiah 31:1–3; Matthew 10:26–31; 2 Timothy 4:16–18]

Therefore prayer must be our first and last response to crisis. While many types of crisis may create fear, decisions should not be made or actions taken based on fear. Our calm confidence is our best witness to our living faith in God. No major decision should be made without reference to the character of God.

The town that neighbored ours in southern Ecuador had the nickname, "Town of the Witches." This was due to a couple of infamous people living there, who for a price would place a curse on specified individuals or households. Many people within this sector feared these witches. We were informed shortly after our move to that region that these witches had placed a curse on our family as well. For our part, this was fully expected as part of the persecution of believers in that region and as an aspect of spiritual warfare. We committed this reality to prayer, asking that God would protect us, trusted that our spiritual protection was in God's hands, and we peacefully carried on. Sometime later a short-term team arrived, with one member who was unusually preoccupied with and fearful of malevolent spiritual forces. In hearing of the cursing witches and experiencing some of the other spiritual darkness of that area, she became overwhelmed with fear of the demonic, took actions accordingly, and was greatly annoyed that we did not partake in such fear.

Each of us is susceptible to different types of fear. For some it may be fear of isolation and for others fear of physical harm, or rejection, or the unknown. Even in the language and culture learning process, numerous cultural and language faux pas occur, and the fear of being laughed at, or of failure, must be overcome. I like to be competent in my work, yet have too many stories to tell from my time of language and culture learning of people at Bible studies just about rolling on the floor with laughter because of a gaffe I was making

> Confronting our fears, committing them to God in prayer, and growing in faith is part of our spiritual journey in mission.

and completely unaware of. And now, decades later, when returning to visit, they retell the stories with embellishment and enjoy yet another time of laughter at my expense. Thankfully, our amazing God worked in spite of my feared inadequacies! With so many possible fears, we know that our decisions cannot be based on them, as we are called to fear God alone. Confronting our fears, committing them to God in prayer, and growing in faith is part of our spiritual journey in mission. Indeed, "Our calm confidence is our best witness to our living faith in God."

3. We affirm that the mission given to us (to make disciples, baptize, and teach) is rooted in God's eternal love for humankind and is therefore more important than a simple consideration for our personal safety. Rather, it includes a willingness to give our all, including our safety and even our lives.

    [Acts 20:22–24; Acts 21:12–14; Romans 14:7–8; 2 Timothy 2:8–10; Revelations 12:11. Also Esther 4:16; Daniel 3:13–18]

    Therefore, while we have a high regard for life, our lives and that of others as God's gift of high value, we do not rule out the possibility of making decisions which might put us in danger or result in suffering or even death. We weigh up the value of our lives in terms of God's great love for us, the ministry that he has given to us, and the lives of those that he has called us to serve.

Loss of life is a very real risk in missionary service. Just recently a colleague serving in Burkina Faso died of dengue fever. Some of us will be asked to give our lives as martyrs, and most of us will be asked to put aside some consideration for our personal well-being. We might not die suddenly from a tropical disease, but

> Some of us will be asked to give our lives as martyrs, and most of us will be asked to put aside some consideration for our personal well-being.

in the course of living among those who have not yet heard the good news, we might be exposing ourselves to toxins on a daily basis. This insidious threat to our well-being is much less dramatic, but still a significant risk. In the course of my years in Ecuador, I gradually began to lose my voice and found speaking painful—not a very practical ailment for an evangelist and teacher who loved to lead worship. I asked God to restore my voice. Despite the prayers of many, seeing an array of specialists and undergoing a battery of tests and treatment, nothing improved my condition. At the Mayo Clinic I was told, "It has to be something in the environment where you are living in Ecuador. You need to leave or risk losing your voice completely and permanently." That was concerning. What good would a voiceless church planter be? The warnings were dire, but despite the risk to my well-being, we were still confident in God's call for us to serve in Latin America. With prayer, we didn't leave Ecuador but moved out of the rural area and into an urban environment (where we were surely exposed to other toxins that may show their effects down the road), and the damage to my voice stopped progressing. But my voice sustained long-term damage. I permanently lost volume. I can't sing. It is still painful to speak. But I have no doubt it was God's will for us to serve him in Ecuador.

4. We acknowledge the potential for extreme physical and mental anguish to workers and their loved ones. Although we would not intentionally seek such experiences, we affirm that it is a great privilege to suffer for Christ.

[Matthew 5:10–12; Acts 5:40–42; Acts 13:50–52; Romans 8:17; 2 Corinthians 11:23–33; 2 Corinthians 12:10; Philippians 3:10–11; 2 Timothy 4:6–8; Hebrews 10:33–34; Hebrews 11:24–26, 32–38; Hebrews 13:12–13; 1 Peter 1:6–9; 1 Peter 4:13–16]

Therefore we seek to rejoice and not to complain if suffering overtakes us.

You may find yourself living in places where significant risks to your physical health are introduced. Are you living in the context of malaria, dengue fever, or where rabid dogs are roaming the streets? If you are bitten by a rabid animal and you are infected with rabies, death is almost certainly in your near future if you are not treated in a timely manner (or barring divine intervention of the miraculous variety). So, there is some degree of real risk introduced in this scenario. While serving in rural Ecuador my wife was attacked by a rabid dog, resulting in puncture wounds in her calf. The shots she needed to prevent the virus from taking hold were at a hospital in the capital city of Quito and needed to be flown to us in a forty-eight-hour window. Normally, this wouldn't have been a problem, but the country was in political crisis, with protesters burning tires on the streets of the capital and police engaging the protesters with tear gas and water cannons outside the Quito airport. So my wife's access to the vaccine was hardly a given. At such points of anguish, risk assessment is no longer a theoretical exercise. Miraculously, God did get the vaccines to us, but that's a story for another time!

5. Consistent with the warning of our loving Savior, we affirm that followers of Christ should expect opposition, persecution, and distressing circumstances as the rule rather than the exception.

    [Mark 13:9–13; Luke 9:23–25; Luke 14:25–35; John 15:18–21; John 16:33; 2 Timothy 3:12–13; 1 Peter 4:12]

    Therefore we should not be surprised by distressing circumstances. We should prepare ourselves, our families, our home churches, and all our coworkers for possible hardships.

There is the risk of persecution when serving cross-culturally in countries or communities where followers of Christ are not welcome. If you are moving to or are ministering in contexts with very few believers, you will likely encounter this reality. The community is resistant to the gospel and antagonistic toward those who are bringing the good news. Likely, you will not be received with open arms by the very people you have come to bring hope. In the context where my family served for several years, this meant that people initially treated us in a cold and sometimes aggressively antagonistic manner. Almost nobody would greet us, few would give us eye contact, and those who did gave us aggressive stares. Local religious leaders proactively tried to mobilize the community to kick us out of town, from the day we arrived to the day we left. I remember vividly having to assess the risk to my family that was real, that harm might come to my family and me if a mob was successfully formed to physically remove us from the community.

In our case, this never came to pass, praise God. However, there are missionaries who have experienced physical persecution, have been kicked out of the country where they were serving, or have been imprisoned or even martyred. All of this necessitates grappling seriously with our theology of risk.

6.   Knowing God's promise to be with us always, we affirm the biblical injunction to obey God's leading regardless of the cost. We also affirm our responsibility to submit ourselves humbly to human authorities, except when doing so would directly contradict God's revealed will.

[Daniel 3:16–20; Daniel 6:10–13; Mark 10:29–30; Acts 4:18–20; Acts 5:27–29; Romans 13:1–7; Ephesians 5:21–22, 6:1, 5; Colossians 3:18–25; 1 Thessalonians 5:12–13; Hebrews 13:7, 17–18; 1 Peter 2:13–18]

Therefore, when we are certain of God's will we will do it, no matter what the cost. However, we will be careful to consider respectfully the advice of host and home country civil authorities, local Christian leaders, mission leaders, family, and leaders of churches. If we are in doubt as to God's will, we will submit willingly to these authorities. If we believe that in order to do God's will we must disregard the urgings of these human agencies, we will seek to maintain a spirit of humility and grace.

After having raised all of our required support, left our jobs, obtained our visas, packed our belongings, and bought our plane tickets, we were excited to finally leave for cross-cultural service. Then we received some unexpected and rather inconvenient news from the missionary team in southern Ecuador. A military conflict had just begun between Peru and Ecuador over a disputed border region and the situation was escalating. We would be delayed indefinitely until the hostilities ended. The team leader explained that even the US State Department had issued a travel ban. We were exasperated. After so many years of preparation, what were we going to do now? We had no jobs, no home, and were more than happy to take the risk and fly to Ecuador anyway. Already we were faced with a significant test of being willing to submit to the advice and decisions of authorities, whether government or mission. At the time, while submitting to the decision of mission leadership, we were disappointed with their decision and not in agreement. In hindsight, they were, of course, absolutely right to require us to wait until the military conflict had deescalated.

> The theological principle of obeying God and submitting to human authority is at play in your life on a daily basis.

For anyone called to serve in a context where the political and religious authorities are antagonistic toward the gospel, this theological principle of obeying God and submitting to human authority is at play in your life on a daily basis. How are we to be wise and courageous in such settings? Having discerning local Christian leaders, among others, to help guide us is hugely helpful as we strive to navigate such complexities.

7. We affirm that we are members of Christ's body, the church. When one suffers, we all suffer. We must in love consider the needs of others before our own needs.

    [John 15:12–13; Acts 9:28–31; Acts 17:5–9; 1 Corinthians 12:12–18; 2 Corinthians 6:3–13; Galatians 6:2; Philippians 2:19–30; 2 Timothy 1:8; 1 John 4:7–12]

    Therefore we will seek to walk alongside others, believers and non-believers, in their suffering and embrace them to the extent we are able. We will reassure them that God understands suffering and has suffered on their behalf in the passion of our Lord Jesus Christ.

I was deeply humbled by two teenage brothers I was discipling who had recently professed faith in Christ. One afternoon we were reading some Bible passages referencing baptism and they asked about the purpose of baptism. So I provided some passages for them to study. That following week they announced that they wanted to be baptized, and they shared this with family and friends. Both young men were employed, and both bosses let the boys know that if they were to be baptized they would lose their jobs. The brothers were the primary wage earners for their family so this was a very serious threat. In addition, their father's side of the family announced that the boys would be disowned if they were baptized.

Fully knowing the cost, these two young men chose to be baptized, and they did so with joy and peace. They both did lose their jobs, and their father's side of the family did disown them.

We need to be keenly aware of the cost of following Christ for those with whom we share the gospel. Local believers and the local church face many risks that the foreign missionary does not. The risks associated with being ostracized from one's community can be particularly acute: losing jobs, children not being allowed to attend school, believers not being allowed to be buried in the town cemetery, being cut off from one's family. These are all realities, and in these circumstances it is critical for the cross-cultural worker to be empathetic with the risk and suffering of our fellow believers, to respond with compassion and care, and to learn from their journey of faith.

> We need to be keenly aware of the cost of following Christ for those with whom we share the gospel.

8. We are confident that our sins are forgiven through Christ, that we have been given eternal life, and that our bodies will be raised incorruptible.

    [Romans 8:14–39; 1 Corinthians 15, esp. v. 58; 1 Timothy 6:12–16; 2 Timothy 1:11–12; 2 Timothy 4:6–8; Hebrews 13:13–14; Revelations 2:8–11]

Therefore all of our decisions should be made in the light of eternity.

For those preparing to serve cross-culturally in mission, questions regarding the riskiness of such a move begin to surface long before boarding the airplane. Internally, within our own hearts and minds, we may wrestle with the wisdom of the decision. Choosing to make such a move raises all sorts of questions about risk, whether real or perceived. Being distant from one's social support and needing to start all over in a new culture introduces the risk of creating a gap in one's social system until new relationships are built. Leaving one's parents, siblings, children, grandchildren, and extended family behind introduces another set of psychosocial risks that are tangible, and cannot simply be replaced by new relationships in a new country. Yet our decisions need to be made in the light of eternity.

We know that our earthly belongings and finances are temporal, and not of comparable worth to items of eternal consequence. Being a missionary and accumulating a lot of money tend to be mutually exclusive, so most missionaries live with a substantial degree of financial uncertainty. How will we make ends meet? Will we ever be able to save up enough to own a home, for retirement, for healthcare, for the education of our children? For most of us, the truth is that we have no certainty beyond the promises of God that our needs will be met, and for the sake of eternity, we have to be willing to live with the risk that our temporal economic situation may be challenging.

> For most of us, the truth is that we have no certainty beyond the promises of God that our needs will be met,

9. We affirm that the Almighty loves to prove his power through the daring faith of those who are led by the Spirit. We also heed Christ's warning not to test God through foolish or unnecessary risks motivated by pride. Biblical examples include those who walked toward danger and those who walked away, both for the sake of their calling.

    [Exodus 14:13–14; 1 Samuel 17:34–37, 45–47; 1 Kings 17:2–5; 1 Kings 18:1–2; Nehemiah 6:10–14; Matthew 4:5–7; Luke 4:28–30; Luke 13:31–33; Acts 4:13; Hebrews 11:32–39; Revelation 7:9–14]

    Therefore, we will let the Spirit of Christ rule our actions and not the fearful reports of various media. We will boldly undertake all that God asks of us. At the same time, we will not presume on God's intervention when it is within our power to act on our own behalf. We will make all reasonable preparations and take all wise precautions.

I once met a family who had just returned from serving two years on another continent and who were quite devastated by their experience. They went out independent of any mission agency. With no plans for the educational needs of their children, their kids were now two years behind in their education. As the couple reflected on the experience, they spoke of the pride they had in telling others that they were "going by faith." They shared how they looked down on those who were sent out by mission agencies that provided planning and safety nets, and how they viewed these missionaries as lacking in their level of faith. After the fact, they felt that they took unnecessary risks for themselves and their children, and their children resented them for it.

It is dangerous for risk-taking and faith to be equivocated. By faith we follow God wherever he guides us, whether that leads us to serve him in a ministry that is perceived as high or low risk. The risk of eternal consequence is in not seeking God's guidance and wisdom and following accordingly.

10. We know that chaotic situations will arise, often when we least expect them. We affirm that wherever possible the decisions that need to be made should be made in community.

    [Acts 15:5–12; Acts 19:29–31; Acts 21:10–14; James 1:2–5, 12]

    Therefore we will seek to be as sensitive as possible to all the relevant input from other stakeholders both locally and globally (mission leadership, team, families, and churches) when chaotic situations arise. Making consensus community decisions will be our goal.

You may find that God has called you to a place where chaotic situations arise. My own missionary experience was in a context of political instability. The protests did not descend to war and foreigners generally were not an intentional target, but there were various coups d'état. This is not the case for many of our colleagues. There are missionaries serving in South Sudan, regularly being evacuated as they try to carry out ministry for Christ in the context of war. There are people living and dying without Christ in Iraq, in Syria, in Afghanistan, and God has called some to bring his good news to those communities. Making decisions in community helps provide wisdom and clarity in the midst of the chaos.

> Making decisions in community helps provide wisdom and clarity in the midst of the chaos.

11. We rest in childlike faith in the assurance that nothing can separate us from God's love, and that whatever risks we must navigate, whatever the outcome, nothing will be wasted and God will still be holding us on the other side, and we will be forever joyously satisfied in him.

    [Romans 8:31–39; Galatians 2:20; Revelation 3:9–12]

    Therefore, when risk taking is called for, we enter into it with great hope in the abiding love and care of our God.

Throughout the years my family served in Ecuador, we were questioned by Ecuadorians about why we would choose to work in Ecuador. People were genuinely perplexed about the choices we made and the risks that were implicit in those choices. How could you willingly leave your extended family and move to a place so far away from them? Who will care for your children? What about all your lifelong friends, all living a world away, why would you voluntarily leave them and risk social isolation? And our decision to move to Ecuador did not make economic sense either, with my wife being from the UK, and myself from the USA, being prime destinations for Ecuadorians to emigrate in search for better jobs. It was counterintuitive that we would move from contexts of greater economic strength to rural Ecuador, where jobs were not plentiful and the economy anything but robust.

> This recurring set of questions that never let up in all our years there provided a wonderful opportunity to share the gospel as the reason why we would chose to take on these real and perceived risks

This recurring set of questions that never let up in all our years there provided a wonderful opportunity to share the gospel as the reason why we would choose to take on these real and perceived risks.

Ultimately, the risks associated with serving in mission only make sense if our decisions to minister are based on God's leading in our lives, and our obedient response to follow God's lead accordingly. In times of trial, when the risks are keenly felt, we take comfort that God knows what he is doing, and has placed us where we are for his kingdom purposes. The mission experience inevitably involves risk, yet our God is great, and nothing can separate us from him. He is compassionate and just and will accompany us on the mission journey. Our God is victorious and he will extend his kingdom.

Discussion Questions

1. What are the risks that you are facing now?
2. What are the risks you anticipate will be coming?
3. What are the theological principles that you can draw on to help you address them?

Geoffrey *W. Hahn* accepted Christ at a young age, and God called him to missions when he was a teenager on a short-term medical mission trip. He completed his BA at Wheaton College, MDiv at Trinity Evangelical Divinity School, and doctorate at Denver Seminary, with a thesis on cross-cultural partnerships. Geoffrey and his wife, Fiona, have two young adult sons. They served in pastoral roles in Chicago area churches and as SIM missionaries in rural and urban settings in Ecuador. In mission leadership Geoffrey has served as a country and area director, and on SIM's International Leadership Team as Director of Ministry Development and currently as a Deputy International Director. Geoffrey seeks to empower others for effective ministry responses to the ever-changing ministry settings and realities in our world.

Scripture: *Micah 6:8 ("He has shown you...")*

Resource: *The Brothers Karamazov,* by Fyodor Dostoevsky (originally published 1880).

CHAPTER 29

Preparing for Intentional Discrimination, Harassment, and Persecution

Wolfgang Häde

As I am writing this chapter, Turkey, the country where I am living and serving, is going through a period of intense political and societal turmoil. Turkish history teaches us that Christians always have been a likely target of public anger in such times. During the last few years, Christians in Turkey went through a rather calm time. But that might change. Are our brothers and sisters in this country prepared for persecution?

It seems to be even more questionable if we as foreign church workers in Turkey are prepared for persecution. Even the "milder forms" of persecution, which the Turkish church is pretty much used to, might be unexpected for workers from Western countries: bad media coverage of Christians in general and missionaries in particular, strong prejudice in society that gives Christians the feeling of not really belonging to Turkey, verbal abuses—just to mention some.

I remember the kind of "preparation for persecution" I went through as a young man in Germany. The leader of our church's youth group took us to a dark underpass to explain to us how Christians in the communist countries have to meet secretly. That was certainly no comprehensive preparation—but at least the impression stuck in my mind.

So how should we prepare global workers for discrimination, harassment, and persecution knowing that the likelihood that they will come across some of those is growing in today's world?

Developing Spiritual Disciplines

Yes, our Lord teaches us not to worry about how we will defend ourselves when persecuted because the Holy Spirit will teach us the words that we need then (Luke 11:11–12)—but we probably will not learn in the midst of persecution how to have a regular devotional time, how to persist in prayer, how to live a pure and forgiving relation with our spouse. If ever possible, spiritual disciplines have to be learned before we come into persecution.

It is true that the Spirit of God gives extra strength when we need it. After my Turkish brother-in-law was martyred, the Turkish police revealed to us that I had been on the murderers' list too and put me under protection. Yes, I sometimes felt closer to heaven in the midst of threats and danger. However, the additional stress of these events simultaneously intensified problems that had been under the surface: a tendency to doubt my own faith, issues in our marriage, and conflicting opinions within our church planting team.

Spiritual disciplines should be learned and practiced before we encounter persecution. When the prophet Daniel faced a ban of any prayer in Babylon, he just continued the discipline that he was used to before the ban: He prayed "three times a day… just as he had done before" (Dan 6:10).

Daniel Waheli worked in a Muslim country in Africa. He reports threats, slander, and finally arrest and deportation. Almost half of his remarkable book however is about the character and the disciplines that church founders in such an environment should develop, like praise, purification, prayer, power, and perseverance.[1] Preparing for discrimination, harassment, and persecution has to start with preparing the spiritual life of the Christian worker. By the way, memorizing Scripture might be one of the indispensable disciplines that help many Christian prisoners to spiritually survive (cf. the testimony of Waheli).[2] We will not be able to begin memorizing Scripture once we don't have a Bible anymore.

> Preparing for discrimination, harassment and persecution has to start with preparing the spiritual life of the Christian worker.

Assuring Christian Identity

In Turkey, physical assaults on Christians happen. But they have been the exception in recent years. However, Christians in Turkey are continuously confronted with a shellfire of verbal attacks. In the media, even in some schoolbooks and as reflected by the prejudice of many Turkish citizens, Christians are presented as followers of an outdated system of belief, as immoral, as second-class citizens. Christian converts from Islam are seen as traitors, as weak people who have been bribed with material promises and cannot be trusted anymore. Christian missionaries are considered spies of Western

---

1   Daniel Waheli, *Freude in Zeiten der Bedrängnis: 12 Prinzipien, Jesus effektiv zu bezeugen—Das Abenteuer einer Familie in Pioniermission* (Nürnberg: VTR, 2014), 121–208.

2   Waheli, 59.

countries, as accomplices of colonialism and as conniving experts in brainwashing young people.[3]

In this respect persecution is "a battle for defining identity" (title of Haede 2012a) of Christians.[4] A state or a society tries to define Christian identity as outdated, weak, deceitful, or just evil. If Christians, including foreign Christian workers, are not aware of this attempt, these false definitions can affect their self-perception. In order to avoid this, Christians in a context of verbal assaults need to focus on assuring their real Christian identity.

> In order to avoid this, Christians in a context of verbal assaults need to focus on assuring their real Christian identity.

As the First Letter of Peter was written to Christians in Anatolia who were suffering predominantly verbal forms of persecution, it is significant that the author focuses on strengthening the identity of his audience.[5] While society perceives the Christians as strange (1 Pet 4:4) and as evildoers (2:12), Peter reminds them that they in fact are special people through their election by God (1:2; 2:4; 2:9), divinely appointed as "obedient children" (1:14), "living stones" (2:4) in a new temple and "a royal priesthood" (2:9).

Christians have been "redeemed from the empty way of life handed down to you from your forefathers" (1 Pet 1:18). So it is no wonder that they become outsiders in society. However, Peter proves that they are not anchorless revolutionaries. He does so by rooting their identity deeply in the Old Testament narrative and in the history of Israel. They now belong to the people of God (1 Pet 2:9–10—cf. Lev 19:6 and Isa 43:21). They are part of a new exodus (cf. 1:13 with Ex 12:11). As the new people of God they are still living as strangers in a spiritual exile (1:1: 2:11–12).

Christians are assured by Peter that suffering is part of their identity because they are united with Christ, and Christ himself suffered (2:20–25). According to Peter the suffering Christians are responsible for avoiding any behavior that might give reasons to be blamed rightfully. Part of the Christian identity is to "live good lives among the pagans" (2:12).

Teaching global workers a strong Bible-based Christian identity is certainly a crucial element of their preparation. Knowing who they are in Christ will be a great help in enduring accusations and slander that try to portray them as bad and dangerous. In addition, they then will be equipped to teach this identity to local believers in contexts of persecution.

---

3   cf. Wolfgang Häde, "Christians in Turkey as Part of a Western Conspiracy? A Turkish Perspective on Christian Missionaries," in *Freedom of Belief and Christian Mission, Regnum Edinburgh Centenary Series 26*, eds. Gravaas, Hans Aage et al (Oxford: Regnum Books, 2015b), 181–189.

4   Wolfgang Haede, "Persecution as a Battle for Defining Identity. Reflections from Turkey," *International Journal for Religious Freedom*, Vol 5/1, 2012a), 87–100.

5   cf. Häde, 2015a, 212–217.

Communicating a Deep Biblical Perspective on Persecution

When I was personally confronted with persecution in Turkey, I was in the process of translating a book from English into German: Glenn Penner's *In the Shadow of the Cross: A Biblical Theology of Persecution and Discipleship* goes through the Bible—literally from Genesis to Revelation—in search of the role persecution has in the big picture of God's history of salvation.[6] To dig into the biblical testimony about persecution was a real and practical help for me in dealing with persecution. Knowing that persecution and martyrdom are a necessary part of God's story with his people I never really had to struggle with the question, "How can a loving God allow such a tragedy?" However, I heard other Christians ask this question when our three brothers were martyred.

Communicating a deep biblical perspective on persecution should certainly be part of the preparation for every global worker. I wonder how many colleges, theological seminaries, or even mission agencies already have obligatory courses on a biblical theology of persecution. Future global workers have to know that suffering in the process of salvation was part of the first promise of a Redeemer (Gen 3:15): The coming Savior would "crush" the head of the serpent, but the enemy would "strike his heel." They have to be taught that the sufferings of the church as the body of Christ are a continuation of his sufferings (Col 1:24), that God has ordained a certain number of martyrs as his ultimate witnesses (Rev 6:11). When Jesus sent his disciples to mission (Matt 10:1–13), he felt obliged to teach them about persecution (Matt 10:14–42). Being the Son of God he certainly knew that ten out of his twelve closest friends would die as martyrs. Global workers have to understand words like to "take his cross" (Matt 10:38) much more literally than we are used to in the West.

> The great danger in persecution is not the threat to the messengers' lives, but the fact that the disciples of Jesus might deny him (Matt 10:32) or love their own lives more than Jesus and neglect their commission (Matt 10:37–38)

Teaching about the biblical importance of persecution should include communicating a strong conviction that the gospel has to be shared whatever the cost. The great danger in persecution is not the threat to the messengers' lives, but the fact that the disciples of Jesus might deny him (Matt 10:32) or love their own lives more than Jesus and neglect their commission (Matt 10:37–38).

Benefitting from Others' Experiences

Global workers in preparation or on the field should be strongly encouraged to read about the lives of suffering Christians and of martyrs of the past and the present.

---

6   Glenn Penner, *In the Shadow of the Cross: A Biblical Theology of Persecution and Discipleship* (Bartlesville, OK: Living Sacrifice, 2004).

When I was confronted with death threats in Turkey, a book about the German pastor Dietrich Bonhoeffer gave me guidance. Just before the outbreak of World War II the German theologian in the summer of 1939 had the opportunity to stay in the United States in order to avoid further persecution by the Hitler regime (I read a different book in 2007).[7] However, Bonhoeffer understood that he had to be in Germany during this crucial time for his nation and returned. Being part of the resistance against Hitler he was arrested and executed in 1945.

Bonhoeffer's testimony helped me to come to the decision to stay in Turkey and be part of the Turkish church in spite of some obvious dangers. Because enduring persecution is a very practical challenge, we need practical examples of brothers and sisters in faith who preceded us. Stories of the early Christian martyrs should be read, but also reports of Christians who live in persecution today. Among the many good books I want to mention the life story of Necati Aydin, one of the martyrs in Turkey and Nil Ripken's impressive exploration of contemporary Christians under severe pressure.[8]

Learning about Convenient Responses to Persecution

When I got death threats in Turkey, I decided to stay. I realized, however, that from a biblical perspective there are no standard answers to the question of how we should respond to persecution. Reg Reimer specifies fleeing, enduring, or advocating as the main three alternative responses.[9]

Unlike most local believers, foreign workers usually have the option to leave the country when persecution starts. However, they may even be confronted with a lack of understanding from their supporters in their home countries when they decide to stay in a dangerous environment. Other workers might feel obliged to endure at any cost though leaving by times can be the better option. Jesus Christ himself advises his followers to leave places where they are not accepted (Matt 10:14) or even to flee from danger (Matt 10:23). The apostles of Jesus do not always insist on staying at certain places (cf. Peter in Acts 12:17). However, Jesus (Matt 16:21–23) and later the Apostle Paul (Acts 21:10–14) rejected shying away from obviously dangerous locations when they knew that God wanted them to be there.

---

7   Eric Metaxas, *Bonhoeffer: Pastor, Agent, Märtyrer und Prophet* 6th ed. (Holzgerlingen: SCM Hänssler. (German translation of Metaxas. *Bonhoeffer: Pastor, Martyr, Prophet, Spy* [2010] 2014), 396–428.
8   Wolfgang Haede, *Faithful until Death—The story of Necati Aydin, a Turkish Martyr for Christ* (Bartlesville, OK: Living Sacrifice, 2012b). Nik Ripken, *The Insanity of God: A True Story of Faith Resurrected* (Nashville, TN: B&H 2013), 137–322.
9   Reg Reimer, "Christian Responses to Suffering, Persecution, and Martyrdom," in *Sorrow and Blood. Christian Mission in Contexts of Suffering, Persecution, and Martyrdom,* eds. William D. Taylor, Antonia Van der Meer, and Reg Reimer (Pasadena, CA: William Carey Library, 2012), 23–30.

Preparation for a context of persecution must raise awareness of the variety of biblical options for responses to persecution. Case studies from other countries can help to practically think through situations that might occur in the future.

Thinking about Church Structures

Tibebe Eshete describes how the Meserete Krestos Church in Ethiopia changed her structures as the persecution by the Marxist regime after the revolution of 1974 increased.[10] New leaders replaced those in prison, cell groups were set up, meeting places rotated. In order to avoid the control of the authorities, meetings would be held on different days during the week and not on Sundays. New converts were not included in the cell groups immediately, but had to go through special follow-up programs. There were certainly more reasons for the astonishing church growth of this and other Ethiopian churches during the Marxist persecution. However, it seems they were well prepared to drop traditional church structures and apply more convenient ones.

It would be helpful for missionary candidates to have a solid biblical theology of the church. That could help to discern which elements of church life are indispensable and which parts of the regular church program might be abandoned if necessary for practical reasons to survive in persecution.

Conclusion

Trusting the Holy Spirit for his guidance in persecution does not exclude a proper preparation of global workers. However, more important than any security check list is to check and foster spiritual disciplines so that workers will be able to continue them in rougher times. A strong focus on who we are in Christ can be a protection again ceaseless verbal attacks on the identity of Christians.

> More important than any security check list is to check and foster spiritual disciplines so that workers will be able to continue them in rougher times.

God's perspective on suffering has to be taught to missionary candidates. They need a good biblical theology of persecution to integrate their experiences of persecution in their walk with Christ. Reading and learning about Christian witnesses who went through persecution before us can equip us to find the convenient response when challenged with threats. It will also be helpful to think about the possible changes in church structure before we encounter persecution.

---

10   Tibebe Eshete, "Marxism and Religion: The Paradox of Church Growth in Ethiopia, 1974-1991," in *Freedom of Belief and Christian Mission*, eds. Hans Gravaas, Aage, et al (Oxford: Regnum Books, 2015), 242–258.

This chapter certainly cannot be exhaustive. However, it is obvious that a proper preparation of global workers for contexts of suffering is indispensable. The number of countries in the work seeing persecution is huge.

Discussion Questions

1. Try to make a one-page draft of a biblical theology of persecution, putting suffering for Christ in the context of the history of salvation!
2. Which biographies of Christians in persecution would you recommend to Christians preparing for a global ministry?
3. Which elements of church structure are indispensable? Which elements could be abandoned in times of persecution?

References

Eshete, Tibebe. 2015. Marxism and Religion: The Paradox of Church Growth in Ethiopia, 1974–1991. In *Freedom of Belief and Christian Mission*. Edinburgh Centenary Series 26., eds. Gravaas, Hans Aage et. al. Regnum. Oxford: Regnum Books.

Haede, Wolfgang. 2012a. Persecution As a Battle for Defining Identity: Reflections from Turkey. *International Journal for Religious Freedom*, Vol 5/1.

———. 2012b. *Faithful until Death: The Story of Necati Aydin, a Turkish Martyr for Christ*. Bartlesville, OK: Living Sacrifice.

———. 2015a. *Anschuldigungen und Antwort des Glaubens—Wahrnehmung von Christen in Türkischen Tageszeitungen und Maßstäbe für eine Christliche Reaktion*. Diss. DTh, University of South Africa, Pretoria.

———. 2015b. "Christians in Turkey as Part of a Western Conspiracy? A Turkish Perspective on Christian Missionaries." In *Freedom of Belief and Christian Mission*, Regnum Edinburgh Centenary Series 26, eds. Gravaas, Hans Aage, et. al., Oxford: Regnum Books.

Metaxas, Eric. [2011] 2014. *Bonhoeffer: Pastor, Agent, Märtyrer und Prophet*, 6th ed., Holzgerlingen: SCM Hänssler. (German translation of Metaxas. Eric. 2010. *Bonhoeffer: Pastor, Martyr, Prophet, Spy*. New York: HarperCollins).

Penner, Glenn M. 2004. *In the Shadow of the Cross: A Biblical Theology of Persecution and Discipleship*. Bartlesville: OK: Living Sacrifice.

Reimer, Reg. 2012. "Christian Responses to Suffering, Persecution, and Martyrdom." In *Sorrow and Blood. Christian Mission in Contexts of Suffering, Persecution, and*

Martyrdom, eds. Taylor, William D., Antonia Van der Meer, and Reg Reimer. Pasadena, CA: William Carey Library.

Ripken, Nik. 2013. *The Insanity of God: A True Story of Faith Resurrected.* Nashville, TN: B&H.

Waheli, Daniel. 2014. *Freude in Zeiten der Bedrängnis: 12 Prinzipien, Jesus effektiv zu bezeugen – Das Abenteuer einer Familie in Pioniermission.* Nürnberg: VTR (English original version: 2013. *Joy under Pressure,* in the meantime a new edition was published: 2015. *Lessons Learned in the Lion's Den: Imprisoned for Sharing Jesus.* Pasadena, CA: William Carey Library).

Wolfgang Häde (DTh, Missiology) is from Germany, and together with his wife Janet, who is from Antioch/Turkey, and their daughter Debora, he has been working in church planting and theological education (with Martin Bucer Seminar) in Turkey since 2001. Necati Aydin, one of the three Christians martyred in Malatya, Turkey, in 2007, was the husband of Janet's sister. Wolfgang authored a book about life and death of Necati (*Faithful until Death— The Story of Necati Aydin, a Turkish Martyr for Christ,* 2012).

Scripture: *Isaiah 43:1b ("Do not fear, for I have redeemed you…")*

Resource: *In the Shadow of the Cross. A Biblical Theology of Persecution and Discipleship,* by Glenn Penner (Bartlesville, OK: Living Sacrifice Books, 2004).

CHAPTER 30

Harassment, Persecution, and Martyrdom on the Field

Antonia Leonora van der Meer

The Christian church continues to grow in the most unlikely and difficult contexts, but simultaneously there is a growing incidence of harassment, persecution, and martyrdom. In the most difficult contexts people keep growing in their faith, in their intimacy with the Lord and in their joy to serve him and reach out to others. This means that we, as members of Christ's body, cannot remain content with just receiving occasional information and saying a short prayer for those who are suffering. We must stand at their side, in our prayers and actions. We must seek to deepen our own relationship with the Lord and thus receive the strength to rejoice amidst suffering.

Without a doubt, being a Christian today in many parts of the world is a high-risk commitment. But then, what's new? The historical norm is that it has always been this way. Few times in history have Christians lived in extended contexts of peace, prosperity, influence, and freedom to practice their faith to its fullest expression. Today it is estimated that some two hundred million followers of Jesus live in contexts where they face harassment, persecution, and the possibility of martyrdom.[1]

The growth of the IS (Daesh in Arabic), and its amazing attraction and influence on people from the younger generations, both in the West and in the East, has become a painful issue which cannot be ignored. According to the UN High Commissioner for Refugees (UNHCR) at the end of 2014 there were an unprecedented 59.5 million people who had been forced to leave their homes. Half of these refugees are children and teenagers. The growth in 2014 of 8.3 million people was the greatest yet registered. In 2014, there was a daily growth of 42.5 thousand people. The crisis in Syria and Iraq is the main cause of this growth.

Not all refugees are Christians, but many are. There are several Christian NGO's and local churches in the Middle East reaching out to these refugees, Christians or not, and many have found new life and hope in Christ.

---

1   William D. Taylor, Antonia van der Meer, and Reg Reimer, eds., *Sorrow and Blood: Christian Mission in Contexts of Suffering, Persecution and Martyrdom* (Pasadena, CA: William Carey Library, 2012).

IS has a problem with Egypt, because of the significant presence and strength of the Christian population. They call them "The People of the Cross," threaten, and seek to kill them continually.

The typical Bible student in the West may never suspect that the biblical texts that deal with pain and suffering might be dealing with suffering for righteousness' sake and because of our Christian witness. This influences how Western Christians view and deal with those who suffer for their faith. We have failed to recognize that persecution is normative for the follower of Christ historically, missiologically, and (most importantly) scripturally.[2]

In 64 countries, with 70 % of the world population there is a lack of religious freedom.

Jesus as Our Model in Suffering

Jesus suffered harassment, persecution, and death to accomplish his mission.

- Jesus gave up his rights and privileges (Phil 2:5–8).
- He accepted humiliation, abandonment, and death on a cross.
- He suffered willingly—for the joy set before him (bringing many from darkness into his kingdom), he endured the Cross (Heb 12:2).
- Jesus prepared his disciples for mission and for suffering (Matt 10:16–20).
- Jesus taught that mission leads to persecution, but persecution cannot prevent people from coming into the light (Matt 24:9, 14).
- Jesus was very open about what he offered and what he expected.
- He taught through his life, his response to suffering, and through his teaching.
- The Sermon on the Mount makes it clear that blessed are those who are persecuted and harassed because of their commitment to Jesus, his kingdom, and his justice (Matt 5:5–6; 9–12).
- Jesus knew that the kingdom of evil would declare war against his church, and taught the disciples how to meet the violence they would suffer (Matt 16:18; 24–26; Mark 6:4; 8:34–38; Luke 9:23–26).
- He sent them as very vulnerable beings, like sheep among wolves.
- He taught us to be shrewd as snakes and innocent as doves. Not violence against violence, but readiness for martyrdom if needs be (Matt 10:16–22).
- The only way to overcome evil is not confronting, but being ready to pay the price.
- He calls us to deny ourselves and follow him to the Cross.
- Suffering the hostility of the world to the kingdom (Matt 10:16, 34–39, John 15:18–20).

---

2   Glenn Penner, "A Biblical Theology of Persecution and Discipleship," in *Sorrow and Blood: Christian Mission in Contexts of Suffering, Persecution and Martyrdom*, eds. William D. Taylor, Antonia van der Meer and Reg Reimer (Pasadena, CA: Wiliam Carey Library, 2012), 72.

- Bearing the cross is the only way to triumph over darkness. Jesus prepared the disciples for global mission among the nations.
- Darkness cannot hinder our work (1 Pet 2:21, Luke 9:23).

Theology of Martyrdom

German theologian Schirrmacher developed the following theses on the theology of martyrdom.

1. The first human being to die was a martyr. Abel is considered a martyr by Jesus (Luke 11:51). According to Hebrews his offering gave evidence that he was a righteous man. Often persecution is caused by envy.
2. The Old Testament prophets were persecuted. They are prototypes of martyrdom (Heb 11:35–38; Jas 5:10). Jesus reminds his disciples "Be happy about it! For a great reward awaits you in heaven" (Matt 5:21).
3. God's people persecute God's people. Israel persecuted the prophets, Jesus, and the apostles. Jesus said "the time is coming when those who kill you will think they are doing a holy service for God" (John 16:2).
4. Christians persecute fellow Christians. Christians have spread death and persecution in the name of their Christian faith. Examples are the Crusades, the Inquisition, and Jewish progroms. The people of God can become his enemies and kill others in his name.
5. Persecution often does not engender unity, but conflict and division among Christians.
6. Acts relates in detail the martyrdom of Stephen, the first New Covenant martyr (Acts 6:8–8:3), and this introduces Saul, who began as persecutor and became a persecuted missionary (Acts 7:58; 8:1–3; 9:1).
7. Jesus is the prototype of the martyr. The prediction of his martyrdom accompanies his earthly ministry. He is presented as model for all Christians (Matt 10:17–19; 16:21; 17:22–23; 26:2).
8. To die for friends is the highest form of love. Jesus taught us to love each other as he has loved us, and he laid down his life for his friends (John 15:12–13).
9. All persecution is directed towards Jesus. Jesus asked Saul: "Why are you persecuting me?" (Acts 9:4). The clearer the church testifies of Jesus, the more it will meet resistance of the Antichrist (Luke 21:12, 17).
10. The suffering of Christians as witnesses is a continuation of the suffering of Christ. Howard Snyder describes the Cross as the guarantee of the church's suffering, not its escape from persecution.
11. Jesus as role model (Heb 2:18; 4:15). Jesus said: "A slave is not greater than the master. Since they persecuted me … they will persecute you" (John 15:20). He sent us as sheep among wolves. He is the Lamb of God sent among wolves to die for others.

12. No church without martyrdom. Suffering is the mark of missions. "We must suffer many hardships to enter the kingdom of God" (Acts 14:22). Before sending the disciples out to preach Jesus spoke about the impending persecution (Matt 10:16–42).

13. The Holy Spirit—consolation in persecution. He is the comforter and gives Christians the strength to endure persecution (John 16:16, 26). "So be happy when you are insulted for being a Christian, for then the glorious Spirit of God rests on you" (1 Pet 4:14).

14. Joy in persecution. "But rejoice, inasmuch as ye are partakers of Christ's sufferings; that, when his glory shall be revealed, ye may be glad with exceeding joy (1 Pet 4:13).

15. Never aspire to persecution. It is God's prerogative, not ours, to determine who is to suffer martyrdom. The believer has no right to pursue martyrdom.

16. It is legitimate to flee persecution. Jesus left Judea for Galilee when the Jews wanted to kill him (John 7:1). He hid when they tried to stone him (John 8:59). The Christians in Acts fled Jerusalem, and Paul escaped from Damascus and from Antioch (Acts 9:25; 14:5–7). A few believers went to meet certain death, Jesus and Paul went to Jerusalem to be arrested. These are special situations, commanded directly by God.

17. Not all suffering is for Christ's sake. "If you suffer, however, it must not be for murder, stealing, making trouble, or prying into other people's affairs" (1 Pet 4:15–16).

18. Pray for the persecutor (Job 31:29; 42:8–9). Jesus told his disciples, "Love your enemies! Pray for those who persecute you" (Matt 5:44–48; Luke 6:27–28). Jesus prayed for those who crucified him, and Stephen prayed, "Lord, don't charge them with this sin."

19. Persecutors become converts. The best known example is Paul, the former persecutor of the church. When we pray for persecuted believers we must pray for their persecutors as well.

20. The fruit of martyrdom. Jesus, when he spoke about persecution said, "This will be your opportunity to tell them about me" (Luke 21:13). Paul shows that his imprisonment does not hinder but further the gospel (Phil 1:12–26). The Lausanne Congress noted that, "Persecution is a storm that is permitted to scatter the seed of the Word, disperse the sower and reaper over many fields."

21. Fruit is not automatic. The experience of the German church under the Third Reich and Communism has not led to revival or church growth. Jesus parable of the sower identifies persecution as just as dangerous to faith as wealth and egotism (Matt 13:3–8, 20–22).

22. Martyrdom accompanies world mission. Missions lead to martyrdom. Jesus sent out the twelve and the seventy with the words, "I am sending you out as sheep among wolves. So be shrewd as snakes and harmless as doves" (Matt 10:16; Luke

10:3). Ananias warned Paul that his ministry would have an immense outcome, but would also bring immense suffering (Acts 9:15–16).[3]

Harassment

In Brazil, with its growing evangelical churches and many evangelicals in position of leadership in society, harassment and persecution may seem a very distant reality. But not if one seeks to serve and reach out to native tribal peoples. Then it becomes common to be refused entry into tribal areas, or when people are serving in projects which had been approved by the government, suddenly this approval is withheld; people are expelled from the villages where they were serving, often with grave forged accusations. But our tribal brothers and sisters give us an example of dedication to whole nights of praise and prayer, and of reaching out to other tribes.

In Colombia the conflict between the government and guerillas has caused a great number of refugees, often because the guerillas want to use their land for planting coca or to force the people to join them or to leave. Christian leaders have especially become targets of such harassment.

Persecution will occur within a broad spectrum, ranging from unjust actions that are intensely hostile, to others that are mildly hostile. Intensely hostile actions can be carried out physically, psychologically, or socially. These actions could include beating, torture, isolation, or imprisonment. Mildly hostile actions would include ridicule, restriction, certain kinds of harassment, or discrimination.[4] Persecution of Christians can be defined as any unjust action of varying levels of hostility perpetrated primarily on the basis of their Christian faith, resulting in varying levels of harm considered from the victim's perspective.[5]

Persecution

There is a clear scriptural link between persecution and discipleship. We are called to follow Christ, denying ourselves and carrying our cross for the reconciliation of the world to the Father. That this journey is set in a context of conflict and suffering is alluded to as early as Genesis 3:15, when the Lord affirms that Satan's judgment will bring deliverance to the offspring of the woman, but it will take place in a process of

---

3   Thomas Schirrmacher, "Theses on a Theology of Martyrdom," in *Suffering, Persecution and Martyrdom*, eds. Christof Sauer and Richard Howell (Johannesburg: AcadSA, 2010), 288–312.

4   Charles Tieszen, "Redefining Persecution," in *Sorrow and Blood – Christian Mission in Contexts of Suffering, Persecution and Martyrdom*, eds. William D. Taylor, Antonia van der Meer and Reg Reimer (Pasadena, CA: Wiliam Carey Library, 2012), 43.

5   Tieszen, 47.

bruising and pain. The deliverance will come through the bruising of the serpent's head, but in the process the heel that bruises him will also be bruised.[6]

As we witness the testimonies of courageous persecuted brothers and sisters, it is worthwhile to reflect on the words of Peter, "For this is a gracious thing, when, mindful of God, one endures sorrows while suffering unjustly" (1 Pet 2:19 ESV). In these words, Peter defines grace as being enabled to endure suffering due to one's faithfulness to God. God has determined to save the world by the foolishness of the Cross of Christ and by the foolishness of the crosses of his children whom he has chosen and called for this very purpose. He will be consistent in using this unique method until he achieves his final goal.[7]

> Peter defines grace as being enabled to endure suffering due to one's faithfulness to God.

There is a growing and violent persecution against Christians in Nigeria, Kenya, and the Sudan. Many young people have been killed, hundreds of young women were abducted and used as slaves or wives of the Boko Haram people. This makes it more difficult to remain in predominantly Muslim areas of these countries. Many families have lost all they had, as well as beloved ones. These brothers and sisters need to know they have not been forgotten by the worldwide church.

Phases of Persecution

- Phase 1: Disinformation
- Phase 2: Discrimination
- Phase 3: Violent Persecution

Initially rumors and disinformation are propagated by the media or word of mouth, which turns public opinion against Christians. When Christians do not have access to public and published opinion in order to rectify this, disinformation is slowly regarded as truth. One striking example is the conviction by the majority of Turks that Protestants in their country are working for the CIA and want to undermine Turkey.

After Phase 1 follows discrimination of Christians as second-class citizens, be it by the state or through their neighborhood. For example, in China the education of children of Christians might be hindered. In Islamic countries the economic status of Christians is lowered, and in India, social aid for the Dalit's is canceled if and when they become Christians.

---

6   Penner, 73.
7   Penner, 74–75.

From all of this emerges fully-fledged persecution which uses various forms of violence, ranging from spontaneous attacks to imprisonment, the death penalty, or murder.[8]

How has persecution developed in India, in the last decades? In 1996, at a conference for evangelical pastors, a pastor asked what should be done about the Hindu extremists. He sought to tell his colleagues that Christians would be severely persecuted. The reaction was total unbelief—India was a secular country and had no state religion, persecution was unbelievable.

But in 1998 Hindu extremists took power in Parliament, and a wave of violence was unleashed throughout the country. From 1999 to 2001 nearly nine hundred acts of violence were recorded against Christians, including rape, church burning, and lootings. Instead of being protected by the police often the Christians were accused of conducting "forced conversions."

How does such a culture of violence develop? Why are Christians so unaware of its coming? There needs to be a power vacuum, which can be filled by clever extremists.

Traditionally the Congress Party of Gandhi and Nehru governed, but in the 1990s it was riddled with corruption. Then there needs to be a strategy to get the extremists into power. The appropriate man was Lal Krishnan Advani. He was concerned about the influence of Christians in the country (in charge of most schools and social work) and concluded that they had power because they were one, had one book, one God. So he reformed Hinduism into a religion of one book—Bhagavad Gita, and one deity—Ram, and one message—hard Hindutva.

Then there is a need to create a series of lies. Advani told the Hindus that the Indian Muslims were trying to displace Hinduism. He created the story that a famous Muslim mosque had been built on the birthplace of the god Ram. And Christians were accused of being CIA backed. Conversion was explained as spiritual violence, and emotional violence, leading to physical violence—converts are seen as being led to disown their parents, their wisdom, and their culture.

There is a need to create a mob. In 1990 Advani created a mass procession through ten states, calling on young men to save Hinduism. In 1992 a mob destroyed the Babri Mosque. The Hindutva movement has between 2.5 and 6 million members and they instigated mobs to close down churches, beat up evangelists, and force converts to renounce their Christian faith. They attack churches and create carefully crafted accusations which frighten the police, who often will not defend the Christians.

And these tactics only work because of loud repetition of the lies. After telling the lies twenty or thirty times people start to believe them. The Hindutva movement has

---

8   Chritof Sauer and Thomas Schirrmacher, "A Global Suvery" in *Sorrow and Blood: Christian Mission in Contexts of Suffering, Persecution and Martyrdom,* eds. William D. Taylor, Antonia van der Meer and Reg Reimer (Pasadena, CA: Wiliam Carey Library, 2012), 12.

created new history books, which teach that Jesus Christ was born in Kashmir and that the Taj Mahal was a Hindu monument (instead of Muslim).[9]

The Sudan has expelled foreign Christians who had official visas for serving and staying in the country but suddenly were treated as criminals. Something similar happened in Morocco some years ago, where the most painful incident was that all foreign people serving an orphanage, who were the only parents the children ever knew, suddenly were expelled in haste leaving crying children behind.

Eritrea is one of the worst countries for Christians to live; there is no freedom and people are subject to arbitrary arrest and put in terrible prisons, often metal containers. There are an estimated 1,200–3,000 people currently in prison on religious grounds. They are not allowed legal counsel or family visits. It is forbidden to pray aloud, sing or read a Bible in prison. Many escape through the Sudan, Libya, and Egypt. Last year twenty-two percent of the boat refugees were Eritreans. Just recently a convoy of Eritreans, seeking to reach Tripoli, were forced to stop by IS militants who kidnapped all eighty-eight Christians. On their way to possible freedom they are subject to physical and sexual abuse.

Christians in Iran have been imprisoned, accused of "acting against national security because they belong to a Christian organization and making propaganda against the Islamic regime, helping to spread Christianity in the country." But this has not stopped them to continue to share their faith and many continue to come to Christ.

Martyrdom

Many Christians still find it hard to believe that martyrdom is a present reality, and they may think that those martyred somehow must have provoked their suffering. How can we understand people killing others in the name of God, in the name of religion? Religion is such a central expression of one's individual and national identity that people feel the need to defend their god, believing their religion was somehow threatened. In the end it is the devil that is behind violence against Christians, because he hates Christ. A pastor in Kurdistan said that people like to speak about the martyrs of the past, but will not risk martyrdom today, and do not take the gospel to any Muslim. He had been criticized for taking converted Muslims into his church.[10]

To suffer and die to accomplish his Father's purposes was not unexpected; Jesus could not be God and do anything else. Weakness, suffering, and sacrifice are God's modus operandi. This is how God accomplishes his work: not through strength or compulsion, but through love and invitation. So as the Servant of God suffers and dies, so do those

---

9   Ronald Boyd-MacMillan, *Faith that Endures* (Grand Rapids, MI: Revell, 2006), 46–56.
10   Boyd-Macmillan, 31–39,

who follow him. This is God's way of reconciling the world to himself. A cross-centered gospel requires cross-carrying messengers.[11]

Many Christians, as well as Yazidi's and other people are being exterminated in Iraq and Syria by the IS. Christians received the option to stay alive if they converted to Islam, as they were refusing, hundreds of thousands have fled, becoming refugees, most of them

> This is how God accomplishes his work: not through strength or compulsion, but through love and invitation.

living in very poor conditions in great refugee camps in Jordan, Lebanon, and Turkey as well as further abroad. Local churches and Christian NGO's continue to serve them and many have come to faith in Jesus. Many others, children and adults, have been brutally killed, heads were put on stakes in the conquered places. Christian leaders who chose to stay have been abducted and killed.

IS continues to kill Christians in Libya In April they released a video where thirty Africans (from Ethiopia) were killed, some of them beheaded at a beach and others shot in their heads in the desert.

Despite the incredible suffering that Middle Eastern Christians endure at present, 11-year-old Iraqi girl Maryam Behnam says that she harbors no bitterness towards those who forced her family out of their home. "I will only ask God to forgive them," she said. Praising God for preserving the lives of her family, she said: "Jesus is my Father, and he is my creator. I have no one else better than him. When [IS] drove us out of our home, his hand was on us and he saved us." Now living in a trailer among other displaced Christians in Erbil, she hopes one day to help those around her, working for Doctors Without Borders. "As Jesus said, 'You've been given freely, you should give freely,'" she said. "This is why we should love them and provide treatment."

The Christian students that were killed at Garissa University in Kenya, by the Al-Shabaab also are martyrs, though they never expected such a death.

The twenty-one Egyptian laborers that were taken to the seaside to be beheaded and killed are an example of faithfulness and a great witness. The public reaction of forgiveness of their families, which were broadcasted on TV, caused a great impact. The Egyptian Bible Society produced a large number of leaflets with an answer of the Christian community to this violence, and they were read and sought for by numerous people of different faiths.

Conclusion

We were never promised a comfortable and easy life, the teaching of Jesus, the apostles, and the Old Testament make it clear that to be faithful to God will mean a continuing struggle against the forces of evil that seek to govern the world. We may know,

---

11   Penner, 73.

nevertheless that when we walk in the way of the Cross, following Jesus, he will never forsake us, will always be with us, and he is mightier than any other power.

Those whose lives and those of their dear ones are under continual threat bear the heavier burden. But the Lord will give them his grace and his strength to persevere.

Our duty is to support them in our prayers and whatever practical way we can—as long as our actions are really appropriate and helpful and do not cause them further suffering. May the Lord help us.

Discussion Questions

1. How has your church or mission community responded to present situations of harassment, persecution, and martyrdom? How has this influenced your ability to serve those who suffer?
2. Has there been an appropriate biblical teaching on the subject? Do you have any plan on how to improve this attitude?
3. What can we learn from Jesus as our model in facing persecution and helping others to deal with it?

References

Boyd-MacMillan, Ronald. 2006. *Faith that Endures*. Grand Rapids, MI: Revell.

Penner, Glenn. 2012. "A Biblical Theology of Persecution and Discipleship." In *Sorrow and Blood: Christian Mission in Contexts of Suffering, Persecution and Martyrdom*, eds. William D. Taylor, Antonia van der Meer and Reg Reimer. Pasadena, CA: Wiliam Carey Library.

Sauer, Christof and Thomas Schirrmacher. 2012. "A Global Survey." In *Sorrow and Blood: Christian Mission in Contexts of Suffering, Persecution and Martyrdom*, eds. William D. Taylor, Antonia van der Meer and Reg Reimer. Pasadena, CA: Wiliam Carey Library.

Schirrmacher, Thomas. 2010. "Theses on a Theology of Martyrdom." In *Suffering, Persecution and Martyrdom*, eds. Christof Sauer and Richard Howell. Johannesburg, SA: AcadSA.

Taylor, William D., Antonia van der Meer, and Reg Reimer, eds. 2012. *Sorrow and Blood: Christian Mission in Contexts of Suffering, Persecution and Martyrdom*. Pasadena, CA: Wiliam Carey Library.

Tieszen, Charles. 2012. "Redefining Persecution." In *Sorrow and Blood: Christian Mission in Contexts of Suffering, Persecution and Martyrdom*, eds. William D. Taylor, Antonia van der Meer and Reg Reimer. Pasadena, CA: William Carey Library.

Antonia Leonora van der Meer, known as Tonica, is Brazilian. She served with student ministry in Brazil and was IFES pioneer for student work in Angola and Mozambique (in times of war). She returned to work at the Evangelical Missions Center for seventeen years, training Brazilian missionaries for holistic service. She helped to start Member Care in Brazil, and is a leader of CIM (Cuidado Integral do Missionário), serving the Brazilian Association for Crosscultural Missions. She did her doctorate in missiology at the Asia Graduate School of Theology. She has published articles and books, like *Sorrow and Blood*.

Scripture: *Psalm 46*, ("God is our refuge and strength..."), *Psalm 139*, and *Isaiah 55:11*

Resources: Several books by Henry Nouwen; *The Cost of Discipleship, by* Dietrich Bonhoeffer (Norwich, UK: SCM Press, 2011 [1937]).

Along the Journey

Caring for Companions

CHAPTER 31

The Reality of Suffering in Mission

David D. Ruíz

> For it has been granted to you on behalf of Christ not only to believe on him, but also to suffer for him. *Philippians 1:29*

Suffering has accompanied the Church of Jesus Christ since its beginning, it is a mark of authenticity of the ministry of those who serve the Lord. We often forget that the Lord Jesus Christ allows suffering in his disciples. He shows his power in the mist of our fragility. Suffering is his stamp of confirmation that we are living in his calling.

The theme of suffering for the sake of the gospel is not a popular one within the church, especially the Iberoamerican church.[1] We speak of suffering in general terms. We speak of the pain of the death of a loved one, of the loss of a job, or of the lack of resources to get something we want. We don't talk about suffering as a consequence of being light in a world of darkness. It seems that we can't remember back very far. Not long ago people in Latin America gave their lives preaching the Word, agonizing daily in the task of being messengers of the Word, as colporteurs or as pastors gone for months at a time in order to take the gospel to the rural areas of our countries, and which extended that suffering to their families.

It has not always been this way. Already around the year 536 BC, Augustine of Hippo felt obliged to write a letter to the pastors explaining the evidence of the reality of the suffering in Christian life and service. He also mentioned the danger of neglecting to teach it, and of expecting instead prosperity and comfort as Christians.

> Hippo wrote that the negligent pastor will not say to his weak sheep, "My child, when you draw near to the fear of God, prepare for trials; Keep a firm heart, be brave." Because whoever says such things is comforting the weak, he is strengthening him in such a way that when he embraces the faith he will stop expecting the prosperity of this century. But if one is encouraged to hope

---

1   Note: Geographical region including Latin America, Hispanic speaking Caribbean, Brazil, Hispanic speaking churches in North America, and Iberian peninsula's counties. For further information see Pietri Uslar, *Arturo, Cuarenta Ensayos* (Caracas, Monte Avila) 1990.

in prosperity, this same prosperity will be that which corrupts him. And when the adversity overcomes him, they will throw him down and finish him.[2]

Christians need someone who can explain to them that it is necessary to suffer in the ministry; that to be a servant of God does not exempt us from suffering by the cross. We need to open our ears to a renewed gospel, not the one corrupted by the search for prosperity. We need to give everything until the gospel reaches the ends of the earth. Note that we are speaking of "Christians," not just missionaries. All of us are exposed to suffering when we begin to be light and to confront a world in darkness with our testimony.

> All of us are exposed to suffering when we begin to be light and to confront a world in darkness with our testimony.

The Bible confirms—through many examples—that suffering is part of the process of discipleship. Very few enter into suffering because we are busy pursuing standards for success, established by the world, and accepted by the church.

In the book of Isaiah, in the third song of the Servant of Yahweh the servant is presented as a disciple in preparation for receiving the commission that the Lord has for him.[3] He is prepared to speak and to listen (50:4), but as a true disciple he learns that his preparation for the task also includes suffering as an integral part of this experience (50:6).

When we see the experience of Apostle Paul, we see that he was someone who was willing to suffer. Acts 9 relates the story of his conversion, the experience with the vision of Jesus Christ that changed the paradigm of his life, that questioned his convictions, and above all gave him a new occupation that also included suffering.

On the Road to Damascus

Paul made the disciples of the Lord suffer. As we read in Acts 9:1; he carried authority from the high priest (9:14), guards, and without a doubt, many chains. In his short experience as a persecutor of the church he was distinguished in his field. Further on, we read like a newspaper headline the credentials of Paul: "All the harm he has done to your people in Jerusalem" (Acts 9:13).

In chapter seven, he observed the martyrdom of Stephen in an improvised torture chamber on the street. There, from this place, Paul saw Stephen's bleeding body as he knelt down, with great effort, with trembling hands and pleaded with the Lord, "Lord, do not charge them with this sin," and then he fell and died. Certainly this image kept

---

2   From *Liturgy of the Hours* (http://www.liturgies.net/Liturgies/Catholic/loh/week24fridayor.htm, April 15, 2016).

3   WC Kaiser, Jr., *Mission in the Old Testament: Israel as a Light to the Nations* (Grand Rapids, MI: Baker Books, 2000), 57.

him awake at night; how is it that Christians can forgive their enemies, in moments like this (Acts 7:58, 60)?

Chapter 8:1,3 lays the framework of the first great persecution of the church: "And Saul was consenting to his death... and Saul made havoc of the church, entering every house, and dragging off men and women, committing them to prison." Certainly the second image that he couldn't erase from his mind was that of the Christians. "How can they continue preaching while they're fleeing?" he must have wondered. And we can imagine that as he hastened their steps to arrive at Damascus, he couldn't understand why it was so difficult to finish off those heretics. It seemed that the more they persecuted them, the more they multiplied. There and then Saul meets Jesus, an unexpected encounter. "Why are you persecuting me?" This is the question he asks, and Paul learns that he has been persecuting, following, and imprisoning God, incarnate in Jesus Christ.

What happened in those three days at Judas' house on Straight street? We can't know for certain, but without a doubt it was a painful time, a pain deeper than anything Saul had experienced in his life. He felt repentance. "How was I capable of doing something like that? How did I stray so far from my interests in defending God that I came to a point of persecuting him?" He certainly also was afraid, imagining all that he had done in his life; he felt the anguish of thinking that everything that he valued in his life had been destroyed, and fear that he had gone too far. He experienced the anguish of knowing that he had erred in his path, like someone who takes the wrong exit, and discovers it when he arrives at a different town.

God took Saul to an extreme point—that somber, powerful, influential young Jew, who becomes blind, alone, sad, repentant, anguished, and fearful. The only thing that Saul could do was pray. During those three days he had been calling out to the Lord, pleading for help in his desperate situation. God described Saul of Tarsus, in this process, with a forceful phrase, "For behold, he is praying."

It is there, in the midst of a desperate situation, needing an answer, that God sends Ananias to console Saul with this revelation: "Go, for he is a chosen instrument of mine to carry my name before the Gentiles and kings and the children of Israel." Then he continues with the methodology of his preparation: "For I will show him how much he must suffer for the sake of my name" (Acts 9:15,16).

God's answer wasn't expected. Paul receives it and begins to understand the meaning of the task to which he has been called. The preparation for it required two qualifying words: "how much" and "necessary"; both related to suffering as part of his preparation for the missions task.

His Lessons in Suffering

God shows Saul that he knows how much he must suffer: God has the measure of our suffering, as we read in 1 Corinthians 10:13, where God allows a measure of temptation for each believer according to what they are able. When he allows suffering, he knows how much we are able to stand. Like the famous "Plimsoll Line," that is painted on the exterior of ships; it helps them to know the limit of how much cargo to load.[4] In the same way, God has painted a similar line on each one of us, depending on the task that he has given us. Survival, in the midst of suffering, doesn't depend on us, but on him who painted the line.

God allows suffering to the measure that we need it: At this point in the life of Saul, when he became the Apostle Paul, he begins to reflect and makes a conclusion about the value of suffering in the Christian life, and in particular, for one's own ministry. Second Corinthians 6:4–10 says:

> But as servants of God we commend ourselves in every way: by great endurance, in afflictions, hardships, calamities, beatings, imprisonments, riots, labors, sleepless nights, hunger; by purity, knowledge, patience, kindness, the Holy Spirit, genuine love; by truthful speech, and the power of God; with the weapons of righteousness for the right hand and for the left; through honor and dishonor, through slander and praise. We are treated as impostors, and yet are true; as unknown, and yet well known; as dying, and behold, we live; as punished, and yet not killed; as sorrowful, yet always rejoicing; as poor, yet making many rich; as having nothing, yet possessing everything.

Finally, he would see it in the perspective of the achievements through suffering, as it was written some time before in 2 Corinthians 4:8–9: "We are afflicted in every way, but not crushed; perplexed, but not driven to despair; persecuted, but not forsaken; struck down, but not destroyed." All of those who are suffering find in the Lord the strength to overcome, not to get out of the situation, but to continue on. Each item in the list brings us to the death of Christ, "So that the life of Christ be manifest in our bodies." So the answer to the question, "How much is it necessary to suffer?" is found in this same passage saying, until "the life of Christ also may be manifested in our body" (2 Cor 4:10).

> All of those who are suffering find in the Lord the strength to overcome, not to get out of the situation, but to continue on.

God allows suffering in the moment that we need it: Suffering comes, many times, when he needs us to stop and examine what we are doing, and not when we have time to do so. Two passages show us that Paul in Corinth receives a word saying that, "No one will attack you to harm you" (Acts 18:10). Nevertheless, in Ephesus, the Spirit tells him to expect suffering and he is ready to follow, even to this (20:22 and 21:11).

Paul's answer to the prophecy of Agabus is that he is ready to walk the path of suffering for Christ's sake: "What are you doing, weeping and breaking my heart? For I am ready not only to be imprisoned but even to die in Jerusalem for the name of the Lord

---

4   The Plimsoll line is a reference mark located on a ship's hull that indicates the maximum depth to which the vessel may be safely immersed when loaded with cargo (on http://oceanservice.noaa.gov/facts/plimsoll-line.html).

Jesus" (Acts 21:13). This answer has nothing of missions' romanticism, but instead it's a decision about his ministry. Paul is ready and willing to accept whatever consequences for the cause of the gospel of Jesus Christ. His conclusion, at this moment in his ministry is: "Whatever God wants to do with me in my ministry, this is the best thing."

Some time ago I heard a missionary who had recently left the field after a long term of service in Sudan. He spoke about his ministry and his struggles. He said that one of the things that had been hardest to forgive was to accept his mission agency's decisions about security in his place of service. He related that when the civil war had begun in that place, he received precise instructions from his superiors to leave within twenty-four hours when an army convoy was evacuating international workers, and he had to do it. He explained with pain the suffering that he and his family felt in that moment, that they were contradicting all that they had preached about trusting in God as they fled at the time of difficulty. They left with strong feelings of frustration and impotence of leaving those they loved, for whom they were willing to do whatever was needed.

God shows us why it is necessary to suffer, and what results from passing through suffering in the ministry. I've chosen four of them. The first is to know Christ in the shadow of the Cross, in the middle of suffering (Phil 3:10). We must first know Christ to let him be known, and this text says that suffering is one of the most effective ways to know him. It is where we see aspects of his face that we could not see in any other way; where we feel his saving presence in moments of anguish, and where our calling is put to the test. We fully confirm that this is what he has sent us to do, and we commit ourselves, even in the midst of suffering, to stay faithful until the end even if it means losing our lives.

Secondly, we must suffer in order to avoid the arrogance of believing ourselves to be more important than the work of God in us (2 Cor 12:7–10). "Therefore I take pleasure in infirmities, in reproaches, in needs, in persecutions, in distresses, for Christ's sake. For when I am weak, then I am strong" (12:10). God has blessed Iberoamerica during the past two decades, as literally thousands of missionaries have left for the field and many have stayed there, doing amazing things. We have taken the knowledge of this missions awakening to many international missions spheres. Time after time we have seen great expectations that there are for this "Iberoamerican missions force," and we have seen the enthusiasm that grows when we share what God is doing among us.

It is very easy to take pride. To start speaking "evangelistically" is to present, sometimes, images of what is happening here, but not necessarily to present the actual reality. This is when suffering makes us remember that in the end, the most important thing that happens with us is not our glorious ministry, but the work that the Lord wants to do in us. It is necessary to suffer in order to see these things clearly.

Thirdly, it is necessary to suffer, in order to give strength and power to our testimony. In Philippians 1:12–14, the Apostle Paul speaks with enthusiasm about his time in prison and his suffering. He says that it turned out for good, and for the furtherance of the gospel. The Christians of Philippi were worried about him and wanted to help him in his suffering. The Ephesians preached Christ with even more fervor. Those all around him see Christ as magnified in his body, and even his enemies, preach Christ. The gospel, then, is in a good spot, because the missionary is in prison. What a tremendous paradox! To be sent to prison so that the gospel can grow. To be taken by force so that the force of the gospel can be evidenced. To take someone to the point of death so that the life of Christ may be manifested in the life of the servant. I don't know if we can understand such paradoxes with the missionary experience we have, but no doubt there are those among us who have lived and are living and can show us with their own lives a photograph of the Apostle Paul laboring in the midst of suffering.

> In the end, the most important thing that happens with us is not our glorious ministry, but the work that the Lord wants to do in us.

Finally, we suffer in order to give the Christian an opportunity to share in the sufferings of Jesus Christ. In Revelation 2:10 the Spirit, writing to the church at Smyrna, says, "Do not fear any of those things which you are about to suffer." Suffering has a part in God's plan. It is however, temporary, and does not continue into eternity. Rather trials demonstrate who comes out victorious.

God shows us that it is necessary to suffer. I love the figure that Paul presents in which suffering is a manifestation of the glory of God (2 Cor 4:7–18). The analogy is the earthen vessel. Suffering is a gradual and continual process in the life of the believer. Each hit that the Lord allows us to take breaks a bit of that fragile vessel. It is a planned suffering. Each piece of that earthenware that is removed leaves a hole. A hole is opened in our life and character when the weight of suffering falls on us. That is where the light of the treasure stored inside can come out. The more hits we take, the more holes, but with more holes, more light! The apostle assures us that to the measure that the outer man is destroyed; the inner man is renewed day after day (2 Cor 4:7–12).

> A hole is opened in our life and character when the weight of suffering falls on us. That is where the light of the treasure stored inside can come out.

This illustration reminds us that closeness to death makes us evaluate our ministry and above all, to experience thanksgiving to God when we see our ministry in "death's perspective;" our achievements, with his victory; and the pride that accumulates in us compared to the humility of the suffering Servant.

Paul wants us to understand that suffering only affects the outer man. The mortal body is wearing out. It's the one that needs to be beat up. In the next chapter he tells us that the inner man is perfected in tribulation. If the outer man is mortal, suffering becomes just a "momentary affliction" (2 Cor 4:17) and the result is that from my deteriorating body the light of the glory of Jesus Christ shines. Sometimes we forget that the ministry of being light to the nations includes suffering.

Are we willing to suffer for the cause of the call? Are we are prepared to walk the calling of God even with the most difficult consequences, to the ends of the earth? Let's think about whether or not we are willing to make Philippians 1:29 our own, "For to you it has been granted on behalf of Christ, not only to believe in him, but also to suffer for his sake."

References

Kaiser, Jr. W.C. 2000. *Mission in the Old Testament: Israel as a Light to the Nations.* Grand Rapids, MI: Baker Books.

Uslar, Pietri. 1990. *Arturo, Cuarenta Ensayos.* Caracas, Monte Avila.

David Ruíz is a pastor and missiologist from Guatemala, married to Dora Amalia. During the last twenty-five years David has been actively involved in the development of the mission movement in Ibero America. He was executive director of the Cooperación Misionera Iberoamericana (COMIBAM) and from 2000–2006 was the fourth International President. David also was International coordinator of Great Commission Roundtable (GCR), and now is associate director of The Mission Commission of the World Evangelical Alliance (WEA) and vice president of Camino Global and Interserve. His book, *Transformación de la Iglesia,* has been serving as a seminal work in Ibero America to rethink the idea of the mission-minded church.

Scripture: *2 Corinthians 4:7–18 ("But we have this treasure in jars of clay...")*

Resource: *El Problema del Dolor* (*The Problem of Pain*), by CS Lewis (New York: HarperCollins Español, 2014 [1940]).

CHAPTER 32

Caring for Those on the Journey

Integral Flow of Care

Detlef Blöecher

Tim welcomed me at the airport as I arrived after a ten-hour flight from visiting one of our missionaries. We hugged each other—it was so great to see him again two and a half years into his first term. We walked out of the airport, hopped into his truck, and off we went through the slow moving traffic of this buzzing metropolis, inching along towards the outskirts and then further on through the vast expanse to his remote place of service, a seven-hour drive on lonely roads. I soaked in the fresh air and enjoyed the bright colors in the blazing sun. Now we had plenty of time to talk and rebuild relationships before we would reach our destination after sunset.

Much had happened in the past years: language learning in this bustling city, his first experience in youth ministry under the supervision of a national pastor, exciting outreach in informal settlements—and finally his assignment to a tiny ministry team in this remote regional town, far off in the mountains with limited social contacts for a bachelor like him. He was given the task of starting a youth ministry. Yet the context was challenging: the young people had to work hard in the fields and local churches felt bound to their traditional church life with little interest in special activities for young people. This was all very new, disturbing the status quo—missionaries had taught them a very conservative form of church and trained a few local evangelists now reinforcing this particular style. Tim's living situation also took its toll, sharing a mud house with many insects and plagued by frequent sicknesses on top of loneliness and cultural misunderstandings.

Once his first reservations had been overcome, words gushed out of his mouth as he openly shared with me one event after the next. I just listened carefully, merely asking a brief question here and then for understanding. At times his voice broke and tears rolled down his cheeks—the stoked up disappointment and frustration begging for release. When we finally reached our destination, he confided to me: "I've had enough. I will quit in a few weeks' time. I just wanted to stay on for your visit." In the following three days we had much to talk, reflect, and pray about, we took time to visit his friends and important places, revisit his experiences and decisions. We shared meals, laughed and cried together, all clothed in times of study in the Word and prayer. We also met his ministry leader who came from a distinct denominational background and had a very different upbringing—their perspectives were light years apart—which led to tragic misunderstandings and unwise decisions… but finally a new perspective grew in Tim's heart, light at the end of a long, dark tunnel. These few days saved the career of this young missionary—with the prospect of a new assignment in another location that I was able to initiate.

It's not just this young missionary crushed in ministry—and rescued by a graceful visit. Bill Taylor states: "Attrition issues are extremely important to me now, for I have witnessed both the visible and the invisible dimension of the iceberg," whose bulk is hidden below the water surface.[1]

There are numerous reasons why missionaries lose sight and finally go home—usually there are several factors combined—and even more workers continue ineffectively in ministry, just too embarrassed to resign and embrace a radical change in person, ministry, or location.[2] Missionaries are our jewels, too precious to lose or gather dust. We should do all to make them sparkle in the light and irradiate the beauty of the creator. What helps missionaries to thrive, grow, and flourish?

This was the key question that led in 2002 to the next WEA global study "ReMAP II—Retaining Missionaries: Agencies Practices," which explored the flipside: good agency practices that help missionaries prosper and be fruitful in ministry.[3] Six hundred and one sending agencies from twenty-three countries with a total of 40,000 long-term cross-cultural workers participated in the survey. Their directors rated their own principles and practices and reported on the fate of their missionaries. The results identified a rich bouquet of factors that contribute to staff longevity, among them: agency's ethos, organizational structure, communication, preparation, personal care, and spiritual issues.[4] Many results have been published in the book *Worth Keeping:*

---

1   William D Taylor, "Examining the Iceberg Called Attrition,." in *Too Valuable to Lose*, ed. William D. Taylor (Pasadena, CA: William Carey Library, 1997), 5.
2   Yet how do we bring them back gracefully, if necessary (Acts 13:13; Phil 2:29)?
3   Rob Hay, et al., *Worth Keeping: Global Perspectives on Best Practice in Missionary Retention* (Pasadena, CA: William Carey Library, 2007).
4   Ethos, i.e., Clear purpose and vision of the agency; Specific work plans and job descriptions; Empowerment of staff; Cooperation in mission; Personal trust throughout the agency. Organizational structure, i.e., Flexible, dynamic organizational structures; Lean administration; Consultative, interactive leadership style; Assignment to gifting; Ongoing improvement of projects; Stable financial support of missionaries. Communication, i.e., Effective communication; Effective systems to handle complaints; Supportive team; Good relationship with sending church and with the local church in place of service. Preparation, i.e., Careful candidate selection, especially regarding Clear calling to ministry by God; Quality pre-field training, especially in Missions; Effective on-field orientation; Intensive language training and cultural studies for new missionaries; Continued Language studies beyond the first term. Personal care, i.e., Effective personal care; Preventative member care and crisis intervention; Good work-rest balance; Continuous training and development of new gifts; Regular personal performance reviews; Staff development in resilience and acceptance of new challenges; Debriefing during home assignment. Spiritual issues, i.e., Maintenance of personal spiritual life; Prayer throughout agency; experience in spiritual warfare.

Global Perspectives on Best Practice in Missionary Retention and on the WEA website www.worldevangelical.org/resources.

The research clearly shows that good agency structures and personal care reduce missionary attrition by a factor of more than five—and this finding is not based on idealistic organizational standards but by the actual performance of a large group of (one-third of all) agencies. Yet missionary retention is not just a matter of a few critical issues but an extensive mesh of many interrelated factors.[5] There is not just one golden way to success but a variety of different routes and models of good practice, and many small steps already make a big difference.

In ReMAP II, mission leaders in general gave only a mediocre rating of their own agency's personal care for their missionaries—which indicates that there is still room for improvement.[6] A few important aspects are summarized in the following:

1. Maintaining Spiritual Life

One of the greatest single factors for missionary retention is our identity in Christ as God's beloved children. This is the core of our life and ministry.[7] It is not so much what we do (which characterizes a servant) but who we are in Christ. He cares for us; in him we find our delight and our fulfillment. We live to his pleasure, to worship him with all our life, with words and deeds. Prayer and vibrant spirituality proved to be one of the key factors in ReMAP II.[8]

> One of the greatest single factors for missionary retention is our identity in Christ as God's beloved children.

A few years ago I came across a survey among cross-cultural Christian workers in the Middle East showing that half of them spent less than ten minutes per day on their personal prayer and Bible reading. This is very little considering their challenging ministry; they spiritually starve to death—no wonder why many leave prematurely.

Our Lord Jesus regularly went to a quiet place to enjoy the company of his heavenly Father, ask for direction and receive his strengthening (Mark 1:35; Luke 5:16, 6:12, 11:1). How can we live on less? Do we take this daily time for prayer, listening, and reading his Word? Some workers may need inspiration through a good sermon (perhaps on MP3), well-thought-out questions to reflect on, worship in community, or a devotional book for reading. I've often changed the format of my quiet time; when it becomes routine I go for a different format so that it stays fresh and inspiring.

---

5   Detlef Bloecher, "Good Agency Practices: Lessons from ReMAP II," *Evangelical Mission Quarterly* (April 2005a), 235.

6   Bloecher 2005a, 19.

7   Kirk Franklin, "Mission and Spirituality," *Connections* 8(1) (April: 12-14, 2009), 13.

8   Jaap Ketelaar, "Spiritual Life," in *Worth Keeping: Global Perspectives on Best Practice in Missionary Retention,* ed. Rob Hay et al. (Pasadena, CA: William Carey Library, 2007), 131.

It is particularly hard for mothers of young children to take a few minutes out of a busy day, i.e., when the children are down a nap or the spouse takes care of them. Mum is the central core of a family; when she loses heart, the family will go home.

Our spirituality is formed by our background, likewise our understanding of the "call."[9] Yet it is extremely important that a sense of God's calling to ministry has grown and confirmed by the home church.[10] When it gets tough, God's assurance is so critical, as John Mark learned the hard way (Acts 13:13).

2. Mentoring

Many younger missionaries have difficulties in finding a daily pattern for their quiet time and a disciplined life in general.[11] They long for mentoring in order to grow spiritually, as a person and in ministry. They want feed-back to reflect on their life and ministry performance and to set realistic goals—how their task makes sense within the whole.

In my experience, the greatest challenge for young missionaries is their impatience: they want to achieve too much in too short time. They are inclined to set utopic goals and get frustrated when things do not move forward quickly. They need an experienced friend who helps them reflect, evaluate, and understand how they are doing. All of us need this, not only young workers.

3. Work-rest Balance

There are so many urgent needs around, so much work to do, and endless opportunities for ministry. How do I set priorities? Where to accept limitations? When do I say no, and how? This is not easy, yet we all need time out for refreshment and peace. What do I do for recreation, to relax, and get newly inspired? How can I develop a hobby?—ideally together with others, like a team sport, aerobic group, music band, learning about local culture, developing an art, or simple reading. The item, "Not being overworked," received the lowest rating in ReMAP II, particularly among missionaries from the global North—proving how all missionaries are struggling with this issue.[12]

---

9   John Amalraj, "What Shapes Our Spirituality in Missions?" *Connections* 8(1) (April:9-12, 2009), 10f.

10   Rob Hay, "Selection," in *Worth Keeping: Global Perspectives on Best Practice in Missionary Retention*, ed. Rob Hay, et al. (Pasadena, CA: William Carey Library, 2007b), 94.

11   Kath Donovan and Ruth Myers, "Reflections on Attrition in Career Missionaries: A Generational Perspective into the Future," in *Too Valuable to Lose*, ed. William D. Taylor (Pasadena, CA: William Carey Library, 1997), 48.

12   In the ReMAP II study 601 mission leaders from twenty countries of the global North and global South (representing 40,000 long-tern missionaries) self-assessed the practices of their own mission agency on a 1 (very poorly done) to 6 (excellent) scale. From the eighty aspects considered, item sixty-one "Missionaries are generally not overworked in the amount of work they do," received the lowest of all ratings (3.51 and even 3.21 from agencies of the global North). Detlef Bloecher, "Continuous Language

In today's world of electronic communication it is particularly difficult to be offline for a few hours and wind down, finding the right balance between work and rest. On a daily basis, weekly (at least one day per week off!), and annually: annual vacation received extremely high rating in ReMAP II.[13] WhatsApp can become a tyranny.[14]

4. Team Building

Missionaries are a particular type of people: strong characters with rich life experience, gifting, and firm theological convictions—otherwise they would not have made it into missions and survived for so long. Yet, how do you glue such edged personalities together into a team? How do we celebrate our diversity—instead of considering it as a threat?

Often missionaries substantiate their personal conviction with Scripture and elevate their personal preference to the rank of doctrinal truth—burdening conflict resolution. Many also have very high expectations towards their team colleagues: if we were obedient to the Lord, they will come to my conclusion, too, and we will live in perfect harmony—yet reality is different.[15] How can we live in grace and consider the other higher than ourselves (Phil 2:3)? Jesus firmly taught: "By this everyone will know that you are my disciples, if you love one another" (John 13:35). Unity is an obligation, not an option.

Today, international teams are the norm in most places. Each nationality has its own strengths and weaknesses, experience and blind spots, preferred leadership style and role expectancy—which adds further dimensions. Two nationalities in a team often lead to tensions; three plus nationalities are conducive to learning and listening to each other. Team building exercises and external consultancy can be valuable tools (Phil 4:2f). Indeed, it requires lots of grace to work together and live out unity in diversity (Eph 4:2).

> Two nationalities in a team often lead to tensions; three plus nationalities are conducive to learning and listening to each other.

In literature we find frequent claims that team conflicts were the prime reasons for missionaries coming home. ReMAP I surveyed this issue carefully and found that only 1/11 of all "returnees for potentially preventable reasons" did so (primarily) because of team conflicts (8.8%)—whereas more came home for health reasons (14.3%), children's education (14.1%), or lack of self-confidence (9.0%).[16]

---

and Cultural Studies Are Indispensable" (https://www.dmgint.de/mission-en/research-papers.html, 2014), 17.

13   Detlef Bloecher, "Good Agency Practices: Lessons Learnt from ReMAP II," *Connections* (June 2004). 19.

14   Especially to new missionaries who need to purposely cut off from home to move into the adopted cultural setting.

15   Amalraj, 11.

16   Bloecher 2007a, 12.

5. Servant Leadership

Celebrating diversity calls for wise, meek leadership, yet leadership style and role models are culturally conditioned. Missionaries have strong ownership in their ministry; many are raising their own support and thus expect a consultative leadership; they want to be included in the decision making and understand its reasons.[17]

Leaders may tend to go for their own vision, title, power, influence, honor. You cannot run a ministry team as a business! Jesus has given us a wonderful example: "I, your Lord and Teacher, have washed your feet, you also should wash one another's feet" (John 13:14). Leadership is about humility and grace, not personal power, influence, or achievement. It is about his kingdom, not ours. Spiritual leaders will give away authority, empower their people, help them grow and achieve their own goals. Leaders find their fulfillment in seeing their staff flourish and grow beyond their own capacity. Peter reminds leaders: "Be shepherds of God's flock that is under your care, watching over them—not because you must, but because you are willing, as God wants you to be… eager to serve; not lording it over those entrusted to you, but being examples to the flock" (1 Pet 5:2f).

6. Participatory Decision Making

The principle of grace also holds true for decision making and ministry in general. Missionaries are very committed to their own ministry, more than to their agency.[18] Yet projects should never be initiated and driven by outsiders. Locals know the situation, needs, and potential (possibly assisted by an outsider); they are the experts, foreigners are the learners. The local community needs to decide what to do and how and which resources to invest: each one has lots to give! It needs to be their project, their initiative, their goal, their effort, their success—which encourages them to set new goals. It requires patience and flexibility, yet it's the only way to ownership, lasting fruit, self-reliance. This counts not only for material projects but also for spiritual insights, what God's Word is saying to them.

> Locals know the situation, needs, and potential (possibly assisted by an outsider); they are the experts, foreigners are the learners.

7. Personal Care

ReMAP II clearly shows that agencies with little member care (MC) suffer very high staff attrition. As the agency's investment in personal care grows, missionary attrition decreases up to an optimum of 5–10% of agency's total personal and financial resources

---

17   Bloecher 2004, 15.
18   Donovan and Myers, 46; Bloecher 2004, 17.

(global North), and 10–20% for agencies from the global South coming from a relational society.[19]

Personal care, however, is not just crisis intervention, but needs also preventative member care which includes: strengthening of personal spiritual life, prayer chains, inspiring communal prayer, making good sermons and spiritual books available, team building, work-life balance, personality testing to understand one's own strengths and weaknesses, as well as tools to grow, acceptance of present personal status (as single or married), and living in reconciled, fulfilling relationships. Moving to another country is stressful and it undermines your self-confidence.

The agency also needs to provide clear work assignments, help to set realistic goals, install clear leadership structures, communicate well with leadership, provide time-out when needed, provide regular feed-back interviews, initiate social team events and good internal communication, arrange team-building exercises, provide regular days off and annual vacation for staff, set up effective systems for handling complaints, provide for satisfactory security, medical care and schooling options for missionary kids, develop hobbies and new gifts, develop life-long learning, assist during transitions, offer new tasks and challenges, teach stress coping tools, etc.. This strengthens the whole person and helps to grow resilience and flexibility.

Curative member care, on the other hand, includes medical care in sickness, specialist care for trauma, burn-out, team conflict, depression, crisis intervention, marriage counseling, missionary kid educational needs, culture shock, conflicts with nationals, resolution of leadership crisis, etc. Many missionaries live in high-risk countries, face a hostile environment, experience violence, are overwhelmed by a heavy work load, extreme poverty, exploitation, and human rights abuse. This puts them under enormous stress. A recent study with a large mission showed that more than 55% of their missionaries in creative access countries suffered from high stress, and most even from multiple causes.[20]

> Preventative and curative care are like the two wings of an airplane: it requires both to fly; one alone will not do.

Agencies that focus on either preventative or curative member care end up with a higher attrition rate than those who provide both in balance.[21] Preventative and curative care are like the two wings of an airplane: it requires both to fly; one alone will not do.

Both types of services require expertise and specialization which few agencies can provide alone, calling for intermission cooperation.[22]

---

19   Detlef Bloecher, "Member Care," in *Worth Keeping: Global Perspectives on Best Practice in Missionary Retention*, ed. Rob Hay et al. (Pasadena, CA: William Carey Library, 2007c), 182ff. Detlef Bloecher, "Member Care: What Makes Missionaries Strong, Healthy, and Flexible" (https://www.dmgint.de/mission-en/research-papers.html, 2011), 3.
20   Detlef Bloecher, "Study on 900 WEC missionarie," (unpublished data, 2012).
21   Bloecher 2007b, 185ff; Bloecher 2011).
22   Bloecher 2007c, 41.

Interestingly, balanced member care reduces missionary attrition for potentially preventable causes as well as unpreventable attrition (latter included: end of the project evacuation, return for medical reasons, retirement, etc.). Comprehensive member care strengthens physical health (immune system), provides hope and faith, optimism and joy, reduces stress, helps people to make good decisions, prevents risky lifestyle (i.e., reckless driving), grows resilience in accepting a new assignment after end of a project, and even when reaching retirement age, etc.[23]

8. Personal Care throughout Whole Life

Research also shows that the risk for missionaries to abandon ministry is the same during all stages of their career.[24] New missionaries initially face cultural adjustment, orientation, and language learning. After two years they move into their ministry assignment and need find the right task. Thereafter team conflicts surface, later burn-out and overwork, after ten years many workers get bored and look for a change. Later it is children's education (teenage years), concern for aging parents, personal health issues, and finally retirement. The predominant reason changes with time, but the combined risk stays roughly the same through the whole life and workers need good care during all phases of life.

9. Life-long Learning and Career Development

Missiological training is as critical as life-long learning.[25] Learning the local language and understanding the culture takes years—in fact, this is a life-long task.[26] We always remain a learner and we never become a local.

Many workers get bored when a task becomes routine. Then they need to move on to a new task—if possible in the same culture—and grow to the next level. A missionary may start as an evangelist, then proceed to church planting, thereafter leadership development, coaching of pastors, theological training, and assisting in the development of the national mission movement. It requires continuous retraining and life-long learning, especially in our rapidly changing world that requires continuous adjustment.

10. Coping with Stress

An extensive study on 900 missionaries of a prestigious mission showed that 49% of their missionaries experience "strong" or "moderate stress"—and many of them from

---

23 Bloecher 2007, c186.
24 Detlef Bloecher, "Research on the Basis of 500 DMG Missionaries, (unpublished data, 2010).
25 Detlef Bloecher, "Training Builds Missionaries Up: Lessons from ReMAP II," *Connections* (4(2), 2005b), 23.
26 Bloecher 2014, 2.

multiple sources.[27] In addition, the majority of workers feel exposed to personal dangers and face major ministry risks.[28] Workers in creative access countries experienced even higher stress levels (up to 87% at least "moderate" or 57% "strong stress"). The percentage was particularly high for workers in church planting, for younger workers, those from the Majority World, from non-English speaking countries, and those with a secular identity.[29] They need care to carry on, debriefing, time out to wind down, and refreshment to continue with their important ministry. They need assistance to extend their stress-coping options.

11. Working through Transitions

Transition is a normal part of life. It is painful to let go a beloved task and to move on to something new, but it's indispensable. It means loss and includes a mourning period for processing. It is painful and we need encouragement to see new opportunities. Going through transitions happens in various phases: first you struggle with denial, then you accept the necessity, work through the process, see some hope, and finally embrace the new. Yet this costs energy and takes time to process. Therefore one should not go through too many transitions simultaneously, otherwise it's overwhelming. What a blessing if another person accompanies you through these changes.

12. Theology of Suffering

We live in a world of suffering and pain.[30] We experience this personally and observe it in society—and many Christians suffer severe persecution, particularly in the global South. Where is God in all this pain and death? This is a crucial question. It is essential to have a sound theology of suffering and this concept needs to be spelled out by our personal experience. Our Lord Jesus went the way of the Cross and he calls us to follow him (Matt 16:24). And Jesus reinforces this teaching: "Remember what I told you: 'A servant is not greater than his master.' If they persecuted me, they will persecute you also" (John 15:20; John 13:16). We have not yet arrived in God's new world.

13. Cooperation and Partnership in Mission

Many issues have been mentioned and they cry for comprehensive personal care, yet no agency has all the resources needed. This calls for intermission cooperation and

---

27   In particular: multiple roles and inappropriate info published in social media.

28   Personal dangers: particularly from general violence, for own religious activities and insensitive info by colleagues. Ministry risks: especially by staff shortage, lack of financial resourcing, visa problems, children's education.

29   Bloecher 2012.

30   William Taylor, Antonia van der Meer, and Reg Reimer, *Sorrow and Blood: Christian Mission in Contexts of Mission, Persecution, and Martyrdom* (Pasadena, CA: William Carey Library, 2013).

partnerships in mission. Research demonstrates that very small agencies lose ten times more workers than agencies with 100+ missionaries.[31] Cross-cultural mission today is a highly complex issue that includes many legal, practical, and missiological issues. It calls for capacity building and specialization of services to keep missionaries running, working together for God's kingdom.

In his book *Doing Member Care Well: Perspectives and Practices from around the World*, Kelly O'Donnell compares member care with a Roman fountain: Water is pumped up to the top level and then flows from one basin to the next.[32] The top level (1) he names "master care:" God's care for his servant. He is our provider and good shepherd. For him we live. He is our joy and purpose of life. 2) The next level he calls "self-care:" Paul reminds Timothy: "Be careful of how you live" (1 Tim 4:16). 3) The third level is for mutual care within a team (and local church). One caring for each other, a central word in the New Testament (John 13:14; Rom 12:16; 15:5–7; Eph 4:32; Col 3:13; 1 Thess 3:13; 1 Pet 4:10). 4) Sender care by the sending church and agency. 5) Specialist care, where O'Donnell refers to physical, medical, interpersonal and team building, financial and logistics, counseling and psychology, crisis and contingency, family and missionary kids, training and career development, spiritual and pastoral. 6) Network care where the member care specialists complement and learn from each other.

I find this model very helpful as it visualizes the right order of services which must not be reversed. Member care is not primarily an art of specialists, but it starts with Christ in the center and our relationship with him. Then it is a matter of our own personal responsibility, mutual care in the work team, and only later the professionals come in. Spirituality lived out in practice.

> Member care is not primarily an art of specialists, but it starts with Christ in the center and our relationship with him.

Senders still have much to contribute. The results of ReMAP I proved that Brazilian evangelical sending agencies lost annually 8.5% of their missionaries for potentially preventable reasons, one-third within four years.[33] This constituted a shock and led mission leaders, church pastors, and Bible school teachers to sit together and work hard on their systems—and eight years later the preventable attrition rate had fallen to 2.6%, one-third of the earlier number.[34]

Many partners can and need to contribute to this flow of care. This is also obvious in the ministry of the Apostle Paul: He was sent by the church in Antiochia (Acts 13:2); he felt accountable to it (Acts 14:27) and also to the church in Jerusalem (Acts 15:2; 21:18). He received most of his financial support from Philippi (Phil 4:15) and later asked the churches in Rome for financial, personal, and logistic support (Rom 15:24), besides receiving much encouragement from his team colleagues (2 Tim 4:9ff). Many

31   Bloecher 2007b, 41.
32   Kelly O'Donnell, "A Member Care model for Best Practice," in *Doing Member Care Well*, ed. Kelly O'Donnell (Pasadena, CA: William Carey Library, 2002), 16.
33   Bloecher 1997,125; Bloecher 2007a, 20.
34   Bloecher 2003, 51; Bloecher 2007a, 20.

parties contributed to it—indeed, it's a continuous life-long flow of care that touches all aspects of life. It is God's mission and senders as well as sent workers are team partners in his way blessing the nations.

Discussion Questions

1. Which missionaries have you witnessed coming home broken with shattered vision and disappointed supporters? What went wrong? What do we learn from their tragic experience? What will you do better the next time?
2. How can I help workers grow, thrive, and develop? What have I learned from this article that I want to put into practice in the next month?
3. How do I care for myself and put 1 Timothy 4:16 into practice? What do I do to keep my relationship with the Lord first?
4. How do I find a good work-rest balance? Which changes do I want to make in the next month?

References

Amalraj, K. John. 2009. "What Shapes Our Spirituality in Missions?" *Connections* 8(1), April:9–12

Blöcher, Detlef and Jonathan Lewis. 1997. "Further Findings in the Research Data." In *Too Valuable to Lose*. Ed. William D. Taylor. Pasadena, CA: William Carey Library.

Blöcher, Detlef. 2003. "ReMAP II Affirms the Maturing of the Younger Mission Movement of the South." *Connections*. October 2003: 48–53.

———. 2004. "Good Agency Practices: Lessons Learnt from ReMAP II." *Connections*. June 2004: 12–25.

———. 2005a. "Good Agency Practices: Lessons from ReMAP II." *Evangelical Mission Quarterly*. April 2005: 228–236.

———. 2005b. "Training Builds Missionaries Up: Lessons from ReMAP II." *Connections* 4(2): 22–25.

———. 2007a. "What ReMAP I Said, Did, and Achieved." In *Worth Keeping: Global Perspectives on Best Practice in Missionary Retention*. Ed. Rob Hay, et al., 9–22. Pasadena, CA: William Carey Library.

———. 2007b, "Agency Size and Partnership." In *Worth Keeping: Global Perspectives on Best Practice in Missionary Retention*. Edited by Rob Hay et al., 39–46. Pasadena, CA: William Carey Library.

———. 2007c. "Member Care." In *Worth Keeping: Global Perspectives on Best Practice in Missionary Retention*. Ed. Rob Hay et al., 181–188. Pasadena, CA: William Carey Library.

———. 2010. "Research on the Basis of 500 DMG Missionaries." Unpublished data.

———. 2011. "Member Care: What Makes Missionaries Strong, Healthy, and Flexible." Https://www.dmgint.de/mission-en/research-papers.html.

———. 2012. "Study on 900 WEC Missionaries." Unpublished data.

———. 2014. "Continuous Language and Cultural Studies Are Indispensable." Https://www.dmgint.de/mission-en/research-papers.html.

Donovan, Kath and Ruth Myers. 1997. "Reflections on Attrition in Career Missionaries. A Generational Perspective into the Future." In *Too Valuable to Lose*, Ed. William D. Taylor, 41–73. Pasadena, CA: William Carey Library.

Franklin, Kirk. 2009. "Mission and Spirituality." *Connections* 8(1), April: 12–14.

Hay, Rob et al. 2007a. *Worth Keeping: Global Perspectives on Best Practice in Missionary Retention*. Pasadena, CA: William Carey Library.

———. 2007b. "Selection." In *Worth Keeping: Global Perspectives on Best Practice in Missionary Retention*. Ed Rob Hay, et al., 93–95. Pasadena, CA: William Carey Library.

Ketelaar, Jaap. 2007. "Spiritual life." In *Worth Keeping: Global Perspectives on Best Practice in Missionary Retention*. Edited by Rob Hay et al. Pasadena, CA: William Carey Library: 131–135.

O'Donnell, Kelly. 2002. "A Member Care Model for Best Practice." In *Doing Member Care Well*. Ed. Kelly O'Donnell, 13–22. Pasadena, CA: William Carey Library.

Taylor, William D. 1997. "Examining the Iceberg called Attrition." In *Too Valuable to Lose*. Ed. William D. Taylor, 3–14. Pasadena, CA: William Carey Library.

Taylor, William D. et al., eds. 2013. *Sorrow and Blood. Christian Mission in Contexts of Mission, Persecution, and Martyrdom*. Pasadena, CA: William Carey Library.

Detlef Blöecher holds a PhD in Physics and worked fifteen years in medical research at various universities in Germany and the Middle East. Since 2000 he is Director of DMG Interpersonal E.V., one of the leading evangelical personnel sending agencies in Germany. Since 2004 he also chairs the Association of Evangelical Missions (AEM), representing 104 evangelical mission agencies in Germany with a total 4,500 missionaries. He is coauthor of the book *Worth Keeping: Global Perspectives on Best Practice in Missionary Retention* (Rob Hay,et. al, ed. William Carey Library, 2007).

Scripture: *John 15:16 ("You did not choose me, but I chose you...")*

Resource: *The Saving Life of Christ*, by W. Ian Thomas (Grand Rapids, MI: Zondervan, 1989 [1961]).

CHAPTER 33

Healers

Laura Mae Gardner

We live in a brutal world—those words come from Gobodo-Madikizela in her book, *A Human Being Died That Night*. "We live in a troubled and tarnished world," said a theologian friend recently. We also live in a world under Satan's control. We who engage in living for Christ and carry on any kind of ministry are in spiritual war every day, day and night. Living in a context of war without a corps of healers is unthinkable. Because the wounds of such a life are seldom understood by non-ministry people, nor are they easily healed, we must think about the kinds of healers we need. But first we must think about the wounds we carry.

The 2012 book, *Sorrow and Blood*, elicited many good comments from many who read early manuscripts. One of these expresses my own feelings well. This respondent says,

> *Sorrow and Blood* takes an unflinching look at the cost of Christian mission in a violent and hostile world. Contributions from around the world tell the awe-inspiring story of missionaries and local believers who have followed their Savior in faithful and sacrificial witness. Theologians help us reflect on the redemptive impact of their suffering for the faith. Advocates advise on how to help without making matters worse. Digesting this epic work will require uncommon fortitude, effort that will be richly rewarded. May God use this volume to rouse his church to take the baton from those who have so valiantly gone before us.[1]

I want to take that baton a little further. I'd like to move from these incredible stories to our response.

However, we can't discuss healers until we acknowledge the wounds we have received. There are many kinds, each one different, but each one cumulative. There are the scars that remain from memories, generational sin, and sinful patterns. We may have experienced the hurt of sexual abuse, perhaps the bewilderment and shame of a

> We can't discuss healers until we acknowledge the wounds we have received.

---

1   Endorsement from Galen Carey in William D. Taylor, et al, *Sorrow and Blood* (Pasadena, CA: William Carey Library, 2012), ix.

son committing suicide, the sadness of irreparable mistakes, and the suffering of failure. We must acknowledge our own sin as well as the impact of sin we have borne. "The old ashes of the sins of my youth are a new fire of sorrow to me" said an unknown author.

There is life stage pain—our children hurt, they grow up and leave us; they are far away. Marital status or singleness, midlife challenges, generational misunderstandings—that are filled with challenges and some sadness. Aging is a series of little deaths, one therapist said.

We must also acknowledge the hurt and suffering around us, such as a colleague's story as a child in South Korea. He tells of the pain that accompanied fear in his war-torn country as well as the pain of hunger.[2] Think of the sadness Korean parents experienced over divided families in North and South Korea. Our colleague's older brother was taken captive when he was sixteen or seventeen and has not been heard from for sixty years. As a parent of sons, I can only imagine the perpetual heartache this must cause.

Ministry has its wounds. See Matthew 21:33–39. In this parable those who were sent to collect the rent from the wine-dressers were obedient, and suffered for it, the last one paying with his life. Obedience in ministry is no guarantee of either success or safety.

> Obedience in ministry is no guarantee of either success or safety.

Other ministry wounds include working year after year without visible results, seeing spiritual children turning back, having evil spoken of the good we have done (Isa 5:20). It includes being surrounded by unfathomable need without resources to alleviate it, about working under corrupt systems and evil people. We experience pain when we see injustice and wounds inflicted on the people we have learned to love. And eventually, when our ministry ends, we must say good-bye to those we've ministered to, knowing we will probably never see them again.

We must not overlook the wounds we experience that are associated specifically with our faith. John the Baptist illustrates this beautifully. John has been a faithful forerunner of the Messiah, who happens to be his cousin. John baptized Jesus, and then stepped aside and invited people to follow Jesus (John 3:27–30). John's faithful stand for righteousness lands him in prison (Matt 14:3–4; Mark 6:17–20), and there he sits. Jesus doesn't seem to care and does nothing to help. So John sends a delegation to Jesus asking, "Are you really the Messiah? Or should we look for someone else?" "Are you who you say you are? I'm beginning to wonder."

"I'm beginning to wonder…" Do we hear the pain and pathos behind those words? There may be times in our life when God seems a stranger to us—or we to him. "I am a stranger with you" or in another version, "I dwell with you as an alien" (Ps 39:12b). While we may hesitate to say we're offended with God, there will be times of bewilderment

---

2   See his story, Taylor 2012, 53.

and wondering where God is, what he is doing. The intimacy we once knew with God is missing.

What might cause us to be offended in our God, or to begin to ask questions like these, or to be on the verge of looking elsewhere for help? I think of seven such situations. They may be intellectual or philosophical or experiential.

The silence of God.   He doesn't answer. How many of us have prayed for a long time without answers to those prayers?

The arrogance of exclusiveness.   One way, one door, one name (Acts 4:12). No other name; I am the way, the truth, and the life. No one comes to God but by Me (John 14:6). You alone, have the words of eternal life, said Peter. (John 6:68). This seems like the height of arrogance to non-Christians! Believers are viewed as uneducated, rigid, religious bigots, and we find that highly uncomfortable.

The tardiness of justice.   The wicked prosper, the righteous suffer. God's people are not exonerated or vindicated. Joseph is a good example of this in the charges laid against him by Potiphar's wife for which he was imprisoned. He was vindicated but never exonerated. Daniel apparently was never released from his long history as a hostage. Habakkuk's words are a cry of pain, "How long, O Lord, how long? You do not avenge me! You tolerate evil!" (Hab 1:2-4). Historically and currently, the persecuted church worldwide is another example of evil that often seems triumphant.

The caprice of mercy.   Some examples from Scripture: paying late-arriving workers a full day's pay, forgiving the publican, the Samaritan woman, the woman taken in adultery, the thief on the cross, watching the rich young ruler go away sadly. His mercy seems very capricious to us.

The unpredictability of God.   Sometimes he works wonders, gives success, heals— and sometimes he doesn't. Just when we think we know what God will do, he doesn't do that. We never know what to expect when we cry out to him.

And then we read about **God's wrath, his anger.** "He is angry with the wicked every day." "God is a righteous judge, a God who expresses his wrath every day" (Ps 7:11). How do we reconcile this description of God with the God of grace, compassion, forgiveness, and unfailing love? We don't understand him.

The unevenness of success in ministry. Some humanitarian caregivers and missionaries work faithfully, entirely without response or apparent success; others meet with instant response, a growing church. How do we understand when faithful efforts are not blessed by God? Many of the prophets were commissioned by God himself, while at the same time they were told they would not be successful—Isaiah, Jeremiah, Ezekiel, among others. Can you imagine working on for forty years (as in Isaiah's case) knowing you would not be successful? (Isa 6:9–10; Ezek 2:5, 7).

In addition to these specific situations there is the poverty, illness, famine, disaster, dissonance, confusion, paradox, and mystery that surrounds us and permeates our lives.

What kind of healer do we need at times like these, when our faith is inadequate? I want someone anchored in God's Word, experienced and trained in responding to human need, someone of character, someone experienced in life, not a novice in life or ministry, someone who has suffered. Compassion and kindness are necessary if this person is going to walk into my heart and life and help me face this pain.

There is a hinge verse in the middle of Psalm 73 that suggests a change of perspective. Verse 16 reads, "When I thought how to understand this [that is, life's injustices and incongruities], it was too painful for me, or oppressive to me, until I went into the sanctuary."

What do we do with this pain, both that which we received long ago, or are experiencing now, or that which we observe? We didn't cause it. We can't change it. There are two choices open to us: we can use it, reap it for the harvest of maturity, grow from it, become more mellow and compassionate toward those in need, more trustful of God. Or we can allow ourselves to become bitter, vindictive, or vengeful. I often think of Genesis 18:25, "Should not the Judge of all the earth do right?" And my heart responds, "Yes, and he does."

> What do we do with this pain, both that which we received long ago, or are experiencing now, or that which we observe?

Several thoughts to consider:

First, I am responsible for my own healing, my growth from pain, progress toward resiliency—just me, no one else can take this responsibility away from me. I must be committed to being as healthy as possible for as long as possible. This does not mean I can always heal myself, but I must be strong enough to seek help and then to benefit from it when it comes.

Secondly, healing agents are all around us, and they are not all human: the color and seasonal aspects of nature, the delight of music and poetry, the value of work, the riches in our storehouse of books, the good memories we have, the sweetness of family, the fragrance of a loving community, and the treasure of good friends.

Third, at times I do need professional healers, e.g., pastors, therapists, caregivers, healthy friends, member care workers. These are the "saints that sustain us; these are 'the faithful of the land; they shall dwell with me'" (Ps 101:6). Others speak "words of life, gentle words that bring life and health" (Prov 15:4). "The tongue can kill or nourish life" (Prov 18:21). It is no sin to need or seek help. In fact, it is a marker of health to know that we need help.

Fourth, our spiritual resources are foundational and inexhaustible; they include the Trinity, the Scriptures, the Holy Spirit, prayer, the rituals of worship, and the sacraments. Dual messages permeate the Scriptures: on the one hand we read of the sinfulness and resulting pain of mankind as a result of the fall—some of which are on-going sinful patterns. On the other hand we are reminded of the glorious, eternal plan of God to bring comfort and healing, and ultimately to rid the earth of all the evil and all the agents of evil.

Fifth, healing is seldom immediate. Most of Jesus' healings were instantaneous, but not all. Mark 8:24, the blind man of Bethsaida said after the initial touch of Jesus, "I see people, but I can't see them very clearly. They look like trees walking around." And then Jesus touched him again and "his sight was completely restored, and he could see everything clearly" (v 25). For most of us, healing is a process, filled with comfort, presence, a pattern, information, continuing encouragement, and hope. Few people are completely whole and healthy. Most of us are in this process of healthful growth of body, mind, spirit, emotions, and relationships. All of us are also in the process of decline as we daily live with the realities of this fallen world, and as our own death draws near.

Sixth, because healing is a long process, many of our human resources grow weary. This is especially true of friends. Professional caregivers are more likely to make time to help us in our journey of healing for much longer periods of time.

Paul Brand (*In The Likeness of God*) says,

> Intense suffering provokes a sudden outpouring of aid, but people soon tire of hearing about depressing conditions. Instead of increasing sensitivity, as a human body does in response to injury, we decrease it. Our focus on the pain turns from "How do I deal with the cause of the pain?: to "How can I silence it?" No longer a motivator and stimulus for action, the pain becomes a dull, ineffective throb. It has worn us down.[3]

Later Brand goes on to say:

> Even as I sense the need of my own body parts, and slow my pace to give them healing rest, so too may I reach out to feel the needs of others: visitors in my home, my office staff, patients in their pain. May my nerves of sensitivity extend beyond the boundaries of my own skin so that I feel their pain as well. Then I will know that my wondrous nervous system is designed as part of wider consciousness, and never knows fulfillment until it opens wide to human need around, and to inspiration from above.[4]

Seventh, we must not short-circuit pain or fail to see its value. Dr. Paul Brand and Philip Yancey coauthored the book, *The Gift of Pain*.[5] The stimulus for the book came from Dr. Brand's work with lepers in India, later in the United States. He discovered that many of the injuries lepers experienced originated because of nerve damage, so if they touched something hot and were burned, they did not feel it until their body was very

---

3   Paul Brand and Philip Yancey, *In the Likeness of God* (Grand Rapids, MI: Zondervan, 2004), 510.
4   Brand 2004, 544.
5   Paul Brand and Philip Yancey, *The Gift of Pain* (Grand Rapids, MI: Zondervan, 1997).

damaged. Together, Dr. Brand and Mr. Yancey extended this concept of the usefulness of physical pain to other kinds of pain—emotional, philosophical, or spiritual. He then moved to emotional responses that were a healing element. Citing Dr. Hans Selye's research on stress, the authors write:

> As Selye summarized his research toward the end of his life, he named vengeance and bitterness as the emotional responses most likely to produce high stress levels (ill health) in human beings. Conversely, he concluded, gratitude is the single response most nourishing to health. Dr. Brand goes on to say, "I find myself agreeing with Selye, in part because a grateful appreciation for pain's many benefits has transformed my own outlook."[6]

Eighth. Healers—who are they? They are all around us. They include friends, colleagues, family, little children. It takes time to develop a healing community, but it is well worth the effort and we must ask. Remember the story of Moses growing weary in his supportive role, so he asked for help from two specific friends, Aaron and Hur (Ex 17:8–15).

But that's not all. Not only do we need to identify the healers around us, but each of us must determine to be an agent of healing.

Some time ago a friend stopped by my office on her way back to her field of service. She had just learned that the level of conflict and anger and division has risen to dangerous levels on her field, and she would walk back into the middle of this situation. I challenged her to go "as an agent of healing." She was taken aback and asked, "What would that look like?"

> Not only do we need to identify the healers around us, but each of us must determine to be an agent of healing.

Agents of healing are characterized by two postures which are knowing clearly what is wrong and how it should be corrected while maintaining genuine love, acceptance, and care. Maturity in life should result in discernment, wisdom, objectivity, and a commitment to bring peace through mediation and wise strategies. Psalm 85:10 says, "Unfailing love and truth have met together. Righteousness and peace have kissed each other."

This peace-making wisdom is further described in James 3:17–18.

> The wisdom that comes from heaven is first of all pure. It is also peace-loving, gentle at all times, and willing to yield to others. It is full of mercy and good deeds. It shows no favoritism and is always sincere. And those who are peacemakers will plant seeds of peace and reap a harvest of goodness. (NLT)

---

6   Brand 1997, 222.

Finally, "There are sicknesses worse than sickness," said one unknown writer. The "dark night of the soul" is one of these.[7] Dark nights will come to most of us. Such profound and often pointless suffering is often followed by despair and feelings of being abandoned by God himself.

Allender and Longman in *The Cry of the Soul* helpfully point us to the ultimate remedy.

> Suffering seems so pointless, meaningless. Rarely can we say honestly, without contrivance, "I see why God allowed this..." More often we are at a loss to comprehend loss. It is a double sorrow—not only do we experience despair, but the despair makes no sense.

> The Cross cuts to the core of all suffering, all loss, all despair by invading it with the cry, "My God, My God." The Cross paradoxically transforms all human sorrow from a horizontal loss to a vertical agony that compels us to ask God who he is. The Lord's cry will never allow us to see human suffering as merely accidental or incidental to life. All loss is bound to God.

> Far more, Jesus' cry of despair also transforms all human suffering as a promise. It is a down payment on hope. Jesus suffered, and so will we. But he has been there before us; he waits for us at the end of our sorrow. He has been perfected and resurrected through suffering; so will we.[8]

"But we see Jesus" (Heb 2:9). He is the final and consummate healer. In him wrong will be made right; we will understand. He is the companion of sufferers.

"The Lord is near to the brokenhearted and saves the crushed in spirit" (Ps 34:18).

"On the Cross they did not crucify an angry man" (an unknown author). Let us allow our sorrow to have its perfecting work in us through the healers around us, and especially through the ministry of the Holy Spirit, and the example of Jesus. Consider him who endured (Heb 12:3). He is the ultimate healer.

So we do live in a ravaged and ravaging world and in a world currently under the power of our arch enemy, Satan. Wounds gained from life and from ministry in this environment are inevitable. Part of our ministry is how we live under fire. So our response to pain and sadness is being observed. As we go through our personal fire, may we be refined and equipped to help others along the way. There is healing, and there are healers. May we honor them, access them, and support them. And as we too are agents of healing, may we share that healing task.

---

7   The concept of the "dark night of the soul" was originated by John of the Cross (1542–1591). His book by that title was written when he was confined for his faith. The concept of the "dark night" describes the work of God upon the soul—not through joy and light, but through sorrow and darkness. The times when God seems absent result in despair. Psalm 42 accurately describes the experience of a person going through the "dark night."

8   Dan Allender and Tremper Longman III, *Cry of the Soul* (Colorado Springs, CO: NavPress, 1994), 158–59.

References

Allender, Dan B. and Tremper Longman III. 1994. *Cry of the Soul*. Colorado Springs, CO: NavPress.

Brand, Paul and Philip Yancey. 1997. *The Gift of Pain*. Grand Rapids, MI: Zondervan.

———. 2004. *In the Likeness of God*. Grand Rapids, MI: Zondervan.

Collins, Kenneth J. 1995. *Soul Care*. Wheaten, IL: Victor Books.

Foster, Richard J. and James Bryan Smith. 1993. *Devotional Classics*. San Francisco, CA: Harper.

Laura Mae Gardner and husband Dick have served in Wycliffe and SIL more than fifty years. These years included completing a New Testament translation, advanced studies, serving as counselors and developers of member care, and in a number of administrative roles. Laura Mae is a pioneer of Member Care, having recently completed the book, *Healthy, Resilient, and Effective in Cross-Cultural Ministry*. She continues to serve on boards, consult with mission organizations and teach seminars and workshops around the world. She is a mother of two and grandmother of eight. She and Dick are "thinking of retiring sometime soon."

Scripture: *Psalm 48:14 ("For this God is our God for ever and ever…")*

Resource: *A Diary of Private Prayer,* by John Baillie (New York: Simon and Schuster, 1996 [1949]).

CHAPTER 34

A Model of Healing and Discipleship

From Brokenness to Wholeness for Three Generations of Global Kingdom Workers and Candidates

Father→ Jesus→ Disciples

Kyle Miller

Seeing the people, he felt compassion for them, because they were distressed and dispirited like sheep without a shepherd. Then he said to his disciples, "The harvest is plentiful, but the workers are few. Therefore, beseech the Lord of the harvest to send out workers into his harvest." Matthew 9:36–38 (NASB)

And So Begins Our Short Journey Together

As global kingdom workers, we are moved by Jesus' appeal to us to appeal in turn to the Father for help with the plentiful harvest, as were Jesus' disciples in Matthew 9, and to us in our day with 7.3 billion people on earth. Even deeper we must admit that it is not only the lost that are "distressed and dispirited," it is often we and our worker candidates that are "distressed and dispirited." Why are we his workers so very distressed and dispirited? Why are we so sadly broken? Why do so many of the models, approaches, and programs that are meant to help us and our candidates fail so quickly as they do? Only by walking with Jesus and in-step with each other on this lifelong journey can we together receive his healing from our past and transformation for the future to redeem our struggles. If this practice becomes a reality in a global kingdom team, then potential ministry candidates will be very drawn to such a team, and will both receive and contribute effectively to the team.

This chapter is shared from our Father's heart, to my heart, to your heart, and then through your heart to the hearts of your ministry teammates and candidates. To plan our journey together, out of the many areas of an individual's brokenness that need Jesus' healing and transformation, let us focus on three areas: our traumas and brokenness that began with our families of origin; our struggles and sins with gender and sexuality, and the history of our failures with God and people. With such a daunting task before us, we need principles and practices that come from deep within God's own personality to address our deep needs. Whenever we need anything, we know that we must "fix our eyes on Jesus" (Heb 12:2), because in Jesus "are hidden all the treasures of wisdom and knowledge" (Col 2:3). So let us plunge in right now to life of Jesus and see how his Father discipled him.

Walking with Our *Father→Jesus→Disciples*

How did our heavenly Father disciple his Son Jesus all of his life in our world? The Father did it minute-by-minute for thirty-three years, and then Jesus passed on that same grace and truth minute-by-minute for three years with his disciples, teaching them often in real time what his Father was teaching him, a holy reality that we will call *Father→Jesus→Disciples*. What the Father did and said to Jesus, Jesus did and said to his disciples. It is that simple, but profound, and not easy to do as wounded and confused as we are. To help us to see and apply these simple but profound principles, we will also briefly examine the parallel *Jesus→Paul→Timothy* discipleship relationships. All of these examples will show us how Jesus' true gospel of grace is actually God's sharing his *grace* with us in the context of *relationship*—him with us, and then us with each other—over the *process* of time. While there are other important ways that God uses to help us heal, this discipleship process is the most important part of God's transforming and freeing us from the past and preparing us for future ministry.

> All of these examples will show us how Jesus' true gospel of grace is actually God's sharing his *grace* with us in the context of *relationship*—him with us, and then us with each other—over the *process* of time.

OldGen, MidGen, NewGen, and Candidates Walking Together?

To apply this to our personal ministry relationships, we will identify three generations of workers—for clarity, let us call them as follows: first, *OldGen,* the oldest generation of workers with the most lifelong maturity and experience; second, *MidGen,* the middle generation that is gaining maturity, experience, and leadership responsibility; and third, the *NewGen,* the youngest generation of workers and potential partners that have the least maturity and experience. All three generations have weaknesses and challenges. Here is one example for each generation—OldGen workers need to obey Jesus and not be called by prideful titles (Matt 23:8–12), MidGen workers need to continue to work heartily for the Lord and not for men (Col 3:23, 24), and NewGen workers need to submit their enthusiasm and ideas to their leaders (1 Pet 5:5) so that their fresh "new wine in new wineskins" (Matt 9:16, 17) approaches can edify all three generations. Relative to this humble discipleship approach, younger believers, those seeking Jesus, NewGen workers, and NewGen candidates are open to genuine OldGen and MidGen workers that are transparent and walking with Jesus Christ.

This God-people-people approach comes from the very nature of our Triune God himself. Our heavenly Father is "above" us as a Father—loving, guiding, guarding, and providing; our Savior and Lord Jesus is "beside" us on the path with earth-empathy—loving, shepherding, and transforming us at each juncture to become like him; and Holy Spirit is "inside" us working 24/7—loving, healing, renewing, and teaching us to think with godly wisdom as Jesus did (1 Cor 2:13–16). So we must learn to live in the "practice of the Presence of God" state, both alone and together with other people in order to work out and to live out the seemingly "impossible mission" of becoming like Jesus while completing the works to which he has called us (Acts 20:24; Eph 2:8–10).

I Am Thankful That We Can Walk and Talk Together

To model this approach, even in a book chapter, my plan is that I will talk with you on our short journey about your lifetime journey as if we were walking side-by-side in conversation. I picture this like real talks in real places I've had on four continents with global kingdom workers just like yourself, as we walk down a quiet snowy street in Eastern Europe, drink strong tea in a loud café in North Africa, wait patiently at a grey departure gate in North America, ride trustingly in the back of a rebel technical with the floor covered in AK-47s as gunfire echoes off the East African mountains, fly high across the cold ocean in coach class, zig-zag through a teeming city in a dangerous tuk-tuk in humid South Asia, or ride a full subway deep under a massive city in urban East Asia. It truly is a journey isn't it? We do it with Jesus and each other, not only in the natural realm, but even more risk and more wonder, in the spiritual realm. So let us pause and pray right now for everyone that is reading or will read this chapter, all around the world.

Walking with Our *Father→Jesus→Disciples*

Following Jesus together, let us learn from his intimate and submitted discipleship relationship with his Father so that he cause pass on his *Father→Jesus→Disciples* model to his disciples for the purpose of healing and growing their lives. From the very start, Jesus was giving his very essence to his disciples. Jesus called the first disciples in Matthew 4, he saw the multitudes coming and so began to teach and counsel the disciples right away in Matthew 5:1–16. He subtly shared eight of his own personality traits that he wanted his disciples to see and to practice in their own lives so that they could humbly pass this on into the lives of their future disciples. Following that for three years, all the way to Matthew 28, we see Jesus living out this *Father→Jesus→Disciples* model with his disciples "horizontally" as he shared what his Father was sharing with him "vertically" by the Spirit. Given our painful brokenness, one of the most comforting aspects of this *Father→Jesus→Disciples* approach can be seen in Hebrews 5:8 where Jesus was described, "Although he was a Son, he learned obedience from the things which he suffered." This was divinely possible only through the 24/7 discipleship that Jesus received from his Father by the Spirit on earth. Thus, if the sinless Son of God and Son of Man Jesus Christ had to be grace-trained in obedience through suffering as a part of his Father's discipleship of him to prepare him for the rigors of his life, suffering, and the Cross, how much more do we as saints that still sin need it? We must see and respond to our past traumas and present suffering as part of our Father's discipleship of us, so that we have something that is naturally unbelievable that we can share with others. Through learning the Father's approach to his Son Jesus we can redeem painful situations for God's glorification and our edification (Heb 12:11), no matter if the suffering is from others' sins, our own sin, or no one's sin at all (John 9:1–5).

> We must see and respond to our past traumas and present suffering as part of our Father's discipleship of us, so that we have something that is naturally unbelievable that we can share with others.

Then There Was the *Jesus→Paul→Timothy* Journey

Another parallel three-generation discipleship model can be seen in the *Jesus→Paul→Timothy* discipleship relationships in the early church. Saul-becoming-Paul's conscious discipleship relationship with Jesus Christ started in a literal flash knocking him down on the Damascus road. Taking Paul through many dangerous and life-threatening circumstances Jesus developed his character in Paul, producing what is currently being called "post-traumatic growth," growth that comes directly from responding wisely to horrible circumstances. Some years later, Paul met Timothy in Ephesus and called Timothy into discipleship to Christ with Paul's mentoring, a lifetime relationship such that Paul would affectionately say to him in 1 Timothy 1:2, "To Timothy, my true child in the faith." Then our three generation model of *Jesus→Paul→Timothy* continues on into the fourth and fifth spiritual generations as each generation accepts the call of being in discipleship under Jesus and to sincerely disciple one another:

> You therefore, my son, be strong in the grace that is in Christ Jesus. The things which you have heard from me in the presence of many witnesses, entrust these to faithful men who will be able to teach others also. (2 Tim 2:1–3)

Jesus' Help for Three Big Things that Can Ruin Our Journey

In the context of this discipleship model, we can find the courage to address our three areas of brokenness, our family traumas, our gender and sexuality difficulties, and worry about our past and fear of future failures. We will need Jesus' courage because in my experience these three areas are root problems for why some long-term workers who have been called and committed to living and sharing the gospel of Jesus Christ so frequently fail to have successful personal lives and kingdom success. Even worse, this failure can result in some invaluable workers eventually quitting kingdom service, often to fall into despair not only about their future in ministry but very tragically even despairing about their future relationship with God at all. Between these three areas there is significant interaction, with trouble in one area flooding into and worsening another area over our life journey. As you read these thoughts, please resist the natural human tendency to think of these issues just in your team members' lives. Rather, let us heed the caution from Ecclesiastes 4:13: "A poor yet wise lad is better than an old and foolish king who no longer knows how to receive instruction." So let us ask Jesus to show us where we are struggling in these three areas, because he knows all about them and he died to be able to redeem in us through his discipleship so we can comfort and teach these truths to others: our unhealed trauma, conflicts, and wrong beliefs stemming from our family of origin; our struggles with gender and sexual identity and resulting destruction; our past failures, present stress, and future fears.

> We will need Jesus' courage because in my experience these three areas are root problems for why some long-term workers who have been called and committed to living and sharing the gospel of Jesus Christ so frequently fail to have successful personal lives and kingdom success.

Our Family Traumas, Patterns, and Wrong Thinking

First, how can our unhealed traumas from our families, our brokenness, and our unique wrong beliefs about God, ourselves, and relationships be healed over time as we walk with Jesus and people? There are two primary reasons why long-term, secure discipleship relationships are necessary in order to begin to bring about body of Christ healing for these deep traumas, conflicts, and wrong beliefs about God, ourselves, and relationships. It was in the context of our past family of origin that these events and damage occurred, so it follows that in God's sovereignty he would begin to heal the traumas, teach healthy relationships, and change our wrong thinking in the context of our present spiritual family of choice—our own church and our three generation kingdom worker teams. Second, because our traumas, conflicts, and wrong thinking happened and grew since we were born, we are blind to the majority of it, blaming others or shaming ourselves, but rarely seeing and addressing our blind spots. Children learn most of their wrong thinking about God and themselves from their parents growing up, so the involvement of OldGens with NewGens and potential candidates is very helpful in facilitating their healing and growth.

One powerful example of this that I see every day is in my counseling with sex trafficking survivors live, on Skype, and on trips. Given the extreme level of their trauma, it is very helpful for these sisters to have long-term and healthy relationships with OldGen women and men. Even before the horror of years of sex trafficking imprisonment, torture, and rape trauma, most all were abused and neglected by their parents, siblings, and extended family, with some girls being sold to traffickers by their own parents in many places around the world. This very *Father→Jesus→Disciples* process with his *Grace→Relationships→Process* at work has been what I have seen counseling survivors of sex trafficking in the US and aboard, and in researching and writing concerning this work for my dissertation-in-process. Just like trafficking survivors need long-term, Jesus-powered safe relationships (*Grace→Relationships→Process*) with *OldGen, MidGen*, and *NewGen* workers, likewise we as global kingdom workers and candidates need them as well to begin to heal and mature together. In other words, as our servants grow in health and maturity, they are able to participate with Jesus in addressing the damage from family of origin in the lives of these women.

Our Silent Gender and Sexuality Struggles

Our deep and mostly secret struggles with gender and sexual identity issues have for many resulted in significant insecurities that often lead to sexual sins with ourselves, virtually, and with others, leading to condemnation from the enemy and producing shame that silences and paralyzes us. Furthermore, it is these very personal struggles that lead to addictions well beyond gender confusion and sexual issues. Eating, drug, alcohol, gambling, stealing, self-injury, and thrill-seeking addictions are often rooted in deep gender and sexual issues. We need safe discipleship relationships within we can open up and begin to admit, some for the first time, that we are struggling with our gender, sexuality, and related sin issues. I have seen that only when a small group of believers is intentionally addressing the early traumas in their lives are they then able and willing to be vulnerable about their deep and hidden insecurities: as a man; as a woman; sexual abuse; bodies, body parts and shame, heterosexual and/or homosexual confusion and temptations, mental lust, sexual sin, pornography, masturbation, and the fears of not knowing how to have a Christ-honoring romantic relationship that could lead to a lifetime of joyful Christian marriage. When a worker does not have a discipleship context with which to begin to work out these "common

> I have seen that only when a small group of believers is intentionally addressing the early traumas in their lives are they then able and willing to be vulnerable about their deep and hidden insecurities:

to man" issues (1 Cor 10:13), then their sense of failure and shame only grows and in turn their spiritual authority, boldness, and vision in ministry correspondingly shrinks.

To be frank, there are not many one-on-one, small group, or ministry team discipleship contexts available in most global workers' lives. Yet, the very fact that you are reading this chapter may indicate that God is calling you to be part the solution, both for yourself and for three generations of workers and candidates around you. I have seen invariably that when believers form intentional relationships such as these to "bear one another's burdens" (Gal 6:2) then miracles been to take place as James the brother of Jesus describes, "Therefore, confess your sins to one another, and pray for one another so that you may be healed. The effective prayer of a righteous man can accomplish much" (Jam 5:16). We all need to have all three generations rally around us and support us and each other so that we can begin to receive that light of Christ into our dark places (2 Cor 4:4–6). Furthermore, it is from these specific miracles of healing, freedom, and transformation that our faith is supernaturally built up, thus giving us great boldness to help others to be believers set free in Christ and reach those that are not yet in Christ to come to claim him as their Savior and their Lord. There is not another area of human frailty more sensitive and terrifying than gender and sexuality, and so when God's restoration begins, and a worker is profoundly changed, they experience a Christ-freedom that they will want to share with anyone they can, a prebeliever, a believer, a worker, their three generation ministry team, or a ministry candidate that is considering join their team (Matt 5:16; Col 3:5–15). If a ministry leader in any of the three generations begins to develop this level of intimacy in discipleship relationship, they will be much more likely to attract strong ministry candidates to their teams, ones that are teachable and can sense the Spirit of the Living God upon their team.

Our History of Failure and Fears of Future Failures

Third, and finally, we must talk about our past, present, and future. While we only live in the present, we carry into the present our accumulated past failures and further create them in our future. As humans, without Jesus-healing, our past history of failures will replicate itself as present stress (fear of sin, rejection, and failure), some of which will self-fulfill and come true. Sadly, even worse, most of this damage is in the biggest domain on the planet, our relationships with people. To address this, we need to meet with OldGen, MidGen, and NewGen colleagues, with God's power and their support, we can break the chain of our personal history of failure and fear. In this *Father→Jesus→Disciples, Jesus→Paul→Timothy* context we can begin to reverse the momentum of history that is repeating itself in our lives and ministries.

Then when we receive this help from Jesus and from other people, he can then begin to redeem these external disasters and internal heartbreaks to transform them into unseen strengths for our life and ministry (2 Cor 12:7–10). Internal character and external relationships that once seemed impossible will become our norm (Matt 19:26); such as living out Jesus' eight personality traits as he outlined in the Beatitudes (Matt 5:1–16), practicing Christ-likeness (Rom 13:9–21), unconditionally loving people (1 Cor 13), and continuously producing more fruit of the Spirit (Gal 5:22, 23; Ps 23:5; Luke 6:35–38) out of our lives and ministries. With brothers and sisters beside us, we can have Christ's reversal of the curse of our past and together with him walk into the future as he brings beauty out of ashes (Isa 61:3). In this context with Jesus and each other, his summary verse in his Beatitudes takes on a whole new *Father→Jesus→Disciples* meaning, "Let your light shine before men in such a way that they may see your good works, and glorify your Father who is in heaven" (Matt 5:16) and be like the godly woman in Proverbs 31:25, "Strength and dignity are her clothing, and she smiles at the future."

After This Walk Together

Let us commit to learning this miraculous, grace-based, and relationship-transmitted approach that our heavenly Father used with Jesus and what Jesus practiced with his disciples. What was passed down from the Father to Jesus, from Jesus to his disciples, and from his disciples, and unstoppably walked down through time through faithful men and women for the past two thousand years has made it possible for us to receive Jesus' blessing along with his disciples from John 14:12, "Truly, truly, I say to you, he who believes in me, the works that I do, he will do also; and greater works than these he will do; because I go to the Father." Maybe some of these "greater works" include Jesus' healing and transformation of our family issues, our gender and sexuality issues, and our failure history that has produced high stress in our present and great fear for our future.

> Maybe some of these "greater works" include Jesus' healing and transformation of our family issues, our gender and sexuality issues, and our failure history that has produced high stress in our present and great fear for our future.

As we conclude our walk together, may I ask you if you believe that this *Father→Jesus→Disciples* life is for you, for your ministry team in all three generations, and for the new candidates that "the Lord of the harvest" wants to send to you to help you join with Paul and say, "That I may finish my course and the ministry which I received from the Lord Jesus" (Acts 20:24)? I commit to do so right now with you, and will continue to pray for you my friend on this hike—I do not know you, but our Father does and will reach you and bless. Please join me and pray and band together under Christ with some team members to do this, then you will begin to receive comfort and growth, so that through you he can bring comfort and growth in others, as we see in 2 Corinthians 1:2–5:

> Blessed be the God and Father of our Lord Jesus Christ, the Father of mercies and God of all comfort, who comforts us in all our affliction so that we will be able to comfort those who are in any affliction with the comfort with which we

ourselves are comforted by God. For just as the sufferings of Christ are ours in abundance, so also our comfort is abundant through Christ.

As we part ways, it is wise to end as we began with Jesus, his words, his appeal to us his disciples to ask his Father for more workers to do his work. Hopefully after our journey together you may read this somewhat differently, with more Jesus-compassion for the distressed and dispirited people on our team, in our cities, and around the world, and with more Jesus-passion for the new candidates that he wants to send to us to join us:

> Seeing the people, he felt compassion for them, because they were distressed and dispirited like sheep without a shepherd. Then he said to his disciples, "The harvest is plentiful, but the workers are few. Therefore, beseech the Lord of the harvest to send out workers into his harvest." Matthew 9:36–38

John and Matthew Homework for Individual and Small Group Study

A *Father→Jesus→Disciples* model from the Gospel of John and the Gospel of Matthew for OldGen-MidGen-NewGen Individual and Discipleship Group Study and Discussion:

1. What do these passages reveal about the *Father→Jesus→Disciples* discipleship relationships? What do the passages reveal about the *Jesus→Paul→Timothy* discipleship relationships?
2. What does this passage reveal about our *OldGen, MidGen, NewGen,* and candidate discipleship relationships?
3. What do these passages reveal about how Jesus Christ can heal and redeem our family traumas and brokenness, our gender and sexuality struggles, and our past failure in our history, present stress, and future fears?

The Gospel of John Passages
1. John 5:30
2. John 8:28, 42
3. John 12:49
4. John 14:6, 7, 10, 16, 18, 26, 28, 30, 31
5. John 15:8, 9
6. John 15:11
7. John 15:14, 15
8. John 15:26, 27

The Gospel of Matthew Passages
1. Matthew 4:19
2. Matthew 5:1–16; all of Matthew 5–7

3. Matthew 9:14–17
4. Matthew 10:1–42
5. Matthew 12:46–50
6. Matthew 22:34–40
7. Matthew 23:1–12
8. Matthew 28:1–10
9. Matthew 28:16–20

References

Allender, Dan. 2014. *The Wounded Heart: Hope for Adult Victims of Childhood Sexual Abuse.* Book & Workbook. Carol Stream, IL: Tyndale House.

Celebrate Recovery Online: http://www.celebraterecovery.com.

Celebrate Recovery International: http://www.celebraterecoveryglobal.com (in twenty-five countries and fifteen languages).

Dever, Mark. 2016. *Discipling: How to Help Others Follow Jesus.* Wheaton, IL: Crossway.

Hodges, Andrew. 2014. *Jesus: An Interview Across Time: A Psychiatrist Looks at Jesus' Humanity.* Birmingham, AL: Village House.

Lawrence, Brother. 1982. *The Practice of the Presence of God.* Springdale, PA: Whitaker House.

McGee, Robert, Pat Springle, and Jay Craddock. 1990. *Your Parents and You.* Houston, TX: Rapha.

Miller, Kyle. 2011. "The Apostle Paul—A Model of Posttraumatic Growth: A Biblical Perspective and Implications for Missions." An unpublished seminary paper for the Ph.D. program, Southwestern Baptist Theological Seminary, Fort Worth, TX. Available from the author at globalcareresponse@gmail.com.

———. 2012. "Jesus Christ's Comfort and Healing for Traumatic Wounds." In *Sorrow and Blood: Christian Mission in Contexts of Suffering, Persecution, and Martyrdom.* Ed. William D. Taylor, Antonia Van der Meer and, Reg Reimer, 445–451. Pasadena, CA: William Carey Library.

———. 2016. "The Healing-Discipleship of Jesus Christ in Matthew: Post-Traumatic Growth through Biblical Counseling for Female Sex Trafficking Survivors." An unfinished Ph.D. dissertation by the author. Table of contents and bibliography available from the author at globalcareresponse@gmail.com.

Willard, Dallas. 2014. *The Great Omission: Reclaiming Jesus' Essential Teachings of Discipleship*. New York: HarperOne.

Yancy, Philip. 2002. *The Jesus I Never Knew*. Grand Rapids, MI: Zondervan.

Kyle Miller grew up in Asia and the USA as a missionary kid, married Terri in 1984; they have grown children Nathan, Kevin, Kristin, and Katherine. At UT-Austin Kyle obtained a bachelor's and two masters' in psychology/counseling, is an LPC-S/LMFT-S counselor, and is finishing his PhD with his dissertation, "The Healing-Discipleship of Jesus Christ in Matthew: Post-Traumatic Growth through Biblical Counseling for Female Sex Trafficking Survivors." Kyle has been providing biblical counseling since 1985 and recently trauma counseling/training in fifteen countries for sex trafficking survivors and their workers and other trauma survivors as the director of Global Care and Response.

Reference: *2 Peter 1:1-4* ("His divine power has given us everything we need for a godly life...")

Resource: *The Practice of the Presence of God, by* Brother Lawrence (Springdale, PA: Whitaker House, 1982).

CHAPTER 35

The Broken, the Wounded Warrior, and Hidden Addictions

Dale Phillips

I am the broken; I am the addicted; I am the wounded warrior; I am on a journey—oh, and, yes, I am a leader in a mission organization. It all began in a little green wooden house in the southern islands of Chile. It was there that my parents brought me home after I was born. My dad was from Alaska and my mom from Kansas; they had met in Canada and were now in Chile as missionaries focused on planting churches. It was just three years later that I heard the children's version of *Pilgrim's Progress* and realized that I wanted to go to heaven. So, in a mission's guest house in Temuco, Chile, I knelt with my mother and accepted Jesus as my Savior.

I grew up in a lovely Christian home with a lot of ministry influence; almost all of my extended family was in full-time ministry. By the time I was thirteen I had read the story of Gladys Aylward and knew that I wanted to be a missionary. During my teen years I worked toward that end and went on mission trips each summer. By the time I was eighteen I had traveled to thirty-two countries and was given much praise for both my Christian character and my heart for evangelism and missions—so much so, that I believed it all, not recognizing the true condition of my heart. In my twenties I married my beautiful bride, had children, and worked for the airlines; always with the goal of becoming a "Real Live Missionary."

In my early thirties our family finally arrived in Eastern Europe as missionaries. My role/job was to solve the problems of our organization as its human resource director. I entered into the worst nightmare of my life. I had always focused on performing for people—being a people-pleaser—yet here my performance wasn't appreciated. Within one year I was in a major internal conflict in my organization. Not only that, but the conflict began to reveal an identity crisis in me that had been buried for a very long time. I now had to cover, hide, and mask who I was. I still needed to perform for the church in the village, and I had to perform for supporters back in our sending country. They could not know of the conflict in my organization. I needed to put on a mask that showed everyone around me that I was fine and moving on in ministry, but inside I felt so lonely and isolated. I did not want to talk to or trust anyone. I felt hurt, valueless, and incredibly ashamed. Here I was, useless in missions. How could this have happened to me? Everyone had always liked me, and now I was not wanted by our organization. To cover the hurt I felt in the organization and the shame I felt in my identity, the masks had to be put on.

Then, one day while on the computer, I accidentally entered the world of pornography. There was no one around to see what I was doing and what I stumbled upon was enticing. That day, in secret, I began a sin cycle of struggling with pornography that endured for years. As a missionary, I wanted out. I knew it was wrong. But as a man, it was so addictive—and nobody knew. I felt so dirty and isolated. I just wanted to tell one person, but the shame in my life was incredibly profound, and I could trust no one. In response to my shame and self-contempt I had to put on a thicker mask to pretend that I was fine. I couldn't tell my wife. She would be so angry. I began to cry out to God, "I am a missionary. I don't even deserve to be here! What were you thinking bringing someone like me to the mission field?" Like Adam and Eve I needed to hide. I needed to cover myself from an intimate walk with God and with anyone else. I felt that my internal identity was a horrible person, struggling with pornography, and carrying a heavy burden of shame. I was now wearing the biggest, heaviest, most concealing mask you could ever wear. I was dead inside, hoping to look alive on the outside, yet desperate for someone to relieve my pain as I continued in my sin cycle.

Did you know that when you wear a mask, only your mask receives love and not you? "You can only love me to the extent to which I trust you with who I am."[1] When a child in my home country goes to his first year of school, there are three things he must learn regarding his identity: his full name, his full address and his mother's telephone number. As believers we must learn the same three things. We must know who we are, where our eternal address is, and how to get in touch with the Father. Yet these core identity issues are where the evil one attacks us continually. When we first accepted Christ, we might have experienced all that Ephesians 1:13–23 tells us. We believe that we are alive to the fullest, and there is great anticipation that God is going to do something astounding in our lives. As we continue to read we encounter Ephesians 2:1–3:

> Did you know that when you wear a mask, only your mask receives love and not you?

> And you were dead in the trespasses and sins in which you once walked, following the course of this world, following the prince of the power of the air, the spirit that is now at work in the sons of disobedience—among whom we all once lived in the passions of our flesh, carrying out the desires of the body and the mind, and were by nature children of wrath, like the rest of mankind.

This was the identity that I was believing about myself, even though these verses are written in past tense. Paul had not written these verses to shame me, but to remind

---

1   Quoted from a personal conversation with Bill Thrall. See also, John Lynch, Bruce McNicol, and Bill Thrall, *The Cure* (San Clemente, CA: CrossSection, 2011).

me of who I am not, of who I am no longer through Christ Jesus; not ever again. The problem is that I live in an evil, fallen world in which the enemy, evil itself, pursues me to try to convince me that this is still my identity. Evil's mission statement is written in John 10:10a: "The thief comes only to steal, kill, and destroy." Evil's hope is that I will not believe the joy of what is true about me as a child of God.

I am so thankful that my true identity is revealed in Ephesians 2:4–9.

> But God, being rich in mercy, because of the great love with which he loved us, even when we were dead in our trespasses, made us alive together with Christ—by grace you have been saved—and raised us up with him and seated us with him in the heavenly places in Christ Jesus, so that in the coming ages he might show the immeasurable riches of his grace in kindness toward us in Christ Jesus. For by grace you have been saved through faith. And this is not your own doing; it is the gift of God, not a result of works, so that no one may boast.

Who am I? I am one that the Father God greatly loves. He is rich (the "pockets-full-to -over-flowing" kind of rich) in mercy. Though I still sin, I am one who is alive with Christ. I am a saint. I am saved by his grace. I did not deserve it, did nothing to earn it, did nothing to initiate it, did nothing to complete it, and I still do nothing in this great work—it is God's great gift to me by his grace. I am raised up together with Christ who has seated me together with Jesus in the heavenly realms right now and forever. He has done all this in order that all creation can watch how he is filled with grace. The amazing part is that he does this by being kind to us through Jesus. In my new identity I can now begin to trust God and others with who I am.

Praise God that he brought someone "safe" into my life that the person behind the mask could begin to trust with who he really was. Just to clarify, a safe place does not mean one where tolerance and acceptance of sin exists. Rather it is a place where we can reveal what has been concealed, and a place where transformation can happen. Transformation did happen in my life. For the first time I began to remove some masks and began to process my own sin cycle in the area of pornography. I was finally able to share about my addiction and my heart with my wife. For the first time in my life, I actually received her love. The breaking of the sin cycle brought incredible joy, not only to my heart but to our marriage. This allowed me to pursue the deeper shame and the true source of my addiction; a secret that I had kept hidden for twenty-five years.

> A safe place does not mean one where tolerance and acceptance of sin exists. Rather it is a place where we can reveal what has been concealed, and a place where transformation can happen.

There are things in our lives that bring us incredible shame, and so we try to keep them hidden. The problem is that those hidden items begin to control us. As Dan Allender states in his book, *The Wounded Heart*, "Hiding the past always involves denial; denial of the past is always a denial of God. To forget your personal history is tantamount to trying to forget yourself and the journey that God has called you to live."[2] God does have us on a journey; it is a journey to know him deeper and more fully. "We sometimes manage to persuade ourselves that God is as pleased as we are with our developing maturity, while in fact his Spirit is gently pushing open doors into the darker regions of our hearts that we pretend don't exist."[3] Larry Crabb says we have to "face the fact that living in a fallen world sometimes exposes people to experiences that no bearer of God's image was ever meant to endure and that our reactions to those experiences are deeply stained with our own fallenness."[4]

For twenty-five years I had held the secret of an experience that no bearer of God's image was ever meant to endure. It was the summer after sixth grade, while on furlough, when we drove across the United States, stopping to visit family and friends. At one of our stops, I became the victim of sexual abuse at the hands of an older teen boy. By the grace of God, the memory is shrouded in time, but unfortunately, contact with this other family meant further encounters with this abuser. I always thought it was my fault and this produced incredible shame that affected the rest of my life, causing me to put on my mask to hide my abuse and trying to earn God's favor through my love for missions during my teen years.

"The damage done through wounding is awful, but minor compared to the dynamics that distort the victim's relationship with God and rob them of the joy of loving and being loved by others."[5] After the first experience, I shut down emotionally. All I could feel was incredible shame. "Shame is an identity issue that attacks our being. It comes from believing lies about ourselves that have been verbally and nonverbally communicated to us through the actions and responses of others."[6] The enemy's strategy as the accuser is to feed us lies though shame messages. I felt dirty, useless, stupid, and unwanted. I was broken. Apart from God, the only internalized emotion that is equal to shame is hatred. I could now only move into self-contempt or others-contempt and I became very angry. I knew this was not what God was looking for so I began to take my masks and weave a whole new pose as a good kid, one who won Christian character awards and loved missions. "The damage of past wounding sets in motion a complex scheme of self-protective defenses that operate largely outside of our awareness, guiding our interactions with others, determining the spouse we select, the jobs we pursue, the theologies we embrace, and the fabric of our entire lives."[7]

> The enemy's strategy as the accuser is to feed us lies though shame messages.

I lived for twenty-five years in my self-protective strategies, living as a Pharisee. Every once in a while people would bump into my hidden wound and I would feel

2   Dan Allender, *The Wounded Heart* (Colorado Springs: Navpress, 1990, Kindle edition), 15.
3   Allender, 9.
4   Allender, 9.
5   Allender, 14.
6   Open Hearts Ministry, *The Journey Leader's Guide*. (Kalamazoo, MI, 2011 https://ohmin.org/), 96.
7   Allender, 20.

excruciating pain leading to anger. I finally discovered that to help control that pain I had to become numb, and thereby I entered the world of pornography. When we feel physical pain we look for some medication to numb ourselves. The same holds true when we feel emotional pain. Whether it is a food disorder, such as overeating, bulimia, or anorexia; whether it is drugs such as alcohol, or amphetamines; whether it is over-exercising, or over-working, or over-spending; whether it is drowning yourself in the work of the church or indulging in pornography, we will find something to numb the pain, and there are the beginnings of addiction. The evil one's strategy is to make me ineffective in ministry. The evil one desires to put me to sleep through wounding that leads to numbing through addiction. May I counterattack the evil one's strategy with Ephesians 5:12–14:

> For it is shameful even to speak of the things that they do in secret. But when anything is exposed by the light, it becomes visible, for anything that becomes visible is light. Therefore it says, "Awake, O sleeper, and arise from the dead, and Christ will shine on you." (ESV)

Isn't that my true desire, that Christ will shine on me? To clarify, it is in community that I was wounded, and through the power of the Cross, in community, I will find healing. I seem to want God to form my character in isolation and show it off in public, but the reality is that God forms my character in community and my character is tested in isolation. As I begin to engage the process of entering my story in community from the stance of my identity in Christ I can truly begin to live out of Ephesians 2:10, "For we are his workmanship, created in Christ Jesus for good works, which God prepared beforehand, for us to do." Because of who I am, I get to do good works; as I rest in who I am, I will do good works. I get to stand complete in Christ and get to do good, because of who I am.

> It is in community that I was wounded, and through the power of the Cross, in community, I will find healing.

Who am I? I am the broken, I am the addicted, I am the wounded warrior, I am on the journey—oh, and, yes, I am a child of God, I am loved, I am chosen, I am saved, redeemed, alive, in his grasp, significant, delighted in, justified, righteous and much, much more.

References

Allender, Dan. 1990. *The Wounded Heart*. Kindle edition. Colorado Springs, CO: Navpress.

Lynch, John, Bruce McNicol, and Bill Thrall. 2011. *The Cure*. San Clemente, CA: CrossSection.

Open Hearts Ministry. 2011. *The Journey Leader's Guide*. Kalamazoo, MI: Open Hearts Ministry.

Dale Phillips was born in Santiago, Chile. He has his master's degree in organizational leadership and has served in various international leadership roles for the past twenty years in the corporate and non-profit sectors. Dale currently serves with ReachGlobal as their Director of Leadership and Organizational Effectiveness. Dale and his wife Carmen have four children and reside on Hilton Head Island, South Carolina.

Scripture: *Ephesians 2:1–10 ("As for you, you were dead in your transgressions and sins...")*

Resource: *The Healing Path: How the Hurts in Your Past Can Lead You to a More Abundant Life,* by Dan B. Allender (Colorado Springs, CO: WaterBrook, 2002). *Healing the Wounded Heart: The Heartache of Sexual Abuse and the Hope of Transformation,* by Dan B. Allender (Ada, MI: Baker Books, 2016).

CHAPTER 36

Serving Those Whose Plans Have Radically Changed

Before Departure or Rapidly Leaving the Field: Medical, Political, or Personal Crisis

Gary Wittevrongel

My early years on the mission field were characterized by numerous painful changes in plans. My wife and I had become isolated from those who knew us well. We were expected as faith missionaries to do much of what was required to get trained, financed, and directed to the field, and doing the work without direct help from others had become a way of life. Unfortunately, my best training in how to help those in missions has come through lessons of my own failures. Really, the primary way I help others now is by helping them to discern and respond to what is going on internally as they face difficulties. I am convinced that the process of redirection after a disruption can become less burdensome or tragic and can even become exciting.

I feel deeply humbled to have been asked to address this subject which is center to my current role of coming alongside missionaries and mission teams so as to increase kingdom effectiveness. Issues of radical changes are a universal experience for all of us as believers, but powerfully so for those who have ventured into mission work because of the significant personal sacrifice, travel, and financial investment made.

In the scope of this article, I cannot cover what is required to lift the burden of any one scenario and there are so many scenarios. There are good books offering strategies for helping missionaries through various challenges. For this short work, I will assume that basic needs for safety, provision, and new opportunity can be met. Here, I will focus on the environment needed to respond well to disruption and the capacity to resolve the pain experienced. If pain is left unresolved during a period of redirection, it will likely result in unhealthy, repetitive, and potentially destructive life choices and patterns.

Resolve (some call this spiritual/emotional healing) is a necessary but often missing experience when life has brought disruption. As resolution from the pain and loss of changed plans happen, the missionary can move with strength and love into what will follow. There are two key considerations I'll mention here: the environment (fellowship of believers) and awareness (the ability to listen and respond to one's heart under the guidance of the Spirit).

The first consideration, environment, includes the full scope of relationships in which the missionary experiences a radical change in plans. For our purposes here, we'll call the needed environment an environment of grace. Pain experienced in radical change is very real and a primary need of anyone who has been hurt or suffered loss is to have the freedom and ability to acknowledge and reveal that it hurts. Missionaries will encounter major disruptions due to the nature of our journey, and our need for resolving the pain in such experiences is exactly the same as every other member of the body of Christ. However, we are often viewed as being somehow on a different level from normal believers. It is as though we move into a place of being super-human when it comes to facing difficulties. It is not helpful to have such an expectation of super-ability assumed on the missionary. If placed in such a position, the missionary will be tempted to perform, to look good, to be tough, and to be seemingly unaffected by loss. Ultimately he/she will be tempted to hide what is happening within and will fall into an unhealthy pattern of not acknowledging and resolving painful issues.

There is a need for an environment of grace which can be made up of other missionaries, caregivers, friends, and family on or off the field, and hopefully the sending church. The number is not critical, but the quality is. To do well in the midst of disruption, a person must have a place that is safe enough for the truth of what is happening within to be openly revealed. The first sign of real health in a situation of painful change is the acknowledgment of the existence of pain. If our environment is not safe, then the tendency will be to mask that pain—to simply cover with more activity, to say that it is just to be expected, or that we will simply not let it stop us or bother us. The truth, though, is that we are not immune to pain and if our environment of relationships is not safe for us, we will move to hide or to numb the pain. Such hiding will result in damaging effects. So, let's agree to this first. Every missionary needs a safe, though not soft, place to actually feel what is happening within and to have safe relationships through which to begin to heal. As a caregiver, fellow missionary, friend, or church, you can become such for a missionary, providing him/her a relationship in which to begin to heal and from which to move toward whatever comes next.

> Every missionary needs a safe, though not soft, place to actually feel what is happening within and to have safe relationships through which to begin to heal.

Obviously, this is a service to missions that cannot be suddenly begun at the point of crisis. The mandate of the church is to be characterized by love (John 13:34, 35) and the actual practice of establishing an environment of grace will take time. But, again, it is not the issue of breadth of the environment, but the quality of the fellowship, the missionary's trusted inner circle. That group of trusted ones can be formed and maintained to the extent to which they desire to trust one another in their immediate issues. Forming and maintaining such a fellowship, where it is safe to be real, where authenticity and vulnerability are applauded, is foundational to serving any missionary, but particularly important for those whose lives have been disrupted. Help to set an environment of grace for your missionary and you'll bring healing, hope, and energy toward what will come next.

Several good works have been written on setting an environment of grace. A few are listed at the end of this article. Establishing an environment of grace is key to every Christian's well-being and growth. Such work is not about missions only, of course, but about the work of the church as a whole. For our work here, it is critical to serving any missionary whose plans have been radically disrupted. An environment of grace will greatly aid them as they look to the future.

The second consideration, awareness, is the ability to come to a conscious acknowledgment of what is happening within one's heart when there is a disruption to plans. The skills of having such awareness will greatly increase the capacity to respond positively rather than react negatively to disruption. What, typically, goes on within? What is it that keeps one from responding well, but instead, reacting out of energy that causes more damage and can end in lack of ability to stay or be redirected well? I believe it is because of unresolved issues resulting from the Fall.

An unresolved issue is any effect of the Fall (my sin, others' sin against me, or an unmet expectation) that has not been resolved through means given to us by God. Such issues, when unresolved, can ignite defensive, often insidious reactions that seem to be justified at the moment. When left without resolve, there are inevitable effects which move the missionary away from healthy responses and into destructive ones. We have the resources available to us in Jesus for resolution, but in the intensity of the disruption, we often fail to access these.

I began to recognize these destructive responses in me on my third mission team while in Eastern Europe in 2003. I had been in mission by that time for nearly twenty years. I received a book, now titled *The Cure*, from the authors. These men had ministered to me in their church for nine years as I healed from my unresolved issues from prior mission assignments. I often heard them give the illustration that when any sin or grave disappointment happens, it has an immediate impact. There is no escaping what happens to me when I am sinned against, when I sin in response, or when life under the Fall deals out painful circumstances. These three are all potent effects of the Fall. But I had always seen myself as tough and able to handle what came. "I won't let that affect me!" was my common response to having my teammates, nationals, or supervisor do something that would deeply hurt me or when illness or visa issues thwarted our hopes. My reaction was to do something so that I felt better (some form of busyness, more work, or withdrawal). Such actions to feel better were actually used to protect myself from pain rather than depend on what Jesus had done to resolve the pain I was feeling.

A wartime analogy regarding unresolved issues was revealed to me while I was working in Bosnia and Herzegovina. Outside my home was evidence of the disastrous conflict which only years before had torn at the infrastructure and at the hearts of all those to whom I now was seeking to minister. In the city where I lived, there seemed to be no haven where the affects of battle were not clearly evident. I walked often (carefully because of the threat of mines) and picked up pieces of jagged metal (shrapnel or shell fragments) that had been propelled out, white hot, at high velocity from artillery shells, mortar shells and grenades. Standing in a field overlooking the city, I had an epiphany: If I had been hit with such destructive weaponry, I could not escape unaffected. It simply was not possible to be unaffected, even if the explosive had been sent by someone who did not intend me to be hit. It was physically impossible to not be damaged by such force. And then, I saw a clearer picture of what I had suffered in life.

So much happens in battle that is destructive and battle is everywhere in this life. Much had happened to me. But I am tempted to say, "It didn't really hurt that much!" "They really didn't intend to hurt me!" or "I won't let that affect me!" But now looking at these artifacts of physical war, it would be absurd to think that I could simply cover the wound, leaving the jagged metal deep in my body, and try to function as normal and healthy. I saw a metaphor for what I had done in my past by attempting to bypass my need for healing from painful events that I had experienced. It simply was not possible to experience the powerful healing offered in the Word of God for those things I chose of cover, ignore, hide, or minimize. I was left with the inevitable, destructive damage of battle and could not move with health into my future. I desperately needed help.

> It simply was not possible to experience the powerful healing offered in the Word of God for those things I chose of cover, ignore, hide, or minimize.

But now, standing in this stark picture of physical destruction, I read this potent book. The authors described a cycle which awakened me to the reality of the power of sin and the Fall and how damage can become an insidious presence, overlooked in the painful events of life. I began to ponder what I was learning and I diagramed the design for healing from the damaging effects of the Fall.

Effects of the Fall & Design for Resolve

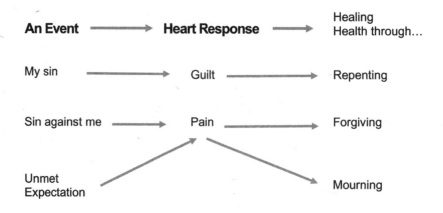

The diagram helped me as I began to awaken to pain/guilt issues in my life and as I help others navigate issues that result from the three damaging effects of the Fall:

- My sin
- Others' sin against me
- My experience of unmet expectations (All of creation is subjected to the Fall)

Like being hit by shrapnel, as I experience damage from any of these, my heart is designed by God to respond and, if unhindered, my heart will feel what God has designed it to feel and it will respond to his provision for resolve.

When I sin, I feel guilt (legitimate shame)

- Guilt is designed by God.
- Its purpose is to turn me toward the completed work of Christ to resolve my sin through grieving and deep-hearted repentance. It is a turning to Christ from my sin.
- It was on the basis of this that I came to Christ in the first place.

When I am sinned against, I will feel pain

- Pain is also designed by God.
- Its purpose is to turn me toward the completed work of Christ to resolve my pain through grieving and eventually deep-hearted forgiving of the other, regardless of their response.
- Earlier in my Christian experience, I had a primarily mechanical sense of forgiving others because it was right to do so. I experienced little of its purpose to heal me from pain and to restore my relationships.

Both forgiveness and repentance are gifts given by God not only to heal my heart but also to heal my relationships. Both depend upon our ability to live in the truth of what has happened and from there, depending on the work of Christ on the cross.

The third aspect of this cycle is that of unmet expectations which are often overlooked or minimized. This is significant for missionaries caught in dramatic disruption of their plans. So many unmet expectations! So much pain!

When I experience unmet expectations (upheaval due to illness, natural disaster, organizational breakdown, financial loss, or political shift) I feel pain that feels much like the pain of being sinned against.

- This pain, too, is designed by God.
- Its purpose also is to turn me toward the completed work of Christ and his presence and comfort (to resolve my pain through mourning Matt 5:4).
- I did not take into account that this pain would also bring me to the inevitable effects, and as a result, I often came to contempt of others and blame them for

things that were simply a result of circumstances beyond our control. This was horribly damaging to our team relationships.

In experiences of the Fall, we are tempted to hide as Adam and Eve did in the garden. Actually, we have developed far beyond fig leaves and even when God asks, "Where are you?" we have carefully worded, often spiritually sounding answers to escape his gaze and the gaze of others. We feel shame and we hide what is going on within, possibly even from ourselves.

When we do not acknowledge our heart's responses of guilt or pain, we will fall in to a pattern of reaction to guilt and pain and we cannot access the provision that Christ has provided through repentance, forgiveness, and mourning (previous diagram).

Cycle of Unresolved Issues

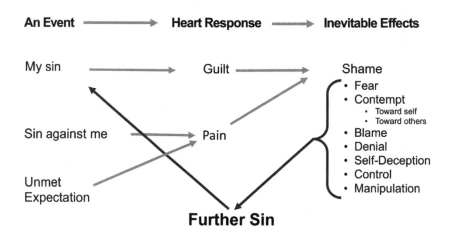

Trying to hide, deny, or minimize my heart's responses, I fail to resolve such issues through Christ's resources, and I will begin to exhibit the inevitable effects as shown in the above diagram.

- Shame - the sense that there is something wrong with me. Shame is a primary response to feeling any of the affects of the Fall (Gen 3:8).
- Then if I continue in hiding, secondary, inevitable effects begin to take hold of me and I begin to react in
  - Fear
  - Blame
  - Contempt (toward self or others)
  - Denial
  - Self-Deception
  - Control / Manipulation

At any point, when I experience any of the three affects of the Fall, if something interrupts a healthy response of moving into repentance, forgiveness, and grief, I will begin to react from the inevitable effects. This, then, results in further sin on my part and the cycle is engaged.

It does not matter where the cycle begins—it can be that I fall into sin and so feel guilt, or that another sins against me and I feel pain, or an unmet expectation is experienced and I feel pain—the results can sadly be the same. Without an awareness of what one is feeling and allowing sorrow and grief, repentance, and forgiveness, I will begin to exhibit these ugly inevitable effects and will enter into further sin, continuing the cycle.

And so an event that could be a means of driving me to the Lord becomes the fuel for greater damage. These cycles of damage can carry on for generations within a family, organization, church, or nation. We cannot avoid experiencing the effects of the Fall just like we would not be able to escape the brutal force of shrapnel. Even pain and guilt from early childhood events have the same potential to send one into the inevitable, destructive effects and can amplify the pain of a present disruptive situation.

This was the case for me. Early in my mission career, I was affected by sin done against me and by unmet expectations on the field, and I reacted negatively far beyond the severity of the disruptive events. Years later, I learned that becoming aware of ugly inevitable effects was very helpful and paying attention to them helped me to look back and find unresolved issues. (Many issues were from my childhood.) It was vital to me to have the opportunity to explore these in a grace environment. Doing so helped me to see how I had fallen into the cycle of unresolved issues. I found help through a well-trained counselor and trusted friends who asked questions that kindly led me into my childhood stories of neglect and abuse. I had hoped these issues were behind me. When I became aware of the damaging inevitable effects in my life, I was able to move toward healing. My ability to respond positively to difficult situations was dramatically improved.

Awareness of one's heart is an absolute necessity if we are to move toward resolve of the pain of disruption of plans. Awareness is very closely attached to the first consideration in this article, the environment or fellowship. The environment allows a safe and strong place to become aware of what is happening within and provides added courage to move toward resolve. Environment and awareness work in conjunction so as to form the means of maturing our hearts so as to respond rather than react to the affects of the Fall. If either is insufficient, then the disruption will likely result in unhealthy, repetitive, and potentially destructive life choices and patterns.

> Environment and awareness work in conjunction so as to form the means of maturing our hearts so as to respond rather than react to the affects of the Fall.

There are also a great many good works on the subject of such personal awareness. They are also listed at the end as resources that have been of great help to me. I now employ many of these as I serve those whose plans have changed radically.

It is my personal desire to help each missionary I encounter to move toward finding an environment in which he/she can be brutally honest with the nature of what is happening both outwardly and within. Once this environment is established in some measure, the next step is to increase their awareness of how they are responding and/or reacting. Finally, it is important to help them move toward resolve of the issues through the resources of repentance, forgiveness, and mourning.

We write in one of our brochures, "Imagine… those things you think may eliminate you from ministry becoming the avenues to your most effective ministry!" It is possible to experience the sudden disruptions common in missions without tragic entrapment in a cycle of unresolved issues. The very event that threatened to undo the missionary can serve as motivation, energized by healing and wholeness and can be passed on to others who are in the midst of a similar experience. Events that evil intended to use for harm (John 10:10) can be redeemed, thus restoring and furthering the work of the kingdom. It is my opinion that such disruptions are a seedbed of great personal and relational growth and hope-giving ministry.

Resources

Concerning Establishing an Environment of Grace

The Cure, by John Lynch, Bill Thrall, Bruce McNicol (San Clemente, CA: Cross Section Ventures, 2011)

Behind the Mask, John Lynch, Bill Thrall, Bruce McNicol (Carol Stream, IL: NavPress, 2005)

Scary Close, Donald Miller (Nashville, TN: Thomas Nelson, 2015)

In the Grip of Grace, Max Lucado (Nashville, TN: Thomas Nelson, 2011)

Transforming Grace, Jerry Bridges (Carol Stream, IL: NavPress, 2008)

Encouragement, Crabb and Allender (Grand Rapids, MI: Zondervan, 2013)

Shame and Grace, Lewis B. Smedes (New York: HarperOne, 2009)

Resources

Concerning Awareness and Unresolved Issues

The Emotionally Healthy Church, Peter Scazzero (Grand Rapids, MI: Zondveran, 2013)

Emotionally Healthy Spirituality, Peter Scazzero (Nashville, TN: Thomas Nelson, 2011)

Waking the Dead, John Eldredge (Nashville, TN: Thomas Nelson, 2006)

Inside Out, Larry Crabb (Carol Stream, IL: NavPress, 2015)

The Cry of the Soul, Dan Allender and Tremper Longman III (Carol Stream, IL: NavPress, 2014)

Abba's Child, Brennan Manning Carol Stream, IL: NavPress, 2015)

The Healing Path, Dan Allender (Colorado Springs, CO: Waterbrook, 2000)

The Wounded Heart, Dan Allender (Carol Stream, IL: NavPress, 2014)

Gary Wittevrongel is a graduate of Wheaton Graduate School with an MA in Cross-Cultural Communication. Gary and his wife Sandy live in North Carolina and travel to serve mission teams and national church leaders. A missionary for thirty years with extensive time living in the Middle East and Eastern Europe, he currently serves with Paraclete Mission Group as a Paraclete Associate. His current role is to come alongside missionaries, mission teams, and nationals to promote deep healing with the goal of increasing kingdom effectiveness. He also serves as an adjunct faculty member for the TrueFaced program, Certificate in High Trust Leadership. Along with colleagues, he and his wife, Sandy, facilitate the Deep Community Experience (DCE is facilitated by a growing number of individuals who have found each other on their journeys toward fuller wholeness in life and mission.)

Scripture: *Ephesians 2:7* ("In order that in the coming ages he might show the incomparable riches of his grace, expressed in his kindness to us in Christ Jesus") emphasis on the kindness of God

Resource: *Healing the Wounded Heart, by* Dan Allender (Carol Stream, IL: NavPress, 2014).

CHAPTER 37

Rest, Recreation, Sabbath

Caring for One's Soul on the Journey

Jim Van Meter

Is the care of our souls being neglected? Often an erroneous assumption is made that goes something like this: "The condition of the soil of my soul will always be good. When I first received Christ as Savior, the seed of the Word of God fell on the good soil of my heart and produced much fruit. Because the soil of my soul/heart was good then, it will always be good and produce much fruit." However, we know from Scripture and gardening, that the condition of soil is not static. Soil must be attended to, nurtured, given opportunity to rest, and supplemented with nutrients when it becomes depleted (Ex 23:11). The quality and condition of the soil is most important. Jesus said the same thing when he taught the parable of the soil in Matthew 13:1–23. The rocky soil, the thorny soil, and the trodden down soil do not produce fruit when the seed falls on these kinds of soil. When seed falls on the "good" soil, it produces an abundant crop. The point Jesus was making is that the quality and condition of the soil of the soul is directly related to fruitfulness and productivity![1]

At the National Pastors Retreat in California in 2008, Ruth Haley Barton from the Transforming Center said, "The most important thing we can do is to be extremely tenacious in the care of our own soul. The best thing we can bring to the work of God is a transformed self, stripped of compulsive behaviors, and then replaced with basic rhythms, rhythms of work and rest, engagement and retreat, solitude and community, Sabbath keeping, and celebration and self-examination."[2] Sadly, 40% of the leaders of one mission agency said that their greatest weakness was the nurture and care of their own soul and relationship with Christ.

Another cause for the neglect of the care of one's soul is that there is a subtle erroneous belief that the great commission task of discipling the nations is equivalent to the great commandment of loving God. Consequently, we can become so preoccupied with

---

1   By "soul" is meant "the real you," the you that was conceived in the heart of God, the you that is more than any job or position, it is the you that longs for relationship and intimacy with its Creator.
2   Ruth Haley Barton, *Strengthening the Soul of Your Leadership* (Downers Grove, IL: IVP Books, 2008), 19.

the work and assume that service is the highest expression of love for Christ. We are committed to the Great Commission, and yet the Lord of the harvest wants our love above all else.

Rest and the Importance of Caring for One's Soul

Rest is central to the Christian life and the cornerstone of the care of one's soul. Rest is an experience that can be enjoyed by faith because it is our heritage. When God rested on the seventh day from his creative works, creation was completed and rest began, because the seventh day has never been completed. This Sabbath rest "was to be entered into by those who respond to his overtures with faith and obedience."[3] The original consecration of this seventh day of rest was for the people of God to leave behind the struggle to live by their own efforts and live out of the gracious provision of God, and celebrate life as a gift of Yahweh, with no efforts of their own needed. The six days of labor would remain under the power of the Fall, "but on the seventh day there was to be relief, renewal, and restoration as an eschatological 'jubilee,' a provision, but promising hope, of complete reconciliation."[4]

> Rest is central to the Christian life and the cornerstone of the care of one's soul. Rest is an experience that can be enjoyed by faith, because it is our heritage.

The writer of the book of Hebrews exhorts the reader, "There remains, then, a Sabbath-rest for the people of God; for those who enter God's rest also rest from their own work, just as God did from his. Let us therefore, make every effort to enter into that rest" (Heb 4:9–11). There is a danger for the people of God to fail to enter that rest because of self-effort, lack of trust and faith, and disobedience. The challenge of discipling the nations is an enormous task, so we are tempted to fulfill the Great Commission and strive unceasingly in our efforts to do so. Whereas, the writer of Hebrews exhorts us to "make every effort" to resist that temptation and desist the ceaseless striving and enter into that place of rest, renewal, and restoration which God intended for all of creation.

However, we need to be encouraged to learn how to better care for our souls. We have forgotten that our Lord, who was sent by the Father with the huge task of redeeming the world, showed us the way to live a life characterized by a rhythm of work and rest and ministry and communion with the Father. In becoming so driven by the task and taking little time to pull back and tend to condition of the soil of our soul, we may be in danger of losing our souls! When the soil of our soul is untended, it becomes trodden down and a hot bed for weeds, thorns, and insects. Souls become unproductive when there is little time and attention given to the care and condition of

---

3   FF Bruce, *The Epistle to the Hebrews* (Grand Rapids, MI: Eerdmans 1964), 74.
4   Ray Anderson, *The Soul of Ministry: Forming Leaders for God's People* (Louisville, KY: Westminster John Knox Press, 1997), 64–65.

one's soul. The consequences of the neglect of that care are many: depletion, plateauing, burnout, depression, weariness, loss of soul or understanding of God's purpose and call, irritability, hoarding of energy, compassion fatigue. That's why Jesus said, "Come to me, all you who are weary and burdened, and *I will give you rest... for your souls*" (Matt 11:28–29, italics mine). Rest is essential to health of the soul, and restoration of a weary soul.

Just as the rhythm of "ebb" and "flow is necessary for much of sea life for rest and the repletion of energy expended during the "flow," there can be no high tide (flow) without the preceding low tide (ebb). Likewise, there is no spiritually powerful work without rest. The ministry journey is long and arduous. It is a marathon and not a race. "Pacing" and "care" of one's soul throughout the journey is critical to learning and enjoying all of God's purposes, not to mention finishing the journey well. Setting the pace takes into account the monitoring of the expenditure of energy as well as the need for repletion, in order to make the purpose, goals, and longevity of the journey possible. So "make every effort" to experience the rest and renewal of the "ebb" of life is of critical importance if we are to experience the intended power of the "flow" from the hand of God's provision.

Why is it so important to give and attention to the care of the soul, when the task is so great? Why take time for the care of one's soul, when there is so much to do?

First, God himself cared for his soul by ceasing from his work of creation on the seventh day. God's creation itself demonstrates his intention and desire that we practice a rhythm and lifestyle of rest. As his image bearers, we are called to rest as he rested. Rest is obvious in the day/night cycle, the seasons (dry and monsoon, winter and summer), the tides of the sea (high and low tides). I had the privilege of living near the ocean for a period of time. One day, I went to the ocean during low tide when the waves were minimal. I saw scores of seals lying on the beach and rocks. As I started to move toward them to get a photograph, someone warned me not to get too close so as to not disturb the seals' rest! Even seals need to rest!

Second, when we rest and the soul is cared for, it gives us the opportunity to reflect upon and assess our work just as God himself assessed his work of creation, and to ask ourselves if what we are doing is really "good." God did not finish the work of creation, but entrusted the on-going process to us humans. As we pull back to rest, we are given insight to assess if our work is aligned with God's purposes and desires for his creation.

> When we rest, we look back and see how God has providentially led us along the way, how he has protected us and provided for us... If we don't enter into the rest that's both symbolized and experienced, our lives will become cluttered, and that will keep us confused. We often labor under the illusion

that everything depends on us or on those around us. But it doesn't. Everything depends on God. And this is the great lesson that rest has to teach us.[5]

Third, Jesus said he is the "way" (John 14:6). The prophet Jeremiah said, "Stand at the crossroads and look; ask for the ancient paths, ask where the good way is, and walk in it and you will find rest for your souls" (Jer 6:16). Dallas Willard says, "My central claim is that we can become like Christ by doing one thing— by following him in the overall style of life he chose for himself. If we have faith in Christ, we must believe that he knew how to live."[6]

Jesus modeled for us the "way" to care for his soul by a lifestyle characterized by both serving and resting. We get a glimpse of Jesus' rhythm for living from Mark 6. The disciples had been chosen and sent out with authority to preach and minister to the needs of the people. When they returned to Jesus, they reported all the wonderful things that had happened. Because there was so much commotion going on around them, Jesus' responded by saying, "Come away with me by yourselves to a quiet place and get some rest" (Mark 6:31). After much ministry, Jesus invites us to be with him and get some rest. This was Jesus' own pattern for caring for his soul.

> Jesus modeled for us the "way" to care for his soul by a life style characterized by both serving and resting.

Fourth, rest and solitude were the spiritual practices where Jesus reflected with the Father in prayer over what had happened in ministry. Communion and solitude with the Father brings rest to our soul, which gives us the strength to face the needs of the multitude. "Compassion is the fruit of solitude and the basis of all ministry. The transformation that takes place in solitude manifests itself in compassion."[7] Compassion is not our natural response to the needs of people, unless we have been alone with the Father, have his heart, and have come to a place of rest in our souls. Jesus could have compassion on the people because he had been with the Father and would have more time with the Father very soon (Mark 6:34, 46).

Following are some foundational spiritual disciplines to assist in the practical care for one's soul in order to cultivate the rhythm of work and rest.

1. Get a good night of sleep. Many times I hear missionaries say, "I only need 5–6 hours of sleep." Archibald Hart in his book *Adrenalin and Stress* says that adults were created basically to get 8–10 hours of sleep.[8] When we are in the habit of sleeping much less than that, adrenalin may be interfering with our basic need for sleep, and in the long run this can be damaging to our health because our bodies were not designed to live on adrenalin day after day. Adrenalin is God's tool to help us cope

---

5   Eugene Peterson, *Conversations: The Message with Its Translator* (Colorado Springs, CO: Nav Press 2007), 1894.

6   Dallas Willard, *The Spirit of the Disciplines* (New York: HarperCollins, 1988), ix.

7   Henri Nouwen, *The Way of the Heart* (New York: Ballantine Books, 1981), 33.

8   Archibald Hart, *Adrenalin and Stress* (Waco, TX: Word Publishers, 1986), 154.

with emergencies and not to be used to help us work more and rest less as a lifestyle. Try getting at least 8–9 hours of sleep each day for a week. Journal your experience at the end of the week.

2. Daily communion and solitude with the Father. Communion with the Father puts our souls at rest because he reminds us again that he is with us and it is his strength, not our own, that we are relying on to face the demands of the day. A day without a time of solitude and silence is to subject ourselves to the noise of both the world around us as well as our own hearts, often missing the opportunity to hear God's still small voice speaking quiet into the storms of the day. Try spending twenty minutes in silence with the Lord each day for a week, listening to what he has to say to you. Journal your thoughts at the end of each day.

3. Weekly Sabbaths. For us in missions, we are often called upon to minister on Sundays, the traditional day of Sabbath for most Christians. The challenge we face is how to observe the purpose of the Sabbath, which is to cease from work. "The important thing is that a particular day is set aside as the Sabbath, and that it is observed faithfully every seven days so that God can imbue us with his rhythm of six days of work and one day of ceasing work."[9] Practice observing the Sabbath for six consecutive weeks, journaling your experience having ceased work one day each week for twenty-four hours, sundown to sundown.

4. Periodic Personal Retreats. A personal retreat is simply a concentrated and consecrated time to be alone with God for a day or two. It is that resting place where we remove ourselves from the demands of our life and give the Lord an opportunity to speak and minister to us in an unhurried setting. It can be anywhere, as long as solitude is possible and distractions are minimal. Jane Rubietta's book *Resting Place* is an excellent guide for that retreat time, with quotes and passages of Scripture to meditate on along with reflection questions and hymns to guide one during the time. Try taking a twenty-four-hour retreat or even a week-long retreat. Journal your experience.

5. Exercise. Exercise a minimum of 150 minutes spread over six consecutive days. This can be working out in a gym, walking, etc. It must be intentionally planned exercise. Journal your experience.

6. Sabbaticals. "Sabbatical years are the biblically-based provision for restoration. When the farmer's field is depleted, it is given a sabbatical—after six years of planting and harvesting, it is left alone for a year so that the nutrients can build up in it. When people in ministry are depleted, they are also given a sabbatical—time apart for the recovery of spiritual and creative energies."[10]

---

9   Marva Dawn, *Keeping the Sabbath Wholly* (Grand Rapids, MI: Eerdmans, 1989), xi.
10   Peterson 1989, 145.

For some unknown reason, missionaries seldom take sabbaticals. After thirty-five years in missions ministry, I had never heard of missionaries taking a sabbatical until a missionary friend shared with me his sabbatical experience. Something stirred in my heart when I heard his story and saw his changed life because I was depleted spiritually and my walk with God had plateaued. After taking this sabbatical, I felt such incredible love from God. I fell in love with the Lord all over again. It isn't that God loved me more, rather my awareness of his love was deepened, love that was not predicated on performance and production. I now know what it is like for my soul to be at rest from having had such an extended time with my loving Father. That rest has become a plumb line, a standard, by which I assess the condition of my soul. When I get off center, I quickly take corrective action.

To take a sabbatical, with the blessing of one's supervisor, take a minimum of two months of time stopping all ministry, and if possible, for as long as six months. This is a time for the restoration of one's soul, doing whatever is life-giving and not obligatory. Journal each day, and restrain the use of the computer to once a week. Report back monthly to a select group of four to six godly people.

So what does it mean and how important is the rest and care for our soul? We are not called to the monastic life or may not have the physical constitution to survive the rigors of the desert like the desert fathers, but we are still responsible for the care of our own souls.

> Precisely because our secular milieu offers us so few spiritual disciplines, we have to develop our own. We have, indeed, to fashion our own "desert" where we can withdraw every day, shake off our compulsions, and dwell in the gentle healing presence of our Lord. Without such a desert we will lose our soul while preaching the gospel to others. But with such a spiritual abode, we will become increasingly conformed to him in whose Name we minister.[11]

As missionaries and leaders, the intentional care of our souls is the single most important thing we can do. As undershepherds, we best lead the sheep to places of green pastures and quiet waters, when we ourselves have been there. When we haven't practiced rhythms of rest and don't know the way to places of rest, then the sheep are impacted because they too don't know where those places of rest are that bring restoration and transformation of the soul. The Good Shepherd is concerned for our souls because a restored soul is directly related to the sheep's welfare. The restoration of a depleted soul is much more arduous than the regular attentiveness to the soul's need for a rhythm of work and rest.

The restoration of a depleted soul is much more arduous than the regular attentiveness to the soul's need for a rhythm of work and rest.

---

11   Nouwen, 30.

References

Anderson, Ray S. 1997. *The Soul of Ministry: Forming Leaders for God's People.* Louisville, KY: Westminister John Knox Press.

Barton, Ruth Haley. 2008. *Strengthening the Soul of Your Leadership.* Downers Grove, IL: IVP Books.

Bruce, F. F. 1964. *The Epistle to the Hebrews.* Grand Rapids: MI, Wm B. Eerdmans Publishing Co.

Buchanan, Mark. 2006. *The Rest of God.* Nashville, TN: W. Publishing Group.

Dawn, Marva. 1989. *Keeping the Sabbath Wholly.* Grand Rapids: MI: Eerdmans.

Hart, Archibald. 1986. *Adrenalin and Stress.* Waco, TX: Word Publishers.

Nouwen, Henri J. M. 1981. *The Way of the Heart.* New York: Ballantine Books.

Peterson, Eugene. 1989. *The Contemplative Pastor.* Grand Rapids, MI: Eerdmans.

―――. 2007. *Conversations: The Message with Its Translator.* Colorado Springs, CO: Nav Press.

Rubietta, Jane. 2005. *Resting Place.* Downers Grove, IL: InterVarsity Press.

Willard, Dallas. 1988. *The Spirit of the Disciplines.* New York: HarperCollins.

Jim Van Meter serves with Paraclete Mission Group. Along with his wife, Leta, he has been in missions since 1970, serving in Indonesia and the Philippines, before serving as Director of Training. His passion is to see missionary effectiveness enhanced. He believes that the care of one's soul is the most important practice the missionary can do as a discipler of nations. He was on the steering committee for the twenty-one-nation missionary retention study (ReMAP2), which resulted in the publication of the book *Worth Keeping.* Jim is a graduate of Dallas Theological Seminary (ThM) and Fuller Seminary (DMin).

Scripture*: John 15:5 ("I am the vine; you are the branches...")*

Resource*: Strengthening the Soul of Your Leadership,* by Ruth Haley Barton (Downers Grove, IL: InterVarsity Press Books, 2008).

Along the Journey

Finishing Well

CHAPTER 38

Finishing Strong and Well

Of Old Shoes, Seasons, Traps, and Antidotes

William D. Taylor

Part One: What Does It Mean to Finish Well?

It's those old shoes that sit to the left of my desk. I turn my head and gaze at them. They stare at me, now dusty, at times dusted, now silent, now talking. They belong to an old marathoner friend of mine who has finished his last race in a life fully lived. Back in the early 90's I had called him on the spur of the moment and asked him to send me a pair of his really old shoes. He laughed, asking why in the world I would request that. I said, "I want tangible shoe-leather evidence of how to finish well after all your years of life, marriage, parenting, cross-cultural ministry, leadership, laughing, loving, and serving." Those shoes would narrate the story of one man who has profoundly shaped me.

A few days later they arrived, snail-mail, in a cardboard box. I sat and held those cracked, worn shoes, thanking God for what they represented. This veteran had begun his marathon with Christ as a teen. He was the promise of his uncle's business in Atlanta, Georgia until he informed his uncle that business was not his passion; Jesus was. The rapid reprisal came; the angry uncle disinherited his nephew. Ironically, he was now free for a God-driven future. The Runner married a life partner in the Race and together they began the marathon of life and ministry; studies at Moody Bible Institute were balanced with pastoral ministry in a Swedish Covenant Church in East Chicago, Indiana; a daughter came into their world; they were turned down by two (get it, two!!) mission agencies for "health reasons." But they persevered; and another sending body took them on in 1938. Following linguistic studies in the then-young Wycliffe Bible Translators program they traveled on a banana boat for Costa Rica. A son was born soon after.

The Race continued. After a decade of service they returned for further study at Wheaton College, sensing the need to upgrade their skill/set and gift/mix. Over the next decades their Race took them to three Latin American countries for ministry, then twelve years as the CEO of his mission agency in the USA. In his fifty-ninth year, he and his wife informed the mission leadership of their desire to transition to a field-based ministry in Spain. They would serve under a much younger man whom the Runner years ago had recruited for Spain. The board was stunned and the chairman admonished him, "Sir, no president of a bank ever returns to become a teller." To which the Runner quietly replied, "I do not work in a bank!"

They served/ran in Spain for five years, developed a strategic camp and conference center west of Madrid, turned it over to Spanish leaders, then returned to the USA. What now? These battle-worn veterans could have opted for retirement but their spirits were strong and the body still had more laps to go. Back in their geographic roots they planted Hispanic churches in the metropolitan Atlanta area. Today some eleven Spanish-speaking churches owe their existence to this vision—by either multiplication or division.

But I'm most impressed with the Runner's deep character. He had a unique combination of natural and spiritual abilities: visionary leadership and administrative gifts, coupled with spiritual insight and sensitive pastoral care, and a robust sense of humor—he could really laugh. He was not threatened by younger or more brilliant leaders and opened space for them to emerge into leadership. He could ask forgiveness. He mentored an unusual number of American and Latin young leaders during his career. He recognized his wife's unusual gift blend and released her for complete parallel fulfillment. He was a strong leader, but servanthood marked his style.

Those old shoes. I cannot get away from them. The Runner's pace slowed down, Alzheimer's took his mind. His life partner was taken by dementia. To the end they were deeply in love with each other, read actively (whether they could remember or not), and into their late 70's taught weekly Bible classes. He once told me that the two of them laughed a lot—at things, at each other, at other people. I have sweet memories of the last conversations with him until That Disease destroyed his keen intellect.

Two lasting memories stay with me. He was seated on his bed in the assisted care home, slowly looked at me in the eyes and said in that shaking voice, "Bill, do you see that lovely lady over there? She's my wife and the most beautiful creature in the world."

The last time I visited him his rheumy eyes caught me coming across the room. He took my hand, looked straight into my eyes, and barely got out the stammering words, "Bill … you … taught … me how to … finish … well. And I'm … trying … to do … that … right … now …." I wept. He died in hospice, age 88, weighing 65 pounds.

Why This Old Shoe Story?

I tell you this story because I, at the tender age of 77, personally need ongoing encouragement to keep my eyes on the Ultimate Goal; not the management goals of an organization or ministry; not the false-self; not those prized, measurable and tangible outcomes, or an ever-increasing profile of apparent success (whether you get there by the authentic route or forcibly carve out your path); nor the self-imposed goals of a society that values high productivity.

But all of us, women and men, younger and older, need to be wary of the traps set out for us. We must never forget the deadly triad enemy—the world, the flesh, and the devil. Some snares will trip us up for a while; we will recover, through confession of sin and restoration, or simply through the natural path of maturation. But other traps are deadly and can destroy our lives and ministries, our integrity and our families. Other things we cannot control, like Alzheimer's.

> The least you can do right now is to know yourself and to anticipate the potential minefields out there, discerning some of the dangers, and learning from those who have battled to finish well.

So let's take a careful gaze at something that may be theory for many of you: finishing well. But look at it this way. The least you can do right now is to know yourself and to anticipate the potential minefields out there, discerning some of the dangers, and learning from those who have battled to finish well.

Three Clarifications—Amplifications

Perhaps the person who has written with most insight on this subject is Bobby Clinton (senior professor of leadership at the School of Intercultural Studies of Fuller Theological Seminary), and I point you to his resources online and in print. He posits that of biblical leaders, only 30% really finished well. That leaves a staggering 70% who did not. And in the church, he suggests that 1/3 finish well, 1/3 finish so-so, and 1/3 finish poorly. [1]

First, in this discussion when we speak of finishing well, we do not just talk about the end of life or at retirement, but at the conclusion of each season of life and ministry. Try it out on yourself. How many "seasons of life, occupation, ministry" have you walked through already? You may be in your mid 30's and I suspect you have already had some three or four of them. They are shorter with each younger generation—simply the reality of shorter assignments (or commitments to a task or team). Others of you in your 40's and 50's may have had twice that many transitions.

So the question comes, how did you finish each season, each assignment? On a scale of one to ten, with ten being optimum, how would you score your season-conclusions?

---

1   For more information start with http://eldose4jesus.blogspot.com/2012/10/finishing-well-dr-j-robert-clinton.html.

This is my sequence just in my first ten years of ministry: seminary study for four years; marriage; IVCF staff in Texas for three years; language school in Costa Rica one year; part-time with Christian Medical Society for three summers; conclusion of our four-year first term of service in Guatemala; doctoral study in Latin American Studies at the University of Texas; back to Guatemala. Well, that took me from my early 20's to my early 30's.

After we served ten more years in Guatemala, we departed in 1985, I at the age of 44, my wife at age 39, and three children approaching 10, 14, 16. I thought I would teach and retire on the faculty of Trinity Evangelical Divinity School. Not! It became clear that for our family that geography and culture was not the best for them. Yvonne's prophetic word confirmed that TEDS would serve as a leverage to get me out of Latin America, but God would pivot me into something totally unexpected.

I then painfully discerned in my gut that my tenure at TEDS would be extraordinarily brief. So we moved and lived four years in a small Arkansas town for the family to make a healthy transition to the USA. I pastored part time what would be a part-time church. Dr. David Howard, my life-long mentor, had spoken tough, wise words in those discerning days, "Bill, God will bless any decision you make that seeks the best for your family."

Yet it was in that bottom of my wrenching losses—Latin America, teaching, missions, pastoral gifting—that God in his mercy gave me what has now become thirty years of service with World Evangelical Alliance Mission Commission. For twenty years I would serve as its executive director and since 2006 continue as senior mentor.

It is right now that I face the reality of the latter laps of the journey. I want to embrace them well and wisely. I must steward my mind, heart, and body in light of their limitations. In the major seasons of my life wherever I experienced a major occupation-geographical change I had envisioned a mountain range before me, and I could anticipate climbing them and descending into the next valley. The Spirit has now shown me, in this latter season of life-ministry, another range into the future, but he has indicated that I will not cross into the next valley; I will only arrive at the foothills. At that point I want to it to be said as was written of David in Acts 13:36: "For David, after he had served the purpose of God in his own generation, fell asleep and was laid with his fathers."

Second, finishing well applies to the termination of each specific job, occupation, or assignment in relation to leadership development and the organization or team with which we have served. I remember so well my father's wisdom as we faced the wrenching farewell from Guatemala: "Bill, leave in a way that they will ask you to return." And I well remember his insightful words when he resigned early as president of his agency and said to me: "Bill, always leave when they want you to stay, instead of trying to stay and they want you to leave."

Allow me to graft in right here the thoughtful reflections of Geoffrey W. Hahn, a coeditor. He says it so well.

I see the challenging spiritual issues in finishing well as relating to faith in our God to be able to carry out his kingdom work through others, a lack of utter dependency on God who alone changes hearts and will not be thwarted in his kingdom work, and a related fear that the ministry will be messed up by neophytes. Additionally, there can be a loss of kingdom perspective in seeing the ministry not as God's but rather as our own, or perhaps viewing the faith of those who come after us as not being as precious as our own (2 Peter 1:1), or pride in our relative spiritual maturity compared to them (Phil 3). The loss of hope in the up and coming generations is also a lack of faith indicator.[2]

I think the fundamental issue that leads to a lack of grace in this matter is likely spiritual pride. Rather than finishing with a pride of superiority that diminishes the faith and perspectives of those who come after us, we should model Paul's enthusiasm for the next generation of Christian leaders:

> Rather than finishing with a pride of superiority that diminishes the faith and perspectives of those who come after us, we should model Paul's enthusiasm for the next generation of Christian leaders.

For this reason, since the day we heard about you, we have not stopped praying for you. We continually ask God to fill you with the knowledge of his will through all the wisdom and understanding that the Spirit gives, so that you may live a life worthy of the Lord and please him in every way: bearing fruit in every good work, growing in the knowledge of God, being strengthened with all power according to his glorious might so that you may have great endurance and patience, and giving joyful thanks to the Father, who has qualified you to share in the inheritance of his holy people in the kingdom of light. (Col 1: 10–12)

One of the key aspects of finishing well relates to leadership development. Too often I see leaders end well in terms of their ministry assignment, but their departure leaves a serious void in leadership capacity for the ministries they led. Too often I see senior leaders surrounding themselves with a leadership team only of other seasoned leaders. While this practice works well in the shorter term for effectiveness and efficiency in carrying out the ministry and feels low risk, in the long term it is a high-risk approach that results in tumultuous transitions. So part of ending well is spending years developing the next generation of leaders that will follow in our footsteps. This, most critically, involves giving developing leaders real responsibility with the corresponding authority to lead. Secondly, it involves giving developmentally-minded feedback (mentoring/coaching/counsel). This requires proactivity and the willingness to build into less seasoned leaders. They will have rough edges, will make mistakes, and will need feedback and support in an environment of gracious relationship with the senior leadership. Paul uses the race metaphor when talking about finishing well.

---

2   Geoffry W Hahn, personal email correspondence with William D. Taylor, December 22, 2015.

We individually at times talk about the Christian life as a marathon, but perhaps more accurately it is a relay.

Another key issue in finishing well is embracing the generations, with their differences, that follow us. This is a key test of being a person characterized by grace. Are we threatened by the generational differences, fearful of what the world will look like under their watch, highly critical and judgmental of the negative traits of the next generation while not seeing the equally negative aspects of our own generation? Or do we speak hope into the future generations, trusting the next generation of followers of Christ? Do we believe that God will powerfully use the next generations to advance his kingdom?

> Do we speak hope into the future generations, trusting the next generation of followers of Christ? Do we believe that God will powerfully use the next generations to advance his kingdom?

And, of course, there are the more personal aspects of finishing well—namely, that some people unwittingly create unnecessary problems or damage their relationships in a way that makes it easier to leave them. If the two ideas above are constant considerations, then it will be less likely that people will damage ministries and relationships as they leave. Rather, they will be excited to see what God does through the people they have invested in.

Third, for most of the rest of this chapter we will speak of the longest-arc of life and ministry, from the start to the very end, at least from your "now to your end." You may be younger, the middle years, or older. You may find yourself in a transition from one of the age categories—those are the most critical periods. Transition well. You may be ahead of me, knowing you are on the last straight stretch to the finish line. What is the nature of that longest arc of life and service? Regardless of where you are now, can you envision what you would want it to be when you "get there" towards the "end?" Wisdom (and folly) mark us all, whoever we are, wherever we serve, in whatever occupation or task. I encourage you to mull over (and let them mull you over) these multifaceted realities of finishing well.

OK, so what does finishing well not mean and what does it really mean?

What it is not? Finishing well does not mean someone who completes his or her personal career, regardless of the vocation, on "top of the success pile" lauded as great examples of modern ministry productivity. Finishing well does not mean banquets celebrating retirement, or biographies, or sharing your secrets to success, nor having your ten-step video programs. It does not mean awards as spell-binding motivational speakers, the writers of self-help books, the evangelical celebrities, the prophetically gifted ones, the great public intercessors, the international missions mobilizers or legendary missionaries. For us it certainly does not mean owning the most toys— though regretfully I do know some missionaries with a lot of toys.

Finally, it does not mean that the high prize is to be given to parents who claim, "I praise God that all my children are on fire for God and serving him in—"

So what does it really mean? It means coming to the end of the life race, perhaps off-camera, quietly, with authentic faith and personal integrity. I personally have two passions in life related to finishing well, and I measure them simply. It means coming to the end of my life still holding to a working conviction of the truth of Christianity, plus integrity in life and towards my wife and my children. At my funeral I want my kids to say, "Dad loved Mom unto the end, was totally faithful to her, and did not sacrifice us on an illegitimate altar of his ministry." That's my prime bottom line. The second passion is to do all I can to contribute toward the goal that every person in every generation in every culture has a legitimate opportunity to hear and understand the gospel of Jesus the Christ in order to make a legitimate decision for or against. It's only fair; this is deep human rights justice.

> It means coming to the end of my life still holding to a working conviction of the truth of Christianity, plus integrity in life and towards my wife and my children.

Finishing well does not mean you must remain a cross-cultural servant nor stay in the same geography/culture all your life. Today's servants already serve with greater mobility, according to global and local needs, based on need and opportunity, skill-set and gift-mix, seeking to expand the kingdom into the tough unreached areas, committed to building up the church of Christ everywhere in the world. Some serve with dedication and giftedness for a season in another culture and language, and then return (for an enormous diversity of reasons) to passport country—but forever changed. The fuller meaning of the Great Commissions equally balance the Great Commandment with the proclamation of the gospel, doing mercy and justice and strengthening the church. Ultimately the key is not vocation nor geography nor role in society, but rather integrity, passion for the living God in Christ, service to the community of faith, and commitment to make Jesus known.

Finishing well is best done in community: your extended family, your spiritual family, and your church family, your colleagues in ministry and your intercessors, your mentors and your fellow believers from different nations and cultures.

Too many of us have been shaped by the image of the Christian life as the Summer or Winter Olympics, and I write these words in the middle of the 2016 Rio Games. We tend to honor and exult in those who jump the highest, run or swim the fastest, endure the most, and above all, those who get the gold, or eight or more of them. Who remembers any bronze medalists of any Olympics, much less those who finished last in any event? (Actually, I really do know the story of some of the last-place finishers and their story is often much more moving.)

I consider our life-long pilgrimage more akin to small-town Paralympics. Here it does not really matter who wins. As those runners, swimmers, and other athletes approach the finish line, perhaps arms and legs flailing in all directions, they cross to the cheer of the coach and crowd. That is our true analogy. The Christian life is Paralympics, and the key is for each of us, regardless of age, gender, and vocation, to cross that final line, flailing. But we have finished; our Coach cheers us. We are all welcomed into the banquet.

Finishing well may mean completing life with broken dreams, unanswered prayers, and unfulfilled desires, with children that may or may not be walking with Christ; it may mean that there are few publicly recognized evidences of high productivity or tangible value. This is particularly a problem for those of us who live in cultures that reward efficiency, effectiveness, and measurable, busy productivity.

It also means that in spite of all of the challenges I have had to grapple with—life and ministry, health and faith, testing by God and temptation by Satan—I shall finish with faith intact and a sense of the loving Father's hand in my life.

In our next section we will take a careful look at traps and antidotes.

Part Two: Of Snares and Antidotes

Over the decades I have carefully studied some of the major snares that we encounter along the journey. Some have called these developmental stoppers. Google the topic and you will find other helpful resources, though our focus is on the topic in the mission context.

All of us have a weak side, and the sooner we recognize it and shore it up, the better off we are. Remember Hebrews 12:1: "Therefore, since we are surrounded by such a great cloud of witnesses, let us throw off everything that hinders and the sin that so easily entangles. And let us run with perseverance the race marked out for us." You may say, "I'm too young for all of this to make sense and it sounds so negative, so why waste my time here?" Well, let me assure you, this is no waste of time; but you may have to take that on faith from someone who has pilgrimaged further along the path and has seen a lot along the way.

> All of us have a weak side, and the sooner we recognize it and shore it up, the better off we are.

Some of the snares which attack us in life and on mission—from obvious to the subtle.

A starting note: keep in mind that the snares are evil relatives and they come at us in combinations, rarely alone. So be wary of the malevolent coalitions. Also, these are not written in any significant order, for their assault against us is personalized to who we are, and the arch enemy certainly knows his tactics.

1. **Financial mismanagement.** Watch out for money problems, particularly if you come from a background of poverty, or if you come from privilege and wealth.

In ministry you are closer to poverty and may have to deal with those realities. Remember Judas. We did not sign up for a high paying job! To be honest, many of us could have made a lot more money had we worked in the marketplace, but that was not God's purpose for us. This is no slam on the marketplace, where God is honored in all honorable vocations. It's a matter of callings and assignments in life.

2. **The subtle invitation to move (or jump ship) from one ministry to another without having completed the previous assignment**. Baldly stated, this might be seen as "grass being greener on the other side of the fence." It's not that God wants us to stay, whatever, in the same job or ministry or occupation. It's the issue of finishing well each season, it's the matter of delicate timing when we contemplate leaving our current assignment. You are free to move when it is best for both current and future tasks. And it also must be good for the entire family. Be very sensitive to the temptation that may come in this subtle guise.

3. **Sexual issues and temptations.** It's unbelievable how one of God's best gifts can so devastate us. Whether single, married, separated, or divorced, sex entraps both women and men today as never before. Many of our younger missionaries come from broken families and have been sexually active prior to encountering Christ in power. Others struggle with gender confusion and may battle this all their lives; others may be freed by God's Spirit through wise counsel and the affirming community of God's people. Temptation patterns can re-emerge later in life and cause a fall. Both single and married men for diverse reasons have tended to succumb to infidelity more than women, but sadly this equation is changing all too rapidly. Not all marital infidelity leads to a broken family, but broken trust is difficult (yet not impossible, thank God!) to recover. Internet porn is destroying too many of our servants, even in remote areas of the world.

4. **Unresolved, systemic family issues.** Due perhaps to the lack of present, authentic, and loving parenting, this vacuum creates psychological and inter-personal problems in our own lives, marriages, and families. These must be addressed with wisdom and courage. Remember, no perfect families exist. Nevertheless, contend for healing and restoration and for establishing new patterns. I admire friends and colleagues who in their 50's are battling heavy stuff in order to be freed. I am saddened when I see friends and colleagues who just don't or can't do their hard work.

5. **Toxic leadership, power abuse.** Most of our colleagues will never get rich, but many find substitutes for distorted significance through power abuse. They themselves may have struggled to submit to authority but then when they got it they abused it. Recent studies in global, cross-cultural mission have documented this destructive leadership toxicity, too often a cause of premature and painful attrition.

6. **Pride and ambition to "get to the top" of the ministry ladder.** It's surprising to many of us that even in mission life we observe the machinations—many times couched in the spiritual language of humility—that some use to work their way into the high echelons of leadership and influence. And they do get there!

Internalize 1 Peter 5:5: "Humble yourselves, therefore, under the mighty hand of God so that at the proper time he may exalt you."

7. **The inability to turn over leadership and authority at the appropriate time;** or at the conclusion of top leadership in the organization; or when facing retirement. There are simply too many examples of men and women in their elder years who just won't let go. The results are self-evident, damaging too many individuals and ministries. In some cases this is called "founder's syndrome." I have also often wondered why so many gifted leaders do not themselves prepare for healthy transitions.

8. **Testing in the middle years of ministry.** At certain points in life, the living God invites his servants into deeper levels of brokenness and suffering. This may come as a result of our own sin, and we reap what we deserve; or it may come at the hand of others. It is always painful. Yet brokenness may also be as a result of a sovereign and complex invitation to follow the path of the suffering Servant. Why does God do this to us? Often he allows this because he's in the process of deconstructing us, of purifying us from our false self, or preparing us for the next stage of ministry. Ironically the next stage might mean ministry from the sidelines, away from the dangerous spotlight. It may mean we will end up walking with a kind of "life limp," as Jacob did after the battle with the angel. I am moved by Isaiah's record that "it pleased the Lord to bruise his servant." In all cases it means the downward path of mobility—to the cross. Henri J.M Nouwen's little book, *In the Name of Jesus: Reflections on Christian Leadership*, speaks powerfully to this topic.

9. **Succumbing to our hidden addictions.** I just Googled this topic and got 622,000 hits on hidden addictions. These afflict believers and non-believers, and there is a lot of material out there. Closer to home in this book, a number of other writers deal with these hidden (to us) weaknesses and sins. We in mission service are not immune to their panoply. I have personally battled some. Thankfully I have a courageous wife who speaks with prophetic truth when she sees these weaknesses taking over.

But it was my daughter Christine, then sixteen, whom God used to break an incipient hidden addiction in my first years with the WEA Mission Commission. It was the love of travel, in part driven by the demands of apparent incessant invitations and commitments. On that memorable day, I had just returned from a "most excellent" trip of ten days—what Yvonne called "Bill saving the world." When Christine came in from school I greeted her with a hug and she simply but pointedly said, "Dad, when are you leaving again?" I was pierced. Saying nothing I went into my little office, picked up the calendar and (pre-Internet) called perhaps eight to ten people who had asked me to speak in the USA and internationally. I explained exactly what had motivated the call to cancel the commitments, and to my encouragement, no one berated me. To the contrary, they affirmed the decision. Two things emerged from that crisis: first, Yvonne and I revisited our eight-point guideline to determine on what basis I would accept a travel engagement; second, I concluded the acid test were I to cancel would be: "If nobody dies if I don't show, I am not that critical to the event."

10. **Coasting to the end** is a peculiar one that describes those who have simply run out of vital energy for the task. Perhaps they are exhausted from Christian life and ministry, or perhaps they quietly struggled with dry rot of the soul. Their spirituality has run out of gas. So they maintain the system, they mark time, go through the routines of ministry and behavior. But their heart is not in it. And neither is the Spirit present.

11. **Serious persecution** will directly affect a lesser number of us, but it cannot be excluded. It is certainly a brutal reality in so many parts of the world, and especially for faithful believers who daily face misinformation, discrimination, intolerance, harassment, physical, and non-physical persecution. In the future we will know more and more martyrs or their family members. In these terrible testing times, will we remain faithful? When we hit "the Wall" of doubt regarding the reality, mercy, and justice of a sovereign God, will we stand steady? We can only pray so as we call on the Spirit to help us.

12. **Spiritual warfare.** Few of us are skilled to discern our unique, personal weak spots where the accuser attacks us. These vulnerable places may have deep roots in our family systems, our own personal brokenness, playing around with the demonic in our earlier years (from Ouija boards to drugs or acid music), or other susceptible zones. Satan's purpose is to destroy, and his warfare is open against us and our children. But one thing you can be sure of, the enemy will throw all he can at you to take you out, and he often attacks the most vulnerable members of our family.

So what are some strong antidotes?

There is good news, however. First of all, the Triune God is on our side: The one God is our Father, his empowering Spirit lives in us, and his Son continually advocates for us before the Father. Let me suggest some brief things to keep in mind, forged in the context of decades of cross-cultural life in Latin America as well global ministry with the World Evangelical Alliance.

1. **Seek the living God above all else.** Cultivate the heart, nurture your inner landscape, the intimate only known by you. Connect daily with the Lord in his work, praying and waiting, listening to the gentle voice. There is no substitute for this on the most regular basis, though it is one of the most difficult spiritual disciplines. Soak in your own preferred mode of prayer but learn other modes to give you depth and breadth.

2. **Identify your personal weaknesses** of character, spirituality, and behavior, and then shore them up. Some of these are "hidden addictions" of mind, will, emotions, and behavior, which we have referenced. God will use different means to reveal them to us and strong relational accountability is here. Remember the "tyranny of the urgent." Those closest to you may help you, but it will hurt!

3. **Develop a sensitive heart to the spectrum of sin** and the ways in which you are vulnerable. Maintain a tender heart to the loving and sovereign Father, Son, and Spirit, and practice a daily lifestyle of confession and repentance.

4. **If you marry, never forget your vows.** I made some mistakes as a husband in my early years of ministry in Latin America. Fortunately they were not "big sin" issues, but were rather a naïve insensitivity to my young bride struggling to learn a foreign language, living in a cross-cultural setting, growing her own identity as a woman and a woman in ministry, and balancing the demands of small children with the expectations of "being a missionary." I was a missionary kid who had returned "home," thus unable to identify with her battles. I learned some hard and good lessons early on. God used Yvonne to show me where I needed to change and grow. There is no substitute for a husband who enhances his wife as a person and partner in life and ministry (and vice versa), and that has been my commitment down through the years.

5. **Be wary of the seduction of travel invitations,** especially when you have children at home. I am thankful for the guidelines Yvonne and I developed early on to control these "glorious invitations to save the world." We also saw too many colleagues who were out there "doing their great ministry thing" but losing their children, or worse, their marriage.

6. **Grow an accountability community,** perhaps from one to three key persons. You cannot be truly accountable to nor fully revelatory to many. Choose carefully with whom you will share your deepest struggles, as not all people can handle such knowledge. Dr. David Howard, my mentor, told me that in all the cases he knew of marital infidelity, the husband and "great leader" had not had true accountability in his personal life.

7. **Be wary of the attacks of the enemy when you are alone,** particularly when you travel in ministry. When I traveled a lot I preferred to have a colleague stay with me in a hotel room so we could help strengthen one another's resolve to avoid toxic TV programs, movies, or corroding Internet temptations.

8. Ask God to help you **develop a prayer shield** of deep friends who will become serious intercessors for you. Some of these will stay with you all your life, while others will be with you for a season.

9. Commit to **building up your inner landscape of transformational spirituality.** Cultivate the heart, above all. Select key writers who touch you deeply. Return to the proven classics of Christian spirituality, and drink deeply from them. Each of us has writers who have shaped us. The most profound impact in my life has come from A.W. Tozer, Henri Nouwen, Dallas Willard, Gerald Sittser, and Eugene Peterson.

10. **Never stop learning,** reading, growing, studying, expanding your horizons. If married, encourage each other to grow as you read and study. Read a diversity of literature and be force yourself to engage literature that makes you think. I have a four-fold reading category: those which make me grow deeper (the hardest

for me to read); those which I read for personal study; those I have to read for global mission ministry and teaching-speaking; those I read for fun to blow the carbon out of my cylinders (old technology language). Finally, in this category of a lifelong learner, develop a lifetime perspective on theology, missiology, ministry, and the cultivation of your inner spiritual landscape.

11. **Commit to being mentored and to mentoring other**s. Mentoring has different dimensions, from an older to a younger, peer mentors, spiritual direction (a different category). Again, I am surprised to see the number of very gifted leaders who do not mentor. Perhaps they do not see the importance or are not gifted for that kind of wisdom rooted in relationship.

Final Thoughts on Finishing Well

We primarily want to encourage you. We yearn to see you, and the deepest part of you, your true self (not the false self) persevering on your own long-distance pilgrimage of God's mission, surviving and thriving with integrity until the end. Finish each season as best as you can.

> We yearn to see you, and the deepest part of you, your true self (not the false self) persevering on your own long-distance pilgrimage of God's mission, surviving and thriving with integrity until the end.

So be strong hearted, be of good cheer. We and that great host of witnesses are with you and for you.

Oh, by the way, that veteran Runner and his shoes that I first wrote of? I so well remember one of my last telephone conversations with him. We concluded the call with my words to him, "Dad, I love you." I still have those old shoes on the bookshelf next to my computer desk." My folks have gone Home now, but the shoes keep on talking.

William D. Taylor was born and raised in Latin America (dual nationality—Costa Rica and USA). His studies include Dip (Moody Bible Institute), BA (University of North Texas), ThM (Dallas Theological Seminary); PhD (University of Texas—Austin). He has served in global mission for fifty years in diverse capacities. He lived in Latin America for thirty years, including seventeen at CAM International at Seminario Teológico Centroamericano. From 1986–2006 he was Executive Director of the Mission Commission of World Evangelical Alliance, now MC Senior Mentor. As president of TaylorGlobalConsult (2011), Bill now invests his life in selective mentoring-apprenticing-life coaching, consulting, writing, teaching and speaking—local and global. He is married to Yvonne, a native Texan, and together they have three Guatemala-born children and seven grandchildren.

Scripture: *Luke 4: 14–21 ("Then Jesus returned to Galilee, filled with the Holy Spirit's power…") and 2 Corinthians 1:3–7 (NLT) ("All praise to God…")*

Resource: *Water from a Deep Well: Christian Spirituality from Early Martyrs to Modern Missionaries*, by Gerald L. Sittser (Downers Grove, IL: InterVarsity Press, 2007).

CHAPTER 39

A Review and a Perspective

The Journey Ends Only When the Destination Arrives

John Amalraj, with Geoffrey W. Hahn and William D. Taylor

The Chinese philosopher Lao Tzu once said, "The journey of a thousand miles begins with one step" (The Way of Lao-Tzu, 604 BC–531 BC). This journey exploring spirituality in missions with authors from different cultures, mother tongues, and traditions has almost taken a decade of our lives from the time the seed of this idea was first discussed. The first round of discussion circa 2007 probably lasted about thirty minutes, but it took thousands of small steps to journey together in bringing a unique publication to completion. Yet in the broader picture of global missiological reflection our attempt to compile a book on spirituality in mission is only the first step. The lifelong journey of spirituality in mission continues.

The spirituality in mission journey is a never-ending one. It starts in Genesis with our first parents, but in particular when Abraham was called by God to take the step of faith, leave his country, and journey across nations to the promised land. By faith he obeyed, and the nations have been blessed. The other patriarchs followed his footsteps. The Hebrews, delivered from slavery, embarked on a journey toward the promised land. Their spirituality was forged on the road as they journeyed through the wilderness. Their journey in spirituality continued in the numerous battles they fought as they gained possession of the promised land. Significantly, and tragically, due to their rebellion the journey included exile from The Land and then a journey back in repentance.

Jesus "set his face" toward Jerusalem on his final journey to the cross as did Paul in his travels across Asia as he headed toward Rome. When Jesus called his disciples to follow him, it was not to join an organization or to be accepted into an institution but to follow him as he journeyed to fulfill the Scriptures and his father's will.

The mission journey continues with the father of the modern mission movement, William Carey, who traveled to Calcutta and made it his final destination. Thousands of others have followed Christ to the ends of the earth. It is in those long life journeys of success and failure, of joy and sorrow, of pain and suffering, that women and men who obeyed the call of God have come to experience their spirituality.

OM founder George Verwer long ago sounded a clarion call to young people in his book *Out of Your Comfort Zone* calling them out of that place of ease. Those of us who made the choice to move out of our comfort zone have risked our very life and future; the results are expressed in the singular ways in which we express our spirituality.

Scripture often portrays spiritual experiences in other imagery apart from that of a journey; it is spoken of the "wilderness or desert experience," "the wedding feast," "the mountain top experience," and more. However, for the three of us on the editorial team, the imagery of "embracing a lifelong journey" seems best to communicate our desire that our global mission community capture and live the reality that our spirituality is not a one-off experience, or even a series of mountain highs; rather it is an ongoing, lifelong experience.

> The imagery of "embracing a lifelong journey" seems best to communicate our desire that our global mission community capture and live the reality that our spirituality is not a one-off experience, or even a series of mountain highs; rather it is an ongoing, lifelong experience.

As we three gave shape to the book, prayed over the writers and then contacted them, then compiled the chapters, reading and editing, we realize that each author has chosen to share an intimate piece of their experiences in their life long journey. Personal experiences are subjective; but they also are reality. Our authors have shared from their heart and written from what they have experienced. The stories and perspectives shared come from the "rubber that meets the road" not those tires that are kept in the showroom.

The most important part of our spiritual journey is the continuing desire to hear our Saviour speak to us. Hearing God's voice is a spiritual milestone for many. Prophets of old have had dreams and visions through which God spoke to them. Others have had the earth shake below them in an earthquake, or the rush of the wind, fire, lightning or thunder, or even the darkness; yet the still small voice is the most common way God speaks to his people. God is not just interested in the display of the spectacular. He speaks quietly in the inner spirit and moves the hearts of people, confirmed by the community of Jesus, to move out in radical obedience to the Great Commission.

Probably all of us parents have driven long distances in our car when inevitably that question kids ask is: "Have we reached our destination?. The answer is "not yet, but we will arrive soon." We the editorial team simply state to you our select readers that as you peruse and reflect on these last few pages that you have not reached the destination. The reality is that you have just taken the first, or next, or a latter step of your quest to understand spirituality in mission. Your journey has just begun; it continues to unfold; it's not over until it's over. Embrace this rich and challenging, at times heavy and hard, lifelong journey of knowing and experiencing God in your day to day life as you obey God's call to be a witness wherever you may go, regardless of your age or gifting, personality or stage in life, ethnicity or geography.

Our prayer is that as you reflect on the contents of this book, you will continue the well-begun journey and meet us in our common destination at the other side of eternity.

The Jews pray a prayer for those who start a journey. Join in this prayer if you will:

> May it be Your will, G-d, our G-d and the G-d of our fathers, that You should lead us in peace and direct our steps in peace, and guide us in peace, and support us in peace, and cause us to reach our destination in life, joy, and peace (If one intends to return immediately, one adds: and return us in peace). Save us from every enemy and ambush, from robbers and wild beasts on the trip, and from all kinds of punishments that rage and come to the world. May You confer blessing upon the work of our hands and grant me grace, kindness, and mercy in Your eyes and in the eyes of all who see us, and bestow upon us abundant kindness and hearken to the voice of our prayer, for You hear the prayers of all. Blessed are You G-d, who hearkens to prayer. (www.chabad.org)

.סוֹלְשָׁל וּכְיִרְדַתְן .סוֹלְשָׁל וּנֵדִיעָצתְן .סוֹלְשָׁל וּכֵילוֹתֵּשׁ .וּניֵתוֹבָא יֵהֹל-אֵנ וּניֵהֹל-אֵ יָ-י רָיֵנֶפָּלְמ וֹצֶר יְהִי
רמוֹא דים רוֹזחל ותעד סאו) .סוֹלְשָׁל וּ הָחָמְשָׁלוּ סִיֵּחָל וּנֵצְפֵּח זוֹחֲמל וּנֵעיּגְתן .סוֹלְשָׁל וּנֵכְמסְתן
תוֹשׁגְרתָמַה תוֹיֵנֶעָרֶפ לָכְמוּ .הָרֶדֶּב תוֹעֶר תוֹיַּחָן סִיֵּטסְלֵו בָרוֹאְנ ביֵוֹא-לָכ רָכֵמ וּנֵליֵצַתן .(סוֹלְשָׁל וּנֵריֵזַחַתן
יָנֵיעְבוּ רָיֵנֵיעָב סִימַחֲרַלוּ דֶסֶחָלוּ נֵחָל (דיחי 'לב) יֵנֵתְתן .וּניֵדָי הֵשֵׂעַמ לָכְב הָכָרָב חַלֵּשׁתְן .סָלוֹעֵל תוֹאָבוּ
יָ-י הָתָא רָוּרָב :הֶפ לָכ תַלֵּפִּת עַמוֹשׁ הָתָא יִכ .וּניֵתָלֵּפִת לוֹק עָמְשׁתְן .סִיֵּבוֹט סִידָסֲח וּנֵלְמגְתן .וּניֵאוֹר לָכ
:הָלֵּפִת עַמוֹשׁ

Alternatively, if you wish you can join this excerpt from the ancient Irish prayer of protection and blessing called "St Patrick's Breastplate":

> Christ be with me, Christ within me,
> Christ behind me, Christ before me,
> Christ beside me, Christ to win me;
> Christ to comfort and restore me;
> Christ beneath me, Christ above me,
> Christ in quiet, Christ in danger,
> Christ in hearts of all that love me,
> Christ in mouth of friend and stranger.[1]

---

1   Read the complete prayer and backdrop here: https://en.wikipedia.org/wiki/Saint_Patrick%27s_ Breastplate If you want to sing it: https://www.youtube.com/watch?v=knY-obH9ZoY

Along the
Journey

Appendix

Annotated Bibliography

Roberta Chiang

Alexander, Donald L. 1988. *Christian Spirituality: Five Views of Sanctification.* Downers Grove, IL: InterVarsity Press. Comparisons of Reformed, Lutheran, Wesleyan, Pentecostal, and contemplative, provides a good and helpful overview of Protestant spiritualities.

Bakke, Jeanette. 2000. *Holy Invitations: Exploring Spiritual Direction.* Grand Rapids, MI: Baker. An excellent introduction to spiritual direction from an evangelical point of view.

Barry, William A. 1991. *Finding God in All Things: A Companion to the Spiritual Exercises of St. Ignatius.* Notre Dame, IN: Ave Maria. Very helpful contemporary discussion of the core spiritual dynamics of the Ignatian Spiritual Exercises, as well as in the area of "finding God in everyday life."

Barry, William A. and William J. Connolly. 1982. *The Practice of Spiritual Direction.* New York: Seabury. Two highly regarded spiritual directors/teachers share practical experiences from their years working out of the Center for Religious Development in Cambridge, MA. *Catholic* point of view, but as a Protestant spiritual director, I highly recommend anything by Barry and Connolly.

Barton, Ruth Haley. 2014. *Life Together in Christ: Experiencing Transformation in Community.* Downers Grove, IL: InterVarsity Press. This author rarely disappoints and neither will this latest book. Barton talks about the rhythms and practices of a spiritual life that will transform any community you are part of. (Other recommended books by this author are: *Invitation to Solitude and Silence: Experience God's Transforming Presence*; *Sacred Rhythms: Arranging our Lives for Spiritual Transformation.*)

Benner, David G. 2002. *Sacred Companions.* Downers Grove, IL: InterVarsity Press. A well-written guidebook that helps the reader understand spiritual friendship and direction. Two excellent sections at the back of the book, "Suggestions for

Further Reading," and an extensive "General Listing," provide a very wide array of choices for further reading on this subject.

Brother Lawrence. 1993. *The Practice of the Presence of God.* New York: Barbour. A spiritual classic, which the author describes as "practicing the presence of God in one single act that does not end."

Casey, Michael. 1996. *Sacred Readings: The Ancient Art of Lectio Divina.* New York: Triumph. The art of prayerful listening set within a Benedictine context; provides coverage of its theological roots with practical application.

Chan, Simon. 1998. *Spiritual Theology: A Systematic Study of the Christian Life.* Downers Grove, IL: InterVarsity Press. Solidly evangelical and broadly ecumenical, this book is a discussion of the theological foundations of spirituality along with the major forms of practices of the spiritual life over the history of the Christian church. This book is described as "the little explored landscape where systematic theology and godly praxis meet." For further interest, the author writes from an Asian cross-cultural point of view, based in Singapore.

Chryssavgis, John. 2000. *Soul Mending: The Art of Spiritual Direction.* Brookline, MA: Holy Cross Orthodox. This book is written from the perspective of Eastern Orthodoxy and has an appendix of seventy-five pages of summaries of the most important patristic sources on spiritual direction.

Demarest, Bruce. 2003. *Soulguide: Following Jesus as Spiritual Director* (Colorado Springs. CO: NavPress. An excellent guide to soul care, from a well-respected evangelical leader in the Christian community. (Other recommended books by this author include: *Seasons of the Soul: Stages of Spiritual Development; Satisfy your Soul: Restoring the Heart of Christian Spirituality*).

Dirks, Morris. 2013. *Forming the Leader's Soul: An Invitation to Spiritual Direction.* Portland, OR: SoulFormation. An invitation to pastors and laity, to participate in "the quiet revolution of spiritual direction." Contains a good recommended reading section, as well as excellent chapter by chapter endnotes.

Driskill, Joseph D. 1999. *Protestant Spiritual Exercises: Theology, History and Practice.* Harrisburg, PA: Morehouse. Geared towards the spiritual leader, particularly clergy, but a very worthwhile read for anyone looking to deepen their spiritual life.

Fenelon, Francois. 1973. *Let Go.* New Kensington, PA. Whitaker Press. Four hundred short letters, written over three hundred years ago; could be read as a devotional. Fenelon is held in high esteem among Christian spiritual directors, and I recommend anything written by him. (*The Seeking Heart*—his works and letters; *The Inner Life*—more mystical, specifically dealing with Madame Guyon, a mystical thinker of the seventeenth century; *The Royal Way of the Cross*—spiritual humility and simplicity.) *Catholic writer.*

Foster, Richard. 1998. *Celebration of Discipline: The Path to Spiritual Growth.* SanFrancisco, CA: HarperSanFrancisco. An excellent introduction to the classic disciplines of Christian spirituality, with three different headings: Inner Disciplines, Outer Disciplines, and Corporate Disciplines. Recommended reading.

_____. 2002. *Prayer: Finding the Heart's True Home.* Grand Rapids, MI: Zondervan. In this author's usual compelling and warm way, he presents a primer on prayers of all kinds—for everyday life, and for spiritual growth.

_____. 1998. *Streams of Living Water.* San Francisco, CA: Harper. Another excellent history of spiritual practices comprising six different traditions: Contemplative; Holiness; Charismatic; Social Justice; Evangelical; Incarnational. There are also two worthwhile Appendices: Critical Turning Points in Church History; Notable Figures and Significant Movements in Church History.

Fryling, Alice. 2009. *Seeking God Together.* Downers Grove, IL. InterVarsity Press. Very practical handbook on the "how to's" of starting a group specifically for the purpose of spiritual direction, within the group.

Green, Thomas H. 1984. *Weeds Among the Wheat.* Notre Dame, IN: Ave Maria. This is one of the best books I've read on the topic of discernment, what it is and how to develop it, while learning to listen to and follow the Holy Spirit. Very valuable for those who are in listening professions. *Catholic.*

_____. 1998. *When the Well Runs Dry: Prayer Beyond the Beginnings.* Notre Dame, IN: Ave Maria. Draws heavily on the *Catholic* mystics tradition, along with Ignatius of Loyola, and is helpful in moving beyond "basic prayers."

Griffin, Emilie. 1997. *Wilderness Time: A Guide for Spiritual Retreat.* San Francisco, CA: HarperSanFrancisco. A good introduction to the use of retreats in spiritual formation. Includes practical information on designing your own retreat, or for those who lead others. Another excellent and reliable book from the Renovare collection of spiritual resources, for the individual or groups.

Guenther, Margaret. 1982. *Holy Listening: The Art of Spiritual Direction.* Cambridge, MA: Cowley. The author pays particular attention to the "art of sitting with women," and equates spiritual direction to midwifery—"birthing the soul." I highly recommend this book. *Episcopalian* so may not sit well with mainline Protestants.

Holt, Bradley P. 2005. *Thirsty for God.* Minneapolis, MN: Augsburg Fortress. This book is an excellent history of spirituality, over the last two millennium, with an updated version providing more focus on the spirituality of Jesus, medieval women mystics, right up to contemporary spirituality. The author very skillfully weaves spiritual practices into the historical context, which makes for engaging reading. Each chapter also contains extensive "suggested reading" with a glossary and time line at the back of the book. Highly recommended.

Hudson, Trevor. 1996. *Christ Following: Ten Signposts to Spirituality*. Grand Rapids, MI: Revell. A cross-cultural pastor to South Africa draws on his experiences both there and from classical spiritual writings, to offer ten disciplines for developing a passion for Christ.

Jones, Cheslyn, Geoffrey Wainwright, Edward Yarnold, eds. 1986. *The Study of Spirituality*. New York: Oxford University Press. *Very* extensive historical and global overview of the spirituality of every major religion through the ages. This book might appeal more to the academic, rather than resonating with personal spiritual growth.

Lane, Beldon C. 1998. *The Solace of Fierce Landscapes: Exploring Desert and Mountain Spirituality*. New York: Oxford. I think this book is brilliant for those ministering in hard places or experiencing hard or dry times, hence the desert metaphor. The author is from a Presbyterian background, teaching in a Jesuit university. *Caution for more conservative Christians.*

Lovelace, Richard. 1979. *Dynamics of Spiritual Life: An Evangelical Theology of Renewal*. Downers Grove, IL: InterVarsity Press. The author describes this book as a manual of spiritual theology. Grounded in the evangelical tradition, he sets out a framework for personal and congregational renewal but with a particular focus on corporate renewal, Christian approaches to the arts, and social concerns.

Moon, Gary W. and David G. Benner, eds. 2004. *Spiritual Direction and the Care of Souls: A Guide to Christian Approaches and Practices*. Downers Grove, IL: InterVarsity Press. The authors provide a careful overview of different denominational practices of spirituality and include chapters on integrating spirituality (i.e., spiritual direction) with pastoral counseling or psychotherapy.

Mulholland, M. Robert Jr. 1993. *Invitation to a Journey: A Road Map for Spiritual Formation*. Downers Grover, IL: InterVarsity Press. The author's "invitation" invites the reader into a gradual, life-long journey with Jesus, with a particular focus on different personality types expressing their spirituality differently.

_____. 2006. *The Deeper Journey: The Spirituality of Discovering Your True Self*. Downers Grove, IL: InterVarsity Press. Richard Rohr describes this book aptly: "Is religion primarily a belonging system or a transformational system?" The author—in all three books—writes very skillfully about the formational journey that ultimately transforms. Highly recommended reading.

_____. 2000. *Shaped by The Word: The Power of Scripture in Spiritual Formation*. Nashville, TN: Upper Room. Robert Mulholland's books—all three—are rooted in Scripture, and all three are a clarion call to a deeper spiritual life. Must-reads for those who want to go from *informational* reading to *formational* reading in Scripture.

Nouwen, Henri. 1981. *The Way of the Heart*. New York: Ballantine Books. Almost anything written by Nouwen will feed your soul and this small book is no different. He talks about a three-fold path to a deepening relationship with the Father: solitude, silence, and prayer.

Reeves, Michael. 2012. *Delighting in the Trinity*. Downers Grove, IL; InterVarsity Press. A small book that *does* delight. It includes an overview of the history of spirituality down through to contemporary spirituality and why the Christian life is rooted in the Trinity.

Ruffing, Janet K. 2000. *Spiritual Direction: Beyond the Beginnings*. Mahwah, NJ: Paulist Press. The author moves beyond the basics of the ministry of spiritual direction to expand on themes of desire and resistance, women's experiences in spiritual direction, "operative theology" in one's own story, transference and countertransference issues, along with other themes. Janet Ruffing is highly regarded in the area of spirituality. *Catholic*.

Seamands, Stephen. 2005. *Ministry in the Image of God*. Downer's Grove, IL. InterVarsity Press. For those in vocational ministry, Seamands demonstrates that *all* of the Trinity must be involved in ministry—the Father, the Son, and the Holy Spirit. Don't be tempted to skim over this book… it is deeper than at first glance.

Sittser, Gerald. 2007. *Water From a Deep Well*. Downers Grove, IL: InterVarsity Press. Another excellent view of the history of spirituality. This book also has its own very worthwhile annotated reading list. Highly recommended.

Smith, Gordon. 2014. *Called to Be Saints*. Downers Grove, IL: InterVarsity Press. A practical guide to learning how to live an abundant life in Christ, but might weigh more on the academic side than the lighter reading side. However, his unswerving view of holiness in daily living makes this book worthwhile reading.

_____. 2003. *The Voice of Jesus: Prayer, Discernment, and the Witness of the Spirit*. Downers Grove, IL: InterVarsity Press. This wonderful book spans the diversity of history and theology from Ignatius of Loyola to John Wesley to Jonathan Edwards and talks about the practicalities of having a closer walk with Jesus by attending to the Spirit.

_____. 2014. *Spiritual Direction: A Guide to Giving and Receiving Direction*. Downers Grove, IL: InterVarsity Press. An excellent apologetic for the art of spiritual direction and why we need a companion along the way to help us grow in discerning God's call in our lives.

Sproul, R.C. 1985. *The Holiness of God.* Wheaton, IL: Tyndale House. A profound investigation into holiness and the dynamics of holiness as it exists in God and is meant to exist in us.

Tan, Siang-Yang, and Douglas Gregg. 1997. *Disciplines of the Holy Spirit.* Grand Rapids, MI: Zondervan. A mainstream evangelical perspective presents attunement with the Holy Spirit as the foundation of Christian spiritual formation.

Thomas a Kempis. 1967. *The Imitation of Christ.* New York: Pyramid. This is described as "the unchallenged masterpiece of devotional literature for the past five hundred years."

Wiederkehr, Macrina. 1995. *The Song of The Seed: A Monastic Way of Tending the Soul.* San Francisco, CA: Harper. A very practical introduction to praying with Scripture, through the practice of *lectio divina*, and from a Benedictine's point of view. Written for groups on retreat or individuals who might wish to journal this experience.

Willard, Dallas. 1998. *The Divine Conspiracy: Rediscovering Our Hidden Life in God.* San Francisco, CA: HarperSanFrancisco. The author presents "discipleship to Jesus" as the very heart of the gospel and reminds his readers that "the good news for humanity is that Jesus is now taking students in the master class of life."

Roberta (Robbi) Bush Chiang is a Canadian who has lived in Hong Kong for twenty-five years with her husband, Samuel, and family of three, while in vocational ministry. They have recently relocated to Texas, where both she and her husband serve The Wycliffe Seed Company. She is a spiritual director by calling and training, her primary passion being the care of souls, along with being an advocate for the Bible-less. Robbi loves all of nature, but particularly trees and rocks of all kinds, likes to read, especially in the areas of history and memoir, and also likes to listen to classical music, her favorites being Beethoven's "Moonlight Sonata," and Ravel's "Bolero."

Scripture: *Psalm 121 ("I lift my eyes to the mountains…")*

Resource: *Shaped by the Word*, by M.Robert Mulholland Jr. (Nashville, TN: Upper Room, 2000), and *The Deeper Journey*, by M.Robert Mulholland Jr. (Downers Grove, IL: InterVarsity Press 2006. Recently, *The Soul of Shame*, by Curt Thompson (Downers Grove, IL: InterVarsity Press, 2015) and *Care of Mind, Care of Spirit*; by Gerald May (New York: Harper Collins, 1992),